Miracle on 34th Street:
The Making of a Christmas Classic

Released in 1947, *Miracle on 34th Street* would go on to join the ranks of the best Christmas movies ever made. The enduring quality of the film is largely due to the inspired performances by Edmund Gwenn as Kris Kringle and Natalie Wood as Susan Walker. (Photofest)

Miracle on 34th Street:
The Making of a Christmas Classic

JEFFREY PAUL THOMPSON

LYONS PRESS

ESSEX, CONNECTICUT

An imprint of Globe Pequot, the trade division of The Rowman & Littlefield Publishing Group, Inc.
4501 Forbes Blvd., Ste. 200
Lanham, MD 20706
www.rowman.com

Distributed by NATIONAL BOOK NETWORK

British Library Cataloguing in Publication Information available

Library of Congress Cataloging-in-Publication Data available

ISBN 978-1-4930-7524-9 (hardcover: alk. paper)
ISBN 978-1-4930-7525-6 (e-book)

∞™ The paper used in this publication meets the minimum requirements of American National Standard for Information Sciences—Permanence of Paper for Printed Library Materials, ANSI/NISO Z39.48-1992.

Contents

This half-sheet poster contains a still of a deleted scene in which Kris is offered venison but politely refuses: "I–just–couldn't," he explains. (Photofest)

C H A P T E R   1

Introduction

Despite having been adapted into a book, at least seven radio dramas, three television movies, a Broadway musical, amateur stage plays, a colorized version, and a feature film remake, it is the original 1947 black-and-white film of *Miracle on 34th Street** (hereafter, *Miracle*) that still remains the favorite version of this modern Christmas classic.* One of the mysteries of the Hollywood studio system during the mid-twentieth century is how so many great films were created from an assembly-line production factory (though, admittedly, there were a lot of failures, as well). There might not be a good explanation, but it happened with *Miracle*—somehow the perfect story, the perfect cast, and the perfect direction came together to create an endearing and enduring Christmas film. The American public's love of the original film seems to echo what Macy's stated when it declined to participate in the 1994 remake: "We feel the original stands on its own and there was nothing to be improved upon.[1]

From the 1930s to the 1950s, the popular culture of Christmas went through a dramatic metamorphosis in America. Perhaps no other period before or since has had so many lasting contributions. Popular Christmas music came into its own with the introduction in 1934 of "Santa Claus is Comin' to Town" and "Winter Wonderland." A flurry of weather-related tunes followed, such as "I've Got My Love to Keep Me Warm," "Winter Weather," "Let It Snow!" "Baby, It's Cold Outside," and, of course, "White Christmas." Cozy songs evoking home, hearth, and family togetherness surfaced, including "Have Yourself a Merry Little Christmas," "I'll Be Home for

---

* *Miracle on 34th Street* went through several title changes from the original story until its final release as a film. This is discussed in detail in chapter 5. To be consistent and avoid confusion, the final title will be used throughout the book instead of the various other titles.

Christmas," and "The Christmas Song (Chestnuts Roasting on an Open Fire)." The period also introduced us to the story—and later the song—of "Rudolph, the Red-Nosed Reindeer" (thanks to national retailer Montgomery Ward), and "Frosty the Snowman" would thumpity-thump-thump onto the scene in 1950. Many of these tunes have consistently dominated the ranks of the most recorded and performed Christmas songs ever since.[2] Some of them, such as "White Christmas" and "The Christmas Song," have practically become required repertoire for any singer who does a Christmas album.

The era also turned out a surprising number of movies that are perennial favorites and have come to define the holiday. Prior to the late 1930s, there really wasn't a "Christmas movie" genre. Of course, Christmas wasn't absent from the cinema. There were dozens of Christmas-themed shorts during the silent era, including several of Charles Dickens's *A Christmas Carol*. Christmas scenes were frequently featured in movies such as *Gone with the Wind* (1939), and in Shirley Temple films such as *Bright Eyes* (1934) and *Stowaway* (1936), for example. But, in general, the Christmas scenes were isolated and not necessarily central to the plot.

Beginning in the late 1930s, this seemed to change dramatically. *A Christmas Carol* certainly got its most lavish treatment to date when MGM did its version starring Reginald Owen and Gene Lockhart, in 1938. Christmas became an integral part of the storylines in big and small productions, such as in romantic comedies like *The Shop Around the Corner* (1940) and *Remember the Night* (1940), and in more dramatic fare illustrating social inequalities, such as *Miracle on Main Street* (1939) and *Beyond Tomorrow* (1940).

As America entered World War II, Hollywood began offering more nostalgic fare. Nothing could help a war-weary nation forget its present woes like movies about Christmas that were "just like the ones [we] used to know," such as *Irving Berlin's Holiday Inn*, which introduced the song "White

"Santa Claus Is Comin' to Town," introduced in 1934, ushered in the golden era of popular Christmas music. (Author's collection)

Charles Dicken's *A Christmas Carol* got a lavish treatment in the 1938 adaptation. Gene Lockhart played Bob Cratchit and Reginald Owen played Ebenezer Scrooge. (Photofest)

The romantic comedy *The Shop Around the Corner* (1940) with James Stewart and Margaret Sullavan takes place in a retail setting during the holiday season, with love conquering all on Christmas Eve. (Photofest)

Christmas" in 1942. The ensuing years brought the turn-of-the-century period musical *Meet Me in St. Louis* (1944), with Judy Garland singing the wistful "Have Yourself a Merry Little Christmas"; *I'll Be Seeing You* (1944), with war veteran Joseph Cotten and Ginger Rogers adjusting to normal life during the holiday season; and *Christmas in Connecticut* (1945), featuring Barbara Stanwyck trying to create the perfect holiday setting. *It's a Wonderful Life*, which made Jimmy Stewart a Christmas icon, came out the following year. *Miracle on 34th Street*, of course, would soon join the pantheon of great Christmas films, and, perhaps, is the epitome of the new genre. Not patently nostalgic—it's a modern story in a modern setting—but it certainly encourages and emphasizes the importance of family, faith, the magic of childhood, and, well, Santa Claus, all of which had been distorted by the modern world, and especially the recent war.

Ever since the merger of the fledgling Twentieth Century Pictures with the faltering Fox Film Corporation in 1935, and the appointment of Darryl F. Zanuck as vice president in charge of production, Twentieth Century-Fox (hereafter, "TCF") had succeeded in becoming one of Hollywood's top studios—if not *the* top studio, especially during war years. Zanuck had developed lovable child actresses Shirley Temple and Jane Withers into some of the industry's biggest stars; launched the careers of matinee idols like Tyrone Power and Henry Fonda; discovered legendary beauties like Gene Tierney and Linda Darnell; created extravagant musicals to showcase the sparkling talents of Betty Grable, Alice Faye, and Carmen Miranda; and kept a handful of well-produced serials going for the fans of the Cisco Kid, Michael Shayne, Charlie Chan, and Mr. Moto. The studio would win its second Academy Award for Best Picture for *How*

Remember the Night (1940), in which big-city prosecutor (Fred MacMurray) takes a shoplifter (Barbara Stanwyck) with him back to his hometown so she doesn't have to spend Christmas in jail. From left to right, Barbara Stanwyck, Beulah Bondi, Fred MacMurray, Sterling Holloway, and Elizabeth Patterson. (Photofest)

Green Was My Valley (1941) (the first was for 1933's *Cavalcade*), and would consistently be nominated for Oscars under Zanuck's leadership thereafter.

By the early 1940s, the studio had developed a robust production schedule of releasing about fifty films per year. About 40 percent of those films were higher-end productions utilizing the studio's best talent, while the other 60 percent consisted of lower-budget films for the serials. Color films were expensive to make because the studio had to license the cameras from Technicolor, so the process was reserved for extravagant musicals like *That Night in Rio* (1941) and *The Gang's All Here* (1943), or highbrow dramas like *Blood and Sand* (1941). Most of the studio's films were released in black-and-white. The production schedule remained the same until 1943, when the economies of war cut the number of films almost in half, down to thirty. All of the popular serials made by the "B" film production unit over at the studio's Western Avenue lot were eliminated during the war and would never be revived.* Other than some cheap crime thrillers that longtime studio producer Sol Wurtzel was churning out, TCF ceased making low-budget movies and concentrated on higher-end fare. This philosophy and reduced release schedule would remain in effect for the rest of the decade.

The 1947 lineup that included *Miracle* was fairly typical during that period. At the first national sales conference following the war, the president of TCF, Spyros Skouras, announced that the company would continue to follow its "established policy" of focusing on four genres of films: 1) adaptations of

Bing Crosby and Marjorie Reynolds introduced the most famous Christmas song of the twentieth century, "White Christmas," in *Irving Berlin's Holiday Inn* (1942). (Photofest)

Judy Garland introduced the wistful (and somewhat melancholy) "Have Yourself a Merry Little Christmas" in the 1944 film *Meet Me in St. Louis* as Margaret O'Brien, who played her younger sister, listened. (Photofest)

---

* The Western Avenue lot was located on the corner of Sunset Boulevard and Western Avenue in Los Angeles. It became the secondary lot when the new lot opened on Pico Boulevard in 1928.

A film that would go on to become a Christmas classic, *It's a Wonderful Life*, came out just six months before *Miracle on 34th Street*. (Photofes)t

One of the major additions to midcentury Christmas culture was Rudolph the Red-Nosed Reindeer. He was introduced in a coloring book by the Montgomery Ward department store in 1939 and then got his own song in 1949. (Author's Collection)

best-selling books; 2) musicals filmed in Technicolor; 3) outdoor pictures filmed in Technicolor; and 4) dramas filmed on location.[3] A total of twenty-five films were released that year, and they were all "A" list productions, even though only eight were filmed in Technicolor. Contrary to later statements made by some members of the cast and crew, *Miracle* was not a "B" picture. It featured a top producer and director, major stars, and was filmed on location, all of which were not characteristic of low-budget movies.

ADAPTATIONS OF BEST-SELLING BOOKS:

The Brasher Doubloon
Daisy Kenyon
*Forever Amber**
The Foxes of Harrow
Gentleman's Agreement
The Ghost and Mrs. Muir
The Late George Apley
Moss Rose
Nightmare Alley

MUSICALS FILMED IN TECHNICOLOR:

Carnival in Costa Rica
I Wonder Who's Kissing Her Now
Mother Wore Tights
*The Shocking Miss Pilgrim***

OUTDOOR PICTURES FILMED IN TECHNICOLOR:

The Homestretch
Bob, Son of Battle

*ALSO FILMED IN TECHNICOLOR

DRAMAS FILMED ON LOCATION:
Boomerang!
*Captain from Castile**
Kiss of Death
Miracle on 34th Street
13 Rue Madeleine

SOL WURTZEL PRODUCTIONS:
Crimson Key
Invisible Wall
Jewels of Brandenburg
Roses Are Red
Second Chance

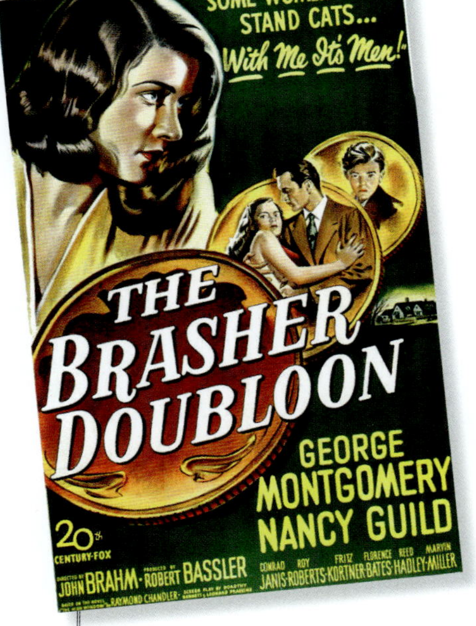

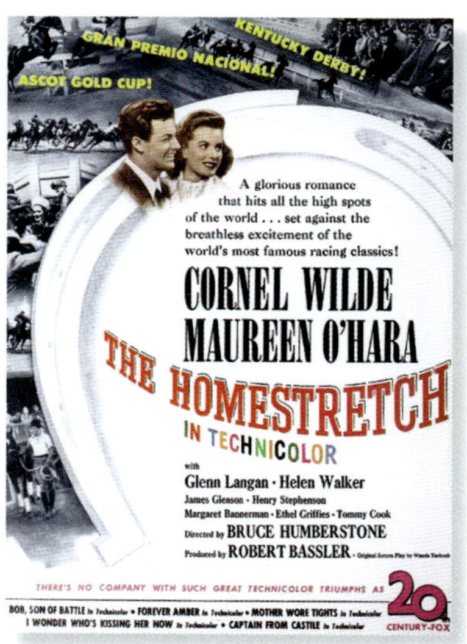

****Released December 31, 1946**

Director George Seaton, left, and writer Valentine Davies, right, on the set of *Miracle on 34th Street*. Although officially Seaton was credited as the screenwriter and Davies was credited with writing the original story, both admitted that developing the narrative was very much a collaborative affair. (Photofest)

The Story

The idea for *Miracle* originated with writer Valentine Davies, but it would take the combined efforts of two other men, namely George Seaton and William Perlberg, for the story to become a motion picture.

Not surprising for the author of a quintessential New York story, Davies was a native New Yorker. Born in 1905 to a fifth-generation New York family, he attended the Horace Mann School in the Bronx. He was then accepted into the University of Michigan, where he was involved in acting and directing campus plays, and where he also wrote a column for *The Michigan Daily*, the school newspaper. He married Elizabeth Strauss, the daughter of the head of the English department, during his senior year. The couple would eventually have two children. After graduation in 1927, the couple returned to New York to join his father in the real estate business. But over the next couple of years it became evident that Davies was not cut out for the real estate business (nor it for him, as he quipped), and he concentrated on his writing.[4]

He completed his first play, titled *Three Times the Hour*, which was staged by producer Brock Pemberton (future founder of the Tony Awards) in 1929. This led him to abandon real estate completely. He went on to study at Yale with professor George Pierce Baker, and wrote another one-act play, *The House of Juke*, which was picked up by publisher Samuel French. His later work as a Hollywood screenwriter was presaged by his stage adaptation of the Earl Derr Biggers's Charlie Chan novel, *Keeper of the Keys* (at the time, the Charlie Chan films were being produced at TCF; incidentally, this turned out to be the only Charlie Chan novel that was never filmed), and a play produced in 1937 called *Blow Ye Winds*, starring a young actor named Henry Fonda. TCF had turned Fonda into a movie star just a couple of years earlier with homespun films like *The Farmer Takes a Wife* (1935) and *Way Down East* (1936).[5]

Despite the success of his plays that he had written for the Broadway stage, it was his short story entitled *The Band Played On*, about the birth of swing music, that attracted the attention of Hollywood. Director William Dieterle, at RKO at the time, brought Davies out to Los Angeles in 1941 to adapt his story into the film *Syncopation* (1942), which featured some of the great big bands of the era, including Harry James, Gene Krupa, and Benny Goodman.[6]

During World War II, Davies enlisted in the US Coast Guard Reserve and served for three and a half years as a personnel officer at the Operating Base in Wilmington, Delaware. It was during this time, in December 1944, that he got the idea for *Miracle*. One day while shopping for a gift for his wife, he was being pushed around by throngs of people. He later recalled that there was "something about the annual pre-Christmas rush [that] stirred in me a vague resentment at the high-pressure commercialization of the Christmas spirit. If there were a Santa Claus, I thought, and he should wander into any modern department store, he'd be a pretty disillusioned old boy."[7]

He started thinking that this might make a good movie, but almost as quickly dismissed the idea, thinking it posed too many problems to work on the screen. Most films feature young, attractive people as the protagonists, and this story would have an old man of dubious mental capacity as the hero. He also feared that "the quicksands of sticky sentimentality" would be "almost inescapable." Reluctantly, he shared the storyline with his wife, who was usually critical of his ideas; but, to his surprise, she really liked it and encouraged him to continue developing the narrative.[8]

A month later, in January 1945, while Davies was on a seven-day leave from the Coast Guard, he met up with his wife Liz and their old college friends, George and Phyllis Seaton, at the Hidden Well Ranch in Las Vegas.[9] While there, Liz suggested that Davies share his story idea with Seaton, who was one of the sixteen staff directors working at TCF at the time.[10] Even though he was reluctant, Davies did so. Seaton really liked it, but had one suggestion right off: Instead of Santa Claus, what about a man who just *thinks* he's Santa Claus.[11] Seaton also expressed interest in making it into a movie.[12]

For the next five months, Davies would work on the story during his off hours in the Coast Guard,[13] which gave him a lot of time to ruminate about the details. Since he had conceived the story as a motion picture, he knew it would have to meet certain criteria in order to be financially successful. Even though the story would be primarily about Santa Claus, it would have to be framed within a love story, starring an actor and actress with box office appeal. The female lead, Doris, would be the antagonist, with a negative experience that has led her not to believe in Santa Claus; and the male lead, Fred, would be the protagonist that would change her mind. Davies believed a love relationship would be "the sharpest way of bringing the two people with widely divergent philosophies together in direct conflict." Ironically, he later noted, many of the scenes that developed the love story did not end up in the final cut of the film, and so, ultimately, it ended up being more focused on Santa Claus after all.[14]

Davies debated whether or not to have Doris be a divorcée. In his first written treatment of *Miracle*, a twenty-page story outline, Fred and Doris are actually married (last name Barton), and they have one daughter named Margaret. Both work at Macy's, where Doris is a personnel manager and Fred is an accountant. Personality-wise, the characters are much the same as they are in the movie. As in the film, conflict arises when Fred takes Margaret to see Santa.* This results in a fight between the two about fantasy and reality and its effects on children, and then Fred reveals that he has quit his job and wants to become a writer and move the family to Maine. Doris, of course, thinks this is ridiculous, and the two decide to separate temporarily, with undertones that it will become permanent.[15] Under this construct, Kris Kringle then works his magic to help save their marriage.

But the idea of Fred and Doris being married did not last long. Davies debated whether or not to have Doris be a widow, but ultimately felt that her "disillusioned, bitter attitude," which she had conveyed to her daughter, "could stem only from a very bitter marital experience and the additional bitter and disillusioning experience of divorce." If her husband had merely died, her bitterness "would have mellowed . . . [in]to something quite different." Davies felt that "If the story says anything at all about divorce, it shows only its shattering effect upon Doris and her daughter."[16] When he wrote the second story outline of *Miracle*, Doris had become a divorcée.

Perhaps surprising to modern audiences, divorce was not uncommon in Hollywood films in the first half of the twentieth century. From the silent era through the early 1940s, divorce was great fodder for dozens of films, both dramas and comedies, such as *Private Lives* (1931), *The Gay Divorcée* (1934), *Dodsworth* (1936), *Stella Dallas* (1925 and 1937), *His Girl Friday* (1940), and *The Philadelphia Story* (1940), to name a few. Divorce was used more sparingly as a plot device during the World War II years, probably because Hollywood was trying to avoid depressing subjects during a dreary era. Nonetheless, Davies did receive some criticism from viewers for this choice. Coincidentally, all of the principal cast members had been affected by divorce in their personal lives: O'Hara had been tricked into a marriage right before coming to America and had to go through a divorce; Payne had divorced actress Anne Shirley just a few years before working on the film; Gwenn had divorced his wife thirty years earlier; and Natalie Wood's mother had divorced her first husband before marrying Natalie's father.

Another challenge Davies had to work through was in creating a realistic Santa Claus character. The first problem was coming up with a name. Davies explained that he ended up choosing "Kris Kringle" because "people in the story would have to call him something, and to have had them call him 'Santa,' for instance, would have implied acceptance of him as Santa Claus immediately. Whereas, having them call him 'Kris,' which is a name not exclusively associ-

---

* To avoid confusion, "Susan" will be used instead of "Margaret" throughout the book, even when referring to the first two synopses.

Modern audiences often think that divorce was a taboo topic during the early years of Hollywood. However, there were many popular films which featured it as a major element of the plot, such as the Fred Astaire and Ginger Rogers musical *The Gay Divorcée* (1934) and the Howard Hawks' comedy *His Girl Friday* (1940)). (Photofest)

ated with Santa Claus, implied the indecision in most people's minds which we wanted to maintain through the story."[17] The name works well because it includes a first and last name (unlike St. Nicholas, for example), and is plausible as a real name in the modern world. Davies originally spelled his name "Chris" in the first story outline, and then switched to "Kris."[18]

A second challenge was how to handle Kris's belief in himself as Santa Claus. Davies later wrote that he had concocted the idea "entirely [as] an example of literary imagination," though the idea of a person believing himself to be someone else was based on several documented cases of such delusions. The discussions about Kris's mental state that ended up in the story were based on actual conversations that Davies had with psychiatrists as to why someone would have such a delusion.[19] Later on, Seaton also discussed the Kris character with his friend Dr. May Romm, who was a psychiatrist practicing in Beverly Hills, and paid her $1,000 for her input.[20] John C. Eagan, MD, was also hired as a technical advisor.[21]

Davies registered his twenty-page story outline containing a synopsis of fifty-two scenes with the Screen Writers Guild on July 3, 1945 (#29243).[22] Since the plan was to turn the story into a movie through Seaton's connection at TCF, a couple of weeks later Davies sold the story to Seaton Productions (which consisted of George and Phyllis Sea-

Developing the character of Kris Kringle posed some challenges for writer Valentine Davies. (Photofest)

THE STORY

George Seaton and William Perlberg worked together on a wide variety of films, including the religious drama *The Song of Bernadette* (1943). Seaton's screenplay was nominated for an Oscar. (Photofest)

George Seaton's dream came true when he was assigned to be the director on *Billy Rose's Diamond Horseshoe* (1945), which was produced by his good friend William Perlberg. (Photofest)

ton) for $7,500 cash, plus 50 percent of the resale price up to $30,000.[23] If the story made it into production, Davies would be credited as the author of the original story, and Seaton would be credited as the screenwriter.

Though only in his mid-thirties, George Seaton had already had a long and varied career in the entertainment industry. He was born George Stenius in 1911 in South Bend, Indiana, but was raised in Detroit and attended Exeter Academy.[24] He had plans to attend Yale but decided to pursue a career in acting instead, and returned to Detroit, where he was hired as an actor in the Jessie Bonstelle Stock Company. He would find fame in the early 1930s as the voice of *The Lone Ranger* on radio, where he would curdle the airwaves with his famous "Hi Ho Silverrr!" He also got a lot of acting experience, since he was also the voice for all of the other male characters on the show.[25]

During the mid-1930s, Stenius made it to New York and tried his hand as a playwright. One of his plays got submitted to MGM, which led to a job with that movie studio. He married Phyllis Loughton, a drama coach at Paramount, in 1936, and the couple would have two children. Around this time he legally changed his last name to Seaton. While at MGM, he worked with Irving Thalberg, and would get a writing credit for the Marx Brothers film *A Day at the Races* (1937). He then worked briefly as a writer at Columbia, where he soon began a long and prosperous partnership with producer William Perlberg. The two ended up moving over to TCF in 1940, where Seaton would become a deft writer on Jack Benny comedies like *Charley's Aunt* (1941) and *The Meanest Man in the World* (1943), and on big, splashy musicals like *That Night in Rio* (1941) and *Moon Over Miami* (1941). In 1943, Perlberg gave Seaton the opportunity to do something more serious when he adapted the religious drama *The Song of Bernadette* (1943) into a screenplay. It was a successful turn, and he ended up getting nominated for an Oscar. The two would start working consistently together on productions at TCF.

But Seaton had some bigger ambitions. He wanted to become a director because "he was disappointed in the way other directors handled his lines."[26] He was most interested in getting his own scripts made into films: "By directing it myself, I can put my ideas on the screen just as I conceive them. It's just the old, old story of getting a thing done the way you want it by doing it yourself. I also feel that having been an actor as well as writing my own screenplays, gives me a distinct advantage in directing."[27] Being a writer and director, though common today, was a bit of an anomaly in the 1940s. Other than a handful of men like Seaton, John Huston, and Preston Sturges, there were not that many writers or directors who did double duty. Seaton was finally given the opportunity to be the writer and the director on the Betty Grable musical *Billy Rose's Diamond Horseshoe* (1945), with William Perlberg as producer.

Even though Davies had worked at TCF before the war, Seaton probably helped him get hired on again as a contract writer in September 1945.[28] During the next six months, he and Seaton worked on the screenplay for *Miracle* in their spare time, and in March 1946 Davies produced a second story outline which was only seven pages long, with descriptions of forty-one scenes.[29] He then spent the next three to four months working on a seventy-eight-page, full-length version of the story, which he completed in July.[30] Even though he was the writer of record, he always made it clear that the development of the story was very much a collaborative effort between him and Seaton.[31] The story was now in a good-enough form to try and sell to TCF. Seaton gave producer Perlberg a copy of the full-length version of the story, which he had told him about previously.[32]

William Perlberg was the third man responsible for getting *Miracle* on the screen, and would be responsible for convincing TCF to finance the picture. He had worked his way up through the motion picture business and was one of seventeen producers on staff at the studio.[33]

Born in 1900 into a Russian-Polish family, Perlberg had emigrated as a child with his family to New York City, and by 1910 they had settled in the Bronx.[34] He graduated from Cornell and married vaudeville star Dagmar Brox of the Brox Sisters in 1928. The couple would have one son. He was hired at the William Morris Agency in New York and worked there for five years before being sent to Los Angeles to open a branch of the agency there.

In 1933, Perlberg joined Columbia Pictures as a casting director. He worked his way up, and eventually became executive assistant to the president of Columbia, Harry Cohn, and then became an executive producer. After his move to TCF in 1940, Perlberg worked on several important pictures, including big musicals like *Hello, Frisco, Hello* (1943) and *State Fair* (1945), and lavish dramas like *The Song of Bernadette* (1943) and *Forever Amber* (1947).[35]

Confident about *Miracle*, Perlberg submitted it to Darryl Zanuck on July 19, 1946.[36] Zanuck, who was the

William Perlberg, the producer who made everything come together for *Miracle on 34th Street*. (Photofest)

THE STORY

Darryl F. Zanuck, vice president in charge of production at Twentieth Century-Fox, gave William Perlberg and George Seaton the green light to make *Miracle on 34th Street*. Following the success of the film, Perlberg was heard saying that he now "believes in Zanuck Claus."* (Photofest)

vice president of TCF in charge of production, clearly remembered that *Miracle* "was not submitted as a story but as a gambling proposition—one of those things that producers usually run away from."[37] As Seaton recounted a quarter-century later, Zanuck told him, "George, you're crazy. Who in the hell is going to care about an old man who thinks he's Santa Claus?"[38] Assistant director Artie Jacobson also remembered that Zanuck just "couldn't see Santa Claus in a court of law in New York City."[39]

Zanuck really wanted Seaton to direct a film based on a story that had appeared in *Reader's Digest* a few years earlier, called *Chicken Every Sunday*, a light comedy/drama about the fortunes and foibles of the Hefferen family in turn-of-the-century Tucson, Arizona. Seaton was not at all interested, calling the story "lousy." So Zanuck struck a deal: He told Seaton he would greenlight *Miracle* if he would agree to do *Chicken*. Seaton reluctantly acquiesced and kept his end of the bargain. As with *Miracle*, he and Davies developed the screenplay together. Eventually, things turned out as Seaton had predicted—*Miracle* was a success and *Chicken* is now forgotten.[40] (To be fair, even though *Chicken Every Sunday* [1949] is not well-remembered, it is a nice little period piece with Dan Dailey and Celeste Holm, and features several of the cast members from *Miracle*, including Natalie Wood, William Frawley, and Porter Hall.[41])

But any hesitance on Zanuck's part was short-lived. Contemporary correspondence indicates that after Zanuck read the original story, he was "very enthusiastic," which is confirmed by the fact that the studio purchased it for a significant sum and moved forward with the production.[42] When Zanuck read the screenplay in early November, he did so "with great pleasure." He was almost effusive in letting Perlberg and Seaton know that he found the treatment to be "excellent, fresh, exciting, and delightful," the story "very honest and believable," and summed it up with the unequivocal "I like it immensely."[43] He was concerned about them capturing the "real *spirit* of the subject," which, if handled correctly, he thought, could potentially be "a masterpiece"; if they didn't, "it would be a horrible bust."[44] Davies would often later quip that apparently "a lot of people believed in Mr. Kringle."[45]

By early August of 1946, the studio was planning on buying the story.[46] The legal department did its due diligence to make sure the story was clear of any liens or encumbrances, and in early September the executive committee recommended moving forward with the purchase.[47] Three weeks later, on September 20, 1946, TCF paid $100,000 for the worldwide rights to the

*Hoffamn, Irving, "Tales of Hoffman," *Hollywood Reporter*, July 2, 1947, p. 3.

story.[48] Seaton subsequently delivered $18,250 of the $100,000 purchase price to Davies, which was less than they had agreed upon, but is probably indicative of the approximately 20/80 percentage of the story and screenplay each one was responsible for creating.[49] The final makeup of the production team was announced in early November 1946.[50]

Even though Seaton had the first version of the screenplay ready for *Miracle* long before shooting began, the story went through several iterations before it reached its final form on the screen.[51] He ended up creating four versions of the screenplay: the original, undated draft; a draft dated November 2, 1946; a second draft, dated November 16, 1946; and the final draft of the script, dated January 2, 1947, which was completed *after* the film crew had returned from shooting in New York. Other than a few revised scenes in February and March, it would be in

One of the first orders of business after purchasing the story of *Miracle on 34th Street* was to have Edmund Gwenn try on Santa suits in the Twentieth Century-Fox wardrobe department in early October 1946, a month before the film went into production. (Western Costume)

its final form. Counting Davies's two synopses, his full-length version of the story, and the subsequent book that he published (discussed in chapter 9), there are eight different versions of the story. The changes in the various versions demonstrate how different the film could have ended up on the screen.

Much of Davies's original story did make it into the film, but there were several additions and subtractions made by Seaton as he worked on the screenplay. One of the most striking elements of *Miracle* is its aim at realism and authenticity. This was a very intentional endeavor. Valentine Davies later stated: "We realized at the outset the necessity of using real names and real places as much as possible because we felt then as we do now that the success of the story was based upon the blend of complete realism and fantasy."[52] During the planning stages, as one critic later noted, they "threw away the book of don'ts in regards to using real names and places."[53]

The initial goal was to incorporate as many real elements as possible and make, in es-

Susan gives Kris a page she has torn from a magazine with the house she wants. The magazine was supposed to be *House Beautiful*, but publisher Hearst wouldn't give permission to use its name. (Photofest)

sence, a docudrama that was grounded in authentic, everyday life. Macy's and Gimbels were featured in Davies's story very early on, and were the most important parties to have on board; luckily, they were not too hard to convince (discussed in chapter 5). But Seaton went further and incorporated several other publications, media personalities, and products into the screenplay, although, despite concerted efforts, none of them ended up appearing in the final film.

Seaton wanted to include actual publications and media personalities in the film which would have given it the look and feel of a documentary. He really wanted newspaper headlines from legitimate news outlets (not tabloids) to be shown during the hearing, and so wrote copy in the style and format of those papers.[54] The headline MACY'S SANTA HAS LUNACY HEARING was supposed to be from the *New York Times*; KRIS KRINGLE KRAZY? KOURT KASE KOMING; 'KALAMITY!' KRY KIDDIES was supposed to be from New York's *Daily News*; and DOCTORS DOUBT SANITY OF SANTA WHO LAUNCHED GOODWILL CAMPAIGN was supposed to be from the *New York World-Telegram*; and it was undecided which paper would feature MACY ADMITS HIS SANTA CLAUS A FRAUD. There were also plans to have a shot of Doris reading about the hearing in the *New York Sun*.

During December while filming was going on, the studio's New York legal office would be busy contacting all of these publications to see if they would be willing to participate. The general sentiment from the newspapers was that, if they had not created the actual content, they did not want it to carry their name. Ultimately, none of the newspapers agreed to lend their names to the production.[55] Surprisingly, perhaps after seeing the success of *Miracle*, some of the newspapers changed their minds for the subsequent TV movies: The *Daily News* allowed its name to be used in the 1955 version, and again in the 1959 version, along with the *New York World-Telegram*.

Seaton tried to incorporate prominent magazines as well. The illustration of Susan's dream house was supposed to have been a page from *House Beautiful* magazine, and he originally intended for the page to feature the floor plan as well. When contacted, *House Beautiful*, a Hearst

publication, wasn't interested in being featured. He
also wanted to feature the December 21, 1946, cover
of *The New Yorker* and "The Talk of the Town" page
in a Sunday brunch scene with Fred and Doris, but
it, too, declined to participate, not wanting its name
on a fabricated article.[56] As a substitute, Earl Wilson, who covered life on Broadway in his column
"It Happened Last Night" for the *New York Post*, was
approached about using his name.[57] He was a good
friend of producer William Perlberg and was eager
to be included in the film.[58] The *New York Post* agreed
to being featured in the film, but required that the
fictional content, a clever little quatrain about Macy's
and Gimbels liking each other, be approved by the
retailers.[59] TCF had decided not to involve the stores
until the film was finalized and so didn't pursue this
angle.

Seaton also tried to incorporate the New York
Daily Mirror syndicated columnist and radio show
host Walter Winchell into the film. He was actually
going to be on-screen in a scene situated right before
Charlie Halloran meets with Judge Harper in his
living room. The scene had Winchell in front of a mi-
crophone delivering the news that Kris Kringle was
going to be tried for lunacy in front of Judge Harper.
Clearly sympathetic to Kris, he declares, "If bringing
back the true Christmas spirit is a form of insanity—
then it's too bad the heads of the big nations are all
so *very, very* SANE!"[60] He then gives a plug from his

Earl Wilson, whose popular column "It Happened
Last Night" ran for decades in the *New York Post*,
was a friend of producer William Perlberg and was
going to be featured in *Miracle on 34th Street* but his
newspaper wouldn't allow it. (Photofest)

sponsor, Jergens lotion. This scene appears to have actually been shot, but got removed during the
final editing of the picture.

To further heighten the realistic tone of the film, Seaton also wanted to feature several
products in the film. He wrote an entire scene about Kris's influence on the commercial market. It
followed the scene where Mr. Gimbel complains to his staff about not coming up with the brilliant
marketing scheme. As Fred and Doris are having Sunday brunch in her apartment, they read in
"The Talk of the Town" section of *The New Yorker* about how Kris has changed the world with his
practice of referring people to other stores. It then turns into a satiric montage, with the following
"anti-commercial" vignettes:

In an attempt to make *Miracle on 34th Street* as realistic as possible, media personality Walter Winchell had a scene where he announces the news of the hearing followed by an advertisement for Jergens. Unfortunately, the scene got cut. (Photofest, Author's collection)

In the second draft of the screenplay, George Seaton wrote a series of satirical "anti-commercials" demonstrating how Kris was influencing the world of commerce. One for Lucky Strike cigarettes encouraged smokers to stay with their current brand. (Author's Collection)

- Shoppers who go to Macy's are sent to Gimbels, and then Gimbels refers them to Wanamaker's, who recommends them to Bloomingdale's, who sends them to Stern's, who suggests they try B. Altman's, who advises them to go to cross-country to J. W. Robinson's in Los Angeles, etc.
- A commercial for Lucky Strike cigarettes urges customers to stay with Camels or Chesterfields or Old Gold if they are satisfied, since there is no pressing need to change.
- The new TCF film *Forever Amber* (1947), (also produced by William Perlberg) is advertised without superlatives such as "greatest" or "stupendous," but is being promoted as one that is "darn good," adding, "We hope you'll like it."
- A commercial for Calvert Whiskey is no longer targeting "men of distinction" and suggests that undistinguished men drink it, too.
- A tailor fitting a man with a jacket tells him it doesn't fit him very well.

To mock the movie industry, George Seaton included an "anti-commercial" for the film *Forever Amber* (1947) in which the audience is told that it isn't the greatest picture ever made, but it's okay. The movie was being produced by William Perlberg at the same time he was producing *Miracle on 34th Street*. (Photofest)

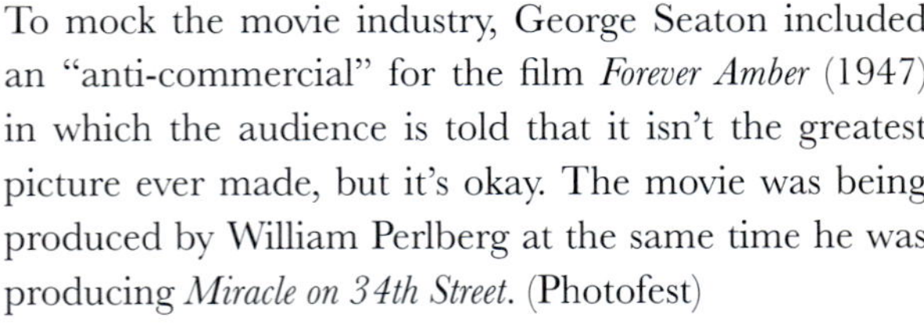

In 1946, Calvert Whiskey was promoting itself to "men of distinction" like actor Adolphe Menjou. George Seaton's parody recommended that undistinguished men should drink it too. (Author's collection)

- A doctor telling a woman that she doesn't need an operation.
- Men in a picket line carrying signs saying that their employer refuses to meet their demands, with the flip side of the signs stating "Maybe we're demanding too much."
- Finally, even *The New Yorker* concedes it's not the best magazine out there, and that there are others that are pretty good.

Canadian Club Whisky was also approached about being featured in the film, probably as a substitute for Calvert Whiskey, but the company declined. As an alternative, apparently TCF proposed using their bottle but obscuring the label in the film. Canadian Club rejected that option as well, indicating that they felt that their bottle was distinctive enough to still be recognizable.[61]

Once the production was approved and under way, Seaton, along with Davies, who was assigned to the project for about two weeks, made revisions to his original screenplay and submitted it to Zanuck.[62] After reading the updated (November 2) draft, Zanuck was only concerned about two things.

First, he was very critical of the Doris character. He found her too cold and harsh, and thought that if any man "ever heard [a mother] give her child the kind of advice Doris does, [he] would start running in the other direction."[63] Subsequently, there was some dialogue that disappeared from the scene where Doris scolds Fred for letting Susan visit Kris. Originally, Doris had a little bit of soliloquy as she gets after Fred for calling her "Susie," because experts have proven that using diminutive forms of names is belittling and psychologically damaging to a child, can cause feelings of insignificance, and can stunt their emotional growth. Fred, in jest, smiles at her and says he doesn't think that Teddy Roosevelt was affected by his name. (Incidentally, Davies didn't like this dialogue because he thought it was too extreme and would turn the audience against Doris.[64]) Seaton removed the lines in his next draft, which certainly softens Doris and keeps her from coming across as too stringent.

Zanuck's second issue was with the "anti-commercials" during the Sunday brunch scene in Doris's apartment. Even though he found the vignettes amusing, Zanuck felt them to be a little over-the-top, and, more importantly, risked "jeopardizing the sincerity and honesty of the balance of the story."[65] Seaton heeded the suggestions, and accordingly, removed the entire montage from the November 16 draft of the script.

There were a few other scenes that changed in these early script revisions. One episode that was clearly debated was in Davies's full-length version of the story, in Seaton's first two versions of the script, but was cut from the third version and not included in Davies's book version. It occurred after Doris invites Kris to dinner. The scene has them exiting Macy's when Kris mentions that he wants to buy a book for Susan. They stop in at a little bookstore and Kris selects the book and pays with a check. After they walk out, the shop owner looks at the check signed "Kris Kringle" and, thinking it's a fake, runs out after him yelling "Stop, thief!" This gets the attention of a police officer, who intervenes. The officer then takes them all down to the West 49th Street police station. Doris calls Fred, who comes down to the station and mediates the situation. Once everything is settled, they go to Doris's apartment for dinner. Kris gives Susan the book—a picture book of the "Pied Piper." Susan skeptically listens to the story but objects, because rats are "hardly musical, and a piper could not be heard all over as large a town as Hamelin."[66] In the film, the entire scene is reduced to Doris telling Mr. Shellhammer what she fears will happen if a police officer asks for Kris's name and he responds, then it's "clang, clang—Bellevue."

Another aspect of the narrative that went through several changes was how to handle

Canadian Club Whisky's distinctive bottle. (Author's collection)

Kris's battery of Mr. Sawyer. In Davies's early versions of the story (the first two synopses and the full-length story), the scene had more levity. Following the photo op with Mr. Macy and Mr. Gimbel, Fred proposes marriage to Doris, and they, along with Kris, go back to Doris's apartment for a celebration dinner. As they are cleaning up, Doris tells Fred that, unfortunately, she has to go to a lecture that evening given by Mr. Sawyer. It is a lecture/study group for Macy's personnel heads. As chairman of the committee, she organized the lecture weeks ago, and is doing the introduction. Furthermore, it would be really in-

During the development of the screenplay, Valentine Davies and George Seaton were at odds on how to handle Kris's battery of Mr. Sawyer. (Photofest)

sulting to Mr. Sawyer, who is close with Mr. Macy. In Davies's first two synopses, Kris is invited to come, but in the full-length treatment, Doris asks Fred to take Kris to a movie and not to mention where she has gone. Fred agrees, and goes to his apartment to grab his coat. While Kris is waiting for Fred, he happens to see a postcard for the event on Doris's desk. It states that Mr. Sawyer will be giving a lecture on "Exploding the Myth of Santa Claus" on Wednesday, December 18, at 8:30 p.m., at McMillan Auditorium on the Columbia University campus. Kris is miffed and leaves without telling Fred.

Kris goes to the auditorium but is not allowed in the front door, and so he goes around the back and enters an unlocked door just as Doris is finishing her introduction. Kris finds himself in the wings of a theater stage with a living room set with a large window and a fireplace. He hears Mr. Sawyer explaining that the Gothic architecture seems incongruous with the subject of his lecture, but the stage set is for a campus play and couldn't be moved.

Sawyer proceeds, stating that Santa Claus represents a generous father figure and people either want to be that figure or want the figure to exist. As he continues, Kris walks behind the set window to the other side of the stage, where he can hear better, and the audience starts laughing. Sawyer doesn't see this and is perplexed at their reaction, but Doris does and starts to panic.

Sawyer continues, saying that people who want to be Santa are compensating for feelings of guilt, and gives examples. Kris starts to fume and gets angrier and angrier with each new comment. His grumblings start to become audible. Sawyer hears them but doesn't know from whom they are coming. He makes the comment "The symbolic significance of the long beard is rather obvious, but it can't be discussed before mixed company," which completely infuriates Kris, who comes out onstage through the chimney on the set. The audience roars with laughter.

Kris tries to defend himself in front of Sawyer, but Sawyer refuses to listen, and, unwittingly, responds to him as "Mr. Kringle," which causes even more of an uproar. Doris tries to intervene, to no avail. Sawyer insists that there will be a discussion after the lecture, and so Kris takes a seat while Sawyer tries to resume. When Sawyer says something with which he doesn't agree, Kris makes facial expressions which amuse the audience. Sawyer tries to continue but just gets more and more flustered. At one point he completely garbles a sentence and Kris, seizing the moment, gets up and asks him how many fingers he is holding up. Sawyer refuses to go on, and Doris is pleading with Kris. Kris insists he just wants to refute Sawyer's "hogwash" and won't leave until he does. Sawyer comes toward Kris with vengeance in mind, and Kris threatens him with his cane (in the first two synopses, Kris just vocally objects and humiliates Sawyer). Sawyer steps backward, trips on a wire, and falls backward, knocking a glass of water off the podium onto his head. While this is all happening, Fred has entered the back of the auditorium and witnesses the event. The next day Sawyer has exaggerated the violence and language that Kris used, and so Mr. Macy has agreed to send him to Bellevue. The ruse to get Kris in the limousine follows. The scene was retained in the book, and a modified version was used in the 1955 TV movie.

Seaton dispensed with Davies's scene when writing the first version of the screenplay and developed an even more farcical approach to the battery by situating it in the cafeteria. Kris and Alfred are having lunch when they overhear Sawyer expostulating on the myth and delusion of Santa Claus (the same speech he gives at Columbia). Kris becomes incensed and threatens to throw a chocolate cream pie in his face. Sawyer gets scared and falls back and hits a tray stand. Sawyer is obviously completely humiliated. An adapted version of this scene surfaced in the 1973 TV movie, with Kris actually throwing a pie in Sawyer's face.

But Seaton had second thoughts and removed the pie scene from the November 16 draft, replacing it with Kris hitting Sawyer in his office. When Seaton shared the new scene with Davies, Davies did not like it. He felt that the previous two versions of the scene were comical, with Kris making a fool out of Sawyer, but that the battery made the scene "heavy." He thought that it would cause Kris "to lose his personality and his crisp charm."[67] Seaton obviously ignored this suggestion, but for good reason: He needed Kris to do something that would get him locked up, and mere humiliation would be insufficient.

A small, but interesting, change was made to the scene where Susan tells Kris her Christmas wish. In Davies's first story outline, Susan overhears Fred and Doris (who are married in that version) discussing their impending separation. Under this gloom, she comes into the living room and pulls out the picture of the house and tells Kris that this is what she wants. In the second story outline and in the book version, the venue was changed to Central Park. One Sunday, Kris takes Susan for a walk, and they make their way to the reindeer pens in the zoo. It is here that

Kris asks Susan about her Christmas wish. The scene is very similar to how it appears in the movie, except for the change in locale, to Susan's bedroom, which Seaton changed in the first version of the screenplay.

Another small but interesting change was made to the Christmas Day scenes. In the first two synopses and the full-length version of the story (and carried over in the book and 1955 TV movie), Susan gets up on Christmas morning and goes into the living room to see if the present she wants is under the tree. When she doesn't find it, she is disappointed, and tells her mother that she doesn't believe in Santa Claus. Doris tries to console her, saying that she was wrong, and that Susan must believe in him.

Meanwhile, Kris, who has been missing since Christmas Eve, makes a triumphal return to the Brooks' Memorial Home, where he can now live, since he has been declared sane by the court. He is to preside over the Christmas-morning festivities. He calls Fred and asks him to bring Doris and Susan out to visit him. Fred hesitates, since they have just broken up, but then acquiesces. There had been a big snowstorm during the night, and Kris suggests the best roads to take. En route, Susan sees her dream house. Seaton changed this scene in his original treatment of the screenplay so that they would drive by *after* the visit to the Brooks' Home, and turned it into the culminating scene. Seaton's change was clever because it allowed one more "Is he or isn't he?" moment. A detail that survived from Davies's first story outline to the final film is the cane left in the corner of the house.

One hurdle that every writer had to jump through at that time was getting script approval from the Motion Picture Association of America Production Code office. In order to remove objectionable content and to avoid costly retakes, the studios were required to submit the script before filming began, as well as any subsequent changes made during the course of production.

When the first 112 pages of the *Miracle* script were submitted in early November 1946, the Production Code office only had some minor objections. It "earnestly" recommended using some product other than whiskey in the "anti-commercial vignette," since "the bulk of the protests on picture content received in this office have to do with drinking." [68] The request was easy to accept since the scene was cut and neither whiskey company wanted to be involved anyway. Surprisingly, there appears to have been no objection to Mrs. Shellhammer's imbibing eight triple-strength martinis.

But the Production Code office wasn't solely concerned with objectionable material. Hollywood had long been opposed to product placement in movies, as the studios did not want their films to become long commercials; hence, for decades, characters in movies only used generic brand products. The office was concerned about the Jergens lotion ad during the Walter Winchell scene.[69] In this case, the Production Code office thought that movie theater owners would object to it being too much like a promotion of the product, and so asked that it be removed. The office also reminded the studio to obtain approval from all living individuals mentioned in the film, such as the allusion to Hollywood restaurateur Michael Romanoff (discussed in chapter 5).

Seaton would continue to work on the script before heading to New York, further refining it during the filming there. The November 16 script had the story pretty much in its final form, and does not differ much from the final, January 2, 1947, script. (There are several plotlines and scenes that were included in all versions of the screenplay, and even filmed, but still ended up on the cutting-room floor. These will be discussed in more detail in chapters 5 and 6.)

TCF script #153 was assigned the production number A-512 on November 8, 1946, and *Miracle* was officially under way.[70] Just two weeks later, the principal cast and crew would be headed to New York to start filming, on Thanksgiving Day.[71]

Maureen O'Hara, Edmund Gwenn, Natalie Wood, and John Payne were perfectly cast in *Miracle on 34th Street*. This is one of only three scenes in which they all appear together. (Author's collection)

The Cast

The casting for *Miracle* was, in itself, a bit of a miracle, in that a couple of the principal and several of the supporting parts were not finalized until right before filiming. Due to scheduling conflicts, vacations, contractual issues, and other commitments, the cast could have ended up being quite different.

The usual practice for casting a motion picture at TCF during the 1940s was to choose from the actors and actresses who were already under contract with the studio. This ended up being the case for Maureen O'Hara and John Payne. Occasionally a studio would borrow a star from another studio when it felt that a film's success hinged on the casting of a certain personality. This, of course, usually involved some level of financial remuneration and/or trading of services of another star at another studio, and so wasn't done unless felt to be absolutely necessary. Even more rare was borrowing actors and actresses for supporting roles, since a studio already had a stable of stars on the payroll that could perform at no additional cost, but such was the case with Edmund Gwenn, who was under contract at MGM, and Natalie Wood, who was under contract at Universal. This was done, as director George Seaton later recalled, because the success of the picture really depended on the right casting of the Kris and Susan roles. "As long as I had Teddy Gwenn and Natalie Wood," he said, "I was willing to compromise on others."[72]

MAUREEN O'HARA (1920–2015), *DORIS WALKER*

The first casting decision that was made—and made very early—was the casting of Maureen O'Hara. She was recommended as a lead when the story was submitted to TCF in July 1946, and

Lew Schreiber, the second-in-command of production at TCF, indicated that he definitely wanted her for the role in mid-August 1946, a month before the purchase of the story was finalized.[73] There is no indication that any other actress was considered for the role.

Maureen O'Hara was born Maureen FitzSimons in 1920 in Dublin, Ireland, to a well-to-do, devout Catholic family (her older sister would become a nun). Her father worked in the clothing industry, and her mother, a fashion designer, was also an accomplished contralto opera singer and actress who had performed in the legitimate theater. Maureen was the second of six children, almost all of whom ended up working in the performing arts and entertainment industries in some capacity.[74]

A very young Maureen O'Hara with her mentor Charles Laughton in 1939. He helped launch her career by casting her in *Jamaica Inn* and *The Hunchback of Notre Dame* (both 1939). The two would remain lifelong friends. (Photofest)

At an early age, Maureen showed an interest in drama. She and her siblings would regularly stage plays at their home for fun.[75] Maureen's mother thought she showed enough dramatic talent that she secretly enrolled her in the Ena Mary Burke School of Elocution and Drama, without telling her husband. Maureen attended regular school during the day, after which she went to the drama school to study acting, singing, dancing, and poetry recitation. It would be a full year before her father knew of her dramatic training. When he did find out, he was none too happy about this decision, as he wanted his daughter to pursue a more practical career. To appease her father, Maureen would later become proficient in shorthand, typing, and bookkeeping, which meant that if necessary, she could work as a secretary as an alternative to acting.[76]

As she grew up, Maureen had plenty of opportunity to hone her dramatic skills. She joined the Rathmines Theatre Company and worked in amateur plays on evenings and weekends. She started winning amateur acting competitions and, at age thirteen, was even invited to perform classical plays on Ireland's only radio station, RTE (Raidio Teilifis Eireann).[77] In 1934, she played Portia in *The Merchant of Venice* and won the Dublin Feis Award, and then, at age fourteen, she was invited to join Dublin's prestigious Abbey Theatre. Initially, she did janitorial work and helped to build and paint sets before she was eventually cast in minor roles. In 1936, she did her final examinations at Trinity College and then went on to become the youngest graduate of the drama course at the Guildhall School of Music and Drama. Six months later she would complete her degree and receive an associateship from the London College of Music and Drama.[78] She was finally offered a lead role in an Abbey Theatre production, but ultimately didn't end up performing it because of a major turn of events.

Maureen's story of being discovered and getting into the movies is the kind that has kept hope springing eternal for many an aspiring actress. One evening when she was seventeen, after attending the Abbey Theatre, Maureen and her parents arrived at the Gresham Hotel in Dublin to have dinner together. As they entered, the manager, a friend of her father's, approached them and wanted to introduce them to entertainer Harry Richman, who was in town for an engagement. Richman, clearly drunk, stumbled from the hotel's bar to greet them. After cordial introductions were made, the FitzSimonses proceeded to the dining room. Richman was the first American that Maureen had ever met and she was not impressed.[79] She did not give the encounter much thought, so much so that a few years later she would tell a *Los Angeles Times* reporter, "I can't remember ever meeting Harry Richman."[80]

But Maureen's striking looks that had helped her win the Dawn Beauty Competition earlier that year clearly made an impression on Richman, even though he was under the influence.[81] Just a week later, on his referral, Elstree Studios contacted her and asked her to do a screen test. Since she had no intention of pursuing a career in the movies, she turned down the offer. Those around her convinced her that this was a once-in-a-lifetime opportunity and that she could always return to the theater if it didn't go anywhere. She relented and went to London with her parents for the test.[82]

Maureen recalls the test being "horrible." They dressed her in a gold lamé gown with accordion pleats that made her look like Mata Hari and caked makeup on her face to make her look much older than she was. She went through the motions of a usual screen test—strutting, picking up a phone, sitting in a chair, etc.—to see how she would look on screen. During her visit, she was given a small walk-on part in Harry Richman's film *Kicking the Moon Around* (1938) that was being filmed the same day.[83]

It just so happened that during this same time, famed actor and co-owner of Mayflower Pictures, Charles Laughton, was looking for an actress for the role of Mary Yellan in his upcoming adaptation of Daphne du Maurier's popular novel, *Jamaica Inn*, to be directed by Alfred Hitchcock. He viewed Maureen's screen test and thought she was overly done up, and had to be at least thirty-five years old. Initially, Laughton was not interested in using her. But, he recalled later, "for a split second [I saw] this extraordinarily beautiful profile which was invisible with all the makeup," and decided to at least meet Maureen.[84] He reached out just as Maureen and her parents were getting ready to return to Ireland and asked if she would be willing to do a second screen test for him, because, he felt, her "possibilities" had not been adequately photographed.[85]

Their first meeting was a bit awkward. Charles Laughton, one of the most famous actors in England, and Erich Pommer, one of the most famous directors in the world (he had discovered Marlene Dietrich a few years previously), as the owners of Mayflower Pictures, were intimately involved in all aspects of their production company. Laughton recalled O'Hara blowing into his office "like a hurricane in a tweed suit," demanding "What d'ya want with me?"

Maureen remembered being asked to do a cold reading of a script, but she politely refused, feeling that she was unprepared. Laughton took her out to lunch and asked her why she wanted to be an actress, and her response, which he still remembered years later, was: "When I was a child I would go down to the garden and talk to the flowers and I would pretend I was the flowers talking back to myself." She did the screen test and then she returned to Ireland for the Christmas holiday. The second test was received *much* more favorably than the first, and, after seeing it, Laughton and Pommer were sufficiently impressed to offer her a seven-year contract with Mayflower.[86]

Maureen returned to London in early 1938 to start work as a screen actress. Laughton wanted her to become comfortable on a movie set, and so cast her in a low-budget musical titled *My Irish Molly* (aka, *Little Miss Molly*) (1938). Though she wasn't too happy with the film, it did give her some experience, which she needed. It would be the first and only time that she would be credited on-screen with her real name, Maureen FitzSimons.[87]

Maureen O'Hara got her first big film role as the girl who discovers suspicious activities while staying at the *Jamaica Inn* (1939). Robert Newton, seen here, co-starred. (Photofest)

Although she only had one film to her name, Laughton thought she was ready for the big time, so she began work on *Jamaica Inn* (1939), directed by Alfred Hitchcock, his final film before heading to America. Before *Jamaica Inn* was released, Laughton told Maureen that her last name was "too long for the marquee" and she would have to change it. He gave her the choice of "O'Hara" or "O'Mara." Maureen protested and said she didn't want to change her name, and refused to pick either one. So Laughton took it upon himself and selected O'Hara, probably due to the popularity of the heroine from *Gone with the Wind*.[88]

By 1939, Mayflower Pictures

Maureen O'Hara got a choice role playing Esmeralda in RKO's production of *The Hunchback of Notre Dame* (1939). (Photofest)

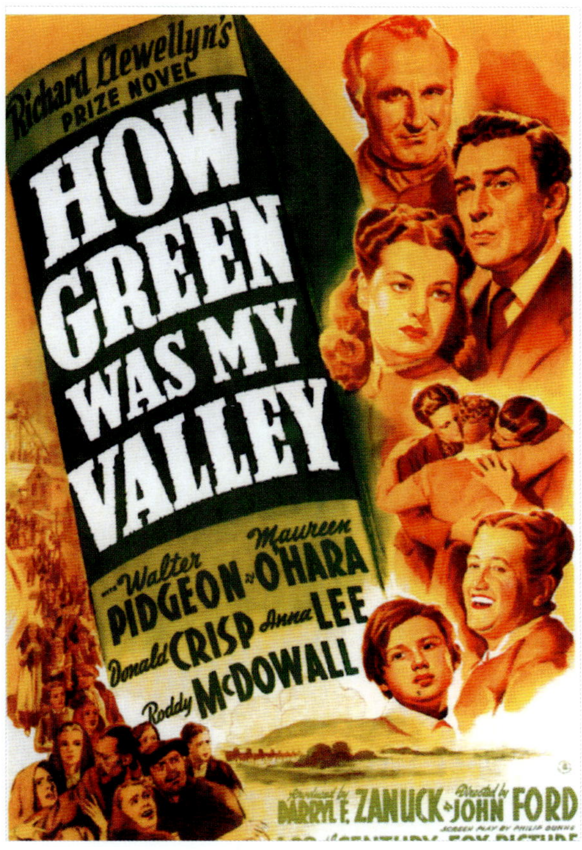

After *Hunchback*, RKO failed to properly capitalize on Maureen O'Hara's talents. Luckily she caught the eye of director John Ford, who cast her in *How Green Was My Valley* (1941). The movie won the Oscar for Best Picture and made O'Hara a bona fide movie star.. (Photofest)

was experiencing financial difficulties, and Laughton and Pommer were looking for a way out. They successfully arranged to be bought out by the American film company RKO. Unbeknownst to O'Hara, this included the purchase of her contract. As part of the deal, Laughton landed her the plum role of Esmeralda to his Quasimodo in a big-budget production of *The Hunchback of Notre Dame* that would be filmed in California. O'Hara left for America with her mother in June 1939.[89]

It was only several months later, after getting settled in Los Angeles, that she was told her contract now belonged to RKO. She was, naturally, quite upset that this was all done behind her back and, moreover, because it meant that she would not be going home to Ireland anytime soon. However, it wasn't all bad news: O'Hara was now represented by Lew Wasserman at MCA, and he renegotiated her contract from $80 per week to $700.[90] O'Hara's acting skills matched her beauty, and *Hunchback* was a huge success, financially and critically. It was undoubtedly this role that caught the attention of Hollywood. Alfred Hitchcock wanted her again for *Rebecca* (1940), and Cecil B. DeMille and Victor Fleming had also requested her.[91] RKO turned them all down and, over the next year, O'Hara would make three lackluster films for her home studio, the most notable being *Dance, Girl, Dance* (1940), which was directed by Hollywood's only female director, Dorothy Arzner, and featured O'Hara in a catfight with a young Lucille Ball. Despite their on-screen quarrel, the two became lifelong friends.

One hiccup in O'Hara's burgeoning career was her marriage to George Brown the day she boarded the *Queen Mary* to come to America in 1939. He had been the production manager at the studio in England.[92] The two had been in a casual dating relationship and she was not that interested in him. On the day she boarded the ship to head to America, he called and asked to see her before she left. Even though she didn't really have the time, he persisted, and O'Hara acquiesced. She showed up at the address he had given and walked in to find that he had arranged a full-blown wedding service. Completely stunned, she was in shock; yet somehow she went through the motions and was suddenly married. She left and boarded the ship, never to see him again. Although the marriage was never consummated, it would take another two years before she was able to get it annulled.[93]

She met her second husband, Will Price, on the set of *Hunchback*, where he was a dialogue coach with directorial aspirations. They would marry at the St. Mary of the Pines Convent in Chatawa, Mississippi, his home state, in late 1941.[94]

In the late 1930s, the head of production at TCF, Darryl Zanuck, was pushing the boundaries of Hollywood's comfort zone with socially conscious pictures like *The Grapes of Wrath* (bringing attention to the plight of Americans acutely affected by the Depression) and *Brigham Young* (a story of religious persecution meant to highlight the then-current treatment of Jews in Europe). Zanuck's next project was an adaptation of Richard Llewellyn's popular 1939 novel, *How Green Was My Valley*, about a small Welsh town and the labor disputes that arise between the coal miners and the owner of the mine. It would be the studio's biggest production of the year, and John Ford, who had been making films there for twenty years, was chosen as the director.

In early 1941, Ford held a party at his home and invited O'Hara to attend. Their interaction at the party was minimal. A few days later, to her surprise, she was invited to TCF to discuss appearing in *Valley*, and she ended up getting the part. O'Hara and Ford would become dear friends and end up making five pictures together.[95]

One sticking point, however, was her contract. RKO had agreed to lend O'Hara, but TCF felt that its investment in O'Hara for such a high-profile production as *Valley* was so substantial that they wanted to have her under contract for future films. In a highly unusual move, O'Hara remained under contract to RKO but also went under contract to TCF.[96] As it turned out, TCF had a much better vision of how to capitalize on O'Hara's talents. She clearly understood this, and in 1944, would renegotiate so she was primarily under contract to TCF, doing one picture a year at RKO (ultimately making fourteen films at TCF compared to only five more at RKO).[97]

Valley was a popular and critical success, with ten Academy Award nominations and five wins, including for Best Picture of 1941. The casting choice of O'Hara was brilliant: It turned her into a star, and was the beginning of her long artistic association with director John Ford. For her next picture, the World War II drama *To the Shores of Tripoli* (1942), she was cast as US Navy nurse Mary Carter, a strong-willed, no-nonsense character, which presaged many of her future hallmark film roles. This was O'Hara's first Technicolor film, which let audiences see her striking titian red hair and hazel green eyes for the first time. The expensive Technicolor process was always reserved for

To the Shores of Tripoli (1942) was the first pairing of Maureen O'Hara and John Payne. They would end up starring in four films together. (Photofest)

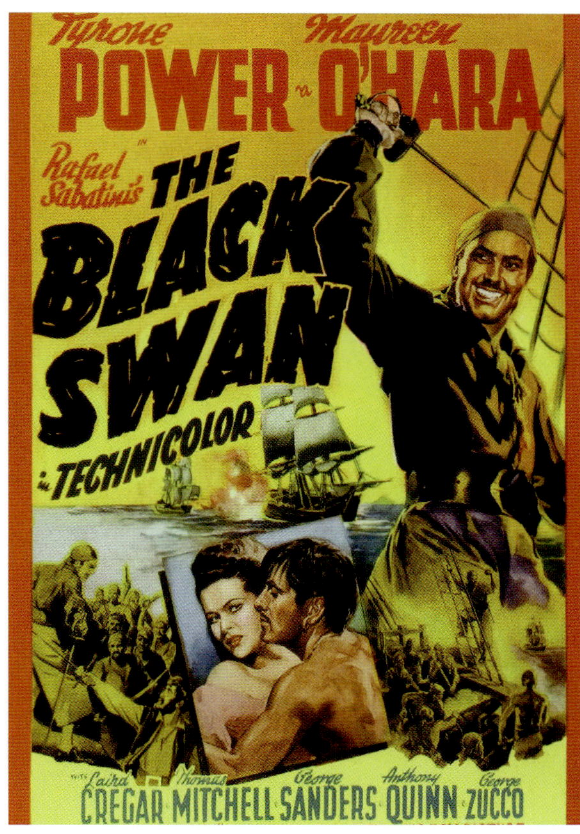

The Black Swan (1942), Maureen O'Hara's second color picture, found her swashbuckling with Twentieth Century-Fox's top male star, Tyrone Power. Her striking red hair and green eyes photographed so beautifully, she was soon crowned the "Queen of Technicolor." (Photofest)

Maureen O'Hara proved her versatility, appearing in period pieces, modern dramas, and even westerns. Here she is with Joel McCrea in *Buffalo Bill* (1944). (Photofest)

As she became one of the studio's leading ladies, she was paired with leading men like Henry Fonda, seen here in the wartime drama *Immortal Sergeant* (1943). (Photofest)

prestige pictures; *Tripoli* is notable because it was one of the few non-musical films to be made in color during the war. It was also the first time she co-starred with John Payne. He became one of O'Hara's "dearest and best friends" in Hollywood. During the filming of *Tripoli* he told her "[to] smile a bit more. You always look like you're angry and stressed out," to which she replied "I am!" He advised her to "stop worrying and just do it [act]."[98] She photographed so

Maureen O'Hara was quite the cover girl in the fall of 1945, appearing on the September issue of *Motion Picture Magazine* and on the October issue of *Photoplay*, the leading movie magazine of the day. (Photofest)

beautifully in this film that she was soon referred to as the "Queen of Technicolor."[99] She was also perceived as an icy cool, prim and proper lady, which resulted in her getting labeled as "Frozen Champagne" in the press, a moniker she absolutely detested.[100]

Over the next few years O'Hara rose to become one of Hollywood's biggest stars, averaging three to four pictures per year, and being paired with top actors such as Tyrone Power, Henry Fonda, Joel McCrea, George Montgomery, and Cornel Wilde. She showed her versatility as an actress in swashbuckling pirate adventures, such as *The Black Swan* (1942) and *The Spanish Main* (1945); modern military dramas, such as *Ten Gentlemen from West Point* (1942) and *Immortal Sergeant* (1943); in a modern Cinderella story with a big band backdrop, in *Do You Love Me* (1946); and in a Western, *Buffalo Bill* (1944).

O'Hara would again be paired with John Payne in

John Payne and Maureen O'Hara made a beautiful couple—and a lucrative one! Due to their successful pairings in *To the Shores of Tripoli* (1942) and *Sentimental Journey* (1946), they were considered solid box office draws that would attract audiences to see *Miracle*. (Author's collection)

Payne and O'Hara starred for the second time together in the tearjerker *Sentimental Journey* (1946). Their on-screen chemistry and the box office success of this picture made them logical choices for *Miracle on 34th Street*. (Photofest)

Sentimental Journey (1946), which, incidentally, used an instrumental version of the popular Les Brown/Doris Day song for its theme. This heart-wrenching film tells the story of a childless couple who adopt a young girl and then—spoiler alert!—the mother dies. Released in March of 1946, it was a huge success, and showcased the chemistry of Payne and O'Hara once again. It became clear that they were a winning team on-screen. For years, even after the triumph of *The Quiet Man* (1952), many fans would come up and tell her that *Sentimental Journey* was their favorite film of hers.[101]

In the spring of 1946, she was at RKO, co-starring with Douglas Fairbanks Jr. in a splashy Technicolor version of *Sinbad the Sailor* (1947). In the summer and early fall of that year, before being cast in *Miracle*, O'Hara was filming the posh, globe-trotting, horse-racing drama *The Homestretch* (1947) for TCF, looking resplendent in the Kay Nelson–designed wardrobe (with some very fetching hats!), again in Technicolor.

Right before *Miracle on 34th Street*, Maureen O'Hara starred in the horse-racing, globe-trotting romance *The Homestretch* (1947), shown here with Glenn Langan. Kay Nelson would design her clothes for both pictures. (Photofest)

O'Hara was planning a trip to Ireland to visit her family there in the fall.[102] She hadn't been back since she had come to America in 1939, and much had changed: She was now married, with a baby girl, Bronwyn (named after her co-star Anna Lee's character in *How Green Was My Valley*).[103] But then O'Hara tripped on the set of *The Homestretch* and was laid up for several days, which delayed filming.[104] Then there was a decision to add an additional love scene, and filming got extended an additional ten days, with completion expected on October 12.[105]

In August, as details were being worked out to purchase the *Miracle* story, TCF ran into a conflict with RKO. The production company would have to be in New York in November and December for on location shooting for *Miracle*, and then back at the studio's lot in January to do interiors. RKO wanted to use O'Hara beginning in January for another picture. The studio lawyers went back and forth ad nauseam over the details in her contract, to see who got to use her services, and if it would be within the time frames they wanted.[106] Luckily, the two studios were able to work out the disagreement, and O'Hara was able to do *Miracle*.

O'Hara departed for the Ireland in late October to visit her family.[107] In later years, O'Hara would claim that she was not informed about the casting decision for *Miracle* until she was in Dublin in November, and that she was forced to cut her trip short to come back to New York to start filming. This seems hard to believe, since her involvement in the film was announced in the press in early October, before she departed.[108] The more likely explanation is that she *did* know about the casting decision, but that the shooting schedule had not been finalized, and/or had not been communicated to her by her agent.

In any event, while O'Hara had planned on taking a six-week vacation in Ireland, she was only gone for about two and half weeks before being summoned back to start filiming.[109] She arrived in New York on November 19, furious about being called back just to play a personnel manager in a silly movie about Santa Claus. These feelings were further compounded by a near-kidnapping incident while she was visiting her family.[110] However, she acquiesced, and after reading the script, her attitude changed. She later recalled feeling that it "was going to be a hit," although she "was not clairvoyant enough to foresee it becoming a classic."[111]

JOHN PAYNE (1912–1989), *FRED GAILEY*

John Payne was recommended for the role of Fred Gailey when *Miracle* was submitted to TCF in July 1946—but he almost didn't get the part.[112] There were a couple of other contenders from the studio's ranks, the first being Dana Andrews.[113]

Andrews had done a few films for United Artists before finding his way to TCF. He first appeared in supporting roles, but his status quickly grew. He got some good roles in *Swamp Water* (1941) and in *Belle Starr* (1941), which was his first pairing with Gene Tierney, and great exposure

Tall (six-foot-three), dark, and handsome looks made John Payne a movie star. By 1942, he was getting more fan mail than Tyrone Power and Victor Mature, two of the studio's biggest leading men. (Photofest)

Dana Andrews was originally slated to play the role of Fred Gailey. (Photofest)

in the film adaptation of one of the most popular plays of the 1930s, *Tobacco Road* (1941). He certainly drew sympathy for his portrayal of the unfortunate victim in *The Ox-Bow Incident* (1943), a nominee for Best Picture.

But it was Andrews's turn as New York police detective Mark McPherson in the elegant whodunit *Laura* (1944), paired for the third time with Tierney, that made him an A-lister. Andrews later credited this success to the fact that fellow contract players Tyrone Power and Henry Fonda were in the service during World War II, allowing him to get the roles that would have gone to them. (Andrews was unable to serve due to health reasons.) As one of the top stars at the studio, he got plum roles opposite Alice Faye and Linda Darnell as a no-good hustler in *Fallen Angel* (1945), and then had a leading role in the drama about GIs coming home after the war, *The Best Years of Our Lives* (1946) for Samuel Goldwyn, which would be one of the most popular films of the year, financially and critically, taking home the Best Picture Oscar. But it was probably his work in the role of Pat Gilbert in the Rodgers and Hammerstein musical, *State Fair* (1945), that helped him to be considered for *Miracle.* He proved that he was just as good in lighter fare as he was at playing a heavy. He was slated to appear in *Miracle* until just a week before filming was to begin, when he was replaced by Payne.[114]

The other actor who was considered for the role of Fred was Mark Stevens. The choice seems a bit surprising—not because he was relative newcomer, but because of his lack of experience in comedy. He had started out at Warner Bros. in the mid-1940s in supporting roles (under the name Steve Richards) in mostly war-themed films, like *Destination Tokyo* (1944), with Cary Grant, and *Passage to Marseille* (1944), with Humphrey Bogart. He got his big break when he came to TCF, where he finally got leading roles in the prison drama *Within These Walls* (1945), and as the tough private eye in one of the better film noirs of the era, *The Dark Corner* (1946), co-starring a young Lucille Ball in arguably the best of her early film roles.

Stevens was probably considered for *Miracle* because of his work in *I Wonder Who's Kissing Her Now* (1947), a glossy Technicolor biopic of turn-of-the-century composer Joseph E. Howard. Co-starring perky June Haver, the role was much lighter and gave him a chance at comedy, in which he proved himself competent; he and Haver had good chemistry, and were paired again two years later for *Oh, You Beautiful Doll* (1949), another musical biopic of another popular songwriter, Fred Fisher. However, as likable as Stevens is in these films, it's hard to see him being able to exude the warmth necessary for the Fred Gailey role, especially since he excelled at playing hard-boiled detectives and policemen, roles that he was drawn to for the rest of his career. When he was proposed for the role, Zanuck vetoed it, stating that Stevens "does not fit the part at all."[115]

Luckily, they settled on John Payne, who was born in 1912 as John Howard Payne in Roanoke, Virginia, the second of three boys.[116] He was the great-nephew of another famous John Howard Payne, who penned the lyrics to one of the most popular songs of the nineteenth century, "Home, Sweet Home." His father, a real estate broker, became a millionaire, and purchased the fifty-acre Fort Lewis farm property north of Roanoke, moving the family there and transforming it into one of the finest estates in Virginia.[117] This would be where Payne would spend most of his youth, learning to ride horses and feed chickens. The property gave him endless opportunities to swim, hike, and explore; according to his mother, his upbringing was fairly idyllic.[118]

In his youth, he was befriended by a local clergyman, Dr. Carl Block. He made such an impression on Payne that for several years he planned on going into the ministry.[119] At age fourteen he went away to attend the Episcopal High School in Washington, DC. The following summer he got a job on a hemp boat in Cuba. The experience was eye-opening, as he learned about the cruder side of life. He learned to fight to protect himself, but, with the ministry still on his mind, stayed away from the girls and booze.[120]

When he returned to school, he found himself engrossed with the pulp fiction of the day. He started writing and, feeling his stories were as good as those he was reading, started submitting them to publishers. Several of his stories were accepted for publication in detective and horror magazines.[121] He was a voracious reader, devouring two to three books a week.[122] He also became interested in aeronautics and tried, unsuccessfully, to build a real glider airplane.[123]

The stock market crash of 1929 devastated his father financially and probably contributed to his death in early 1930. This, of course, changed the Paynes' family life dramatically. Payne had transferred to Mercersburg Academy in Pennsylvania, where he completed his schooling. It would not be until after his graduation that he would learn of his family's financial ruin. There was enough money to support his mother, but Fort Lewis had to be sold. Payne's inheritance amounted to $1,000 and some AT&T stock.[124]

Payne initially decided to attend Roanoke College in order to remain close to his mother.[125] He became unsatisfied at Roanoke, and so applied to MIT, but didn't get in. Payne then decided to go to Columbia University in New York in 1933, and major in journalism. While at Columbia, in addition to his journalism classes, he took drama and Shakespeare classes, and also enrolled in voice lessons at Juilliard.[126] Through faculty connections at Columbia, he got a role in a production of *Hamlet* at the Little Theater in Roxbury, Connecticut, as well as small singing gigs on radio shows at CBS.[127] He ended up selling his AT&T stock to pay for his tuition during his second year at Columbia. He then took a variety of jobs, including being a switchboard operator; a bouncer at a chop suey restaurant; a wrestler at exhibition matches (using the names "Alexei Petroff, Savage of the Steppes" and "Tiger

Jack Payne"); a babysitter; and a singer at Minsky's burlesque theater, the latter being so tawdry that he only lasted a few nights.[128]

During one of his wrestling matches, he broke his ankle. This turned out to be a blessing. One evening he got a telegram from a theatrical agent he had met at a party some months before offering him a job as a stock player in a traveling Shubert show in Detroit.[129] Payne took it, as it offered a chance to be on the road and earn a steady salary of $40 per week.[130] The experience was great, but he eventually tired of being on the road and returned to New York by the fall of 1935. His timing was impeccable. His agent had found another job for him in the new Broadway musical *At Home Abroad*, which gave him a good-enough salary to get a decent apartment and, for a time, own a car.[131]

But Payne almost lost his chance to go to Hollywood. One night after the show, a man approached him, saying, "I just saw the show, Payne—I'm Sam Goldwyn. You're pretty good." Thinking this was a joke, Payne retorted, "I ought to be. I'm Clark Gable." Payne then went to his dressing room to change. When he got there, he kept thinking about the man's garb. He'd been wearing a very fine suit from an impeccable tailor, so that man probably really was Samuel Goldwyn! He rushed back down just in time to catch Goldwyn before he exited. He was offered a $350 per week contract with Goldwyn Studios; he accepted, and was off to California.[132]

Though Goldwyn brought him to Hollywood, Payne only appeared in one film at his studio, the soap opera–ish *Dodsworth* (1936). During his time there, he ran into the mogul twice. The first time, Goldwyn asked to see his teeth. Upon inspection, he said, "Tsk, tsk. Have them capped and straightened at once." Payne did get a cleaning and some fillings done, but nothing major. When he ran into Goldwyn the next time, he was asked to see his teeth again. Goldwyn declared, "Hmm . . . a thousand percent better. You see? Now you can *smile*."[133]

When his contract expired, Payne said he was offered a renewal, but turned it down after he heard his voice on film, because it sounded squeaky and high-pitched. He was embarrassed and feared that he would suffer the same fate as silent film star John Gilbert, whose voice didn't match his looks when sound movies came along, and it ruined his career. So Payne took some time off and worked with a vocal coach and succeeded in lowering his singing voice by a

One of Payne's earliest roles was in *College Swing* (1938), an all-star cast that included his future co-star Betty Grable. From left to right: Payne, Gracie Allen, George Burns, Martha Raye, Bob Hope, Florence George, Ben Blue, Betty Grable, and Jackie Coogan. (Photofest)

whole octave, as well as deepening his speaking voice.[134] The decision ended up being a smart one, as his singing voice would become one of his biggest assets.

Payne then jumped around from studio to studio. He got third billing in a smaller 1937 TCF film, *Fair Warning*, and then ended up at Paramount, where his most notable entry was in a George Burns/Gracie Allen picture called *College Swing* (1938) that, coincidentally, also featured his up-and-coming future co-star, Betty Grable. He then went under contract at Warner Bros. and got a nice break when Dick Powell refused to perform in the Busby Berkeley film, *Garden of the Moon* (1938). The role went to Payne, and he started getting noticed. He also got top billing in a couple of "B" pictures, including *Kid Nightingale* (1939) (about a singing boxer) opposite Jane Wyman, and *King of the Lumberjacks* (1940). *Wings of the Navy* (1939) with Olivia de Havilland was another highlight of his time there, professionally and personally, since he got to be around real aircraft.

It was following his departure from Warner Bros. and signing on at TCF in 1940 that his career really took off. His first film as a contract player at the studio was *Star Dust* (1940), a Cinderella story about a young actress, played by Linda Darnell, making it big in Hollywood. Tyrone Power was originally going to star in the picture but he didn't want to do it, and so the studio decided to replace him with Payne, who was equally tall, dark, and handsome.[135] When Power enlisted in the army,

Payne got a great break when Dick Powell refused to appear in the film *Garden of the Moon* (1938). However, despite appearing in several films at Warner Brothers, the studio failed to make him a star. Here he is with Margaret Lindsay. (Photofest)

John Payne's first role at Twentieth Century-Fox was in the Hollywood Cinderella story *Star Dust* (1940) with Linda Darnell.

With a good singing voice and skilled in light comedy, Payne became a natural for musicals and starred in some of the era's best. Here he is with Sonja Henie in *Sun Valley Serenade* (1941). (Photofest)

TCF decided to groom Payne to fill in during the interim.[136] He went on to appear in *Tin Pan Alley* (1940) with the studio's biggest blonde, Alice Faye, and again with young ingénue Betty Grable, also in her first starring role after years in supporting roles, and with whom he would be paired frequently in the near future.

He proved himself adept at musical comedy and was subsequently cast with Alice and Betty and Sonja Henie in some of the era's finest musicals, including *Sun Valley Serenade* (1941), *Week-End in Havana* (1941), and *Springtime in the Rockies* (1942), among others.

He got a big boost to his career when he was given a straight dramatic role opposite Claudette Colbert in *Remember the Day* (1942). While making *Springtime in the Rockies*, he expressed his desire to stop doing "escapist" fare and get into "hard-hitting, realistic" pictures.[137] By October of 1942, he had become the studio's most popular star, receiving upwards of six thousand fan letters per month.[138] TCF had successfully petitioned the US government to defer his enlistment in the armed forces until after *Hello, Frisco, Hello* (1943) was completed.[139] He participated in war bond drives and raised millions for the government before officially serving as an air flight instructor in the US Army Air Corps.

In 1937, he had met and married actress Anne Shirley, who had just made a big splash as *Anne of Green Gables* (1934). (In an odd move, she legally changed her

Payne became one of Twentieth Century-Fox's biggest stars and was paired with the studio's top talent. Here he is in the lavish musical *Week-End in Havana* (1941) with Alice Faye. (Photofest)

Payne and actress Gloria DeHaven got married on December 28, 1944, after courting for several months. DeHaven would accompany Payne to New York for the filming of *Miracle*, where sightings of the celebrity couple caused quite a stir. (Photofest)

A great smile and an affable personality made John Payne a major movie star. (Photofest)

Payne got top billing when he starred with Betty Grable and Victor Mature in the boxing-themed musical *Footlight Serenade* (1942). (Photofest)

name from Dawn O'Day to that of the *Gables* character!)[140] The two seemed to be happily married, and were considered at the time "Hollywood's foremost young couple."[141] They welcomed a little girl, Julie Anne, into the world in 1940. As it turned out, their union was not a match made in heaven. During the filming of *To the Shores of Tripoli* (1942), while dining at Romanoff's one evening, Shirley told him she was leaving him.[142] It came as a complete surprise to Payne, and back on the set, he found himself bawling in O'Hara's dressing room. He had had no idea that she was so unhappy.[143] It was a shock to the Hollywood community in general, where the press had held them up as a picture of marital bliss.[144] The two never publicly dis-

After returning from WWII, John Payne wanted to get away from musicals and so was cast in the lavish drama *The Razor's Edge* (1946) with Gene Tierney.

cussed the particulars of their divorce.

After his release from the army in September of 1944, Payne wanted to settle down and get married again.[145] Following his divorce from Shirley, he had been seen around town with Jane Russell, Sheila Ryan, and June Havoc, but nothing permanent came of those relationships.[146] One evening he was lined up with MGM actress Gloria DeHaven by Alan and Sue Ladd. They were giving a party and suggested the two come as a couple. The proposed match was a success, and they were married a few months later, in December.[147] Although the couple would have two children together, it would be a rocky marriage, with DeHaven wanting to continue her acting career. They would separate and reconcile a few times during their marriage. One public reconciliation occurred in October, right before *Miracle* went into production.[148]

Despite his desires to do more straight dramatic fare, TCF cast him in two more musical pictures, *The Dolly Sisters* (1945) and *Wake Up and Dream* (1946), in which he introduced the song "Give Me the Simple Life." Following those assignments, he was teamed with O'Hara for the second time in a purely dramatic film, *Sentimental Journey* (1946), and he got a nice role in the studio's big prestige picture of 1946, *The Razor's Edge*. He would next be cast in *Miracle*. His transition was successful, and he never did another film musical. He was also doing well financially, receiving a salary of $2,750 per week.[149]

Payne's versatility in drama and comedy was necessary, since *Miracle*'s story involves a mix of levity and seriousness. Payne and O'Hara had good chemistry and made a nice couple, but the two were ultimately chosen because they had been solid box office draws in the two previous films they had done together, *To the Shores of Tripoli* (1942) and *Sentimental Journey* (1946).[150] *Miracle*'s story "charmed and fascinated" Payne, and, according to one observer, he "would knock himself out" trying to get the character just right.[151]

EDMUND GWENN (1877–1959), *KRIS KRINGLE*

Director George Seaton knew that the casting of Kris Kringle was one of the most crucial choices if *Miracle* was going to succeed. He needed to have just the right actor. Edmund Gwenn was a natural choice, since his physical characteristics fit the bill, and he had proven himself capable of playing a broad range of roles during his decade in Hollywood.[152] He was being considered for the role very early on when the story was submitted to TCF in July 1946, with a "strong recommendation" that he be chosen for the part.[153]

Edmund Gwenn was born Edmund John Kellaway in the London borough of Wandsworth in 1877, the eldest son of a government civil servant.[154] He attended St. Olave's School and King's College, London.[155] As a boy, his favorite sports were rugby and boxing.[156] He was also fascinated by the sea and all things sailing, and considered joining the navy, but his mother steered him away, fearing brawls, liquor, and shipwrecks would not be good for her son.[157] His father expected Gwenn to follow in his professional footsteps, but Gwenn saw the civil service as a "continent of unexplored boredom."[158] His father was irate when Gwenn expressed an interest in the theater at age seventeen, viewing that world as a "sink of iniquity."[159] Gwenn later recalled, "In a scene without parallel in Victorian melodrama," his father "quite literally showed him the door."

Edmund Gwenn as he appeared in 1946 without his Santa suit, his beard, or hairpiece. (Photofest)

Although Gwenn really had no experience, having only acted in a few amateur plays, he took off nonetheless, and, being desperate, took whatever roles he could get. Fitting for his circumstances at the time, the first London play he appeared in was the comedy *Rogue and Vagabond* in 1895, by which point he had assumed the stage name of Gwenn, probably to avoid potentially bringing shame to his family's name.[160] Gwenn's younger brother Arthur would follow him into the theater, adopting Chesney as his stage name.[161]

For the next several years Gwenn traveled around the United Kingdom, performing Shakespeare and old melodramas, and each "Christmas found him in that perennial British favorite, a series of pantomimes."[162] In 1899, he finally made his debut in London's West End in *A Jealous Mistake*. In 1901, he married Minnie Terry, the niece of the famous British actress Ellen Terry, before heading off to Australia and New Zealand to perform there for a year, although he ended up staying for three.[163]

Upon his return to England in 1904, he took some small roles, and then one day, much to his surprise, he received an invitation from none other than George Bernard Shaw, asking him to play the leading role of Henry Straker in *Man and Superman*. Shaw was duly impressed and cast Gwenn in his next five plays, becoming his professional godfather.[164] From that moment on, Gwenn was in demand on the London stage, and appeared in dozens of plays by the likes of

J. M. Barrie, J. B. Priestley, Henrik Ibsen, Arthur Conan Doyle, and W. Somerset Maugham. He would remain a preeminent actor on the London stage for the next four decades.

He and his wife divorced before he enlisted in the British Armed Forces during World War I. His wartime duties included delivering supplies to the front lines, and he ultimately advanced to the rank of captain.[165] Upon his return, he got back into the theater in 1919, resuming his life as an actor. He made his New York stage debut in 1922 in a couple of plays, but then returned to London.

Gwenn had dabbled in film during the early years of cinema, with his most prolific effort being *The Skin Game* (1920), in which he reprised the Hornblower role he had played onstage. With the advent of sound movies, he started appearing more regularly, including in two of Alfred Hitchcock's early films: the sound version of *The Skin Game* (1931) and *Strauss' Great Waltz* (aka, *Waltzes from Vienna*) (1934).

In 1935, he returned to New York to star on Broadway in *Laburnum Grove*, reprising a role as a counterfeiter that he had made famous on the London stage, when Hollywood came calling.[166] MGM signed Gwenn as a contract player, and he started showing his versatility as a doctor in the sci-fi thriller *The Walking Dead* (1936), with Boris Karloff; as John Bonnyfeather in *Anthony Adverse* (1936); as Mr. Bennet in *Pride and Prejudice* (1940), with Greer Garson and Laurence Olivier; as a foil to Jack Benny in *Charley's Aunt* (1941) and *The Meanest Man in the World* (1943); and as an assassin in Hitchcock's *Foreign Correspondent* (1940). During his first decade in Hollywood, he appeared in over thirty movies while still returning to London to do legitimate theater through-

Edmund Gwenn, playing Katharine Hepburn's father, joins up with Hepburn and Cary Grant as a trio of con artists in *Sylvia Scarlett* (1935). (Photofest)

Edmund Gwenn as the beneficent grandfather John Bonnyfeather in the grand adaptation of Hervey Allen's best-selling novel, *Anthony Adverse* (1936). (Photofest)

John Jones (Joel McCrea) almost meets his death when would-be assassin Rowley (Edmund Gwenn) convinces him to climb the cathedral tower in Alfred Hitchcock's *Foreign Correspondent* (1940). (Photofest)

Edmund Gwenn showed his versatility when he played the bitter, drunk father in *Bob, Son of Battle* (1947) (aka, *Thunder in the Valley* or *Shepherd of the Valley*), which he filmed just a few months before *Miracle*. The role is in direct contrast to his Kris Kringle role. (Photofest)

Though he had no children of his own, Edmund Gwenn got a taste of life as a father with five daughters when he played Mr. Bennet in the first film adaptation of Jane Austen's *Pride and Prejudice* (1940). Mary Boland played Mrs. Bennet. (Photofest)

Edmund Gwenn became good friends with Lassie; they appeared in three films together. Here he is in the first one, *Lassie Come Home* (1943). (Photofest)

Always an asset in period pieces, Edmund Gwenn co-starred with Lana Turner in *Green Dolphin Street* (1947), right before filming *Miracle*. (Photofest)

out the late 1930s. He starred on Broadway in 1942 as Dr. Chebutykin in Chekhov's *The Three Sisters*, with Katharine Cornell, Ruth Gordon, and Judith Anderson, which *Time* magazine called "a dream production by anybody's reckoning—the most glittering cast the theater has seen, commercially, in this generation."[167] He had settled down at the Beverly Wilshire Hotel at the outbreak of World War II, and decided to stay permanently when his home of thirty years was bombed in London and he lost everything.[168]

Gwenn had been up in southern Utah during the summer and back in the studio in the early fall of 1946, filming the awkwardly titled *Bob, Son of Battle* (1947) (which was later rereleased under two different titles: *Thunder in the Valley* and *Shepherd of the Valley*), for TCF. He plays a mean old codger that stands in stark contrast to the gentleness he displays as Kris Kringle. No wonder the *New York Times* would remark that he "plays saints and villains with equal aplomb and appeal."[169] He was in California and had started filming *Green Dolphin Street* (1947) with Lana Turner at MGM when he got the offer to be in *Miracle*. Apparently Seaton approached Gwenn about the role and then Gwenn had to seek permission from MGM, where he was under contract. Luckily there were no upcoming projects for him, and so the studio allowed him to do it.[170] Gwenn's participation in the film was announced in early October, at the same time as O'Hara's.[171] Apparently, Gwenn was so excited after reading the script that he called Seaton right away and blurted "When do we start?"[172] In early October, long before production officially started, Gwenn was trying on Santa suits in the studio's wardrobe department.[173]

Natalie Wood (1938–1981), *Susan Walker*

Natalie Wood was not cast in *Miracle* until just days before the production went to New York. The role of Susan was the second casting decision that Seaton felt was essential for the success of the film.[174] Natalie had signed a contract with Universal just six months earlier, which TCF tried to buy out, but ultimately, the studio was only able to get her on loan. Her initial loan would cover two films, *Miracle* and *The Ghost and Mrs. Muir* (1947), which would be filmed concurrently.

Natalie was born in 1938 in San Francisco to struggling Russian immigrants, Nicholas and Marie Zacharenko.[175] She had one sister, ten years her senior, from her mother's previous marriage.[176] Perhaps she was too young to have had an identity crisis, but she must have experienced at least some level of confusion over her name. At the time of her birth, the name registered with the state of California was "Natalie Zacharenko." She appears to have been christened "Natalia Nikolaevna Zacharenko" in the Russian Orthodox Church, "Nikolaevna" being the Russian patronymic for "daughter of Nicholas."[177] When her

Natalie Wood was practically a veteran with five films to her credit when this portrait was taken around the time that *Miracle on 34th Street* premiered in theaters. (Photofest)

parents applied for American citizenship in 1940, she was identified as "Natalie Nicholas Zacharenko," the patronymic being anglicized, inadvertently giving her a male middle name.[178] On that same application, her parents changed their last name to Gurdin, choosing the name of a family friend, apparently in an effort to have a more American-sounding name.[179]

Her legal name would become Natalie Nicholas Gurdin, but from a very early age, her family called her "Natasha." Five years later, her mother used "Natasha Gurdin" as Natalie's legal name

Natalie Wood's family moved to picturesque Santa Rosa in 1942 where she would be "discovered" and make her first appearance in the film *Happy Land* (1943), which was shot here. (Photofest)

Alfred Hitchcock shot *Shadow of a Doubt* (1943) in Santa Rosa right before Natalie Wood's family moved there. Coincidentally, two of *Shadow*'s stars, Teresa Wright and Macdonald Carey, would co-star as Doris and Fred in the 1955 TV movie version of *Miracle on 34th Street*. (Photofest)

Inspired by the discovery of Edna May Wonacott by Alfred Hitchcock, Natalie Wood's mother tried to make the same thing happen for her daughter. Edna May, center, is surrounded by her classmates who are holding autographed photos of her, which sold for $5 each during a World War II war bond drive. (Photofest)

when she signed the contract for her daughter's first significant film role in *Tomorrow is Forever* (1946). At the same time, she signed her own name as "Mary Gurdin."[180] It was for this film that Natalie's last name would be changed to "Wood" by producer William Goetz, naming her after director Sam Wood, who directed the Marx Brothers in *A Night at the Opera* (1935). Years later, she complained that she "hated it," and would have preferred "Woods," because at least that would conjure up pretty images of "trees and forests."[181] "Natasha Gurdin, professionally known as Natalie Wood," is how her name appeared on the loan agreement between Universal and TCF.[182]

With the outbreak of World War II, fearing that San Francisco would be bombed, the Gurdins moved out of the city and down the Peninsula, to Sunnyvale. They liked to get out in the country and would vacation with other expatriates, appropriately, in the Russian River Valley, north of San Francisco. After one such trip in late September 1942, on a whim, Natalie's mother decided to buy a house in Santa Rosa and relocate the family there permanently.[183] The move ended up being providential, since this is where Natalie would have her film debut.[184]

The picturesque little town of Santa Rosa was getting a lot of attention from Hollywood in the early 1940s. In 1942, Alfred Hitchcock, affiliated with Universal at the time, had chosen it as the backdrop for his jarring thriller *Shadow of a Doubt* (1943), which starred Joseph Cotten as nice uncle Charlie who comes for a visit and is warmly received by his family, until his nieces start getting suspicious of him. One of the nieces was played by ten-year-old Edna May Wonacott. Edna May was the daughter of the local grocer, and happened to be in downtown Santa Rosa with her cousins when Hitchcock and his producer were scouting for locations. They spotted her and thought she would be perfect for the role of Ann Newton.[185] After a screen test, she got the role, and subsequently became a local celebrity as the "Cinderella Girl." Upon her return from Universal Studios, where she had been filming for a couple of months, Santa Rosa hosted an "Edna May Day" celebration as part of a war bond drive on October 24, just a month after the Gurdins' arrival.[186]

When Hollywood came calling again the following summer, the town was more than eager to accommodate TCF for their oddly titled film, *Happy Land* (1943), about a father, played by Don Ameche, who reminisces via flashbacks about his son, who has just been killed in World War II. Natalie's mother, inspired by the discovery of Edna May, was hoping that history would repeat itself and that her daughter would make it into the movies as well. Within the first few days of filming, Marie had dolled Natalie up and followed the film crew around in an attempt to get her daughter noticed. The Gurdins had rented a trailer to the film crew to use as a dressing room for the outdoor scenes, which probably provided additional justification for Marie hanging around the set.[187] Once she had identified Irving Pichel as the director, she told Natalie to "go over there and sit on that man's lap and sing him your songs."[188]

Even at this young age, Natalie captivated those around her. The director remembered her coming up to him and saying "Mr. Pichel, can I be in the movies?" To which he replied, "You don't want to be in the movies." She paused and changed the subject by saying "that her name was Natasha Gurdin, that her birthday was July 20, that her parents were Russian, and that she would like to sing me a Russian song, if I would like to hear it. Assuring her that I would be enchanted, she did, and I was."[189]

The ruse worked, and Natalie got her first role as the little girl who drops her ice-cream cone in the opening shots of the film. She is only seen for a few seconds and her face is obscured, so if you blink, you will miss her. Ann Rutherford, one of the stars of the film, had an "indelible memory" of the "delicious three-year-old" (although she was actually almost five) on the set, and would give her

Natalie Wood's mother groomed her to look like child star Margaret O'Brien when she took her to auditions. (Photofest)

THE CAST

Natalie Wood's first starring role featured her alongside Orson Welles as a World War II orphan refugee in *Tomorrow is Forever* (1946) (Photofest)

Natalie's second role of consequence was in the comedy *The Bride Wore Boots* (1946). A complete departure from her role in *Tomorrow is Forever*, Natalie just had to play a cute little girl. Here she is with Barbara Stanwyck who played her mother and Gregory Muradian who played her brother. (Photofest)

big hugs and show her off to the rest of the cast and crew, a memory Natalie remembered as well.[190] Director Pichel, self-admittedly, was so enamored with Natalie that, over the next few years, he kept in contact with her, sending gifts for her birthday and for Christmas.[191]

The local reception by Santa Rosa was positive enough that TCF decided to return in the fall of 1943 to film *The Sullivans* (1944), a story about a family that lost several sons during World War II (a popular theme). Marie Gurdin, no doubt, tried to get her daughter on-screen again, but to no avail. She continued to feel that Pichel would be the key to her daughter's success, however, and kept abreast of his projects through the movie magazines. She also kept a correspondence going with him through letters purportedly written by Natalie. When Marie learned that his next film, *A Medal for Benny* (1945), starring Dorothy Lamour, had a role for a young girl, she decided this was the time to act. Natalie had just completed kindergarten, and once again, Maria uprooted the family and moved to Los Angeles in May of 1944, with the hope that Natalie would get that role.[192]

Upon arriving in LA, Marie contacted Pichel to let him know that they had relocated and Natalie was ready to make her film debut. Stunned, Pichel feared that "he was a modern Pied Piper who had, however unwittingly, piped the child out of her Hamelin home." He was afraid that he would be leading Natalie down a path of misery, as he was very against children becoming actors, feeling that it robbed them of a normal childhood.[193] He was firm with Marie and tried to dissuade her from pursuing a film career for her daughter. Needless to say, Natalie did not get a role in *A Medal for Benny*.

Undaunted, Marie groomed her daughter to look like then-current child star sensation Margaret O'Brien, and started making the rounds of auditions for the next eight months, but with no success. She then read about Pichel's next project, titled *Tomorrow is Forever* (1946), which would star Claudette Colbert and Orson Welles. The plot centered on a soldier who never returns from World War I and the tragedy that ensues. The film had a role for a young girl to play an Austrian war refugee. Marie somehow finagled to get Natalie into the audition without the director's knowledge. Pichel was chagrined when he saw her come into the room, but was relieved that her audition "was not very good."[194] During the tryout, he had asked her to cry on cue, since it would be necessary for some of the scenes, but she was unable to do so.

Later, when Marie found out why Natalie didn't get the part, she called and pleaded with Pichel to let her try again the following day, which he reluctantly agreed to do. Natalie's sister and mother coached her for the next twenty-four hours, getting her to think of sad things, like the day her dog died. Right before the scene, her mother apparently took her aside and ripped the wings off a butterfly in front of her, and, as expected, Natalie burst into tears.[195]

Pichel recalled that she "came in again, played the scene—and broke our hearts . . . the tears seeming to come from 'the depth of some divine despair.' " He concluded, "After that second test, there was never any question—Natasha, rechristened Natalie Wood, was 'in the movies.' Where, I am bound to say, she so obviously belongs."[196]

Filming took place in the spring of 1945, and Natalie gave an amazing performance. She was able to re-create what she had done in the audition and was believable as the young refugee suffering from PTSD. She had to speak some of her lines in German, which she delivered convincingly, probably due to the fact that she had grown up bilingual, speaking English and Russian.[197] Her authentic emotional responses and the persona she conveyed were far beyond the skills of most first-time movie actresses, let alone a six-year-old girl. Years later, her co-star Orson Welles commented, "I've had a lot of experience with child

Casting Natalie Wood in *The Ghost and Mrs. Muir* (1947) with Gene Tierney almost prevented her from appearing in *Miracle on 34th Street*. (Photofest)

actors, but Natalie was far and away the most memorable—even more so than Liz Taylor [who was featured in his 1944 adaptation of *Jane Eyre*]. She was a professional when I first saw her. I guess she was born a professional."[198] There seems to be some basis for Welles's assessment of her natural abilities. As an adult, Natalie remembered that when she was "a very young child, acting was just like playing house or playing with dolls," and came very effortlessly.[199]

Following the filming of *Tomorrow is Forever*, Pichel decided to do a comedy for his next picture. Starring Robert Cummings and Barbara Stanwyck, it focused on a marriage with one spouse who loves riding horses and the other who does not, and the strife that ensues. He cast Natalie in the role of their daughter, but it would be completely different from her first film. In *The Bride Wore Boots* (1946), all Natalie had to do was be a cute little girl, which she did very well. Even though both films were not released until 1946 (*Tomorrow* in January and *Bride* in May), Natalie was already starting to get noticed. *Life* magazine showed up at her home and did a feature on her that appeared in the November 26, 1945, issue. A few months later, *Look* magazine did the same in its March 19, 1946, issue.

Natalie's performances in these two films, which director George Seaton certainly saw, were the ones that influenced his choice of her for *Miracle*. Years later, assistant director Artie Jacobson claimed that he was the one who first suggested that Seaton cast Natalie in the role.[200] Along with O'Hara, Payne, and Gwenn, Natalie's name was recommended for the role when TCF was considering the purchase of the *Miracle* story in July 1946.[201]

As of November 1, Jacobson was making screen tests of three girls who were being considered for the role of Susan. One complication that almost kept Natalie from appearing in *Miracle* was that director Joseph Mankiewicz really wanted her for *The Ghost and Mrs. Muir* (1947), and the filming schedules were going to overlap (*Miracle* was slated for November 26 through February 22; *Ghost* for December 4 through March 7).[202] Jacobson inquired if Natalie would be needed during the courtroom scenes in *Miracle*, which were scheduled to be filmed last; when the answer was "Probably not," he thought he could finagle it for her to appear in both.

The final decision was not made until Seaton had seen all of the screen tests.[203] Apparently Seaton did like Natalie's test, and the scheduling conflicts were resolved, because Natalie's participation in *The Ghost and Mrs. Muir* was announced in the press on November 9, and *Miracle*, a couple of weeks later.[204] The final loan agreement with Universal gave her a compensation of $250 per week until December 7, at which time her rate would go up to $300 per week, and would cover all travel expenses.[205] Natalie Wood was en route to New York via plane on November 22.[206]

Supporting Cast (in alphabetical order)

The cast of supporting character actors in *Miracle* is proof that one does not need a lot of screen time to make movie history. *Variety* later declared the film to be "an actor's holiday, providing any

number of choice roles that are played to the hilt.”[207] Lela
Bliss (Mrs. Shellhammer), Alvin Greenman (Alfred), and little
Bobby Hyatt (Thomas Mara Jr.) all had small roles, but gave
indelible performances despite appearing for only a few minutes in the film. Years later, O’Hara shared her enthusiasm for
her co-stars when she said, “I marvel at the expert casting of
the supporting players in *Miracle*, including William Frawley,
Porter Hall, and Thelma Ritter. Believe me, when *those* people
did their scenes, you didn’t go and lock yourself in the dressing room! You’d stay around and watch! Thelma Ritter *always*
had an audience.”[208] Director George Seaton would hire
many of these actors in his other films in subsequent years.

Jack Albertson (1907–1981), *Al Golden*

The actor who portrayed the unassuming postal worker
(who isn’t even called by his name in the film), who unintentionally helps prove Kris Kringle’s legitimacy by forwarding thousands
of letters to the courthouse, was just beginning his long career
in film and television. Born Harold Bernard Albertson in Massachusetts, Jack began his career onstage in vaudeville, working
with the likes of Milton Berle, Bert Lahr, and Phil Silvers. His
small part in *Miracle*, one of only two film appearances in the
1940s, helped pave the way for his entrée into film and television.

Jack Albertson’s role as the postal
worker in *Miracle on 34th Street* was just
the beginning of a long career in film
and television. In the mid-1960s he won
a Tony for appearing in the play *The
Subject was Roses* and would reprise the
role with his co-star Martin Sheen on
the big screen. (Photofest)

Beginning in 1950, Albertson started appearing with reg-
ularity in supporting roles in films and on television shows. He popped up in a wide variety of lighter
fare, including Disney’s kids’ movies (*The Shaggy Dog*, 1959; *Son of Flubber*, 1963); Doris Day comedies
(*Teacher’s Pet*, 1958; *Lover Come Back*, 1961); and Elvis Presley musicals (*Roustabout*, 1964; *Kissin’ Cousins*,
1964), with the occasional serious drama thrown into the mix, such as *Days of Wine and Roses* (1962).

Albertson continued acting onstage, appearing on Broadway in the mid-1960s in the play *The
Subject Was Roses*, and winning a Tony for his performance. He reprised the role in the 1968 film (which
co-starred a very young Martin Sheen, who also reprised his stage role), and won the Academy Award
for Best Supporting Actor. Bigger roles in bigger films followed, such as Grandpa Joe in *Willy Wonka
and the Chocolate Factory* (1971), and as one of the passengers on the cruise ship disaster film, *The Poseidon
Adventure* (1972). In the 1970s, he created the lovable curmudgeon character Ed Brown in the sitcom
Chico and the Man, and would win an Emmy for his work. Albertson’s last film role was as the voice of
Amos Slade in the Disney animated feature, *The Fox and the Hound* (1981). He is one of only a handful
of actors who have won the “Triple Crown of Acting” by winning a Tony, an Oscar, and an Emmy.[209]

Harry Antrim (1884–1967), *Mr. Macy*

Although there were many department stores in the 1940s that were still owned and operated by their namesake families, Macy's was not one of them. There was a real Rowland Hussey Macy, but he had died back in 1877, and his heirs had sold out to the Straus family in the nineteenth century. But for fiction's sake, it made more sense to resurrect R. H. Macy for *Miracle*. One thing that *was* real was Mr. Macy's office, as they filmed in the actual office of Jack Straus, then-president of the store.[210]

Fred Lewis had originally been hired in early December 1946 to play the role of Mr. Macy, but had to withdraw due to illness.[211] Luckily, Harry Antrim was available, and fit the bill perfectly as president of the world's largest store.[212]

Antrim was a seasoned performer, having started in his teens as an entertainer on the vaudeville circuits. Though a Chicago native, he had made his way to New York as early as 1903, and was in a duo with Yetta Peters in sketches and shows with titles such as *A Meal Under Difficulties* and *The Frolicsome Lambs*.[213] Antrim would spend the next quarter-century touring the country doing comedy and song-and-dance sketches. When he later went solo, a reviewer summed up one of his thirteen-minute acts this way: "A 'nut' comedian, sings ragtime, talks, does imitations of animals and mechanical imitations—drawing corks, etc., burlesque, cello playing, tin whistle. Fast and effective act."[214] Other notices commended him as an adept comedian, noting that he "is quite capable and diligent in eccentric comicalities" and an "exuberant young fellow" who is "a whirlwind of laughter."[215] He later married Betsy Vale and they performed, on and off, as a duo on the famous Pantages theater circuit.[216]

As vaudeville waned in popularity, Antrim successfully moved into legitimate theater. In the mid-1930s, he found himself in California, where he landed a role at the Pasadena Playhouse, as well as a handful of small film roles.[217] Clearly not satisfied with his reception in Hollywood, he returned to the New York stage in the late 1930s and appeared in several plays, mostly comedies. He would only reenter the world of film with the offer to appear in *Miracle*, and, for the next twenty years, would become a staple character actor in Hollywood films and television, with his deep, sonorous voice always making an impression. Antrim had over a hundred varied roles in everything from *The Heiress* (1949), which featured Olivia de Havilland in her Oscar-winning performance, to Disney's *The Monkey's Uncle* (1965), which would be his last movie appearance. He was frequently a guest star on dozens of television shows in the 1950s and 1960s, including *I Love Lucy*, *Bonanza*, and *The Andy Griffith Show*, among others.

Lela Bliss (1896–1980), *Mrs. Shellhammer*

Even with only a few minutes of screen time, Bliss created one of the most humorous characters in *Miracle* as the tipsy Mrs. Shellhammer. Who hasn't mimicked her elongated, high-pitched "Hello-o-o" at least once?

Lela May Bliss was born in Los Angeles and ended up in the early 1920s doing vaudeville comedy sketches with actor (and future husband) Harry Hayden.[218] The two made the rounds on the various theater circuits with their act, and were married in Denver while on the road, in 1923.[219] They would have two sons.[220]

The couple settled in New York, where both found success on the stage. Bliss appeared in the role of Ethel Brander in the first production of the Otto Harbach/Oscar Hammerstein II musical *Rose-Marie* on Broadway, in 1924.[221] Husband Harry became involved with the productions of famous theater impresario David Belasco.[222] The couple continued to do their vaudeville comedy sketches through the end of the decade as Harry Hayden and Company.[223]

By the early 1930s, the couple had relocated to Los Angeles, where they took over the Miniature Theater on Robertson Boulevard in Beverly Hills, rechristening it as the Bliss-Hayden School of the Theater,

Lela Bliss had a varied career on the stage and in film and television that spanned decades. Toward the end of her career, she appeared in the famous first season of *The Twilight Zone*, in the episode "Time Enough At Last," with Burgess Meredith as the man who just wants to read. (Photofest)

with the goal of "developing and exploiting new talent and to provide consecutive playing experience for those who definitely qualify for the theater."[224] They accomplished this by staging plays in their little theater that would run for a few weeks at a time, giving students the chance to play before a live audience. They also gave students a lot of practical advice, and their connections in the entertainment industry helped many of them get roles in movies. Bliss and Hayden were highly involved in the productions and would often play roles in the shows themselves.[225]

Their extensive theatrical experience helped them both land small parts in films, with Bliss debuting in *Hitch Hike to Heaven* (1936).[226] Bliss made a handful of screen appearances in the late 1930s and early 1940s, while still running the acting school. The year 1946 ended up being a good one for her, with featured roles in the romantic comedy *Without Reservations* (1946), with John Wayne and Claudette Colbert, and in the evil-twin-sister mystery *The Dark Mirror* (1946), with Olivia de Havilland. Right before doing *Miracle*, Bliss got signed to appear in the period musical drama about Robert and Clara Schumann, *Song of Love* (1947), with Katharine Hepburn.[227]

The couple would run the drama school until the mid-1950s. Several aspiring actresses, including Marilyn Monroe and Betty White, got some of their early acting experience here.[228] Bliss and Hayden got into television early on as a married couple on the 1950s sitcom, *The Stu Erwin Show*. Hayden passed away in 1955, with over 250 film and TV credits to his name, but Bliss continued acting in film and on television throughout the 1950s and 1960s, including a recurring role on the 1950s sitcom *Blondie*, and a role in a famous episode from *The Twilight Zone*'s first season, "Time Enough at Last."[229]

Jerome Cowan played Miles Archer opposite Humphrey Bogart's Sam Spade in John Huston's private-eye classic, *The Maltese Falcon* (1941), one of his best-known roles. (Photofest)

Jerome Cowan (1897–1972), *Thomas Mara*

Sporting his distinctive signature pencil mustache, Cowan was a constant fixture in film and television from the 1930s through the 1960s. Born in Norwich, Connecticut, as Jerome Palmer Cowan, he liked the outdoors and was involved in horseback riding, boating, and swimming.[230] By age nineteen he was working as an insurance clerk in Hartford, and a few years later, in 1920, he married Helen Louise Gillespie in New York, who would later work as a stage actress under the name Helen Dodge.[231] The couple would eventually have two daughters. Cowan, understandably, lost interest in the insurance industry and got a job as the master of ceremonies at a vaudeville house in Hartford.[232] Apparently smitten with the theater bug, he decided to make a career change.

In the early 1920s, Cowan would perform in plays such as *The Blimp* and *We've Got to Have Money,* and in vaudeville acts like a musical sketch with Lillian Russell's daughter Dorothy, titled *My Evening Star.*[233] When he wasn't acting, he worked as a waiter.[234] He became a stock player at the Rialto Theatre in Hoboken, New Jersey, in 1926, and went to Birmingham, Alabama, in the fall of 1929 for an engagement.[235] In 1930, he found himself in a scandalous production of *Frankie and Johnnie* on Long Island, where local law enforcement arrested the cast and manager because the plot involved a brothel (even though it was a nineteenth-century one).[236]

In the early 1930s, Cowan started appearing regularly in plays on the Great White Way, with featured billing, such as *Marathon,* where his name was the fourth one down.[237] In 1935, Cowan, who had excelled in comedy, was cast in the George Abbott production *Boy Meets Girl,* which was a parody of the goings-on at a movie studio. The show was a hit and a big money-maker, and gave a huge boost to his career.[238] The success of the show got him noticed by Samuel Goldwyn, who, just a few months after signing John Payne, brought Cowan to Hollywood and gave him a part in *Beloved Enemy* (1936), starring Merle Oberon.[239] Goldwyn was impressed enough with Cowan that he bought out his two remaining stage contracts and offered him one with the studio.[240]

Over the next decade, Cowan would appear in over fifty films, including comedies, dramas, and Westerns, his most prolific being *The Maltese Falcon* (1941), playing Miles Archer to Humphrey Bogart's Sam Spade. Before appearing in *Miracle,* he had a connection with William

Perlberg and George Seaton with *The Song of Bernadette* (1943): Perlberg was the producer, Seaton was the screenwriter, and Cowan portrayed Louis Napoleon III.

Cowan was not cast as the district attorney in *Miracle* until right before the filming of the courtroom scenes.[241] Some have claimed that the Mr. Mara character was supposed to be an incarnation of Thomas E. Dewey, the former tough-on-crime district attorney and the then-current governor of New York. Like Mr. Mara, Dewey wore a pencil mustache and was a Republican, and invoking him would certainly have been in line with the film's aim at realism, but these may just be coincidences. Cowan was wearing his mustache long before his role in *Miracle*, and Mr. Mara had to be a Republican in order for the punchline to work as to why he wouldn't vote for Judge Harper. Furthermore, neither Davies nor Seaton nor the contemporary documentation ever mentioned that Mara was based on Dewey, so the similarity may or may not be happenstance.[242]

Just a few months after completing *Miracle*, Cowan found himself in another film with Natalie Wood, called *Driftwood* (1947). He would continue to have supporting roles in films throughout the 1940s, including a recurring role as Dagwood's boss in the *Blondie* movies. In the 1950s, he returned to Broadway to appear in several George Abbott productions, such as *Say Darling*, *Lunatics and Lovers*, and *My Three Angels*.[243] Throughout the next two decades, he made dozens of guest appearances on television, including the "playhouse" anthologies, and on almost every major show of the era, from *77 Sunset Strip* to *Bonanza* to *Green Acres*.

Like Lela Bliss, he also appeared in another famous episode from the first season of *The Twilight Zone*. Called "The Sixteen-Millimeter Shrine," Cowan played an aging movie actor opposite Ida Lupino. During the 1960–1961 season, he scored a permanent role as Tab Hunter's boss on *The Tab Hunter Show*, but, unfortunately, that show only lasted one season. During the 1960s, he also made a few appearances on the big screen, including in *Penelope* (1966), which starred an all-grown-up Natalie Wood, and in Elvis Presley's version of *Frankie and Johnnie* (1966) (no record of any arrests for this production). By the end of his career, Cowan would have more than two hundred film and TV credits to his name.

Mary Field (1909–1996), *mother of the Dutch girl*

Field had scored a conspicuous role early in her career as the mother in the 1937 adaptation of *The Prince and the Pauper* starring Errol Flynn. Unfortunately, she was never able to succeed in scoring many substantial roles after that. By the time she was cast in *Miracle*, she had made over a hundred appearances in films mostly playing bit parts as secretaries, nurses, maids, shopgirls, and the like. Dawning an elegant fur coat and hat ensemble, the role of the mother of the little Dutch girl allowed her to be more patrician than she usually was. Incidentally, she appeared in three other movies starring Maureen O'Hara: *How Green Was My Valley* (1941), *Sentimental Journey* (1946), and *Sitting Pretty* (1948).

William Frawley (1887–1966), *Charlie Halloran*

William Frawley, who was a veteran actor of vaudeville, theater, and film, was just on the cusp of superstardom when he appeared in *Miracle*. Just a few years later he would become one of the stars of the hit television show *I Love Lucy* as Fred Mertz. Here he is with co-stars Vivian Vance (left), Lucille Ball (right), and Desi Arnaz. (Photofest)

There is no doubt that William Frawley was the first person to sing "Silver Bells," albeit off-key, in the film *The Lemon Drop Kid* (1951). (Author's collection)

Fans of *I Love Lucy* will instantly recognize Frawley as the irascible Fred Mertz from the classic television show. Hailing from Burlington, Iowa, Frawley grew up in a good Irish-Catholic family. He played baseball and football as a kid, and had a lifelong fascination with the world of sports. Having a good singing voice, he got involved in local theater in his youth. Then, while working in Chicago in his early twenties, he and his brother Paul decided to form an act as the Frawley Brothers, much to their mother's chagrin, as she despised the world of theater. After a brief stint, his brother broke up the act and headed to New York, where he became a popular actor on the New York stage.[244]

Frawley then teamed up with piano player Franz Rath and toured the vaudeville circuit with an act titled "A Man, a Piano and a Nut."[245] He claimed throughout his life to have been the first person to sing "My Melancholy Baby" and "Carolina in the Morning"; although there is some debate as to whether this is technically true, he certainly popularized both.[246] (One song which he did sing for the first time—and with which there is no debate—is "Silver Bells" in the 1951 film, *The Lemon Drop Kid*.)

Frawley met and married Edna Louise Broedt, and they toured on the famed Orpheum theater circuit as a comedy duo. After they separated in 1921, he headed to New York and became a stage actor, mostly in musicals. In the early 1930s, when he was in his mid-forties, he headed to California and landed a contract with Paramount. Over the next decade, he would be cast as cops, mugs, heavies, con artists—most any role that a middle-aged, bald guy could play. By the mid-1940s, he had appeared in over eighty movies.

Frawley was cast in *Miracle* in early January 1947, giving him about a month to learn his lines.[247]

He was perfect as the cigar-chomping politico that guides Judge Harper through the complicated realities and consequences of his decision.

Following *Miracle*, Frawley would continue to appear in bit parts up until the early 1950s. At about the time when most people are looking at retirement, he got the biggest break of his career when he was cast as Fred Mertz in the new *I Love Lucy* TV show, which turned him into a household name. Instead of calling it quits after *Lucy*, he took another role as Bub O'Casey on *My Three Sons*, working well into his seventies. Frawley was a good actor—apparently the gruff character of Charlie Halloran was much closer to the real Frawley than the lovable Fred Mertz or Bub, but we never knew!

Robert Gist (1917–1998), *window dresser*

Gist was performing in the long-running (it was two years into its over-four-year run) hit Broadway comedy *Harvey*, about a wealthy man and his invisible rabbit, when he landed the role in *Miracle*. His portrayal of the wary window dresser—who puts the reindeer in the wrong order in the opening scene—was his film debut. He would appear in the original cast of another landmark Broadway play, *The Caine Mutiny Court-Martial*, in 1954. Gist would go on to appear in supporting roles in about twenty more films and dozens of TV shows, including roles in Hitchcock's *Strangers on a Train* (1951) and Blake Edwards's *Operation Petticoat* (1959).

In the early 1960s, Gist got interested in doing work on the other side of the camera, and successfully transitioned to becoming a director. He directed twenty episodes of the final 1960–1961 season of the *Peter Gunn* television series, and then found work throughout the rest of the decade doing episodes of major TV shows like *Dr. Kildare*, *The Twilight Zone*, *Star Trek*, *Mission: Impossible*, and *Hawaii Five-O*. He made one feature film, the adaptation of Norman Mailer's *An American Dream* (1966), starring Janet Leigh and Stuart Whitman.

In the early 1970s, Gist transitioned to academia and took a position at the University of Alberta at Edmonton in the radio and television department, where he worked on developing educational television, as well as doing some writing.[248] In 1973, he left Canada for New York and worked as one of the professionals hired by Columbia University for its intensive summer seminar, to help train minority students in journalism and broadcasting.[249] He then took a position at the Australian Film and TV School and taught there for several years.[250] He was briefly married to actress Agnes Moorehead in the 1950s.[251]

Alvin Greenman (1930–2016), *Alfred*

As a native New Yorker, Alvin Greenman was able to get the accent just right as the teenage custodian from Brooklyn. Technically a child actor, Greenman made his screen debut in *Miracle* at age sixteen, turning seventeen during the production. For some reason, in the publicity materials, "Albert" got substituted for "Alfred" on the cast list, even though it is clearly "Alfred" in the script and film (someone obviously made a mistake).

In the early versions of the story, there is no Alfred character, but there is a janitor in the locker-room scene, and a character named Eddie, who is being treated by Mr. Sawyer. In the November 16 draft of the script, the janitor and Eddie were combined into the Alfred character. Alfred also had an additional scene that got cut. It occurred when Kris ducks out of Macy's so that Fred and Doris can spend the evening together. Fred comes into the locker room and Alfred tells him that Kris left twenty minutes earlier (discussed in detail in chapter 5).

Upon the completion of *Miracle*, TCF had an option to sign Greenman to a term contract for up to thirty days after the release of the film, but did not follow through.[252] Greenman went on to become the assistant director of the Henry Street Settlement's children's theater in New York.[253] He continued to appear in some small parts in TCF films, such as *Mr. Belvedere Goes to College* (1949) and *We're Not Married* (1952). In 1951, TCF signed him for another featured role in *Down Among the Sheltering Palms* (1953), an attempt to capitalize on the popularity of the musical *South Pacific* playing on Broadway at the time, and he got a good notice in *Variety* for it.[254]

Over the next decade, Greenman got small roles in several films and on television, including an opportunity to work with some of his *Miracle* friends (William Perlberg, George Seaton, and Thelma Ritter) in *The Proud and the Profane* (1957). The World War II drama, with William Holden and Deborah Kerr, focused on a woman searching for her lost husband, and gave Greenman the opportunity to play Santa Claus again.

Greenman ultimately decided to quit acting and make a career behind the camera as a script supervisor. He would spend the next few decades in this capacity, supervising the script for high-profile films like *The Longest Yard* (1974) and *The Karate Kid* (1984). In 1994, while working as the script supervisor on the John Ritter/Markie Post sitcom, *Hearts Afire*, he was asked to don the red suit again and play Santa in the episode "The Perfect Christmas."[255] This coincided with the release of the feature film remake of *Miracle on 34th Street*, in which Greenman appeared in a cameo as Alfred the doorman. He would be the only actor to appear in both the original 1947 film and in the 1994 remake.

Porter Hall (1888–1953), *Mr. Sawyer*

With a face that seemed as if he was destined to play cantankerous, stubborn, or obnoxious characters, Hall certainly made it a reality. Born Clifford Porter Hall in Cincinnati, he attended the University of Cincinnati, worked as a steelworker, and then joined a Shakespearean troupe before ending up on Broadway in 1926 in the original theatrical production of *The

Porter Hall was one of the great character actors of the mid-twentieth century and ended up being in lots of classic films. Here he is in his first film appearance in *The Thin Man* (1934) with, from left to right, Myrna Loy, William Powell, and Minna Gombell. (Photofest)

Great Gatsby, directed by George Cukor. In 1927, he married Geraldine Hall, and then spent another seven years as a stage actor in New York before heading to Hollywood, where he snagged the role as the lawyer in the popular mystery thriller *The Thin Man* (1934), with William Powell and Myrna Loy. Over his next twenty years in Hollywood, he would appear in more than seventy-five movies, including such classics as *Mr. Smith Goes to Washington* (1939), *His Girl Friday* (1940), *Double Indemnity* (1944), and *Going My Way* (1945).[256] Hall was involved in an automobile accident right before *Miracle* went into production. Luckily he was able to recover in time, and joined the company for filming in New York.[257]

Theresa Harris (1905–1986), *Cleo*

George Seaton was fighting racism in a low-key manner when he cast Harris to play Cleo in early January 1947.[258] Demure Harris had been appearing in movies since the late 1920s, although many of her roles went uncredited. By 1933, however, she managed to get good supporting roles in Warner Bros.' *Baby Face*, opposite Barbara Stanwyck, and in RKO's *Professional Sweetheart*, with Ginger Rogers. She worked consistently in the 1930s and 1940s, though often in minor roles. When writing the screenplay, director Seaton was adamant that he did not want the Cleo character to be "a hundred and eighty pounds of 'How y'all, honeychile,'" which would perpetuate the stereotypical Black mammy persona. He seems to have had Harris in mind when he describes Cleo as "pleasant, trim, and intelligent," which Harris effectively portrayed in the role, even if her screen time was brief.[259] Harris would continue working through the late 1950s, appearing in more than sixty films.

George Seaton was subtly fighting racism by using demure Theresa Harris as Doris Walker's housekeeper. (Author's collection)

Percy Helton (1894–1971), *drunk Santa Claus*

Helton debuted on Broadway in 1897, at the age of three, appearing in an act with his father. He continued onstage for over half a century, co-starring with the likes of Helen Hayes and Peggy Wood, and worked with George M. Cohan for five years. He also found success in film, with

Percy Helton, who plays the drunk Santa Claus in *Miracle*, appeared in another classic, *White Christmas* (1954), as the train conductor who checks Phil Davis's (Danny Kaye) and Bob Wallace's (Bing Crosby) tickets as they get on the train headed to New York. Or is it Vermont? (Photofest)

his first credits dating back to the silent era, He would appear in hundreds of film and television roles, including *How to Marry a Millionaire* (1953), *Jailhouse Rock* (1957), *Butch Cassidy and the Sundance Kid* (1969), and almost every popular TV show in the 1950s and 1960s. Helton had another supporting role in another holiday film favorite as the train conductor who checks Danny Kaye and Bing Crosby's tickets as they board the train in Florida, in *White Christmas*.[260]

Back in the late teens and early twenties, Herbert Heyes was one of Fox's heartthrobs of the silent screen. (Author's collection)

Herbert H. Heyes (1889–1958), *Mr. Gimbel*

When Heyes appeared in *Miracle* he looked every bit the part of a distinguished department store owner. You could hardly guess that he was once a huge matinee idol of the silent era. Heyes had been hired by Fox Film Corporation in 1916 to co-star with filmdom's original vamp, Theda Bara, in such films as *Under Two Flags*, *The Vixen*, and *Salomé* (all 1918), among others. He then left Hollywood in the mid-1920s to pursue the fledgling medium of radio, and return to his roots in the legitimate theater. Heyes returned to film in the early 1940s and focused on character roles. Unlike the fictitious Mr. Macy, there actually was a real Mr. Gimbel who was running Gimbels at the time *Miracle* was being made. To add to the authenticity of the film, he was asked to play himself, but turned down the offer, something he later regretted, and so Heyes was cast.[261] Heyes ended up getting a twofer: He would reprise the role of Mr. Gimbel in the 1955 TV movie version, the only actor from the original cast to do so. He would continue working in film and television until just a few years before his death. One of his most famous roles was that of the factory owner who tries to help his nephew, played by Montgomery Clift, in *A Place in the Sun* (1951).

Robert "Bobby" Hyatt (1939–2007), *Thomas Mara Jr.*

Cute little Bobby Hyatt got the endearing role of cute little Thomas Mara Jr. just days before the courtroom scenes were filmed.[262] It was an inspired choice, with his innocent testimony under oath helping to establish the veracity of Kris Kringle. *Miracle* was Bobby's second credited role, although he had previously appeared in a couple of other movies as an extra. His adorable appearance in *Miracle* certainly boosted his career, and he worked steadily as a child actor, appearing in more than twenty-five films in several genres, from musicals such as *Give My Regards to Broadway* (1948) to film noirs like *The Dark Past* (1949) to historical dramas such as *Les Misérables* (1952), which found him once again cast alongside Edmund Gwenn.

He also found success on television, with noteworthy roles such as Tiny Tim in a 1949 adaptation of *A Christmas Carol*, narrated by Vincent Price, and as Tom Sawyer in "The Adventures of Huckleberry Finn" on the *Climax* anthology series in 1955. He also appeared as Natalie Wood's brother in the short-lived 1953 sitcom *The Pride of the Family* which starred Fay Wray as their mother. He would continue to guest-star on several TV shows through the early 1960s, from *Father Knows Best*, and *Leave It to Beaver*, to *Cheyenne* and *Combat!* As an adult, he turned to screenwriting and directing, and succeeded in having several of his screenplays produced into films.

Gene Lockhart appeared in the lavish 1938 adaptation of Charles Dicken's *A Christmas Carol* as Bob Cratchit. It was a family affair, with his wife Kathleen playing Mrs. Cratchit and his daughter June playing Belinda. (Photofest)

Gene Lockhart (1891–1957), *Judge Henry X. Harper*

A few years younger than Edmund Gwenn, Lockhart followed much the same career path. He was born Eugene Lockhart in London, Ontario, Canada, into a musical family. At age seven, his father joined the Canadian Kilties Band and toured the British Isles as a Scottish baritone. His family traveled with the band, and so young Lockhart was enrolled in the Brompton Oratory school in London.[263] Upon his return to Canada, he attended St. Michael's school and the De La Salle College in Toronto. He went on to become an excellent athlete, winning the Canadian one-mile swimming championship in 1909, as well as playing on the Toronto Argonauts football team from 1910 to 1913. He continued to be a swimmer throughout his life.[264]

Encouraged by his mother, Lockhart landed

A talented writer as well as an actor, Gene Lockhart wrote the lyrics to the 1920 hit "The World is Waiting for the Sunrise," which became a standard. (Author's collection)

a job in a local theatrical troupe in Chautauqua, New York, for a season before scoring a part on Broadway in the musical *The Riviera Girl* in 1917. To diversify, he started writing his own material. He wrote the book and lyrics for a musical titled *Heigh-Ho* in 1920, which featured the soon-to-be-standard song "The World is Waiting for the Sunrise." He wrote several plays and a few hundred sketches that were performed in vaudeville and on the radio. He worked in Boston, performing in Gilbert and Sullivan operettas, and would become a regular on the New York stage through the early 1930s. He married British actress Kathleen Arthur in 1924, and had daughter, June, a year later (she went on to become a famous actress in iconic television series like *Lassie* and *Lost in Space*).[265]

In 1933, Lockhart appeared as Uncle Sid opposite George M. Cohan in Eugene O'Neill's comedy *Ah, Wilderness*, a role that finally got him noticed by Hollywood, and RKO ended up signing him to a contract. Like Gwenn, he became an unlikely movie star as a rotund, older, middle-aged man, but worked it to his advantage. He could play heavies, as he did in his Oscar-nominated performance as Regis in the thriller *Algiers* (1938), or be endearingly pitiable, as he was as Bob Cratchit in *A Christmas Carol* (1938), which, incidentally, turned into a family affair, with his wife and daughter appearing as Mrs. Cratchit and Belinda Cratchit.

He worked consistently while in Hollywood, and by the mid-1940s had appeared in over seventy films, occasionally returning to do theater in New York. He was no stranger at TCF, where he had recently appeared in *The House on 92nd Street* (1945) and *Leave Her to Heaven* (1945), and in the Betty Grable feminist picture, *The Shocking Miss Pilgrim* (1947), which was directed by George Seaton. He was cast in *Miracle* quite late in the production schedule, in January 1947, just four weeks before the courtroom scenes were filmed.[266]

In Lockhart's next role after *Miracle*, he was teamed again with Maureen O'Hara, playing her father in *The Foxes of Harrow* (1947). He would continue to be a venerable character actor for the next decade, appearing in over thirty more films. He would assume the role of Willy Loman after originator Lee J. Cobb's departure in *The Death of a Salesman* on Broadway in 1949, to rave reviews.[267] One of his last film roles was as the Starkeeper in the musical *Carousel* (1956).

Thelma Ritter (1905–1969), *mother of Peter*

Miracle marked the screen debut of Thelma Ritter as the flustered mother trying to find a toy fire engine, to no avail, declaring that if "Macy's ain't got any, nobody's got any." Her character in *Miracle* gave audiences a taste of the no-nonsense voice of reason that she would often play in subsequent years, usually as a counterbalance to a leading star's emotional foibles.

A Brooklyn native, Ritter was interested in the theater from an early age, and took every opportunity to perform. While attending the Manual Training High School, she got bit parts around New York. After graduation, she worked to earn money to attend the American Academy of Dramatic Arts. After two years there, she got a job in a stock theater company in Elizabeth, New Jersey, where she "was the maid in the family, the friend of the family, the passing pedestrian, or just anything that stood around and said nothing."[268] After a few years, she eventually made her debut on Broadway in *The Shelf*, in 1926.

The following year, she met Joe Moran, who had recently graduated from Johns Hopkins as a liberal arts major and, at the invitation of a friend, decided to try his hand at being an actor. The two met, and while he "was a goner the first time [he] saw her," it took her some time to come around to liking him.[269] They eventually married and spent the next five years as starving actors.

Then one day, Joe entered a contest for writing commercial jingles, and won. He started entering all kinds of advertising competitions and kept winning. His skills were noticed, and he was soon hired by the firm of Young & Rubicam and became an executive there, leaving the theater world behind. The Morans eventually moved to Forest Hills, Long Island, had two children, and were enjoying serene suburban living.[270]

But by 1944, Thelma wanted to get back into show business. She made the rounds of auditions for radio shows and finally got some parts on the air over the next few years. In 1946, while appearing on the Mollé Mystery Theatre, she heard that George and Phyllis Seaton were coming to New York to film *Miracle*.[271] Phyllis had lived in the same apartment building where the Morans lived when they were first married, and they had remained friends. George asked Thelma if she would do a walk-on part "to bring him luck."[272] She acquiesced, and although she was only on-screen for about three minutes, it was enough time to make an indelible impression and prove that she could deliver a deadpan line like no one else. The dailies were sent back to Los Angeles, and when Darryl Zanuck saw Ritter, he called Seaton and was desperate to know "who is that woman. . . . I just showed [the footage] to Joe Mankiewicz and we want her for *A Letter to Three Wives*."[273]

When Thelma saw *Miracle* for the first time at a movie theater, she sat in the balcony behind two women. When her scene came on, one of the women said, "Get the face on that one!" Thelma "shuddered happily. She had achieved her goal—to be outstanding in her own way."[274] Her appearance in *Miracle* launched her career as one of Hollywood's best character actresses and a long association with TCF, doing half of her films at that studio. During the next quarter-century, she would appear in thirty films, including *All About Eve* (1950), *Rear Window* (1954), *Pillow Talk* (1959), *The Birdman of Alcatraz* 1962), and *Move Over, Darling* (1963). She would ultimately be nominated for six Academy Awards, but, unfortunately, would never win. She quipped, "I'm the William Jennings Bryan of the acting profession, always nominated—never elected."[275]

Thelma Ritter, who was an experienced theater and radio actress, was asked by her old friend George Seaton to play the bit part of Peter's mother. It launched her film career. (Photofest)

James Seay (1914–1992), *Dr. Pierce*

With his good looks and Hollywood chin, Seay seemed destined for stardom. He was discovered by Cecil B. DeMille while acting in a play at the famed Pasadena Playhouse.[276] He succeeded in getting a contract with Paramount in 1939, and briefly used the stage name Michael Rand. He had appeared in bit parts in several films before DeMille finally gave him a good role in the Gary Cooper film, *North West Mounted Police* (1940). He had appeared in over three dozen films by the time he was cast in *Miracle*, getting the role just a week before filming began.[277]

In Davies's original story, and through several versions of the script, Dr. Pierce's role was much bigger and more important than it ended up being in the final version of the film. For example, originally the opening scenes had Dr. Pierce and Kris discussing his mental condition and attending the parade with his son where he sees Kris on the float. Dr. Pierce also originally provided more background information on Kris during his discussion with Doris and Mr. Shellhammer and was one of the witnesses at the trial. The reasons for minimizing the character were not fully articulated.

Seay never succeeded in becoming a leading man, but he worked consistently for the next quarter-century in film and television. He got recurring roles in two 1950s TV Westerns: as Judge Spicer in *The Legend of Wyatt Earp* and as the sheriff in *Fury*. He would guest-star in over a hundred TV shows from the 1950s through the early 1970s, everything from *Perry Mason* to *Death Valley Days* to *Gomer Pyle: USMC*.

Ann Staunton (1919–1994), *Mrs. Mara*

Born Virginia Ann Koerlin in New York, Ann worked as a showgirl and model there before making her way to Los Angeles in the early 1940s.[278] She first appeared in the low-budget film *Prisoner of Japan* (1942), in which she got a good notice in the *Los Angeles Times* as an actress with "much promise," although it didn't lead to more film roles.[279] Her personal life was much more interesting than her screen life. She apparently dated Mickey Rooney, and ended up marrying former Olympian rugby player and sportswriter Dick Hyland in the early 1940s, but the marriage only lasted a few years.[280] She appeared in several notable films at TCF in the mid-1940s, including *The Razor's Edge* (1946), *Daisy Kenyon* (1947), *Call Northside 777* (1948), and *The Snake Pit* (1948). She continued to work as an actress until the early 1970s, guest-starring on television shows like *Alfred Hitchcock Presents*, *Leave It to Beaver*, and *Perry Mason*, among others, before retiring.

Anthony Sydes (1941–2015), *Peter*

As the little boy who just wants a fire engine that his mother can't find at Macy's, Anthony Sydes was undeniably cute as little Peter, who blurts out his wish to Santa without taking a breath. He was just five years old when he appeared in *Miracle*. His first role was in the TCF drama *Claudio and David* (1946), with Robert Young and Dorothy McGuire. He worked as a child actor until he was in his teens, appearing in seventeen features, including several high-profile films like

Cheaper by the Dozen (1950), *Belles on Their Toes* (1952), and *Lust for Life* (1956). Maureen O'Hara was his mother in *Sitting Pretty* (1948), and he appeared with Natalie Wood in two other movies, *Driftwood* (1947) and *Chicken Every Sunday* (1949). In the late 1950s, he joined the army and did tours in Vietnam, Italy, and Germany, and was a recipient of the Purple Heart. He retired from the military after twenty years and started A&A Auction Gallery in Santa Cruz, California. He was the father of four children.[281] His younger sister would also go into acting and would be known as perky Cindy Carol, most famous for playing the titular character in *Gidget Goes to Rome* (1963).

Philip Tonge (1898–1959), *Mr. Shellhammer*

As his accent indicates, Philip Asheton Tonge was born in London. He started performing as a child actor at a very young age, and worked consistently through his teens. In 1914, he emigrated to the United States to appear in the play *Highway of Life*, which was an adaptation of Charles Dickens's *David Copperfield*. He continued to get parts in several plays through the early 1920s, includ-

Anthony Sydes would appear with Natalie Wood in another George Seaton movie a couple years later, *Chicken Every Sunday* (1949). (Photofest)

ing in Jerome Kern's *The Bunch and Judy*, which starred Fred Astaire and his sister Adele. In 1923 he married Anna Hahn and, a year later, got a job as an actor at the Boston Repertory Theater, where he spent the next two years. He returned to New York where his friend Noel Coward ended up casting him in five of his plays during the 1930s and 1940s, such as the original productions of *Hay Fever* and *Blithe Spirit*. His three decades as a veteran actor on Broadway certainly helped Tonge get the role in *Miracle*. He continued appearing in legitimate theater through the early 1950s, before completely transitioning to roles in Hollywood, where he finished his career. He appeared in several high-profile films, such as *Hans Christian Andersen* (1952) with Danny Kaye, the horror classic *House of Wax* (1953) with Vincent Price, and Billy Wilder's adaptation of Agatha Christie's *Witness for the Prosecution* (1957). Tonge also guest-starred on several TV shows throughout the 1950s, from *Perry Mason* to *Lassie*. When he died he was married to his second wife, Lyda Ridout.[282]

CAST AND CREW OF THE ORIGINAL 1947 FEATURE FILM

The following cast and crew information was compiled from the on-screen credits, the pressbook, the press release, the filming location information sheet, and the "Call Bureau Cast Service" list.[283] The latter was the most comprehensive, and was the basis for the order and classification below. Anyone else not on this list would have been considered an extra. Some character names which were not listed in these sources were identified in the script or in the film and added for clarity.

PRINCIPAL AND SUPPORTING CAST

Maureen O'Hara (Doris Walker)

John Payne (Fred Gailey)

Edmund Gwenn (Kris Kringle)

Gene Lockhart (Judge Henry X. Harper)

Natalie Wood (Susan Walker)

Porter Hall (Mr. Sawyer)

William Frawley (Charles Halloran)

Jerome Cowan (Thomas Mara)

Philip Tonge (Mr. Shellhammer)

James Seay (Dr. Pierce)

Harry Antrim (Mr. Macy)

Thelma Ritter (Mother of Peter)

Mary Field (Mother of Dutch girl)

Theresa Harris (Cleo)

Alvin Greenman (Alfred)

BIT PARTS

Ann Staunton (Mrs. Mara)

Robert Hyatt (Thomas Mara Jr.)

Richard Irving (Reporter)

Jeff Corey (Reporter)

Anne O'Neal (Secretary)

Lela Bliss (Mrs. Shellhammer)

Anthony Sydes (Peter)

William Forrest (Dr. Rogers)

Alvin Hammer (Mr. Mara's assistant)

Joseph McInerney (Bailiff)

Ida McGuire (Drum majorette)

Percy Helton (Drunk Santa Claus)

Jane Green (Mrs. Harper)

Marlene Lyden (Dutch girl)

Dorothy Gilchrist (Secretary)

Irene Shirley (Secretary)

Guy Thomajan (Post Office employee, Lou)

Jack Albertson (Post Office employee, Al Golden)

Herbert H. Heyes (Mr. Gimbel)

Stephen Roberts (Guard)

Robert Lynn (Salesman)

Fran Lee (Customer)

Robert Gist (Window dresser)

Jack Gargan (Chauffeur)

Brick Sullivan (Guard)

Walden Boyle (Judge's clerk)

Teddy Driver (Terry)

Patty Smith (Alice)

Robert Karnes (Intern)

Basil Walker (Intern)

Jean O'Donnell (Secretary)

Walden Boyle (Judge's clerk)

CREW

Producer: William Perlberg

Director: George Seaton

Assistant director: Arthur Jacobson

Screenplay by: George Seaton

Original story by: Valentine Davies

Production manager: Charles Hall

Musical direction: Alfred Newman

Music: Cyril Mockridge

Orchestral arrangements: Edward Powell

Directors of photography:

Charles Clarke, Lloyd Ahern

Art direction: Richard Day, Richard Irvine

Set decoration: Thomas Little, Ernest Lansing

Film editor: Robert Simpson

Wardrobe direction: Charles LeMaire

Costumes designed by: Kay Nelson

Makeup artist: Ben Nye

Special photo effects: Fred Sersen

Sound: Arthur L. Kirbach, Roger Heman

Key grip: Faxon

This is where the miracle happened: looking down 34th Street from Seventh Avenue. The Empire State Building is on the right. (Author's collection)

Macy's, Gimbels, and 34th Street

Three instrumental "characters" that appear in *Miracle* are Macy's, Gimbels, and the 34th Street shopping district. It's not difficult to see why Valentine Davies chose Macy's as the setting for his story. As the biggest and most famous store in the United States, it epitomized the commercialism that Kris is trying to counterbalance. Even by 1946, Macy's had a long history in New York that went back to 1858, when its namesake, Rowland Hussey Macy, opened a fifty-foot storefront at 204–206 Sixth Avenue, near 14th Street, in Lower Manhattan.

Rowland had had a rather unlucky streak most of his life up until that time. He was born into a long-established Quaker family on Nantucket Island off the coast of Massachusetts in 1822, where his father ran a bookstore. At the age of fifteen, he became a sailor and traveled the world aboard a whaling ship for the next four years. When he returned, he made his way to Boston and worked as a printer, and then, with the help of his brother, he opened a notions shop in 1844. They tried to make a go of it for two years, but with no success. He opened another store, married, and started his family.

News of the Gold Rush enticed Rowland to head to California with hopes of opening a store there, where all of those miners could spend their money. He set out with his brother and they eventually opened a store in Marysville, some forty miles north of Sacramento. This is where Macy & Company was born, but the venture was not successful, only lasting six months. He returned to Boston, where another brother, who had opened two stores, let him take over the management of the store that was located thirty-five miles north, in Haverhill, in 1851. Rowland ran the store for a few years but ran into difficulties, and it failed in 1855. In 1857, he joined his brother-in-law Sam Houghton out in Wisconsin, where they tried to make it in real estate, but that failed too, and so he returned to the East.[284]

Rowland then decided to head to New York City. He opened the equivalent of an upscale fabric store, which also sold notions and other essentials for making clothing. Though this was long before ready-to-wear clothing became standard, he also carried some manufactured items like underwear and handkerchiefs. Things didn't get off to a great start when both a large theft and a gas fire occurred during the first two years, but the store survived.[285] It was around this time that Rowland adopted a star as a symbol for his store, apparently based on a tattoo on his arm that he had received during his days as a sailor.[286] One propitious move was the hiring of young Margaret Getchell in 1862. She had some great ideas, such as adding new lines of merchandise and decorating the store's windows at Christmas, that helped to turn the store into a huge success. She rose quickly through the ranks and became one of the top executives at the store, and one of the earliest female executives in America.[287]

There was a real R. H. Macy, but he died back in 1877 long before there was a *Miracle on 34th Street*. (Author's collection)

Rowland had picked a good location for his store. As New York City kept growing, the center of retail activity, previously located around City Hall in Lower Manhattan, kept moving northward. As leases came up on adjacent properties, Rowland rented them for his expanding emporium; by 1877, Macy's was comprised of a hodgepodge of eleven separate storefronts.[288] As the nineteenth century progressed, the area from 8th Street to 23rd Street along Sixth Avenue became the most fashionable shopping district in New York, known as "The Ladies' Mile," and Rowland's store was right in the middle of it.[289]

In 1874, Rowland was approached by Lazarus Straus, a wholesaler of china, glassware, and silver. Lazarus had emigrated to America and settled in Georgia in 1852. After the Civil War, he decided to move the family up north to New York, where he and his two sons, Isidor and Nathan, started their firm, L. Straus & Son. The business was doing well, supplying inventory to several retailers, but Lazarus wanted to lease space at Macy's, and so approached Rowland, who agreed to the venture. The deal was mutually beneficial, as the china and glassware department quickly became one of the best-selling departments at the store.[290]

Almost twenty years after opening his New York store, Rowland died in 1877 at the age of only fifty-four. The store passed to his two junior partners, Abiel LaForge and his nephew, Robert Valentine, but both of them would die soon thereafter, in 1878 and 1879, respectively. Rowland's own son was not fit to take over the store, and so it passed into the hands of a distant cousin named Charles Webster. Webster, who was fairly inexperienced, hired Jerome Wheeler to help manage the enterprise. There was some internal friction, which caused Wheeler to eventually depart. The Strauses, who were very interested in becoming stakeholders in Macy's, bought a 45 percent share of the company in 1888, and then bought Webster out completely in 1896.[291] The sale to the Straus family was a boon to the company. They immediately expanded the 14th Street store by opening a huge stand-alone men's shop. By the turn of the century, it was becoming apparent that they needed a newer and bigger venue, and they sensed that Midtown Manhattan was the place to be.

During the nineteenth century, the area in and around 34th Street was called "The Tenderloin," the notorious center of New York's night life, with theaters, dance halls, bars, gambling houses, and the like. A fun little fact about that era is that Thomas Edison projected the first motion picture in America in 1896 in Koster & Bial's Music Hall, which stood where Macy's now stands.[292] The population growth was continuing to push the city ever northward, and it made sense for retail to follow. The Strauses decided to build a brand-new store, and selected 34th Street and Broadway as the site. They started buying up land and were successful at obtaining the acreage they wanted, except for one little building in the corner of the property. The asking price was originally $250,000, but when word got out that it was for the new Macy's store, an agent from one of their competitor stores, Siegel-Cooper, offered $375,000, and the seller accepted it. The agent then turned around and tried to sell the property to the Strauses, who promptly refused, and just designed their store around the existing building; hence the "notch" at the corner of 34th Street and Broadway.[293] Even though Macy's doesn't own that small building, since the mid-twentieth century the store has rented the space above it to hold "The World's Largest Store" sign. The groundbreaking for the Herald Square store took place in 1901. The new nine-story megastore was designed by the firm of De Lemos & Cordes, and was completed just in time for the Christmas shopping season in 1902. The tenth floor, added in 1910, increased floor space to one million square feet.[294]

When Macy's announced its new store, other retailers soon followed. The first was Saks & Company, which opened its elegant, bowed-facade store known as Saks-34th, right across the street, just weeks before Macy's.[295] Many others soon moved into the area. B. Altman started construction of a new store at Fifth Avenue and 34th Street in 1905; Best & Company moved in at Fifth Avenue and 35th Street in 1910; and Lord & Taylor built its new flagship store at Fifth Avenue and 38th Street in 1914.[296] This influx of new stores quickly changed the tenor of the neighborhood, as the unsavory nightspots moved elsewhere and the Midtown shopping district emerged. It was around this time that Fifth Avenue became synonymous with high fashion.[297]

Isidor and Nathan guided the company through the move to Midtown Manhattan, and the store was a huge success. Tragedy struck the Straus family in 1912 when Isidor and his wife Ida were passengers on the *Titanic* and went down with the ship. This left Macy's in the hands of Nathan and Isidor's sons, Jesse, Percy, and Herbert. In 1913, the two factions of the family decided to divide up the family businesses: Isidor's sons bought out Nathan's interest in Macy's, while Nathan's family assumed all interest in the L. Straus & Son wholesale business, and in the Abraham & Straus department store in Brooklyn, which they partially owned.[298] Jesse Straus became the president of Macy's for the next twenty years, until he became the ambassador to France in 1933. Percy took the helm for the next six years, during which time both Herbert and Jesse passed away.[299] In 1940, Jesse's son Jack became president, and remained in that role until he retired in 1968.[300] "Mr. Macy" in *Miracle* is based on him.

The Mr. Macy character in the film was based on the then-current president of the store, Jack Straus, shown here as he appeared in 1946. For authenticity, they used Straus's office as Mr. Macy's office in the film. (Author's collection)

The Herald Square store went through major expansions in the 1920s and 1930s. In 1924, the same year as the first parade, a twenty-story annex was built to the west, providing an additional half-million square feet of floor space, making it worthy of the moniker "the largest store in the world."[301] In 1928 and 1931, two more additions would extend the store all the way to Seventh Avenue and provide yet another half-million square feet of floor space, completing the current footprint of the flagship store.[302]

It was during the 1920s that Macy's became a real powerhouse and the number-one retailer in New York. Macy's famous slogan, "It's Smart to be Thrifty"—coined by their own advertising genius Bernice Fitz-Gibbon—was used for decades (and it can be seen briefly in *Miracle* on the store facade). In the film, Mr. Macy instructs his underlings to expand the referral program to their other stores in San Francisco, Toledo, Newark, and Atlanta. The stores to which he is referring were not fictional: Macy's phenomenal success in New York had led the company to expand across the country. Macy's had acquired Lasalle & Koch in Toledo in 1924; Davison-Paxon-Stokes in Atlanta in 1925; Bamberger's in Newark in 1929; and O'Connor, Moffat & Company in San Francisco in 1945. They continued to operate some of those stores under their original nameplates for many years.[303] In the spring of 1947, during the making of *Miracle*, Macy's

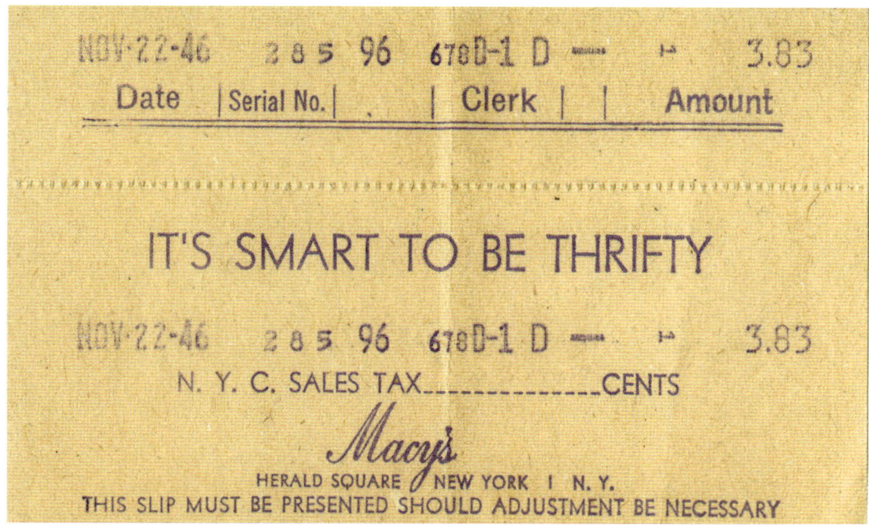

This receipt, issued just days before the *Miracle* company arrived at Macy's, carries the store's famous motto. The day before, the store had registered over $1.2 million in sales. The 1946 Christmas shopping season would be groundbreaking with sales surpassing $1 million on seven separate days and almost reaching $1.5 million on two of those days. (Author's collection)

acquired John Taylor Dry Goods in Kansas City.[304]

By 1946, the Midtown shopping district was visited by 250 million people annually and accounted for 40 percent of retail sales in Manhattan.[305] The biggest attraction was Macy's, which had become *the* grand emporium in America, a city within a city that attracted a clientele from the wealthy elite to the bargain hunter. With more than 400,000 items in stock (not counting different colors and sizes, they were quick to point out), its 180 departments carried everything from fine furniture to livestock (!). It had the world's largest bookstore, with over 18,000 titles on hand, and its 11,000-square-foot china and glassware department (obviously dear to the Strauses) sold more dinnerware than any other store in the world.[306] In short, you could find almost anything you needed at Macy's—except coffins (Macy's never got into funeral wares).

An average of 150,000 people came through the store every day, adding up to 45 million transactions per year.[307] The staff was 11,000 strong and would almost double to 21,000 during the holiday season. And the 1946 Christmas season was an extremely good one, sales-wise: Even before the Christmas shopping season officially began, the store had a record sales day on November 14, when it did $1,000,000 in sales (a "normal" day would bring in about $250,000). It was only the fifth time in its history that this had happened.[308] That season, there would be a total of seven million-dollar days, with two days approaching sales of $1,500,000.[309] Macy's would learn a thing or two from the movie experience. Influenced by *Miracle*, life imitated art when Macy's employed a "Miss Christine Kringle" to refer shoppers to other stores if Macy's didn't carry the merchandise they were seeking.[310]

Gimbels served as the other major attraction in the 34th Street shopping district. The story of Gimbels is another one of the great rags-to-riches stories of the nineteenth century. Adam Gimbel emigrated from his native Bavaria (part of modern-day Germany) to the United States via New Orleans in 1840. He made his way up the Mississippi and settled in Vincennes, Indiana,

Situated between 32nd and 33rd Streets on Sixth Avenue, Gimbels was a New York institution for three-quarters of a century. (Author's collection)

 MACY'S, GIMBELS, AND 34TH STREET

where he opened a dry-goods store in 1842. He married and had a prodigious brood of fourteen children, with four daughters and seven sons surviving to adulthood, many of whom joined him in the family business.

The Gimbels had a thriving retail business for almost half a century in Vincennes, and eventually decided to expand the business by opening another store in Danville, Illinois, in 1881. By 1886, they were looking to expand again. But father Adam, who was getting on in years, decided to retire from the business and move to Philadelphia. The Gimbel sons, interested in continuing the family business, felt that the burgeoning railroad system expanding across the United States would be key to continued growth in the retail industry, and were exploring various cities for expansion. Anticipating that Milwaukee, Wisconsin, was going to become the next major railroad hub, they decided to establish a store there in 1887; a few years later, they sold off their interests in the Vincennes and Danville stores. Although Milwaukee never developed into a huge transportation hub (Chicago took that honor), the Gimbels did build the largest department store in that city, a landmark there for almost a hundred years.[311]

By 1893, the Gimbel sons were looking at another expansion. They felt that Midwestern cities, like Chicago and St. Louis, couldn't handle additional retail competition, but a great opportunity arose in Philadelphia, where their parents had relocated. Haines and Company was a struggling store that was looking for a buyout, and the Gimbels seized the opportunity. They purchased Haines for $1,000,000 in 1894, and established their store at Ninth and Market Streets. Gimbels would expand again when it entered the Pittsburgh market by purchasing the Kaufmann & Baer store in 1925.[312] These are the stores Mr. Gimbel refers to in *Miracle*.

Following the death of their father, Adam, in 1896, the Gimbel brothers had their eye on the Big Apple. Herald Square was quickly becoming a shopping mecca, and Gimbels wanted to get in on the game. Then–vice president Bernard Gimbel (grandson of Adam) took the initiative and successfully convinced the family to break into the New York market. The Gimbel brothers moved forward and commissioned famed architect Daniel Burnham (his credits included the Flatiron Building in New York, Marshall Field's store in Chicago, and John Wanamaker's store in Philadelphia) to build an eleven-story, one-million-square-foot structure covering approximately half of a city block. Like Macy's, the new Gimbels store was built on the site of a theater, the Eagle, which was famous for being the venue of the first production in America of Gilbert and Sullivan's *H.M.S. Pinafore*.[313]

The store opened for business in 1910, and was considered an upstart in New York. Macy's, which had dominated the Midtown Manhattan shopping district for almost a decade by then, now had a serious competitor, even though the Gimbels store was only half the size of Macy's after its expansion.[314] Gimbels never became glamorous, remaining focused on middle-class buyers by carrying quality merchandise at reasonable prices. It had a well-known bargain basement that was the largest in New York, and always offered amazing deals. But a few years later, in 1923, Gimbels was able to enter the luxury market when Horace Saks ran into some financial difficulties when trying to open his second store on Fifth Avenue. Bernard Gimbel proposed to buy the Saks company and allow Horace to remain as president, which he gladly accepted. This allowed him to proceed with the creation of Saks Fifth Avenue. Gimbels took control and operated the Saks-34th store, which acted as a buffer between Gimbels and Macy's until the mid-1960s.[315]

One of the major elements of *Miracle* is the rivalry between Macy's and Gimbels, which was one of the great retail rivalries in the country. Most cities had two leading department stores vying for the same customers, and Macy's and Gimbels filled those roles in Manhattan. The origins of the feud are a bit hazy. Some say it began when

At the time *Miracle* was made, there wasn't a real R. H. Macy, but there was a real Mr. Gimbel. Bernard Gimbel, seen here, was asked to play himself but turned it down, which he later regretted. The role went to Herbert Heyes, who played Mr. Gimbel in the 1947 film and in the 1955 TV movie. (Photofest)

Gimbels opened their store in 1910 and lured some of Macy's executive talent away. Others say it started as a publicity gag which the stores kept going for notoriety's sake. Another source claims it originated with entertainer Eddie Cantor in a comedy sketch, when he was asked to reveal some deep, dark secret, and he replied, "Does Macy tell Gimbel?" In any case, the phrase entered American lingo as a popular response if someone was asking another to divulge a secret.[316] Whatever the origins, as the two biggest retailers in the 34th Street shopping district, competition was fierce. They were essentially fighting for the same customers, since both stores carried similar lines and types of merchandise. Even though Macy's was a significantly larger operation, a good sale at Gimbels would have Macy's clientele running across the street. The rivalry was good-natured, and its continuance certainly kept both names in the public consciousness.

In an attempt to stiffen the competition, Gimbels hired Bernice Fitz-Gibbon, the famed advertising executive that had coined the "It's Smart to Be Thrifty" slogan for Macy's in the 1920s. She had gone to Wanamaker's after working at Macy's, before being lured to Gimbels. Fitz-Gibbon was equally effective for Gimbels, coming up with the slogan "Nobody but Nobody Undersells Gimbels" in the mid-1940s. She is credited with introducing the repetition of a pronoun for emphasis as a literary device.[317] The slogan was included in the *Miracle* script during Kris's photo op with Mr. Macy and Mr. Gimbel, when they start arguing about who will supply the X-ray machine. After saying he could get it for cost, Mr. Gimbel was supposed to say, "Nobody but nobody undersells Gimbels." It's not clear why the clever use of this slogan was cut, especially since Fitz-Gibbon was the studio's contact at Gimbels during the filming of *Miracle*.[318]

In addition to Macy's and Gimbels, several other New York retailers recognized the marketing value of being featured in a film, and enthusiastically embraced participation in *Miracle*.[319] Due to the fact that all the other stores mentioned throughout the film are now defunct (with the exception of Bloomingdale's), some viewers might assume that these were fictional names created for the movie, but they were not. Every store mentioned was a going concern at the time. When Kris tells Peter's mother she can find a fire engine, he recommends she go to Schoenfeld's, which was a real toy store, but he did get the address wrong: He said it was over on Lexington Avenue, when its real location was at 630 Fifth Avenue.[320]

All of the stores featured in the *R. H. Macy & Company Shopping Guide for the Convenience of Our Customers* were real as well. Bloomingdale's had been a New York institution since 1872, and had always been located on the Upper East Side, on Lexington Avenue and 59th Street. In the 1940s, Bloomingdale's catered to conservative middle-class families; it wasn't until the 1950s that it transformed itself into "Bloomies" and became a serious arbiter of the trendy and hip.

Hearns was a store with a long history in New York, dating back to 1827. Before the arrival of Gimbels in New York, Hearns was Macy's big rival in the late nineteenth and early twentieth centuries, when both were located in Lower Manhattan. In 1946, it still had a store on Fifth Avenue and 14th Street, one up in the Bronx, and one in Newark.[321]

Stern's, which had been around since 1867, had moved to Midtown Manhattan in 1913, and was located at 41 West 42nd Street, near the New York Public Library. Prior to World War I, Stern's had focused on high-end imported merchandise but, due to supply chain issues during the war, changed their focus, and by the 1940s carried more mid-range merchandise. Stern's was known for throwing flashy events frequented by celebrities and became known as "the show business store."[322]

McCreery & Company was just east of Macy's on Fifth Avenue and 34th Street, and, incidentally, was prominently featured in another 1947 film, *Life with Father*. TCF had reached out to a couple of other stores, McCutcheon's and Wanamaker's, but they never agreed, and so do not appear in the film.[323]

Macy's and Gimbels would continue to be mainstays of the 34th Street shopping district for decades after. However, both stores were seriously affected during the consolidation and collapse of the department store business model in the 1980s and 1990s. Unfortunately, Gimbels would not survive (although its Saks Fifth Avenue division did), but would be fondly remembered during its demise with references to its cinematic ties in headlines such as "No More Miracles on 34th Street, Gimbels Gone."[324] Following its closure, the Gimbels 33rd Street store was renovated and reopened as a mall, and the classic Sixth Avenue facade is now clad with glass panels, making the building unrecognizable. Macy's ended up being part of a few mergers and acquisitions before it was transformed into a national retailer. A major renovation of the Herald Square store in 2012 has helped it maintain its status as a shopping mecca.

Thanksgiving Day was the first day of filming for *Miracle on 34th Street* and this was one of the first shots at 77th and Central Park West where the parade begins and Doris and Kris first meet. (Photofest)

The Production

One of the essential elements that contributed to the realistic feel of *Miracle* was filming on location in New York. During its thirty-year history, the studio had occasionally sent productions on location when they were big-budget films and the story called for it. For example, Henry King, one of the studio's top directors, often campaigned to do his films on location, and so his upcoming film, *Captain from Castile*, would be shot in Mexico in early 1947. But for most films, shooting on location was unnecessary. The studio's expansive almost-300 acre backlot in west Los Angeles had about every conceivable set for every conceivable movie, from a Western town to a French village to a modern residential street. There were even two "New York" streets: an "Old" New York street consisting of brownstones and a "New" New York street consisting of 1930s and 1940s *moderne* apartment buildings and storefronts.

While much of *Miracle* could easily have been filmed on the backlot, including even the parade shots, TCF had started a trend of doing more films, especially crime dramas, on location, to add to the visual veracity of the stories, with *The House on 92nd Street* (1945), *13 Rue Madeleine* (1947), and *Boomerang!* (1947) being recent examples. Other studios had been featuring real places in films as well, such as New York's Waldorf Astoria Hotel in *Weekend at the Waldorf* and the famous Stork Club getting a namesake movie, both released in 1945. Though *Miracle* is a far cry thematically from the film noirs of the period, it had the same aim. Shooting *Miracle* in New York certainly added to the realism of the story.

There was another reason, as well. In the mid-1940s, TCF started shooting films away from Los Angeles primarily as a cost-cutting measure. The costs of filming in California had soared due to rising construction costs, demands from writers, and higher salaries for cast and crew. *Variety* later noted that the costs to make a typical movie were up 63 percent from 1946 to 1947 alone.[325] *The House on 92nd Street* and *13 Rue Madeleine* had provided a huge boon to the Eastern film industry, and New York wanted to attract more productions in order to lure back the film industry that had largely abandoned the Eastern Seaboard a quarter-century earlier.[326] The mayor and city administration were very cooperative, and the local unions were a cheaper solution due to the rising costs in California, and so it ended up being a win-win situation for both groups. It also provided a chance to get away from all the labor unrest in Los Angeles that was giving the studios so many headaches. The authenticity provided by shooting on location was the added bonus that such filming provided.

An element of utmost importance was the participation of Macy's and Gimbels, since they were both key to the story—Macy's, in particular, because their Thanksgiving Day parade plays such a pivotal role in the narrative. In Davies's first story outline, he had gone generic by using "Tracy's" and "Grimble's" as the names of the stores, but had changed them to the real names when he did the second story outline. George Seaton remembered the studio suggesting he use made-up names like "Tracy's" and "Trimbels" (probably to avoid getting permissions), but he rejected that because it sounded "too fairyland like."[327] (Incidentally, the studio had played with the Macy name in the 1942 film *Life Begins at Eight-Thirty*, which features a drunk Santa Claus who gets fired at the Marcy Herald Square store.)

So, in late August, before TCF had purchased the story, the legal department reached out to Macy's to see if they would be willing to be involved with the film. It was probably no surprise when the retailer agreed to cooperate.[328] Macy's knew the value of a motion picture tie-in: The company's brainchild a few years before had involved developing the wardrobe for the United Artists release, *Walter Wanger's Vogues of 1938* (1937), and then offering those clothing lines in their store.[329] This initial approval gave TCF enough confidence to proceed with the project.

Seaton remembers reaching out to the Gimbels public relations department after production had started. When the store found out Macy's was involved in the project, the answer was a flat-out "no." Not willing to give up, Seaton made an appointment with store president Bernard Gimbel directly. Gimbel read the script and was willing to have his store participate, with the following suggestions: He wanted Gimbels to be the star of the show instead of Macy's, and he wanted the setting moved to Philadelphia, where Gimbels sponsored that city's big Thanksgiving Day parade. Wanamaker's, Gimbels's big competitor in Philadelphia, could then be featured as the rival store. Seaton was unwilling to concede on a total change in location since he had already worked everything out in New York. Gimbel was even offered the opportunity to play himself in the film, but turned it down, a decision he later regretted.[330] After his suggestions were rejected, Gimbel debated participation, but ultimately accepted, making a final decision on November 27, the day before filming began; he even agreed to have his own office filmed.[331] The final script was

Despite some complications, Kay Nelson was able to get Maureen O'Hara's costumes ready for this wardrobe continuity photo right before filming started on Thanksgiving Day in front of the American Museum of Natural History. Notes indicate that her coat was camel hair, her hat was tan beaver cloth with a brown satin sequin trim band, her shoes were brown kid leather, her silk scarf was green and brown, her gloves were tan, and her purse was tan leather. (Western Costume)

sent to both stores for approval, but TCF decided not to invite further comment from either until the film was completed.[332]

The cast and crew started assembling in New York during the days before Thanksgiving. O'Hara arrived on November 19, ahead of the rest, because she needed to do wardrobe fittings.[333] Kay Nelson, one of the studio's staff costume designers, was assigned to do *Miracle*. Nelson had been at TCF since the early 1940s and had had the opportunity to work on a variety of films. She had designed stunning showgirl costumes for Betty Grable in *Billy Rose's Diamond Horseshoe* (1945), created an elegant wardrobe for Gene Tierney as the rich-girl-gone-bad in *Leave Her to Heaven* (1945), and dressed everyday people in film noirs like *The Dark Corner* (1946) and *Boomerang!* (1947). She had also worked on Maureen O'Hara's last three pictures (*Do You Love Me*, 1946; *Sentimental Journey*, 1946; and *The Homestretch*, 1947), all of which featured O'Hara as a fashion plate in exquisite sartorial splendor. Nelson's experience doing wardrobe for contemporary pictures and having worked with O'Hara made her an ideal choice for *Miracle*.

Nelson's biggest challenge would be designing O'Hara's wardrobe. Normally, a custom wardrobe is created for the main stars of a picture. To be true to the character of Doris Walker as a department store executive who gets a 10 percent employee discount, a decision was made to dress O'Hara in off-the-rack, ready-to-wear clothes that would be available at Macy's. This also made sense from a practical standpoint, since O'Hara was in Ireland and wasn't available to do fittings at the studio in Los Angeles anyway. When O'Hara arrived in New York, she spent the whole first week getting her costumes ready.[334] She and Nelson went on several shopping expeditions around New York, only to find that most ready-to-wear women's clothing was not made for tall women like O'Hara, at five-foot-eight. Nelson was suddenly scrambling to find seamstresses who could make custom copies of ready-to-wear suits and dresses and have them ready in about one week's time. This delayed the production by two days.[335]

One interesting side note is the Hollywood Production Code's concerns about the wardrobe. When TCF submitted the initial screenplay for approval in November 1946, the Production Code office reminded the studio, first and foremost, that the women's costumes were to be modest and not too revealing; they were particularly concerned about plunging necklines. This concern was most certainly due to the ongoing problems the Office had encountered with Jane Russell's revealing outfits in *The Outlaw* (1943). Presumably in response to this dictum, Nelson designed all of O'Hara's costumes with extremely high necklines. With O'Hara's wardrobe issues resolved, filming could begin.

Unlike most movies, where scenes are shot in a haphazard order, depending on a variety of factors, *Miracle* was actually shot fairly chronologically as it appears on the screen, with the parade scenes shot first. In Davies's first outline of the *Miracle* story, there actually was no parade scene. Instead, the story opened with Doris and Mr. Shellhammer surveying the Santa they had hired for the toy department. His beard is slipping off and his padding is falling out and the

MACY'S THANKSGIVING DAY PARADE LINEUP FOR 1946*

The New York Guard's 17th Infantry Band
The Golden Eagle float with a 20-foot wingspan accompanied by
"15 gorgeous maidens in Colonial costumes"
The Fireman Float
The Prodigious Pilgrim balloon (40 feet tall), "accompanied by 20 babes in Puritan dress"
The Popeye and Olive Oyl float
The Hey Diddle Diddle float
The Snowman float
The Pinocchio float
The Ferko String Band
The Panda Bear balloon (38 feet tall and 30 feet wide)
The "Comedy Model T Ford" which "explodes, disintegrates, and rears up on its hind wheels"
The Twin Giraffes float
Hopalong Cassidy on his horse with the Western Boy and Girls
and a "Genu-wine wagon from the days of the '49ers"
The Old Lady in the Shoe float with her ten kids
The Scottish bagpipe band in kilts
The Ice-Cream Cone balloon (44 feet tall)
The Donald Duck on a Pirate Ship float
The Pink Elephant Slide float
The Ringmaster float
The St. Louis Cardinal Baseball Player balloon (46 feet tall)
The Nimble Tumblers on the Trampoline float
The Three Men in a Tub float
The Candy Cane balloon (41 feet tall)
St. Nicholas Band of Jersey City
The Santa Claus float

*Due to conflicting and/or unavailable sources, this list is an approximation of the order of the parade.

disappointed children can tell he's a phony. Doris and Mr. Shellhammer know they need to find a replacement, and quick. She then calls a theatrical agent for a referral and gets Kris Kringle to be their Santa. Davies created the parade scenes for his second story outline, and they stayed in throughout all of the revisions. The movie would certainly have been much easier to film if the action had been kept in the toy department. By retaining the parade as part of the story, it provided another reason for the company to go to New York, because it would save the cost of replicating it in Los Angeles.

The Macy's Thanksgiving Day Parade has become such an integral part of the American popular landscape that it's hard to imagine Thanksgiving without it. Although very little logical connection exists today between department stores and parades, the two were heavily entwined during the early twentieth century.[336] This originated in the fact that window dressers relied heavily on crepe paper to make attractive displays in the large plate-glass windows, one of the principal methods of marketing merchandise at the time. The skills these window dressers acquired using crepe paper and drapery translated easily into making floats for parades. Many a retailer across the United States was finding that store-sponsored parades provided excellent opportunities for advertising. Gimbels had actually started a Thanksgiving Day parade in 1920 in Philadelphia.[337] Macy's started their parade in 1924, the same year that Hudson's department store started one in Detroit. The Hollywood Chamber of Commerce first sponsored the Hollywood Christmas Parade in 1931. Most parades are no longer sponsored by retailers, but Macy's has continued to find marketing value in their parade, especially after they transitioned from being a retailer in select markets to a national one.

The 1924 parade was an elaborate affair, with floats and marching bands, and was deemed a big-enough success that Macy's continued sponsoring the parade year after year. From the beginning, it was focused on Santa Claus and the unveiling of the Macy's Christmas windows as the culminating event. For the first decade, the parade was called the Macy's Christmas Parade; in 1935, the name was changed to the Macy's Thanksgiving Day Parade, the name it's been known by ever since.[338]

One of the signature elements of the parade—the massive balloons—was not introduced until 1927, and the number usually varied between five to ten per year.[339] Up until 1932, when the balloons arrived in front of Macy's at Herald Square, they were released and floated away. With intentionally slow leaks, the balloons could stay afloat in the air for up to a week, and would usually end up somewhere in the greater New York metro area. Macy's would attach an envelope which included information on the cash reward for a balloon's return. But as airplanes became more common in the early 1930s, the balloons started to cause problems. In 1931, Felix the Cat almost collided with an airplane, and in 1932, Tom-Cat almost caused another plane disaster, and so Macy's stopped releasing the balloons the following year. In 1933, Macy's released 5,200 small balloons, 200 of which had Macy's signature red star and, if found, could be redeemed for merchandise.[340] Due to World War II, the parade was on hiatus from 1942 to 1944, with Macy's

Edmund Gwenn was Santa Claus in the 1946 Macy's Thanksgiving Day Parade. His portrayal was so well liked that other department stores started requesting his services. (Author's collection)

The panda bear balloon arrives in front of Macy's on 34th Street where the parade route ended. The Empire State Building can be seen in the background. (Photofest)

donating the rubber balloons to help with the war effort.[341] By 1946, the parade was a New York City institution, with its twentieth incarnation.

TCF had received permission from Macy's to photograph the parade from all angles. While that seemed to be easy enough to do from the sidelines, they also needed to get footage from higher angles, for the scene of Susan and Fred watching the parade from his apartment, and also from the middle of the parade route. The scouting crew went up and down Central Park West inquiring with several apartment dwellers whether they could film from their windows, such as an apartment on the third floor of the building at 253 West 58th Street.[342] O'Hara remembered rehearsing the pre-parade scenes in the days before Thanksgiving so everyone would know where to go and what to do.[343]

The first day of filming was on Thanksgiving Day. O'Hara, who had just come from temperate Ireland, remembered it being "bitterly cold" all day, even though the reported temperature was fairly moderate for winter: The high that day was at 48, and the low at 30 degrees Fahrenheit.[344] The 1946 parade marked some significant changes from the past. Since its inception, the parade route had always started

Cowboy star William Boyd, better known as Hopalong Cassidy, was the big attraction in the 1946 Macy's Thanksgiving Day Parade. Twentieth Century-Fox had no intention of promoting another studio's star and so he doesn't show up in *Miracle*. His popularity caused him to be invited back to host the 1951 parade, shown here. (Photofest)

Susan divulges some insider information when she tells Fred that the baseball player balloon "was a clown last year. They just changed the head and painted him different." In honor of the seventieth anniversary of the film, the baseball player balloon was re-created and appeared in the 2017 parade. The parade footage was shot in New York along Central Park West and then, through movie magic, projected to appear to be in the window on the set of Fred's apartment on Stage 14 on the Twentieth Century-Fox lot in Los Angeles where Fred and Susan's interaction was filmed. Note the absent projection in the photo on the right. (Photofest)

at or above 110th Street; in 1945, they had moved it down to 106th Street. Beginning in 1946, the parade's starting point was moved down to 77th Street, by the American Museum of Natural History, drastically reducing the parade route (which is where it has remained ever since).[345] The parade went down Central Park West, through Columbus Circle, and continued down Broadway, turning west on 34th Street and ending in front of Macy's. The first two parades had been morning affairs, but for most of the 1920s and 1930s, the parade had become an afternoon event, starting at 1:00 or 2:00 p.m. In 1941 and 1945, it was moved up to 11:45 a.m., and on November 28, 1946, they started even earlier, at 10:00 a.m., with scheduled arrival in front of Macy's to be at 11:15 a.m.

The production used a total of fourteen cameras to film along the parade route.[346] There were four cameras placed at the staging area at 77th Street and Central Park West, to capture the opening scenes with the drunk Santa Claus and Doris meeting Kris. Cameras were placed in apartment and office windows along Central Park West, at Columbus Circle, and at Times Square; four cameras were at the prime filming location in front of Macy's on Herald Square, alongside the NBC cameras.[347]

Things did not go off without a hitch. Assistant director Artie Jacobson remembered placing cameras in five apartment windows. One key spot was almost lost when a man got mad about not being able to watch the parade because his wife had rented out their window without telling him. Some additional cash quickly resolved the situation.[348] At another of the rented apartments, a mother changed her mind and said she wasn't going to allow filming because her child was sick. Even though she threatened to telephone the police, the cameraman entered the apartment, got the shots he needed, and left before she could make the call.[349] A third apartment on Central Park West that provided "a perfect view" of the parade was rented for two days on condition that the cameramen would vacate the premises from noon until 2:30 p.m. to accommodate a baby's napping schedule.[350]

The principal camera was installed on top of a station wagon that held director George Seaton and assistant director Artie Jacobson. It allowed them "to shoot certain scenes, and then we could beat the parade by twenty blocks and get some more angles before we wound up on 34th Street."[351] Because the cameras were actually placed in the parade, the floats and marching bands had to maneuver around or even over them in some instances. The biggest problem was keeping things flowing and not having huge gaps during the parade scenes.[352]

All new balloons had been created for the parade in 1945 and then repurposed in 1946. Susan gives away a secret of the Macy's parade when, in response to Fred's comment, "Looks like they're having a little trouble with the baseball player," Susan knowingly replies, "He was a clown last year. They just changed the head and painted him different." The 1946 parade featured a total of five balloons, including the 46-foot-tall baseball player (purportedly a St. Louis Cardinal), a panda bear that was 38 feet tall and 30 feet wide, a 41-foot-tall candy cane, a 44-foot-tall ice-cream cone, and a 40-foot-tall pilgrim balloon, "accompanied by 20 babes in Puritan dress."[353]

The Prodigious Pilgrim balloon, passing through Times Square (the Astor Hotel can be seen on the right), was 40 feet tall and was "accompanied by 20 babes in Puritan dress." (Photofest)

Along with the six* marching bands and sixteen floats, the major attraction of the parade that year was cowboy film star William Boyd, better known as his alter ego, Hopalong Cassidy. He appeared with his horse and a whole contingent of cowboys and cowgirls, as well as a "genuwine wagon from the "days of the '49ers." The reason that he was not included in the footage in *Miracle* is certainly because he was not a TCF star. The same was true for Popeye and Donald Duck.

It was announced in advance that Edmund Gwenn, Maureen O'Hara, and John Payne would appear in the parade, but, of the three, only Gwenn did (and apparently not everyone got the word—the *New York Times* reported that Santa's identity was only revealed afterwards!).[354] Just like in the movie, he actually rode on the float as Santa Claus down the parade route. When the float arrived at Macy's, Gwenn climbed up on the marquee and was introduced by Philip

---

*Contemporary sources only identify four of the six bands that appeared in the parade that year.

Luckily Twentieth Century-Fox did not have to hire extras for this scene! Gwenn was Santa Claus in the 1946 Macy's Thanksgiving Day Parade. Upon arriving at Macy's on 34th Street, he got off the float and climbed on the canopy with the assistance of fellow actor Philip Tonge to unveil the store's windows, which were based on *The Nutcracker* ballet. The Spike Jones version of *The Nutcracker Suite* with lyrics played on the loudspeakers. (Photofest)

Tonge.[355] Then, to the crowd's delight, he unveiled Macy's windows, which showcased mechanical displays based on "The Nutcracker Prince," designed by Lilla Belle Pitts, a music professor at Columbia University. The windows were unveiled with the cute/annoying version of *The Nutcracker Suite* by Spike Jones and His City Slickers playing on the loudspeakers.[356]

One amusing story came out years later. As they were getting ready for filming the parade that day, Seaton suddenly remembered that Gwenn had a bladder problem and might need to relieve himself during the parade. It became incumbent on assistant director Artie Jacobson to figure something out, and so he "rigged a funnel with a long pipe trailing out of the sleigh."[357] When Seaton told Gwenn what they had contrived, he adamantly refused the accommodation, declaring with British decorum, "I wouldn't think of it." When Gwenn arrived at Macy's and concluded the unveiling of the windows, cinematographer Charles Clarke, unaware of Gwenn's condition, wanted to get one more shot of Gwenn and the crowds. Seaton told him no because Gwenn needed to find a restroom. However, when Gwenn heard what Clarke wanted, he acquiesced and remained up on the marquee for the shot.[358] Then, practically doubled over, he had to be quickly escorted to the men's room.[359]

The crew ended up filming over 15,000 feet of parade footage—about two hours and forty-five minutes' worth, almost twice as long as the completed movie—because there obviously would not be any option to do retakes.[360] Ultimately, only a few minutes ended up in the final cut of the film. Even though the parade had first been locally televised in 1939 on NBC for one hour (for the tens of people who had television sets at that time), the sequences filmed by TCF for use in *Miracle* provided the first footage that most Americans would have seen of the parade.[361] Certainly encouraged by *Miracle*'s success, for the 1948 parade, NBC decided to make it a national broadcast, beginning a Thanksgiving Day television tradition for millions of Americans.[362]

With the difficult parade scenes completed, the crew moved to filming inside Macy's, where the theme that year was "The Greatest Christmas Show on Earth." On the Friday and Saturday following Thanksgiving, the crew was still finalizing administrative details, like getting the day-player contracts signed for people like Thelma Ritter.[363] Macy's was open late (until 9:00 p.m.) both days, and so it is unclear how much, if any, filming got done that weekend. The plan was to do all of the camera and lighting setups and other preparations before the store opened to the public at 9:45 a.m. Some scenes, such as those that required background crowds, would be filmed during the day, while scenes featuring just the cast would be done after the store closed, at 6:00 p.m.[364] Charles Hall, the unit production manager, worked closely with public relations manager Norman Neubert of the display department and a Macy's buyer, who was on hand to help prop man Bill Siddell in case he needed anything from the store's inventory.[365]

The most essential filming location in the store was Macy's North Pole Annex. In 1946, it was installed on the seventh floor, where the rug department was located. Leo Mars, an actor in his seventies who had followed a career path in the theater similar to Gwenn's, was in charge of the operation. In fact, he was exactly what Susan accuses Kris of being: a nice old man with fake whiskers. To play Santa at Macy's was the most prestigious Santa gig around, and a lot of older actors sought the position. Each applicant had to have a physical exam to make sure he was in good health. The costume was expensive, at $175, and each actor would be stuffed and coiffed accordingly. The artificial whiskers were cleaned once a week. Mars instructed his subordinates to be "jovial," "not ask personal questions," and to "promise nothing," giving the children a lollipop before they left (Kris was going completely against store policy when he promised Peter that fire engine!).[366] Five actors were hired for the six-week season, with three Santas working at any given time on three separate thrones. Due to the design flow of the setup, the 27,000 children that came through each week only met one Santa, and were none the wiser about the other two. Each Santa would work for sixty minutes and then get thirty minutes off. The sign seen in the movie during the photo op with Mr. Macy and Mr. Gimbel—that reads "Will be back in a little while.

While filming at Macy's, Edmund Gwenn took some time to get into the role by working in the real North Pole Annex as a Santa Claus. (Author's collection)

I'm feeding my reindeer"—was actually the line used by the actors when they went off shift.

As part of his research for the role, Edmund Gwenn insisted on actually playing Santa Claus for a few hours each day, and took this role very seriously. When he was on the throne, he would ask each child what he or she wanted, taking down their names and addresses with the intention of sending them the desired gift. One day, director Seaton went into the office at Macy's that Gwenn was using as his dressing room and saw him going over the list. Gwenn came to one kid who had asked for twelve presents and blurted out, "Greedy little bugger, isn't he?"[367] Months later, before *Miracle* was released, there was an item in the *Hollywood Reporter* about some banter overheard on a Hollywood set about Gwenn: "Things must have been pretty tough for the old boy. D'you know that when I was back in New York around Christmas he was working as a Santa Claus at Macy's!"[368]

Cinematographer Charles Clarke remembers seeing Thelma Ritter for the first time when she showed up for her scenes. She seemed a little nervous, since she had only done theater and radio, and had never been in a movie. He offered some comforting words about how everyone makes mistakes and that the crew was there for her. It seemed to give her the confidence she needed for her first film role. He was really glad when such a down-to-earth woman became a big movie star a few years later.[369]

Following the Thelma Ritter scene, where Peter asks Kris for a fire engine, three short clips were filmed of Kris offering similar advice to other parents, such as "You'll find just what

Kris's shopping advice has made Peter's mother (Thelma Ritter) a new devotée of Macy's and she wants Mr. Shellhammer (Philip Tonge) to know about it! This scene gives a nice glimpse of Macy's interior in 1946. Little Peter (Anthony Sydes) is in tow. (Photofest)

you want at FAO Schwarz—$6.75”; “Bloomingdale’s has exactly what the little girl wants—$2.49”; and “Go to Stern’s on 42nd Street; they have them, and they’re worth every penny.” These were followed by a scene in Mr. Shellhammer’s office with a woman with a Southern accent praising the new policy, calling it “almost Southern,” and then his secretary coming in to tell him there are six more women who want to thank him.

During the filming on the seventh floor, Seaton hired a clown to amuse a crowd of shoppers and secretly filmed them in order to get some authentic reactions. Several people ended up being prominently

In this deleted scene, a woman from the South is telling Mr. Shellhammer that it’s “almost Southern” the way that Macy’s is sending customers to other stores. It preceded his secretary telling him there are six more women who want to thank him. (AMPAS)

The scenes of Macy’s North Pole Annex were shot on the seventh Floor of Macy’s Herald Square store in New York and on a re-created set on Stage B on the studio’s lot in Los Angeles. Can you tell the difference? After visiting the set, Jack Straus, the president of Macy’s, couldn’t. (Photofest)

Things come to a head when Doris sees Fred introducing Susan to Kris. (Photofest)

featured in the shot and were offered a $10 bill and a release form to appear in the film. One woman from Brooklyn was completely taken by surprise and asked what it was for; she was told, "Madame, you've just been in a movie, and this is your pay." She exclaimed, "My goodness, I only came here to buy a rug."[370] With an average of 150,000 customers per day (and even more in December), the areas where the crew was filming often became too crowded, and the crew would have to pick up and move to another area of the store.[371] O'Hara remembered that "once word got round that we were working in the store, we couldn't go anywhere without a squad of police."[372]

As filming got under way, one issue that became readily apparent was the need for more electricity. Despite the fact that Macy's had its own power plant that supplied the twenty-two million kilowatt-hours of electricity required to light and heat the twenty-five acres of floor space, it just wasn't enough to power the big klieg lights.[373] To get more power, they used one of the elevator shafts and ran cables directly down to the generator in the basement.[374] This, in turn, caused issues for the crowd scenes. The fire department wouldn't let cables be on the floor for

Mr. Shellhammer instructs Kris on how to push toys on undecided children. The scene was shot in the women's locker room at Macy's. (Photofest)

fear of tripping, and was concerned that the bright lights would blind people coming off the escalators. Consequently, cables were attached to the walls, and rheostats were put on the lights to control their brightness.[375] The lights also caused problems in the women's locker room, where they filmed the scene with Kris and Alfred: They got so hot that they set off the sprinkler system, more than once soaking the cast and crew.[376] One group that was not concerned about all these hassles was the New York electricians' union, as its members ended up being very well compensated with overtime pay.[377]

Miracle also showed some of the

non-public areas at Macy's. The employee cafeteria was used for the scene with Alfred and Kris. At that time, the cafeteria served five thousand meals a day at cost to employees.[378] The establishing shot of Kris picking up his tray and walking across the room was shot at Macy's. However, the close-up shot of Kris and Alfred at the table was filmed back on Stage 14 on the TCF lot. The art department replicated the set quite well, except for one detail: The knob on the radiator suddenly disappears when Kris sits down.

This scene, shot at Macy's, allowed store employees to see firsthand how tiring moviemaking can be with retake after retake. Doris is on her way to Mr. Macy's office, which was filmed in the real office of the president, Jack Straus. (Photofest)

The thirteenth floor, which is where the executive offices were located, also figures prominently in the film. The office of Macy's president was actually used for Mr. Macy's office in the movie.[379] During the filming on the thirteenth floor, Macy's employees were stunned at how long it took to shoot the scenes, and had compassion for the extras in the elevator who had to just stand there for hours and hours during the retakes.[380] The scenes in Doris's office were shot at the store, but a replica set was also created for some retakes on the studio lot.[381] There is a nice glimpse of the advertising department shown during the scene of the compilation of the *R. H. Macy & Company Shopping Guide for the Convenience of Our Customers*.

Mr. Sawyer's office was shot in the toy reserve on the fifth floor, but it was also replicated back on the studio's soundstage. It is interesting to note the evolution of the mental health exam questions. In the first three screenplays, Mr. Sawyer asks Kris who is president of the United States, and he responds correctly with "Harry Truman." In the final screenplay, the question is changed to: Who was the first president of the United States? This was probably done so that the film wouldn't be dated should there be a delay in release. What is a little inexplicable is Kris's assertion to Doris that Mr. Sawyer would not know that Daniel D. Tompkins was the vice president under John Quincy Adams. Seaton introduced the line in the November 16 screenplay, but initially he used the name of O. Max Gardner, who was President Truman's Under Secretary of the Treasury. Again, presumably in an effort not to date the film, the name was changed to a historical figure. However, even though Daniel D. Tompkins was indeed a vice president, he was in that office under James Monroe, not John Quincy Adams; Adams's vice president was John C. Calhoun. Clearly a mistake, but a fact that is bit arcane, so most people wouldn't have known whether it was true or not. A likely explanation is that an assistant just read the wrong line in an almanac, and no one double-checked it.

O'Hara had fond memories of being at the store. Working on their third picture together, she and Payne had become good friends. For all the times he had teased her for being glum on the sets of *To the Shores of Tripoli* and *Sentimental Journey*, she "made sure to greet him with a big, joking smile" every morning on the set of *Miracle*, to demonstrate her changed attitude.[382] In the evenings when they were filming, she and Natalie had free rein to wander around and try clothes and shoes on, and look at all the toys.[383] She probably ran into some clothing that looked familiar during those evenings: Macy's had teamed up with RKO designer Edward Stevenson to create an exclusive line of clothing inspired by the costumes from O'Hara's soon-to-be-released movie, *Sinbad the Sailor* (1947).[384] She was able to get much of her Christmas shopping done without having to deal with other shoppers.[385] On the evenings when they weren't shooting, O'Hara remembers walking up and down Fifth Avenue with Payne and Gwenn to look at the decorated store windows. She loved seeing the reactions of people when they saw Gwenn looking in; she "knew then that he was going to make a splash as Santa Claus."[386]

The final film does not show as much of Macy's interior as was originally intended. One major scene that featured the famous wooden escalators and helped develop the romantic relationship between Fred and Doris would be completely cut from the final film. In the script, the scene is preceded by Mr. Gimbel complaining about the success of Macy's new marketing strategy, followed by the other deleted scene of Fred and Doris having Sunday brunch in her apartment. In the escalator scene, Kris is finishing his shift on the seventh floor and saying good night to everyone when he runs into Fred. Fred explains that he has tickets to go see *Annie Get Your Gun* and has just asked Doris to join him, but she declined because she has to work late. They get on the escalator and continue their conversation as they descend to the main floor. Fred complains about how difficult it is to spend time with her because she just wants to work and then asks Kris if he wants to go to the play with him. Kris also declines the offer, and so Fred proposes that they go grab dinner and then play a game of chess instead, to which Kris agrees. They get off the escalator, and there is a shot of a large crowd of shoppers on the main floor. Kris then heads to the locker room, passing Mr. Sawyer on the way and asking him how his nails are coming along. Kris then slips out the back with the hope that Doris and Fred will spend the evening together looking for him. After a long wait, Fred goes into the locker room

Kris tells Doris "Christmas isn't just a day—it's a frame of mind—and that's what's been changing." Many of the offices were shot on the thirteenth floor at Macy's and replicated back on the Twentieth Century-Fox lot for retakes. (Photofest)

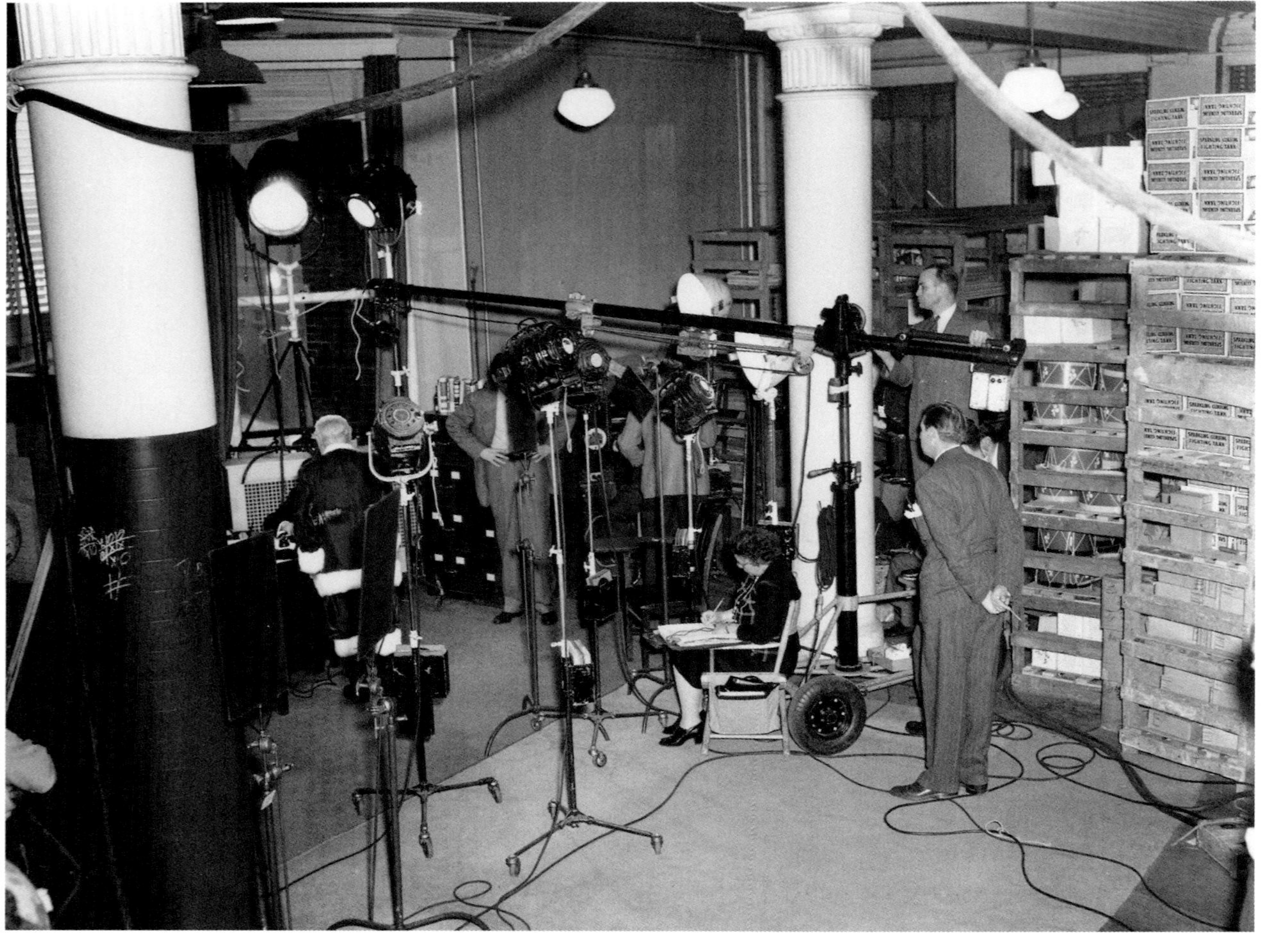

Kris confronts Dr. Sawyer in his office and bonks him on the head. This was filmed in the Toy Reserve on the fifth floor at Macy's; note the drums in crates and boxes marked "Sparkling Climbing Fighting Tanks" on the right side. (Author's collection)

and finds Alfred, who tells him that Kris already left. Fred then returns to Doris's office to inform her that Kris is missing. Concerned that Kris might be in trouble, the two start making phone calls to hospitals and police stations, and end up spending the entire evening together. With no leads, they finally give up and go home. Additional scenes that continued this plotline would be filmed back in Los Angeles.

Preparing for the escalator scene turned out to be quite a technical challenge. It called for one continuous shot of the camera following the actors as they descended on the escalator. This meant that the camera had to roll backward in front of the actors on the floor and then transition onto and down the escalators while remaining steady. This, of course, could not be done with a camera on the standard straight dolly tracks. One of the ingenious grips came up with the idea of putting the camera on a dolly with a folding leg with a wheel (similar to the landing wheel of an airplane) that could pop up or down depending on the contours of the floor. This would allow the camera to get on and off the escalators while maintaining a steady shot. The next problem

In this deleted scene, Doris turns down tickets to the theater with Fred because she has to work late. Fred then asks Kris to join him for dinner, but then Kris disappears. Fred comes back to Doris's office to tell her that they need to go looking for him, shown here. Kris's ruse forces Fred and Doris to spend the evening together. (Photofest)

was the lighting. Cinematographer Charles Clarke later noted that this kind of scene is always problematic because it is very difficult to obtain uniform lighting in spaces that have obstructions above (like other escalators).[387] Lastly, they had to assemble four hundred extras on the main floor. It was a very complicated undertaking, but the rigged dolly worked just as designed. However, when the film was developed, they realized that the cameraman had kept the lens too low, so when they got to the main floor, only the backs of Gwenn and Payne were seen and none of the extras. That one shot cost $38,000 and they couldn't use it.[388]

When they had completed the filming at Macy's, producer Perlberg asked Jack Straus if there was anything he could do as a thank-you. Straus responded, "Yes, I'd like that little whistle your assistant director, Artie Jacobson, blows when he wants silence." Finding the request a bit odd, Perlberg pressed for a reason, and Straus explained, "Well, that little whistle has gotten more respect from Macy employees than anyone around here."[389]

The crew filmed at several other locations around New York. The opening sequence has Kris walking down Madison Avenue between 62nd Street and 61st Street. The Lillian Schary Waldman Interior Decoration store was located at 19 East 61st Street. This was a real business, and had been located there since 1941.[390] In Seaton's original version of the screenplay, the store was identified as "Foster's, 'Long Island's oldest department store,' " which made sense when the scene that followed was at the Brooks' Memorial Home. In the November 16 screenplay, he had changed it to being a small side-street toy shop. In the final script, the type of store is not specifically designated.

One exterior that was filmed but ultimately cut from the film was of Bellevue Hospital at the corner of First Avenue and 29th Street. After Kris is tricked into believing he is going to get a picture with the mayor, there was supposed to be a shot of the limousine pulling up to Bellevue. The unit manager, Charles Hall, was supposed to make the arrangements for permission to film there, but he failed to do so. He hadn't told anyone, and so made himself scarce the morning of the shoot. The film crew arrived and started setting up and then, inexplicably, the Bellevue guards chased them away. Seaton made do by filming the limousine approaching, getting as close as possible without raising the ire of the guards, and then doing a wide shot to show the building. Only later did they learn why the crew was so unwelcome: The staff at Bellevue was none too pleased with the negative portrayal of their institution in Billy Wilder's 1945 film, *The Lost Weekend*, and they had not allowed filming on their premises ever since.[391]

The New York County Supreme Courthouse, located at 30 Centre Street in Lower Manhattan, was used as the locale for Kris's sanity hearing. Filming took place on December 11 in the rotunda for a couple of scenes. One is the scene where Mr. Sawyer approaches Fred to ask him to drop the matter. The scene was originally filmed with Sawyer exiting the elevator, and the elevator operator was clearly in the shot. A couple of weeks later, that elevator operator decided to make a little trouble. He had been paid a nominal fee (probably $10) for his two-second appearance in the film, but the crew had failed to get a receipt from him. He then resorted to extortion by claiming that he hadn't been paid, and refused to sign the release allowing him to be photographed unless he was paid $500. The studio flatly refused and contacted the film editor Robert Simpson, who had an easy solution: He suggested just cutting the operator out of the film, which is precisely what happened.[392] Another scene shot here has Kris arriving on the first day of the hearing. Apparently, the cameraman forgot to check the brightness of the lighting; as Kris walks up to Alfred, you can see a shadow of the camera on the column. The exterior and the rotunda were the only parts of the building that were filmed, as the courtroom was replicated back on Stage 14, on the studio lot.

Susan's dream house was also located in the greater New York metropolitan area. It wasn't on the way back from Great Neck to Manhattan; it was rather out of the way, up in Port Washington, which is adjacent to Manhasset on Long Island (where Fred says he wants one of those "junior partner" homes). The actual house is located at 24 Derby Road. The crew went up there to film the scene and only needed to do a few shots in front of the house, since the interiors of the car and house were all shot back in Los Angeles. The camera crew set up their cameras and, during filming, it was so cold that the cameras actually froze. As they were trying to figure out what to do, a woman by the name of Vaughn Mele, who lived in one of the homes across the street, invited everyone into her home to warm up. O'Hara remembers that the camera got the place of preference closest to the fireplace so it could thaw. As a thank-you, O'Hara took Mele and her husband out to the famous "21" Club in Manhattan for dinner, but Vaughn was so starstruck "that she couldn't eat a bite and only drank a glass of milk!"[393] And for anyone who has been wondering where the Brooks' Memorial Home is located, it's time to stop. It was not a real building, but just a special effects shot done back at the studio.[394]

It wasn't all work while the company was in New York. O'Hara kept a busy schedule doing many "movie star" activities while there. She stayed at the elegant Sherry-Netherland Hotel right across from Central Park, and so was close to everything.[395] She had arrived just in time to attend the world premiere of the studio's prestige production of W. Somerset Maugham's *The Razor's Edge* (1946), which was held at the Roxy Theatre on November 20. This was a significant

It was so cold the day the cast and crew went out to 24 Derby Road in Port Washington on Long Island to shoot Susan running up to her dream house that the camera froze. Maureen O'Hara is wearing her personal nutria fur coat. (Western Costume)

event because it was the first movie premiere since the war to bring the glitz and glamour back. The movie stars, the evening gowns, the furs, the jewels, the tuxedos, the limousines, and the red carpets were all there, a sign that life was finally getting back to normal in the Big Apple.

O'Hara, dressed in an elegant high-neck black evening gown, attended with escort Homer Harmon, along with lots of celebrities, including Tyrone Power, Gene Tierney, Clifton Webb, Frank Sinatra, and Myrna Loy.[396] One person notably absent was John Payne, one of the stars of the film, who hadn't made it to New York yet. Other notable guests included the Duke and Duchess of Wind-

Twentieth Century-Fox's prestige production of *The Razor's Edge* (1946) got a huge gala premiere at the Roxy Theatre in New York right before *Miracle* started filming. Several stars attended, including Tyrone Power and his wife Annabella, (center) and Gene Tierney (right), all greeted by Ben Grauer. (Photofest)

sor, who caused quite a stir when they got up and left before the film was over, and US Secretary of State James Byrnes. At the after-party held at the Terrace Room at the Plaza Hotel, O'Hara appeared "very subdued" and was hardly recognized by any of the non-Hollywood crowd.[397] A few weeks later, RKO hosted a cocktail reception in O'Hara's honor at the Cottage Room at the Hampshire House hotel in honor of the release of her upcoming film, *Sinbad the Sailor* (1947).[398]

O'Hara was also invited to attend the Christmas luncheon of the Associated Motion Picture Advertisers, which was held on December 13 at the Town Hall Club. Ernest W. Fredman, British trade paper editor, was the principal speaker and guest of honor. O'Hara was joined by her mentor and good friend, Charles Laughton, as well as Martha Scott and Simone Simon. O'Hara was selected to draw the door prize.[399] TCF instructed O'Hara to extend her stay in New York until December 22, but then, with everything apparently wrapped up, she was back in Los Angeles on December 19 for Christmas.[400]

Payne had brought his wife, actress Gloria DeHaven, along with him to New York so the two could enjoy some time together. They had fun roaming around Chinatown, Little Italy, and the Lower East Side, and being seen at the Stork Club.[401] They also frequented several of the other famous nightclubs while they were there. Payne left New York on December 16 on a TWA flight that had to make an emergency landing in Columbus, Ohio, due to a failed engine.[402] Luckily, there were no injuries. The rest of the *Miracle* company had departed by December 18. Filming in New York was done.

One issue that was percolating while the company was in New York was what to call this movie. As appropriate and perfect as the title *Miracle on 34th Street* seems to be, it actually wasn't chosen until about a month before principal photography was completed. Movies often have a working title that ends up being very different from the release title, but few films have had as many title changes in so short a time as *Miracle* did. When Valentine Davies wrote his first story outline and filed it with the Writers Guild on July 3, 1945, he gave it the character-focused title "Mr. Kringle." Two weeks later when he sold it to Seaton Productions, he indicated (inexplicably) in the contract that the story was also known by the very fitting title (in both senses), "Christmas Present."[403] Then, when he submitted the completed story to TCF a year later, he changed the title to the seem-

Maureen O'Hara stayed at the exclusive Sherry-Netherland Hotel on Fifth Avenue while in New York. (Author's collection)

ingly generic "This Is the Time," but, fortunately, he gave it context. On the title page, he explains that this is in reference to one of Fred's lines in Charles Dickens's *A Christmas Carol*: Fred declares to his uncle Scrooge that Christmas is the time "when men and women seem by one consent to open their hearts freely . . . and I say God bless it." All three titles were referenced when TCF was considering purchasing the story during the summer of 1946, but "This Is the Time" was the one that was ultimately used on the purchase contract, dated September 20, 1946, with an acknowledgment that it was also known under the other two titles.[404]

But none of these titles lasted for long. By early October 1946, when the studio announced the decision to cast Maureen O'Hara and Edmund Gwenn in the picture, the reported title was the romantic *My Heart Tells Me*, which was a title borrowed from the song Betty Grable had popularized in the 1943 film, *Sweet Rosie O'Grady*, which had become one of the most-played songs on the radio at the time.[405] This was in line with what the studio had done previously when it used the title of an already-popular song for O'Hara and Payne's previous collaboration, released earlier that year, the box-office-smash tearjerker, *Sentimental Journey*. The first two drafts of the script (the undated version and the November 2 version) were both titled *My Heart Tells Me*.[406] Then, just a couple of weeks later, on November 14, the studio announced that the title had been changed to the somewhat romantic but still vague *The Big Heart* (which, incidentally, ended up being the release title in the United Kingdom).[407] Darryl Zanuck was "crazy about the title," because it had a similar feel to *Sentimental Journey*. The November press release announcing Natalie Wood's participation in the film went out under that title.

But by early December, plans were afoot at the studio to change it yet again.[408] It is around this time that "Miracle on 34th Street" appears to have first surfaced, although it is not clear who came up with it. Seaton discussed it as a possible title with a friend, who didn't like it, and suggested as alternatives "Miracle at Macy's" or "Miracle on Herald Square." He particularly liked the latter because the use of "herald" hinted at the Christmas theme of the story.[409] Even though it is very similar in name, there is no indication that the 1939 Christmas-themed film *Miracle on Main Street* came up in the discussions, although it certainly would have when it came time for TCF to check the availability of the title.

If any of these title suggestions made it up to the studio management, they fell on deaf ears—at least initially. Just as filming was wrapping up in New York on December 17, the studio announced the new title change, this time to the odd *It's Only Human*.[410] The new title appeared both on the plot synopsis in the press release issued on December 30, 1946, and on the final version of the script, dated January 2, and remained in effect while principal photography resumed back on the studio lot.

But that title didn't last for long. By January 10, 1947, when final screen credits were due, the title was suddenly changed to *The Miracle on 34th Street*, and it became official. The studio ultimately decided to drop "The" and announced the final release title on January 23, 1947, as *Miracle on 34th Street* (although at least one internal studio memo dated January 27 still referred to it as "tentatively entitled").[411] *The Hollywood Reporter* assumed that this was because TCF had found great box-office appeal when film titles featured real street addresses, like *The House on 92nd Street* (1945) and *13 Rue Madeleine* (1947). The constant change was dizzying: "We are assured this is the final title," quipped one seemingly relieved reporter.[412]

The cast and crew had taken two weeks off for the Christmas break, but were back at the studio at the beginning of the new year. Wardrobe fittings occupied the first few days of the month, with filming starting back up on Monday, January 6. Most of the sets were built on Stage 14, and art directors Richard Day and Richard Irvine, along with set decorators Thomas Little and Ernest Lansing, had been busy finishing all the interior sets, including Fred's and Doris's apartments and the courtroom.* One really interesting change was the decor of Doris's apartment. In Davies's original story, he described her apartment as "very modernly furnished," to match the kind of woman she is, and in Seaton's final screenplay, he indicated that he, too, wanted the apartment to be "modern, in good taste, neat—but rather cold." Probably in response to Zanuck's critique that the Doris character was too off-putting, Seaton completely changed the art direction. Instead of a contemporary decor, he went with a very traditional Early American theme, which was very popular at the time. It certainly provides a more warm and homey feel than modern decor would have, and softens the perception of her character to a certain extent.

The next three weeks (until January 27) were devoted almost exclusively to filming the scenes in Doris's and Fred's apartments. These scenes were probably filmed first because they featured Wood, who was filming *The Ghost and Mrs. Muir* simultaneously, so the production needed to get her scenes completed as soon as possible. In addition to the handful of scenes that do appear in the film, a few additional scenes were filmed that didn't make the final cut. One such scene is rather amusing and it's a little surprising that it wasn't retained: After Fred offers his apartment to Kris, and Doris calls Mr. Shellhammer, all four main characters sit down to dinner. Fred goes

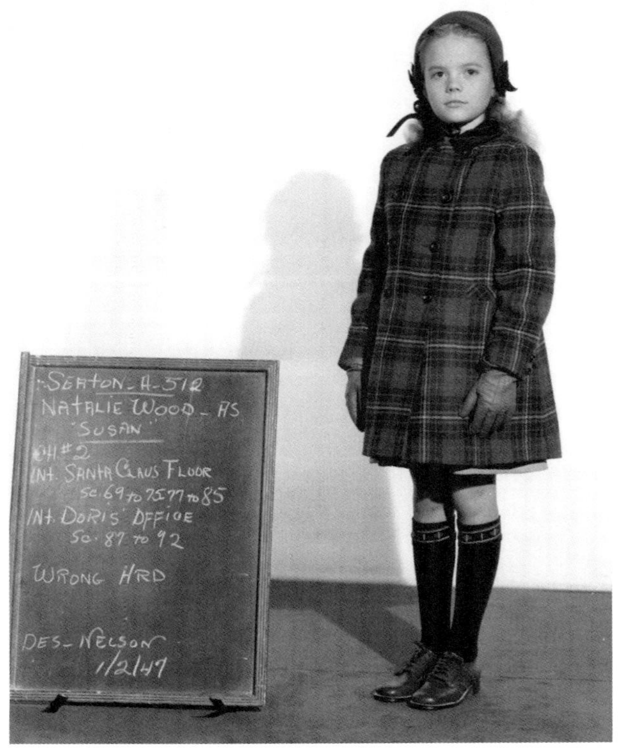

The Twentieth Century-Fox wardrobe department made sure all costumes were properly documented when the company returned to the studio in January 1947, like this outfit worn by Natalie Wood. Notes indicate that the dress was made of turquoise jersey; the coat was red-and-green-plaid wool; the hat was green felt; the gloves, red kid; the socks and shoes were brown, the latter being from Natalie's personal wardrobe. (Western costume)

---

* See appendix B for a full list of sets and filming dates at the studio.

Following Zanuck's recommendation to make Doris a more likable character, director Seaton decided to change the decor of Doris's apartment from "modern . . . but rather cold" to a cozy Early American theme. (Photofest)

This deleted scene, which was in the script right after Doris speaks to Mr. and Mrs. Shellhammer about Kris staying with them, had Fred bringing out some venison steaks for dinner. When offered to Kris, he declines saying "Venison—you understand. I—just—couldn't." This amusing scene was included in the 1955 TV movie. (Photofest)

into the kitchen and brings out the main course, venison, given to him (he announces) by a coworker. Susan asks what that is. Doris tells her that it is deer meat, and she can have some eggs if she doesn't like it. Kris politely declines, declaring that he is not a vegetarian, but, "Venison—you understand. I—just—couldn't."[413] This scene was included in the 1955 TV movie.

Even though Seaton had drastically changed the Sunday brunch scene by removing the anti-commercial montage, he did keep it in the story. In the final script, Fred and Doris are in her apartment and Doris picks up *The New Yorker* and reads about how Kris's actions have had a widespread influence for good. Doris then declares that it is a bit ridiculous to think that such behavior will solve all of the world's problems. At the same time, Susan and about six other children are acting like animals and being corralled by her friend Homer. They are pretending that the zoo has just burned down, so now they have to find a new zoo. Susan gets behind a chair and acts like a monkey. Doris is a bit torn, because these childhood fantasies go against everything that she has taught Susan—and yet Susan has found a new vitality that she hasn't had before. She doesn't want to admit that Kris might be a good influence on Susan. Meanwhile, Fred is watching Doris and seems to pick up on her thoughts. She goes into the kitchen to do the dishes, and avoid Fred. This scene, too, was cut.

Another major scene filmed on the apartment sets was the continuation of Kris's disappearance scheme, filmed on location earlier at Macy's. While Doris and Fred have been making calls to locate Kris, he has been in Susan's room learning how to blow bubbles with bubble gum and singing her to sleep with "To Market."

He returns to Fred's apartment, and then Fred walks in to find Kris picking bubble gum out of his beard. Fred is perturbed to find Kris there, since they have spent the whole evening trying to find him. Kris, however, is delighted to hear that his little scheme of getting them together worked. Fred feels obligated to tell Doris, and so he goes to her apartment. She invites him in for some coffee and, while he is explaining Kris's matchmaking efforts, Susan awakes from a nightmare and screams, calling for Uncle Fred. He rushes in to comfort her and then sings her back to sleep. Bothered that her daughter would call for Fred and not her, Doris is visibly upset. Fred tries to comfort Doris and encourages her to have a good cry. Kris sees all of this from the bedroom window and dances with joy.

While on set, Maureen O'Hara, Natalie Wood, and John Payne examine the production crossplot which indicated what, when, and where everything would be filmed and who needed to be there. (Author's collection)

When it came time to film the bubble gum scene, it came out that Gwenn, to everyone's surprise, had never chewed gum and didn't know how to blow a bubble. Natalie was well versed in the practice and took the opportunity to teach him. "We're never too old to learn," he declared.[414] When the cameras were ready to roll, Natalie required about five minutes to chew the gum to get it to the perfect consistency so she could blow a big bubble.[415] Of this entire sequence, only the singing of "To Market," the bubble gum blowing, and the subsequent beard-picking would survive in the final cut of the film.

On the days when they weren't shooting the apartment scenes on Stage 14, they were on Stage B, where the Macy's North Pole Annex had been re-created in exacting detail in order to do close-up shots.[416] The set was furnished with stuffed animals and toys sent from Macy's in New York:

Susan reprises her monkey impersonation during the deleted Sunday brunch scene. (Photofest)

In this deleted scene, Fred comes back to his apartment after trying to find Kris for hours, only to find him picking bubble gum out of his beard. A little miffed, he then realizes that this was all a ruse orchestrated by Kris so that he and Doris could spend more time together. (Photofest)

After Fred finds Kris back at his apartment, he goes over to tell Doris he is safe. She invites him in for a cup of coffee when Susan wakes up from her nightmare. (Author's collection)

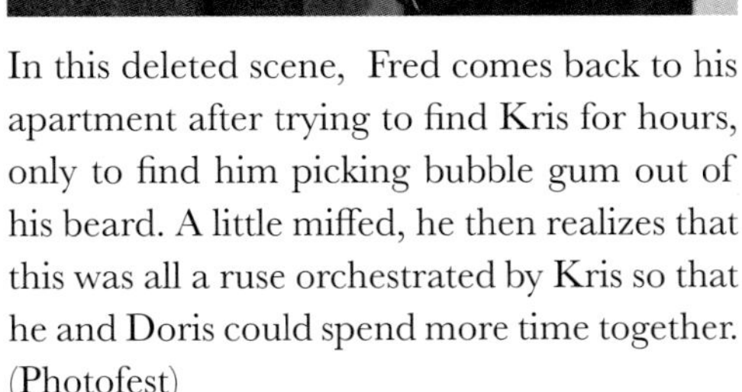

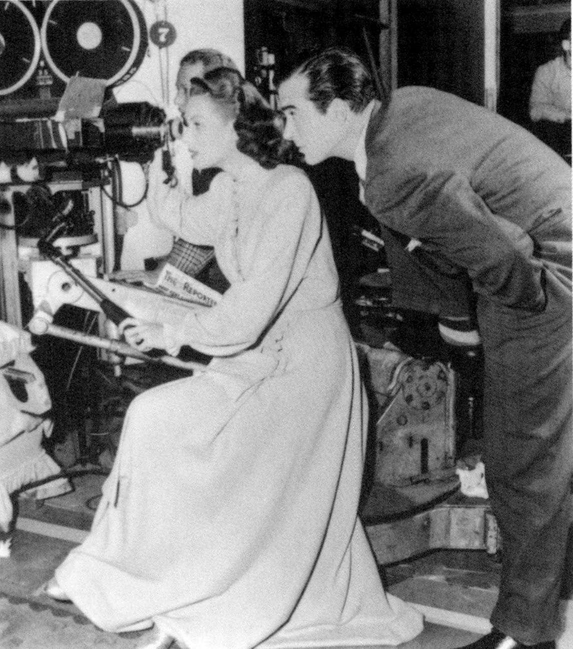

This deleted scene had Fred singing Susan back to sleep after she awakes from a nightmare. The proposed songs included "You Tell Me Your Dream, I'll Tell You Mine" and "The Japanese Sandman." This would have given audiences another chance to hear Payne's singing voice since he had eschewed roles in musicals. (Photofest)

Maureen O'Hara wants to see what the camera sees and has caught John Payne's attention. This photo was taken during the filming of Susan's nightmare scene that was deleted. O'Hara's bathrobe was made of powder-blue flannel. (Photofest) the big stuffed teddy and panda bears were overstock, and Macy's was more than happy to get rid of them.[417] Jack Straus, the president of Macy's, came out to the studio to inspect the replica set and was utterly amazed at how accurate it was.[418] Seaton called in 175 children to be extras for the scene, and Thelma Ritter and Philip Tonge came out to Los Angeles, presumably to do close-ups and/or retakes.[419] The scene with Marlene Lyden as the little Dutch girl was shot here. O'Hara would later comment that she wasn't aware that this set had been reconstructed on the lot, which would make sense if all of her Annex scenes were shot in New York.[420]

Natalie kept a busy schedule. In addition to filming *Miracle*, on some days she was also doing scenes for *The Ghost and Mrs. Muir* (1947). She would be on one set in the morning and then on the other in the afternoon, switching from nineteenth-century England to

Natalie Wood and John Payne go over the script on the set. The tender relationship conveyed by the two actors is one of the highlights of the film. (Photofest)

Director George Seaton, in the middle with suit and tie, directs a scene in Doris's apartment. Cinematographer Charles Clarke is on the right. (Author's collection)

Some of the 175 children that worked as extras got to meet Santa on the re-created set of Macy's North Pole Annex on Stage B on the Twentieth Century-Fox lot. (Photofest)

modern New York within hours.[421] She also had to fit in the mandatory schooling. Natalie's mother insisted on a private tutor for her daughter while the other children met in the classroom held in the Old Writers' Building on the TCF lot. Bobby Hyatt remembers Marie Gurdin not allowing Natalie to associate with him (or anyone else) who wasn't an important adult at the studio who could advance her career. However, he remembered Marie Gurdin as a very funny woman, and said that she always reminded him of a real-life version of Natasha from *The Rocky and Bullwinkle Show*.[422] He also remembers Gwenn stopping by the classroom and doing a funny dance in the doorway that caused laughter among all of the kids and, consequently, made it hard to focus on schoolwork.[423]

Some delays occurred at the end of January. Payne got the flu, and then Natalie got a bad cold, and both were out for over a week, which meant some rearranging of the shooting schedule.[424] It was the second time during the filming that Natalie had had an ailment. Back in New York, she had become fascinated with revolving doors and kept playing on them as if they were merry-go-rounds, until she got her foot stuck and ended up with a bad bruise.[425]

The first week in February was mostly spent on Stage 6, filming the interior scenes of the Brooks' Memorial Home and of Bellevue Hospital. Originally, the Brooks' Home and Dr. Pierce had much bigger roles. The opening scene in Davies's original story had Kris sitting in his room at the retirement home, which looked like Santa's workshop, fixing toys. Dr. Pierce comes in to tell him, reluctantly, that he can no longer live there because the board of directors has decreed that residents must be completely sane, and since he calls himself Kris Kringle, there are doubts about his mental state. Kris rejects the idea that he is crazy and chooses to leave rather than go to an asylum.

During their conversation, he asks Dr. Pierce what he would like for Christmas. Dr. Pierce responds that he wants an X-ray machine, and if Kris can get it for him, then he'll know that Kris is Santa Claus. Kris then announces that he will stay with his friend, who is the zookeeper at the Central Park Zoo. This scene remained in the first two drafts of the screenplay and in the published book; however, in the November 16 draft, Seaton repurposed some of these elements to create a different scene. He inserted it in the middle of the story, after Kris accepts Fred's invitation to stay with him. Fred and Kris drive out to the Brooks' Home to collect his things from Kris's full-of-toys room, where Dr. Pierce expresses his wish for the X-ray machine. But in the end, Kris's room was never filmed,

On the set, Natlaie Wood called O'Hara "Mama Maureen" and everyone called Natalie "the little old lady." O'Hara, who appeared with many child actors through the years, declared that Natalie was the "finest, most professional young actress in the picture business."* (Photofest)

---

*O'Hara, Maureen, "Feature Audio Commentary by Maureen O'Hara, (August 24, 2006)." *Miracle on 34th Street*, Los Angeles: Twentieth Century Fox Home Entertainment, 2-disc DVD set, 2006.

and the interaction with Dr. Pierce takes place in the sitting room.

One detail that Davies stressed to Seaton was to ensure that the Brooks' Home was not portrayed as a mental institution. He was concerned that the audience might infer as much when Doris first makes the phone call and asks for a doctor, and then this would be compounded in the next scene, when Dr. Pierce and Doris discuss Kris's delusion. Davies successfully campaigned to add "for the Aged" to "Brooks' Memorial Home" on Kris's employment card, and then have Doris clarify with her secretary that "it's a home for old people" when she makes the call. These small additions solved the problem.[426]

After Kris has accepted Fred's offer to stay with him, Fred drives Kris out to the Brooks' Home to get his things. While there, Dr. Pierce says he'll believe in Santa Claus if he gets an X-ray machine. On the car ride back, Fred tells Kris what happened to Susan's father. Both scenes were cut from the film, but not before the publicity materials went out. (Photofest)

The episode concluded with Fred and Kris driving back to Manhattan, during which Fred tells Kris about Doris's ex-husband. They were married in college, and then after graduation, "he developed a strong aversion to work and a great affinity for the bottle." Soon after Susan was born, he took off and hadn't been heard from since. This is followed by the scene of Fred and Kris getting ready for bed and Fred asking whether Kris sleeps with his beard inside or out. The driving scene made it all the way to the final script, but did not end up in the final cut of the film; however, some elements of this sequence were incorporated into the 1973 TV movie and the 1994 feature film.

Dr. Pierce's original role also included him being in the parade scenes and holding a longer discussion with Doris about Kris. In the first and second versions of the screenplay, Dr. Pierce brings his son to the parade, and together they see Kris on the float, which makes Kris's claims about himself more credible. Dr. Pierce also has a longer conversation and provides more background information about Kris while talking to Doris and Mr. Shellhammer at Macy's. Dr.

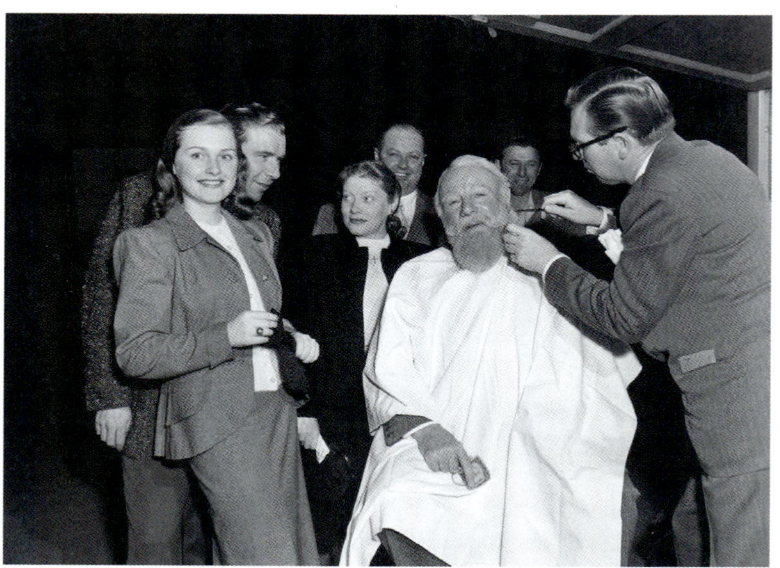

Edmund Gwenn gets some special attention to his beard on set. Director George Seaton is on the left. (Author's collection)

The interior of the Brooks' Home was shot on Stage 6 while the exterior was a special effects shot. Susan, saddened by not seeing the gift she wished for under the tree, did receive a "Baby Beautiful" doll made by the Ideal Toy Company. The doll was only in production for a couple of years and has become a sought-after collector's item because of her appearance in *Miracle*. (Author's collection)

Pierce tells them that he thinks that Kris had an unhappy childhood and that his family was poor and couldn't afford any toys, and so, by acting like Santa Claus, he is making up for that. He also confirms that Kris's name is really Kris Kringle, explaining that it's a cutesy name, like a girl he knew whose family name was "Tree" and so, for fun, they named her "Olive." Although these tidbits were in the final script, they also didn't make it into the final film. This was probably due to Davies's insistence that less is more. He felt that they needed to show that Kris was not crazy and then leave it at that, instead of trying to logically prove it to the audience. It would then be a matter of faith and not common sense that he is Santa Claus. As Davies wrote in a letter to Seaton, "The less explanation there is . . . about Kris's past . . . the better off we are."[427] Dr. Pierce popped up

A little glimpse into Natalie Wood's dressing room trailer on the soundstage at the studio. (Author's collection)

John Payne tries out a pogo stick in front of Natalie Wood on the soundstage at the studio. The "honey wagon" trailers used for the stars' dressing rooms can be seen in the background. (Author's collection)

again in the original story during the hearing, where he testified on Kris's behalf. This was preserved in the book.[428]

The interior scenes at Bellevue were also filmed that first week of February on Stage 6. In addition to the scene with Fred visiting Kris in the sitting room, a scene was filmed of him failing the mental health test. Clearly deflated, Kris is sitting across the desk from Dr. Rogers, who asks him to name the first president of the United States, and he says Calvin Coolidge; he asks him how much 2 x 5 equals, and he responds 8; and finally, he asks him how many days there are in the week, and Kris says it depends on whether it's a leap year or not.[429]

Although the courtroom was re-created on Stage 14 back at Twentieth Century-Fox, it looks remarkably similar to the real ones at the New York County Supreme Courthouse in Manhattan. Gene Lockhart was great as Judge Harper. (Photofest)

In the earliest versions of the story, the Central Park Zoo, the zookeeper, and the reindeer all figured prominently, but these parts were eventually completely eliminated. After leaving the Brooks' Home (when that scene was at the beginning of the story), Kris is found wandering through the Central Park Zoo. A father and his son are standing by the reindeer pen and are trying to feed them with peanuts, to get their attention, but to no avail. As Kris approaches, the shy reindeer are unusually responsive to him, coming over to him immediately when he offers them some carrot tops. While there, Kris hears strains of "Jingle Bells" and wanders over to Central Park West, where he sees that preparations are under way for the parade. While this scene is in the full-length version of the story, in the book, and in all versions of the screenplay, it did not end up in the film. Some of the New York newspapers mention filming in Central Park, but it's unclear whether these are references to the parade scenes or to this scene.[430] The reindeer were slated to be filmed in Ventura County back in California, but it doesn't appear that that filming ever took place.[431] Parts of this scene were incorporated into the 1973 TV movie and the 1994 feature film.

The courtroom scenes were some of the last ones to be shot, which took place from February 10–15, 1947, on Stage 14. The set was based on the New York County Supreme Courthouse, and replicated the wainscoting, tall ceilings, and white plaster walls of one of the courtrooms. The only real difference is that, in the real courthouse, the doors at the back of the courtrooms are offset and not in the center of the back wall, as they are in the film. The set

Edmund Gwenn as Kris Kringle, gets ready on the courtroom set on Stage 14 to testify on his own behalf that he really is Santa Claus. (Photofest)

designer also added a few extra rows of benches for visitors, since a hearing involving Santa Claus would obviously attract a lot of spectators.

All the courtroom scenes were filmed in six days. Cinematographer Charles Clarke, who had been with the production from the beginning, had to leave two weeks before filming was completed—he was required to go down to Mexico to do camera work on *Captain from Castile* (1947)—so the courtroom scenes were shot by Lloyd Ahern.[432] Most of the actors in the minor roles, such as William Frawley and Jerome Cowan, were only hired a few days before the scenes were filmed.[433] Bobby Hyatt, who played Thomas Mara Jr., remembers Seaton working with him and making him think he was part of the creative process in order to get a good performance. Seaton asked Bobby what he thought would be an appropriate response if someone asked him why he believed in Santa Claus. Hyatt remembered coming up with the line "Because my daddy told me so." Seaton was enthusiastic about that, and said he would use it in the film. However, it turns out Seaton was just a good manipulator and had fed the line to him: It was in Davies's original story and in every version of the script, long before Bobby was hired for the part.

One aspect of the courtroom scenes that was debated early on was how long Kris would remain in a state of depression. In one version of the script, Doris's involvement in sending Kris to Bellevue was not cleared up until Susan writes him the letter, a forced (and trite) plot device based on misunderstanding. Davies did not want him depressed during the hearing because he feared it would seriously dampen the tone of those scenes, and Fred would have a hard time defending a client who wants to be put away. Davies suggested that once Doris finds out what had happened, that she let Kris know through Fred that she was not involved. This would allow him to bounce back and be in good spirits during the hearing. Receiving the letter from Susan would only makes things better.[434]

When Davies and Seaton were working out the proceedings of the hearing, they deliberately wrote themselves "into a corner."[435] The goal was to have the evidence mount overwhelmingly against Kris, to the point where his case appears to be a lost cause. They had Judge Harper talk to Charlie Halloran behind closed doors to explain why the judge would prolong a hearing that would normally be open and shut. Then they decided to have Mr. Macy perjure himself to provide some hope for Kris. The idea was that when all seemed lost, fate would step in—albeit, in a very logical way—and save the day via the United States Post Office. Which, incidentally, brings up another historical inaccuracy that pops up during Fred's legal argument. He incorrectly states that the United States Post Office was founded on July 26, 1776. This is the date written in the script, so it was not a mistake made by Payne. The correct date is July 26, 1775, a year *before* the American Revolution took place. There is no explanation other than somebody misread the date or just assumed that the Post Office could not have come into existence before the United States was formed in 1776. Close inspection also reveals another gaff: Some of the articles in the newspapers that flash across the screen discuss the hearing in the past tense *before* it begins. These were clearly originally intended to be seen after the first day of the proceedings.

The prop department had to create 50,000 letters and get 5,000 of them addressed, sealed, stamped, and postmarked in case they were needed for close-up shots in this scene. (Photofest)

The prop department had a tall order when it came to supplying fifty thousand envelopes for the courtroom scene. In case they were needed for close-up shots, five thousand of them were actually addressed, stamped, and taken to the post office in New York to get canceled. The addressing of the envelopes alone took three men about a week to do.[436] There is one continuity error in the scene: Look for the lamp on Judge Harper's desk that disappears once the men start dumping the bags of letters. Even though she is not in it, this was O'Hara's favorite scene in the movie.[437] Subsequently, she got involved with a toy campaign for needy children in conjunction with the post office.[438]

The scenes in Judge Harper's living room and chambers were shot February 19-20. Seaton had a little fun in naming Judge Henry X. Harper: The "X" stands for the X a voter marks on a ballot, a sly reference to the judge's upcoming reelection campaign.[439] Another interesting trait about the judge's character was conveyed through the decoration of the Harpers' living room set on Stage 6. Seaton wanted his living room to have "modest furnishings [to] reveal that he is an honest judge."[440] The scenes in the judge's chambers were shot on Stage 3. Aiming for authenticity, Seaton had insisted on and obtained the actual New York state form for mental competency hearings and used it on-screen.[441]

Susan's dream house was real; well, at least the exterior was. The interior was built on the Twentieth Century-Fox lot in Los Angeles. (Photofest)

As mentioned earlier, rarely is a movie shot sequentially, but *Miracle*, for the most part, was filmed in order. Case in point is the scene of Susan's dream house, appropriately called the "Christmas House" on the studio records, which was one of the last scenes shot. The exterior had been filmed on location back in New York, but the interiors were all built on a soundstage. The scene was filmed entirely in one day, February 21.

On February 22, the sign and the exterior of the Brooks' Memorial Home would be filmed as a special effect. That would be the last day of principal photography, even though there would be some retakes and added scenes. Gwenn hosted a fancy cast and crew party catered by the famous Beverly Hills restaurant, Chasen's.[442] Natalie attended the soirée and saw Gwenn out of costume for the first time. She later recalled, "I really did think that Edmund Gwenn was Santa. I had never seen him without his beard. . . . At the end, during the set party, I saw this strange man, without the beard, and I just couldn't [put] it together."[443] O'Hara then flew to Cleveland that weekend to do some fund-raising for the Greek Relief Fund, and then took a much-needed vacation with her husband at Arrowhead Hot Springs.[444] Gwenn checked into Cedars-Sinai Hospital on February 27 for a couple of weeks due to some chronic health problems, but he didn't get as much rest as he had anticipated; apparently he had to re-record some of his lines from his hospital bed![445]

Even though the principal photography was over, *Miracle* would still go through quite a few changes. During the last week of February, Seaton made some additions and revisions. He wrote a scene with Kris arriving at the courthouse and being told by the police officer that he couldn't enter the courtroom with his cane because it could be a weapon. There is no indication that the scene was ever filmed. He then revised the scene in the Maras' apartment and filmed it on February 28.

On March 1, a couple of additional scenes were filmed. They took care of the minor process shot of Doris walking into her apartment during the parade. But the bigger event of the day was re-shooting the scene of Dr. Pierce coming to Macy's and meeting with Doris, Mr. Shellhammer, and Mr. Sawyer. Some of Doris's office scenes had been shot on location in New York, but her office had been re-created on Stage 3, which is where this retake was done. The retake includes Dr. Pierce confirming that Kris has a delusion for good, and then makes the allusion to the Hollywood restaurateur who believes he is a Russian prince, despite overwhelming evidence to the contrary.

Romanoff's was the famous restaurant owned by that "highly respected citizen" Michael Romanoff referred to by Dr. Pierce. Romanoff claimed to be a Russian prince and was a staple personality in Los Angeles for decades. He made cameo appearances in over a dozen films from the 1930s to the 1960s, including in *Arch of Triumph* (1948) and *Move Over, Darling* (1963). (Author's collection)

The oblique reference was to Michael Romanoff, the proprietor of Romanoff's, a celebrity restaurant located on Rodeo Drive in Beverly Hills frequented by a coterie of movie stars. A con man who hobnobbed with the rich and famous on two continents, Romanoff was neither royal nor Russian, but no one really seemed to care. (His real name was Harry F. Gerguson, he was from Brooklyn, and everything about his background was suspect.)[446] His restaurant, which opened in 1940, funded with money from friends like Cary Grant and Darryl Zanuck, became a power center in Hollywood. It was the place to see and be seen, where deals were made and careers launched or dashed. Movie stars could take their temperature on their popularity by whether or not they had to wait for a table.[447] The line about Mike Romanoff had appeared in Davies's full-length version of the story and made it through all the revisions, to the final screenplay, but the studio's legal team was concerned that it might result in a lawsuit. It was going to be deleted unless Romanoff gave his consent. Seaton must have really wanted to keep it in, because the studio did reach out to Romanoff, and he actually signed a waiver (!) late in January, indicating he had no objection to the lines in the film.[448]

The very, very last scene for *Miracle* was filmed on March 31, on Stage 14. It was a retake of Fred and Doris's breakup at her apartment. Their romantic relationship had gone through a series of changes before its final incarnation on the screen. In Davies's original story, the romance develops at a faster pace and involves an engagement. The day after Kris's scheme to get Fred and Doris to spend the evening together, Fred goes shopping on Fifth Avenue for a sapphire ring for Doris. One retailer says that they don't have anything like that, but to check at Cartier; Fred politely says that Cartier just sent him there. He is starting to realize just how influential Kris is becoming throughout New York City. Fred then goes to Macy's toy department and sees Mr. Macy and Mr. Gimbel shaking hands, which Doris proclaims the "Miracle of Miracles." Once the photo op is done, Fred pulls Doris aside and proposes to her with the engagement ring. Kris very happily sees all of this go down from his throne.

In Seaton's first version of the screenplay, he moved the proposal to much later in the story, placing it after the first day of the hearing. Before the hearing starts, Fred pulls out the ring and shows it to Kris, and tells Kris he is going to pop the question. That evening, Fred shows up to Doris's apartment with a big Christmas tree ("If it's not big enough to make you move furniture, it's not a Christmas tree," he explains), and the ring is in his pocket. He sets the Christmas tree down and is about to propose when Doris asks him how his law firm feels about him defending Kris, and he tells her that he quit. There was a much longer discussion between the two of them about believing in each other and whether this marriage would work or not. This scene made it all of the way to the final January 2 script. During the retake, the Christmas tree and the proposal got cut, along with much of the dialogue, but the condensed scene was still able to convey that they had broken up. In doing this, Seaton subsequently made their engagement the culminating event of Christmas Day.

One cinematic device that figured more prominently in *Miracle* than most movies was the use of "inserts." An insert is a close-up shot of an object or printed matter, such as the department store advertisements, the newspaper headlines, or the letter that Susan writes to Kris (which most certainly was not in Natalie's handwriting). Preparation on these started in late December, but they couldn't be filmed until permission from the various stores, newspapers, and magazines came through, which didn't end up happening in several instances.[449] Most of these inserts were probably filmed sometime in February or March.

Close examination of the inserts reveals some fun facts. The newspaper copy seen at the beginning of the film right before the page is turned to reveal the advertisement for the Macy's Thanksgiving Day parade was cobbled together mostly from old issues of the *New York Times*. Several of the articles are from the July 27, 1933, issue, but the page also includes articles from the July 20, 1933, and the December 23, 1932, issues. They were all made generic by removing any notable references, such as "War on Kidnapping by Federal Forces," which is really titled "Roosevelt Orders War on Kidnapping by Federal Forces."[450]

Another fun fact is that whoever prepared Kris's employment card for the insert shot took the list of reindeer from the original version of the "Account of a Visit from St. Nicholas ('Twas the Night Before Christmas)" without first consulting the script. In the poem, the reindeer that is now commonly referred to as "Donner" was spelled "Donder," but in the script for the opening sequence, where Kris is correcting the order of the reindeer, Seaton spells it "Donner," and that is clearly what Kris says on-screen. A trifling detail, but a fun one nonetheless. There is no other explanation for the discrepancy.

With principal photography completed, retakes done, and insert shots finished, *Miracle* was ready to go on to the post-production phase. Surprisingly, due to significant editing, the film would end up being quite different than it had been just a few weeks before.

Fred was supposed to sing Susan back to sleep after she awakens from a nightmare in a deleted scene. Could this be John Payne practicing while Edmund Gwenn and Natalie Wood listen? (Photofest)

Post-Production

The first screening of *Miracle* was at a preview during the third week of March in Glendale. Although just a few miles from downtown Los Angeles, it was considered far enough away from the big city to be a typical American audience. The film "got cheers" from the crowd and loud applause during the courtroom scene, and the comment cards were "amazing."[451] Years later, Seaton recalled that practically all of the feedback cards gave the film an "excellent" rating, an anomaly in all his years as a filmmaker, and a phenomenon he had not seen before or since. With the soundtrack and final edits completed, *Miracle* was in its final form and ready for another preview, which was held in the town of Pomona on April 17.[452] Darryl Zanuck, who had missed the preview in March, made sure to attend this one after hearing about the audience's enthusiastic response. After that screening, which had an equally appreciative audience, he walked out into the lobby, approached Seaton, and said, "You win. I never thought it would come out like this."[453]

Director Seaton and film editor Robert Simpson then went to work tightening up the film. They ended up cutting out about twenty minutes of footage, meaning that *Miracle* could have been an almost two-hour movie. The end result is that the romance and relationship between Fred and Doris, originally deemed necessary for commercial viability, ended up being considerably downplayed, shifting more of the focus to Kris and Susan. The following scenes had made it through all of the script revisions and were filmed but did not make the final cut:

- Kris giving shopping advice to three other Macy's customers.
- The Southern woman complimenting Mr. Shellhammer in his office on Macy's new policy.
- Kris politely refusing to eat venison at Doris's apartment.
- Fred and Kris going out to the Brooks' Home to get his things and see Dr. Pierce.
- Fred and Kris in the car on the way back from the Brooks' Home, where Fred tells him about Susan's father.

This deleted scene had Dr. Rogers administering the mental health test to Kris, who intentionally answers the questions incorrectly. (Author's collection)

- The Sunday brunch scene with Susan pretending to be a monkey.
- Kris and Fred descending the escalator at Macy's and then Kris slipping out to trick Fred and Doris into spending the evening together. (Incidentally, cinematographer Charles Clarke always thought that this was a necessary scene and pleaded for years to get it put back in the movie.)[454]
- Fred returning to his apartment and finding Kris picking the bubble gum out of his beard.
- Doris inviting Fred in for coffee, followed by Susan's nightmare.
- The limousine with Mr. Sawyer and Kris pulling up to Bellevue Hospital.
- Kris failing the mental health test in Dr. Rogers's office at Bellevue.
- The Walter Winchell radio spot.

Once a motion picture has had its final edit and is "locked," usually the next step is the scoring. Though preparations for the soundtrack, such as legal clearances, had begun when production got under way in the fall of 1946, the music wouldn't be finalized and recorded until April 9, 1947.[455]

The scene in Doris's apartment during the hearing originally included Fred proposing to Doris with a ring. It was changed at the last minute but not before a picture of the original scene was included in the lobby card set. (Author's collection)

The soundtrack for Miracle is minimal, and could even be characterized as sparse, with several scenes containing no music at all (only a few critics would even notice the music, but, when they did, called it "unobtrusively good").456 A good portion of it is "source music" (i.e., music originating from a source in the movie, such as on the radio, that a character would hear), contributing to the film's aim at realism, with only the occasional use of music for dramatic effect. Cyril Mockridge, longtime TCF staff musical director, was in charge of the music, and was aided by studio arrangers Jack Virgil, Urban Thielmann, and Edward Powell. This team created a delightfully fanciful and effective score that used forty-nine different cues, including original themes, traditional and popular Christmas songs, patriotic marches, and nursery rhymes.457

British-born Mockridge, a veteran of World War I and classically trained at the Royal Academy of Music in London, emigrated to the United States in the 1920s, and arrived at TCF in the mid-1930s. Over the next two decades, he would score dozens of films. By the mid-1940s, his credits included *How Green Was My Valley* (1941), *The Ox-Bow Incident* (1943), *and My Darling Clementine* (1946).

After the famous TCF fanfare, written by Alfred Newman, a bright and upbeat theme plays over the opening credits. Composed by Mockridge, this is one of the only pieces of original music used in the film. With a bouncy, upbeat tempo, soaring strings, and jingle bells in the background, it is certainly evocative of sleigh rides and snow, and the fun Christmas adventure the audience is about to have. The theme appears three more times in the film: when Susan is blowing bubble gum with Kris; when Macy's employees are creating the shopping guides; and at the close of the film.

The second original piece of music used in the film is a dreamy little motif titled "The House," referencing Susan's dream home. It is first heard when Susan shows Kris the picture of the house she wants from the magazine, and then is repeated during scenes that hint her wish will come true, such as when Fred and Kris are talking about Doris and Susan before bedtime, and when Doris adds her "I believe in you too" postscript to Susan's letter. And it's reprised, of course, when they find that house on Christmas Day.

While it's not surprising that Christmas music would appear in *Miracle*, it is surprising how understated it is. Like all studio music departments of the era, economy was key; using public domain music to avoid licensing fees was the better path, and so out-of-copyright Christmas music is found throughout the film. As soon as the parade begins, "Jingle Bells" is introduced and plays a supporting role throughout the film. The James L. Pierpont tune from 1857 has long been associated with Christmas, even though it's not necessarily a Christmas song (there is no mention of the holiday in the lyrics), and acts as the perfect tie-in to the Santa Claus storyline. With arrangements by the studio's Mockridge, Virgil, and Powell, it is used over fifteen times in the movie, including a brassy orchestration during the parade scenes, a dissonant version during the newspaper montage during the trial, and a bright countermelody at the end of the film (signaling that the spirit of Christmas has triumphed after all).

A less prominent use of Christmas music is found in a series of music box arrangements by studio arranger Urban Thielmann.[458] These are used almost exclusively as source background music at Macy's North Pole Annex, when the children are visiting Santa Claus. Listen for "Good King Wenceslas," "Hark! The Herald Angels Sing," and "The First Nowell." The somber—yet surprisingly appropriate—"God Rest Ye Merry Gentlemen" is heard when Dr. Sawyer tricks Kris into getting into the car to go to Bellevue.

Perhaps the most appropriate music cue used in the film is "Santa Claus Is Comin' to Town." It was written by composer J. Fred Coots and lyricist Haven Gillespie and first published and recorded in 1934. Even though the song was only a little more than a decade old, by the mid-1940s, it was so popular that it was quickly becoming a Christmas standard. Some musicologists point to this song as the beginning of modern popular Christmas music, and it has gone on to become one of the most recorded songs of the genre. The studio paid $100 to license the song for *Miracle*.[459] A marching band arrangement is used during the Thanksgiving Day parade scenes (intertwined with John Philip Sousa's "Sabre and Spurs" and E. E. Bagley's "National Emblem March"), and a swinging big band version is heard on the record player at the Brooks' Home on Christmas Day.

The TCF legal files show a surprising number of music pieces that were originally considered for the parade scenes but, for various reasons, were not used. A variety of marching band songs were investigated, including "Stars and Stripes Forever," "The Washington Post March," "Semper Fidelis," "Yale Boola Song," "Stein Song," "Notre Dame Victory March," and "On the Mall." Ultimately, only the two marches mentioned above are heard during the parade, probably because the others were still under copyright and would have required licensing fees.[460]

Although several marches were considered for the parade scenes, patriotic favorites "Sabre and Spurs" and "National Emblem March" were selected to convey the sounds of the marching bands which have been a hallmark feature of the Macy's Thanksgiving Day Parade for decades. (Author's collection)

Kris: Hello! I'm happy you came.

Dutch girl: Oh, you are Santa Claus!

Kris: Well, yes, of course.

Dutch girl: I knew it. I knew you would understand me.

Kris: Naturally. Tell me what you would like from Santa Claus.

Dutch girl: Nothing. I have everything. I just want to stay with this lovely lady.

Kris: Do you want to sing something for me?

Even though neither had a very good Dutch accent, Gwenn and Marlene Lyden created one of the most memorable scenes in the film that triggers Susan's belief. Above is a translation of their exchange before singing the song. (Photofest)

The most memorable song in the film is when Kris and the little Dutch girl sing "Sinterklaas Kapoentje" together, which sparks Susan's belief in Santa Claus. The song is a traditional song from the Netherlands that dates back to medieval times, and is sung when Saint Nicholas arrives by boat on his saint day, December 6. The lawyers made sure that the tune was in the public domain.[461] Here are the Dutch lyrics and the English translation that TCF provided to the Production Code office for clearance:

Dutch:

Sinterklaas Kapoentje
Geef wat in mijn (m'm) scho entje
Geef wat in mijn (m'm) laarsje
Dank u Sinterklaasje.

English translation:

Santa Claus Capuchio
Put it in my shoe, Ho Ho
Put it in my boot, Ho Ho
Thank you dear Santa Claus.

Several nursery rhymes were also incorporated into the soundtrack to enhance the childlike fantasy aspect of the film. These, too, are music box arrangements by Thielmann and play in the background at Macy's while children are lined up to see Santa Claus. Listen for "Mary Had a Little Lamb," "Twinkle, Twinkle, Little Star," "The Farmer in the Dell," "Here We Go 'Round the Mulberry Bush," and "Sing a Song of Sixpence." The other nursery rhyme that is used in the film is "To Market," which Kris uses to sing Susan to sleep. The rhyme is sung to a tune written specifically for *Miracle*.[462]

At least two pop songs were considered for a "vocal visual" (to be sung on-screen) in

Susan's nightmare scene. After she wakes up and screams, Fred, who is in the living room with Doris, rushes in to comfort her. The script calls for the song to be "a popular tune with a 'Good night' angle," and suggests using the 1920 hit "Japanese Sandman."[463] The legal files show that there was an earlier investigation to use the standard "You Tell Me Your Dream, I'll Tell You Mine."[464] The song, originally published in 1899 with music by Charles N. Daniels and lyrics by Seymour Rice and Albert H. Brown, became a big hit at the turn of the century. In 1929, lyricist Gus Kahn had reworked the lyrics, and it was his version that the studio was adamant about using. Had the scene been included, it would have been a nod to John Payne's days as a musical singing star.

Kris sings "To Market" to Susan to get her to fall asleep. The studio's music staff composed an original tune to sing to the verse of the old nursery rhyme. (Photofest)

The 1945 hit "Candy" (by Mack David, Joan Whitney, and Alex Kramer), popularized by Johnny Mercer, Jo Stafford, and the Pied Pipers, was also considered for use in the film.[465] It is not clear where the song would have been included, but since the lyrics have more of a romantic bent, perhaps it would have been used to accent one of the scenes with Doris and Fred.

And if you've always wondered what song Susan is practicing on the piano while Doris is

"The Japanese Sandman" and "You Tell Me Your Dream, I'll Tell You Mine" were both considered as songs for Fred to sing to Susan after she awakes from a nightmare in a scene that was deleted from the film. (Author's collection)

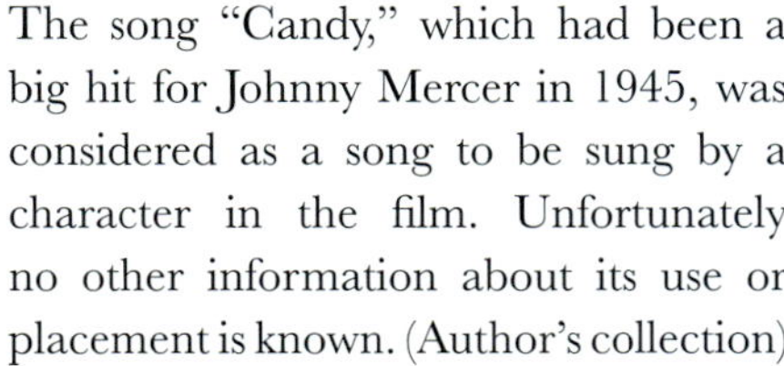

The song "Candy," which had been a big hit for Johnny Mercer in 1945, was considered as a song to be sung by a character in the film. Unfortunately no other information about its use or placement is known. (Author's collection)

When the film was released, the censorship board in Ohio objected to this scene because Santa Claus (played by Percy Helton) is drunk. (Photofest)

on the phone, the wait is over: It is Chopin's "Prelude, Opus 28, No. 7."

The last hurdle for every motion picture made in Hollywood at that time was to receive final approval from the Motion Picture Association of America Production Code office. Since all of the Production Code office's requirements about modest clothing, product placement, and references to living people were met, there were no major problems with *Miracle*, and the Motion Picture Association of America would grant the certificate of approval on April 29.[466]

But even after receiving approval from the MPAA, a film could be subject to religious and regional film boards. For example, the Catholic Church's National Legion of Decency was an organization whose ratings could influence the success of a motion picture. Anything less than an "A" rating would signify that the movie had objectionable content and indicate to Catholics that they shouldn't see it. The Legion gave *Miracle* a "B" rating for portraying "the acceptability of divorce."[467] Another objection came from the film board in Ohio regarding the Thanksgiving Day parade scene with the drunken Santa Claus, who justifies himself by saying, "Oh, it's cold—a man has got to do something to keep warm."[468] The board apparently felt that it wasn't fitting for Santa to be depicted in an inebriated state, but also, state liquor law prohibited Santa from being used in advertising. (Whether or not the scene was deleted for exhibition in Ohio is unknown.)[469] The scene's dialogue, luckily, was kept intact for general release, and provides one of the many memorable one-liners in the film.

With the film negative shipped to New York on April 19, 1947, and the copyright registration filed, it was time for the publicity department to get to work.[470]

Final editing of *Miracle* continued even after the publicity materials had been created and sent out. This set of lobby cards contains three images of scenes that were cut from the final film. Can you identify them? (Author's collection)

CHAPTER 7

Publicity, Premiere, and Awards

For decades, film historians have been utterly perplexed as to why such a quintessential Christmas movie was released at the beginning of summer instead of in the fall, when it would have been more thematically appropriate. They have proposed all kinds of theories, such as: the studio wasn't confident in the film and wanted it to play longer, to build up momentum before Christmas; movie attendance is higher during the summer and, hence, the film would be more profitable; or "Christmas in June" would provide great publicity and be an attraction during the summer heat for moviegoers.

Some of these theories developed contemporaneously and some were promulgated years later by the likes of George Seaton, Maureen O'Hara, and Natalie Wood, even though they had no personal knowledge about the film's release, having already moved on to other projects.[471] In any event, the various theories that have been proposed are all wrong. In general, movie attendance during the summer of 1947 was low, with many theater owners believing that the hot weather was making beaches and amusement parks bigger attractions than movies.[472] Films in the 1940s rarely played in theaters for more than a few weeks, let alone a few months, so trying to build up momentum would have been useless. Lastly, TCF was not planning on a "Christmas in June" campaign, clearly evident in the advertising art. The truth is, as anyone would logically expect, when *Miracle* was in the midst of filming at Macy's in December 1946, the original marketing plan was to release it during the Thanksgiving and Christmas holiday season of 1947, when it would be the "most appropriate."[473]

However, that plan was interrupted by a prolonged disruption in the studio system. Hollywood had gone on strike during the final months of World War II, and there were ripple effects for the next couple of years.[474] It had taken Hollywood several decades to develop into a union industry, but, by the 1930s, unionization was fairly complete, with card-carrying members found throughout the industry. Right as the war was wrapping up and the film industry was looking forward to returning to normalcy, a jurisdictional dispute arose between the unions. The issue was whether set decorators should continue to be represented by the Screen Set Designers, a local of the Painters' union, which was part of the Conference of Studio Unions (CSU), or whether they belonged to the Property Craftsmen, a local of the International Alliance of Theatrical Stage Employees (IATSE). Some set decorators went on strike and soon several other factions in Hollywood followed suit. The strike would last eight months. As it progressed, things got particularly (and unusually) violent that fall especially at the Warner Bros. lot. Though the strike ended on October 30 of that year, it took a special committee of the American Federation of Labor (AFL) to finally resolve the matter in December, when they ruled that set decorators belonged to the Painters' union, but then deemed that the construction of sets, which had been under the CSU, now belonged with IATSE. This, of course, upset the carpenters, who asked the AFL for a clarification, which was finally issued on August 16, 1946, giving all construction work to the CSU. IATSE balked at the ruling, and the carpenters went on strike. The demonstrations got as equally violent as those of a year earlier. TCF had to deal with picket lines at its Western Avenue studio in Hollywood and in front of its west Los Angeles lot in late October and early November, just as *Miracle* was getting under way.

All of this labor unrest disrupted production in many—and sometimes unexpected—ways. For example, the technicians at the Technicolor lab went on strike, and so, suddenly, there was a shortage of color film prints available to show in theaters during the holiday season. TCF was the hardest hit of the studios, with its November and December Technicolor releases (*Margie* and *The Shocking Miss Pilgrim*) held up, as were the releases for late winter and early spring, *Carnival in Costa Rica* (1947) and another Maureen O'Hara film, *The Homestretch* (1947).[475] Understanding this background gives Charlie Halloran's in-film comments to Judge Harper about the "CIO and the AF of L" a little more context.

The studio started to scramble, and rearranged the release schedule for the next few months. *Miracle* was not on the release schedule as of December 18, but a couple of days later, it was announced that it would be released in the summer.[476] Since *Miracle* would be completed in April and was being filmed in black-and-white, it would not be affected by the Technicolor strike. In January, the studio clarified that the film would be released in June, a decision it stood by through February.[477] Chaos apparently reigned at the studio during March and April, because all films were pulled off the release schedule, and only the low-budget Sol Wurtzel thrillers and a rerelease of *Alexander's Ragtime Band* (1938) were announced.[478]

But then, with the Technicolor print crisis subsiding, TCF changed its mind and decided to push the release for *Miracle* back to the fall, as originally intended, so that it would be in general distribution leading up to Christmas. The studio chose September 19 as the definite release date.[479] This change made sense, especially in light of the novelization of *Miracle* that Valentine Davies was writing, which was to be published in conjunction with the film's release (see discussion in chapter 9). But then on April 26, the studio abruptly changed the release date and moved it up to premiere on June 4, with an undetermined general release date.[480] With only a little over a month to do publicity (instead of the usual four to five months), Charles Schlaifer, head of the TCF publicity department, moved full steam ahead. *Miracle* was slated to open at the studio's flagship Roxy Theatre in New York City, and he only had about a month to create the buzz for it.

Once the *Miracle* film had made it to New York and was viewed by the studio executives and stockholders at the annual meeting, the first order of business was to screen it for Macy's and Gimbels.[481] After reviewing the script back in January, neither store had had any involvement with the film, which had been on purpose, as the studio didn't want any interference during the creative process. However, now that the film was finished, Macy's and Gimbels needed to see it as soon as possible because, if either one balked at anything, the whole movie might need to be reworked.

A screening for the executives of both retailers was held on April 29, 1947. Meanwhile, back in Hollywood, there was a screening for the press at the Academy Awards Theatre that same week. There was not any advance notice regarding the film's genre or content, and yet it was still extremely well received. The audience "enjoyed every minute of it," and, at the conclusion, it received a "hearty round of applause"—a response that was extremely rare for jaded entertainment reporters who see a lot of movies.[482] The reviews that came out following the screening were unanimously positive. *Variety* called it "one of the most appealing, heart-warming films to come out of Hollywood in many a day," and thought that the supporting roles were "played to the hilt." Its reviewer liked Payne and O'Hara, was "surprise[d]" by Natalie Wood's "standout, natural portrayal," and was prophetic in stating that Gwenn's performance was the best of his career.[483] *The Hollywood Reporter*, as well, found it to be a "delightful surprise hit," gushing that "these are all gorgeous characters," and found that "Natalie Wood impresses as a totally unactorish child."[484] *The Film Daily* was very vocal in stating: "We have something to shout about. And we feel we can shout loud and long," because *Miracle* deserved it.[485] The critics thought the film would do very well through word-of-mouth.

Unlike today, when most films are released simultaneously in thousands of theaters on the same day and date, movies in the 1940s would usually premiere at a movie palace in New York and/or Los Angeles, playing there exclusively for a few weeks. The film would then be put in a limited release in the big downtown theaters of other large cities. It could take several months for a film to make it into general release and into smaller neighborhood theaters. Like every other TCF film at that time, *Miracle* followed this release pattern. Had the September 19 release date been retained, the film would have been playing across the country in November and December, just in time for Christmas.

Schlaifer had been working on the campaign at least since March, and had already placed an article on O'Hara in the weekly newspaper magazine *This Week*, but he now had to get things in high gear, and very quickly.[486] Since the movie was not going to be released at Christmas, he chose to put no indication of its holiday theme in the advertising—no holly, no candy canes, and certainly no Santa. Instead, the advance campaign emphasized the "human elements" and used taglines such as the vague "Meet the Man Behind the Miracle," the generic "A Miracle of Laughter! A Miracle of Tenderness! A Miracle of Entertainment," and the rather trite "The Heart Story of Today . . . Tomorrow . . . and Always."[487] The poster art was on the bland side, with illustrated profiles that were not-so-great likenesses of O'Hara and Payne looking at each other, and an extremely small image of Wood hugging Gwenn (which, incidentally, would become the exclusive piece of art used for the film's later home video release). In their first two movies together, *To the Shores of Tripoli* (1942) and *Sentimental Journey* (1946), Payne had received top billing, but O'Hara got top billing in *Miracle*, a sign of her rising popularity and box office draw. The size of the actors' names in the advertising of the film was contractually defined. Whatever the size of the film title, O'Hara's and Payne's names would be 90 percent of that size; Gwenn's would be 35 percent of it; and the principal supporting cast's names (Gene Lockhart, Natalie Wood, Porter Hall, William Frawley, Jerome Cowan, and Philip Tonge) would be 15 percent of that size, with guaranteed screen credit and inclusion on all advertising materials.[488]

Much of the original advertising art was intentionally vague about the story. This "insert" poster is one of the few pieces that at least indicates that it involves a parade. (Author's collection)

A special five-minute teaser trailer was even created for *Miracle*, unique enough that there were advertisements just to go see it apart from the movie![489] It featured studio executives sitting in a projection room watching a trailer that describes the film as "Hilarious! Romantic! Delightful! Charming! Tender!" and "Exciting!" Then the studio head yells at the projectionist to turn it off. He scolds his underlings, saying that a picture can't be all of those things, and that it should give the public an idea of what the story is all about (the joke being, of course, that this trailer doesn't do that at all). He then storms out and runs into several movie stars on the lot (Rex Harrison, Anne Baxter, Peggy Ann Garner, and Dick Haymes), who separately describe the film in disparate terms, just like the trailer had done. The studio head then goes back into the theater and watches the film in its entirety; by the end, he also agrees that it is all of those things. In line with *Miracle*'s aim at realism, the trailer was actually filmed on the TCF lot in the Little Theater and on Avenue G (but, it should be noted, the executives were played by actors).[490] The trailer is clever, and a fun a little glimpse into the Hollywood of the 1940s.

Since *Miracle* was moved up for release in June, there was no reference to its Christmas theme in the three-sheet poster. (Photofest)

The teaser trailer had been created to supplement a standard trailer.[491] It was supposed to be shown in theaters two weeks before *Miracle* started its run, with the standard trailer being shown one week before. But theater owners complained that it was too long. Most trailers at the time were about ninety seconds to two minutes in run time, meaning that two or three trailers could be shown in the same time as this one. The feedback was so negative that the studio just dropped the teaser trailer and sent out the two-minute version (which was actually just the last part of the teaser).[492]

Publicity really got under way in mid-May. Another preview was held for Macy's on May 9 as part of its "Friendly Forty" club. It included a private dinner party at the Pennsylvania Hotel, with three hundred people attending.[493] The TCF publicity team then started traveling across the country to do special preview screenings in places like Minneapolis and Des Moines; they also held meetings with the regional exhibitors to discuss the marketing strategy for *Miracle* and *The Ghost and Mrs. Muir*, along with some long-term goals.[494] A sneak preview was held at the Roxy Theatre on May 16, and the response from the audience was phenomenal. A total of 1,005 comment cards were turned in, with 789 rating it as "Excellent," 181 rating it as "Good," twenty-eight rating it as "Fair," and only eight rating it as "Poor."[495] Regional previews were held in twelve other big cities that week, as well, mostly in the Northeast and Midwest.[496]

One of the biggest coups of the publicity campaign was incorporating all of the retailers in the 34th Street shopping district. The area was one of the busiest pedestrian areas of New York City, with 250 million annual visitors, and it accounted for almost 40 percent of retail sales in Manhattan.[497] Macy's had agreed to underwrite the advertising campaign, but it was not focused solely on its store.[498] Since the idea of *Miracle* had not originated with Macy's or Gimbels, an important aspect of the publicity was to avoid the appearance that the film was merely a piece of propaganda for either store.[499] This is probably why other businesses were invited to join the campaign. The theme was "34th Street Midtown Salutes 'Miracle on 34th Street.' " Banners were strung across 34th Street, as well as shield decorations on a hundred lampposts all the way up and down the street, which was the first time that the city had ever allowed such a thing.[500] The John David store on Herald Square and Spear's Furniture on 34th Street both put huge banners up with the theme.[501] Hotels, banks, restaurants, and stores for blocks around 34th Street featured flags on their roofs and signs in their windows. There were even lithographs on delivery trucks.[502] In addition, a half-million three-by-five-inch special heralds carrying the message "McCreery [or another store] Salutes A Miracle of Screen Entertainment Value!" were distributed, mailed, handed out in person, or included in outgoing packages.[503] Gimbels put an ad in the *New York Times* stating that "Nobody but Nobody could salute 'Miracle on 34th Street' with more enthusiasm than the Miracle on 33rd Street."[504]

For its part, Macy's decorated its 34th Street windows based on the theme of the history of the store, and had signs in every window promoting the film. The store also projected a trailer of the film on a continuous loop on one of their upstairs floors.

Despite the bland advertising art that indicated nothing about the story, audiences flocked to see *Miracle on 34th Street*. This six-sheet poster was one of the largest ones exhibitors could buy. (Author's collection)

Macy's bought three full-page ads in New York newspapers, advertising the film.[505] Macy's also bought ads in eighty cities (with populations of 100,000 or more) to run after *Miracle* had opened in those cities, inviting people to come to New York, and to be sure to visit Macy's during their trip.[506] The store also mailed an additional 180,000 heralds to customers on their mailing list and distributed 10,000 more each day in the store.[507]

On the day before the premiere, Macy's coordinated advertising on station WOR of the Mutual Broadcasting System, a key station that reached about twenty million homes from Philadelphia to Boston. Making arrangements was fairly easy to do, since Macy's owned the station.[508] This marked the first time the station had participated in a full-blown advertising campaign for a movie.[509] The tribute started at 6:45 a.m. on June 3, with eleven different programs making mention of *Miracle* throughout the day, until 6:15 p.m.[510] There was a mention of the film at least every twenty minutes, totaling two and a half hours of dedicated advertising of the film.[511] The station's mobile unit broadcast from 34th Street, stopping in at participating stores. The station even sponsored a special letter contest, asking listeners to send a letter describing "the closest thing to a miracle that [had] happened to them."[512] The radio coverage worked, and *Miracle* got mentioned on fifteen other local and national shows, with Kate Smith and Ted Collins giving enthusiastic endorsements on their shows.[513] All of the trade papers were utterly impressed with the comprehensive publicity campaign, naming it one of the best of the year; *Variety* noted that it was the biggest campaign since *The Razor's Edge* (1946), six months previously.[514]

Miracle premiered at New York's Roxy Theatre on Wednesday, June 4, with the first showing at 10:30 a.m.[515] The Roxy Theatre, located at 50th Street and Seventh Avenue, and connected to the Taft Hotel, was the flagship theater of the TCF theater chain. Built in 1927 in an exuberant Spanish-Gothic style, it was the definition of a movie palace. Everything was grand, from the entrance rotunda to the lounges to the sweeping staircase to the cavernous auditorium with usherettes and 5,886 seats.[516] Tickets cost between 80 cents and $1.50 (higher prices for evening shows), which was considerably more than the average national movie ticket price of 34 cents.[517]

In the 1940s, as a holdover from the vaudeville days, the Roxy was still putting on a stage show as an added attraction to accompany the movies. Moreover, a new stage show was created for each new movie. For *Miracle*, the program included comedian Jerry Lester delivering a few jokes (just a few years before he would go on to fame as the host of *Broadway Open House*, the first late-night talk show on TV); an act featuring the famous Salici Puppets, who could sing, dance, and do acrobatics; pianist Jan August, who had just had a hit with "Misirlou"; and Art Lund singing his recent hit songs, the #1 "Mam'selle" and "Blue Skies."[518] About two weeks into the run of the show, an amusing episode concerning studio egos occurred. During his introduction to "Mam'selle," Lund would mention, as was customary for singers at the time, that a recording of the song was available on MGM Records. TCF got wind of this and did not like the fact that he was mentioning a competitor in its theater—even though the song was from the TCF film *The Razor's Edge*. Lund was thereafter prohibited from uttering "MGM Records" for the remainder of the show; he could only say that the song had been recorded.[519] The show also featured the Roxy's own dance troupe, the Gae Foster Roxyettes.[520]

Even though the studio decided not to do a big, glitzy, formal premiere, there was an impressive turnout for the first showing on Wednesday morning. Patrons lined up four deep in front of the theater. Borough president Hugo E. Rogers bought the first ticket, and P. Raymond Haulenbach was there, representing the 34th Street Midtown Association.[521] Noticeably absent was anybody connected with the making of the film—none of the movie stars, and not even the director, George Seaton (he was up in Alaska for a summer vacation).[522] A total of 21,171 people saw *Miracle* on its opening day. Apparently, hot-weather attractions did not draw too many people away. The response from the audience was impressive; after every screening, they would break into applause. A. L. Balaban, the managing director of the Roxy, was a bit overwhelmed, stating, "Never in all my years in this business have I observed such an audience reaction. They leave [the] theater visibly happier."[523]

Among the patrons the first few days were 12,000 Macy employees, who were admitted to screenings in batches of 2,000, at the reduced ticket price of 55 cents.[524] Valentine Davies's brother Clarence attended one of the screenings with the employees and reported on the event. He

Miracle on 34th Street premiered at the Roxy Theatre on June 4, 1947 and played there for a month. Exactly 21,171 people saw it on opening day. This photo, looking east down 50th Street, was taken on that day in the early afternoon.

The Roxy Theatre entrance, at the corner of 50th Street and Seventh Avenue, was Twentieth Century-Fox's flagship theater in New York. This is as it appeared in the 1930s before the marquee was updated. (Author's collection)

The Roxy's cavernous auditorium had almost 6,000 seats. (Author's colection)

The Roxy's rotunda lobby was grand indeed! (Author's collection)

The Roxy's proscenium. (Author's collection)

said the Macyites "screamed delightedly" when they saw the recognizable interiors of the store, they "applauded loudly" when the cafeteria came on-screen, and they "laughed scornfully" when Mr. Macy "cheerfully" gives Doris and Mr. Shellhammer a bonus; apparently this was too much of a fantasy for their willing suspension of disbelief.[525]

Miracle would play for a month, with phenomenal ticket sales the first week alone bringing in $125,000.[526] In comparison, there were eighteen first-run theaters in and around Broadway.

Popular comedian Jerry Lester was part of the stage show at the Roxy Theatre during *Miracle on 34th Street*'s run there in June 1947. (Photofest)

Art Lund sang his recent #1 hit "Mam'selle" during the stage show at the Roxy, but Twentieth Century-Fox wouldn't let him mention that it was on rival MGM's record label. (Photofest)

Pianist Jan August rounded out the musical offerings during the Roxy stage show. (Photofest)

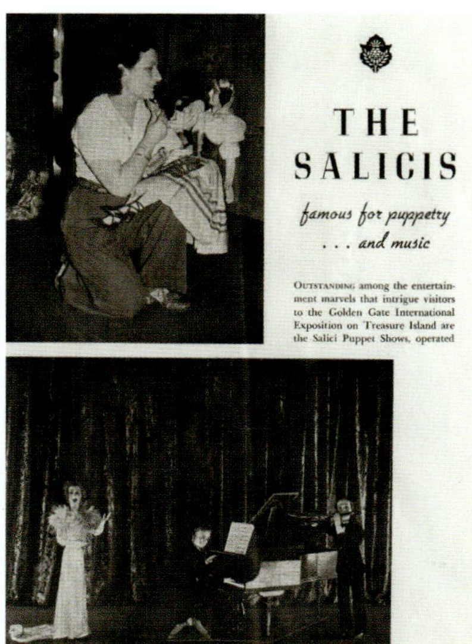

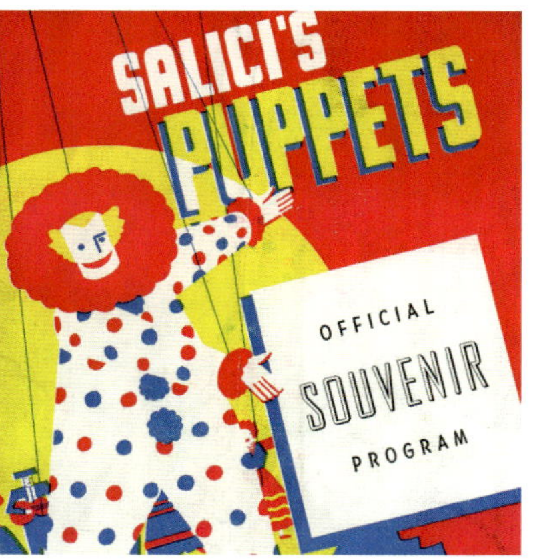

Part of the stage show at the Roxy included a performance by the famous Salici Puppets. They could sing, they could dance, and they could do acrobatics. They had been performing in Europe for 200 years and had only made their American debut a few years earlier. (Author's collection)

Great Expectations (1947) was playing at Radio City Music Hall (the only other theater comparable in size to the Roxy) and brought in $130,000 in its third week. The rest of the theaters (which were much smaller) were bringing in less than $70,000 that week, with most bringing in a half or a third as much. *Miracle*'s second week earnings would dip a little, blamed on the hot weather that made outdoor activities more attractive, but it brought in a strong $101,000.[527] The third week brought in a respectable $94,000, and the last week was a still-impressive $71,000. The last screening at the Roxy was on July 1.[528] *Miracle* had been preceded by *The Brasher Doubloon* (1947), an adaptation of a Raymond Chandler novel with George Montgomery as Philip Marlowe, and was followed by another mystery, *Moss Rose* (1947), set in the Victorian era and starring Victor Mature and Ethel Barrymore, which opened on July 2.[529]

Even though *Miracle* was not originally slated to open anywhere else until it had a proven track record in New York, the studio decided to release it in four other cities the week following the New York premiere. This caused some headaches for the publicity department, because it didn't get the advertising materials delivered on time.[530] *Miracle* opened in Boston at the Metropolitan, in Chicago at the Woods, in Pittsburgh at the Harris, and at four theaters in Los Angeles: the Chinese, Loew's State, the Uptown, and the Loyola.[531] The following week, another eight cities were added to the release schedule, including San Francisco, Dallas, Toledo, and Salt Lake City.[532] By the middle of July, *Miracle* was still only in limited release in these few key cities.[533]

The *Miracle* publicity campaign was helped nationally by leading consumer research service Meyer and the National Retail Dry Goods Association (NRDGA), with its 7,500 member stores. Both encouraged retailers to do a *Miracle* tie-in promotion, because it's "not just for Macy and Gimbel, but for all stores. Why? Because the department store is demonstrated as a community institution—with a soul! Store personnel are naturally and humanly portrayed, and the part played by department stores in the lives of children at Christmas carries a mighty public relations message."[534] Many successful retailer tie-in campaigns were launched across the country, especially in the cities with Macy's- and Gimbels-affiliated stores.[535] This ruffled some theater owners, such as the Associated Theatre Owners of Indiana, who felt that they should be compensated for the free advertising that Macy's and Gimbels received, with fifty-one mentions in the film.[536]

Miracle was gradually rolled out across the country during the rest of the summer and into the early fall. While the film was well received across the country, it did not do well in some areas, including San Francisco, Detroit, and in several small towns, for unknown reasons.[537] Financially speaking, the film did very well. It had cost $1.5 million to make, and, based on the TCF seventy-eight-week amortization schedule, was considered well ahead of the game, having recouped all of its costs in just thirteen weeks.[538] It would end up grossing $2,650,000 in its first run, making it the forty-fifth-biggest moneymaker of 1947. To put it in context, the highest-grossing movie that year was *The Best Years of Our Lives*, bringing in $11,500,000, which was well ahead of any other film. Only fifteen pictures made more than $4,000,000.[539]

By early November, after *Miracle* had finished its initial run, it was re-booked in over a thousand theaters to play during the holiday season. So, despite all the mayhem surrounding its release, it did end up playing in theaters at Christmastime in 1947 after all![540] *Miracle* was released internationally and dubbed in at least two foreign languages (French and Spanish). By the time it made it to many of the foreign markets, it was close to Christmastime, so they got to exploit the holiday aspect of the film. Unlike the American advertising, this resulted in some very eye-catching poster art, such as the Danish and Italian posters. The film would continue to be booked in theaters from the late 1940s through the mid-1950s, when it started airing on television. These repeat bookings allowed many more people to see the film; by 1951, it was estimated to have been seen by 75 million people.[541]

The critical reviews for *Miracle* were unanimously positive (a filmmaker's dream), and used glowing words all the way around: "delightful," "original," "charming," "fresh," "captivating," "sparkling, "engaging," "beguiling," and even "magical." Almost every reviewer was impressed by the unique story, and several, like Rose Felswick of the *New York Journal-American*, thought Seaton "handled the fantasy angle of the story so realistically that it never once becomes fantastic."[542] Some pointed out that it is not patently a fantasy, because it "never denies or affirms" whether Kris is Santa Claus, so "you can look at it any way you want to."[543] Another critic observed as much—that we don't know if Kris "is right or wrong, mad or sane. We only hope he is right. For the crowning uncertainty is an inspired one."[544] One concern from the beginning was keeping the sentimentality in check: *Newsweek* recognized that it "could have been all treacle and bubble gum, and too cute for words," but successfully avoided that.[545]

Practically every reviewer had high praise for the character actors, declaring the film "an actor's holiday," in which they "click incisively in brief characterizations."[546] Edmund Gwenn was universally loved in the role, and the *New York Times* even went so far as to propose that "if ever the real Santa wants to step down, Mr. Gwenn is the man for the job."[547] Hedda Hopper took Hollywood to task for not giving him top billing; after all, she pointed out, "he's absolutely dominant in every scene—he is the picture."[548] Many reviewers were particularly impressed with the child actors, especially Natalie Wood, whom one critic referred to as "properly terrifying" in her realistic portrayal of Susan.[549] Alvin Greenman and Robert Hyatt were also identified as particularly endearing. All of these great character performances probably influenced Lee Mortimer of the *Daily Mirror* to declare it "one of the most human photoplays ever."[550] Louella Parsons of the *Los Angeles Examiner* cautioned, "If you don't LOVE, LOVE, LOVE 'Miracle on 34th Street,' run to a doctor—there's something radically wrong with your heart."[551] Even usually crusty Bosley Crowther of the *New York Times* recommended it to those who have "grown weary of the monotonies of the screen," as "the freshest picture in a long time, and maybe even the best comedy of the year."[552]

One of the most insightful reviews was by Cecilia Ager of the *New York Post*'s "PM Magazine." She found it to be very much "an inside story for New Yorkers" that "merrily . . . chops down our mighty metropolis to the size of a friendly small town, making for the moment neigh-

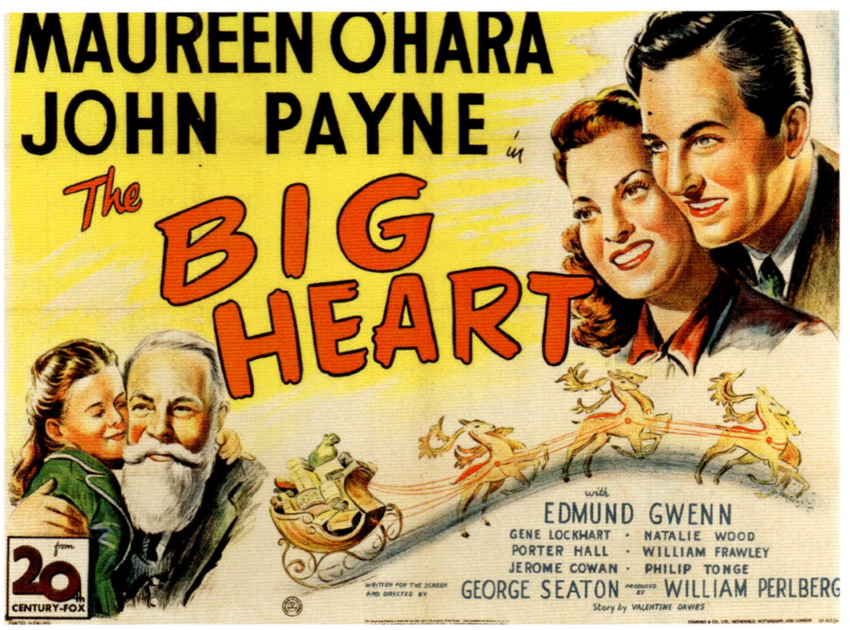

Miracle was released in the UK as *The Big Heart*, one of its working titles. (Author's collection)

When *Miracle* was released in Denmark, there was no question that this was a Christmas movie: The title was *Do You Believe in Santa Claus?* (Author's collection)

The title was not changed when the film was released in Italian, as seen on this poster. (Author's collection)

This Italian poster is one of the best examples of advertising art that actually conveys what *Miracle* is all about. (Author's collection)

For the Spanish herald handbill, the title was changed to *You Can Also Live by Wishing*.

bors of us all." She then tackles the commercial aspect of the film, stating that it is a complete fantasy—first, that a Macy's Santa would have higher ideals than his employer; second, that such ideals would cause any bother in Macy's management; third, that there is an R. H. Macy; and fourth, that customers would start viewing Macy's as a benevolent institution. She thinks one of the miracles of the film is that it "induc[es] us to feel sympathy for" Macy's. She feels that it all works, because it was "played straight."[553] Kate Cameron of the *Daily News* observed that, even though the setting was a department store, "there is no taint of commercialism about it."[554]

Perhaps the highest praise came from John Mason Brown. He had been a drama critic for two major New York papers, head of the drama department at the Brooklyn Institute for the Arts and Sciences, a lecturer at Columbia, and host of the *Of Man and Books* program on CBS; and he was currently the writer of the column "Seeing Things" for the *Saturday Review of Literature.* He had praised the film in his column, comparing it to the famous 1897 editorial in the *New York Sun*, titled "Yes, Virginia, There Is a Santa Claus."[555] At the opening lecture of the Western College for Women lecture series, he lauded the output of the British film industry, including such productions as *Henry V* (1944), *Great Expectations* (1947), and *Brief Encounter* (1945), and then went on to lambaste Hollywood for glamorizing everything. He felt that the only movies currently made in Hollywood that deserved merit were *Life with Father* (1947) and *Miracle on 34th Street.*[556] Another critic, from the *New York Post*, Archer Winsten, concurred that *Miracle* was "proof that 20th Century-Fox is Europe's only competitor this year in the production of excellent films."[557]

Really, the only negative comments made about the film were slight, and mentioned by just a couple of reviewers. They included criticism that the film was released in June, "with bland disregard for seasonal timing," and that the Doris–Fred romance was perhaps a bit stiff and underdeveloped.[558] But even those reservations did not keep the likes of *Life* magazine from naming *Miracle* as "Movie of the Week."

Boxoffice magazine would publish, as a regular feature, a summary of a film's reviews for theater owners to see how it was being received. *Miracle* got positive reviews from every major trade paper, giving it a "14+" rating. Very few films ever received a rating that high. Other films at the time that received consistently positive reviews included *The Best Years of Our Lives* (1946) (14+), *Song of the South* (1946) (14+), *The Jolson Story* (1946) (14+), *It's a Wonderful Life* (1946) (13+), *Blue Skies* (1946) (13+), and *Boomerang!* (1947) (11+).[559] Perhaps Eileen Creelman of the *New York Sun* summed it up the most succinctly when she stated that it was an example of "Hollywood at its best."[560]

The positive reaction of the critics was a good omen that the awards season would be very kind to *Miracle.* The first award it won was *Boxoffice* magazine's Blue Ribbon Award in July 1947. Beginning in 1932, the award had been given monthly to the best family film selected by the National Screen Council.[561] As 1947 was winding up, *Miracle* appeared on several lists of the "Best Films of the Year," including in the *Film Daily*, the *New York Times*, and the *Los Angeles Times*.[562] It came in as the fifth-best film of the year (behind *The Best Years of Our Lives, The Jolson*

Story, *Life with Father*, and *The Yearling*) in the *Film Daily*'s annual poll of 352 critics from across the nation.[563] It was nominated for Best Picture of the Year by the New York Film Critics Circle and by the Protestant Motion Picture Council—but lost to *Gentleman's Agreement* and *The Yearling*, respectively.[564] The National Board of Review selected *Miracle* as the second-most-entertaining film of 1947 (behind *Great Expectations*).[565] It thus deserves recognition as one of the few films that has been deemed both a critical and a commercial success.[566]

Natalie Wood became the first person to be honored for her participation in the film when she won the "The Most Talented Juvenile Motion Picture Star of 1947" from *Parents' Magazine*.[567] *Look* magazine (one of America's most popular magazines at the time) honored the film at its seventh annual Achievement Awards. The awards ceremony was broadcast on Bob Hope's radio show on February 3, 1948, from Hollywood. Edmund Gwenn won a special award for his performance. When he accepted, Gwenn graciously said that "the credit doesn't really belong to me, it belongs to the man who made this film, George Seaton."[568] Seaton received his award right after Gwenn for his dual role as writer and director of a screenplay. *Miracle* was also accorded the honor of being on the magazine's list of the fifteen best movies of the year.[569]

But these accolades were just a buildup to the bigger ceremonies. The Hollywood Foreign Press Association banquet was held on Wednesday, March 10, 1948, at the Roosevelt Hotel on Hollywood Boulevard, with three hundred in attendance.[570] Walter Pidgeon was the emcee, and Maureen O'Hara was the hostess for the evening. That year, four new awards had been added, bringing the total up to twelve. Gwenn was the winner of the Best Supporting Actor award, and Seaton won the inaugural award for Best Screen Story.[571]

Ten days later, *Miracle* would score big again at the Academy Awards. The Oscars were held at the massive Shrine Auditorium in Los Angeles on Saturday, March 20, 1948, with more than three thousand of Hollywood's elite attending. It was a special evening, as it marked the twentieth anniversary of the awards ceremony, and it proved to be a big night for TCF, which had a total of twenty-two nominations across all the major categories. *Miracle* had been nominated for four awards, including Best Picture.

Valentine Davies had been nominated for "Best Writing (Motion Picture Story)." He was up against another lighthearted Christmas-themed story, *It Happened on Fifth Avenue*; the TCF film noir, *Kiss of Death*; a Dorothy Parker story, *Smash-up: A Story of a Woman*; and a French entry, *A Cage of Nightingales*. Davies ended up winning. After the ceremony, studio head Zanuck wrote a personal note to Davies, declaring, "There is no question but what your story was the best original story of the year. I would have been really outraged if you hadn't received it."[572]

George Seaton was nominated for "Best Writing (Screenplay)," but was up against four heavy dramas. Two were scathing indictments of anti-Semitism and prejudice, *Gentleman's Agreement* (adapted by famous playwright Moss Hart) and John Paxton's *Crossfire*; the other two were the docudrama *Boomerang!*, about the murder of a small-town minister, and the adaptation of Charles Dickens's *Great Expectations*, by David Lean. In addition, *Gentleman's Agreement* and *Boomer-*

The December 13th, 1947, issue of the British film magazine *Picture Show* got to capitalize on the Christmas theme of *Miracle*. Note that the film was released in the UK under one of its working titles, *The Big Heart*, as indicated in the lower right corner of the cover. (Author's collection)

Miracle was one of nine films to be considered one of the "best movies of the month" and turned into a short story for *Movie Story* magazine's July 1947 issue. (Author's collection)

Miracle got the cover and was the lead story in *The Best Screen Stories of 1947*, which contained abridgements in story form of twenty motion pictures released that year. The Academy of Motion Picture Arts and Sciences thought the story was pretty good, too, and gave it Oscars for best story and screenplay. (Author's collection)

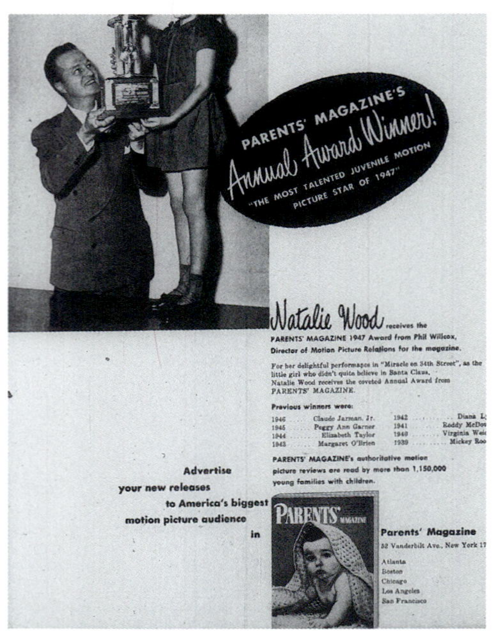

Natalie Wood was the first member of the cast to win an award for the film from *Parents' Magazine* as "The Most Talented Juvenile Motion Picture Star of 1947." (Author's collection)

Maureen O'Hara was the official hostess at the Golden Globes in 1948. Here she is (from left to right) with George Seaton, Elia Kazan, and Max Steiner. (Photofest)

Presaging his success at the Oscars, Edmund Gwenn won a Golden Globe for his performance in *Miracle*. Here he is with Howard Hill (left), vice president of the Hollywood Foreign Correspondents Association, and composer Max Steiner (right) who won for *Life with Father*. (Photofest)

It was a happy night for the men who made Kris Kringle come to life on the screen, Edmund Gwenn and George Seaton. (Author's collection)

Miracle on 34th Street lost to *Gentleman's Agreement*, but at least the Best Picture Oscar was kept in the family since both were made by Twentieth Century-Fox. The studio was the biggest winner of the night walking away with seven Academy Awards. (Photofest)

ang! were both made by his own studio. With such stiff competition, it is impressive that his comedy won, but it did, and Seaton walked away with the Oscar.

Gwenn was up for "Best Supporting Actor." Gwenn was beloved by the other members of the cast, who were definitely happy when he was nominated, but they did think it was a bit unfair that he was the only one.[573] Seaton was delighted with his performance, "because he played it almost as a proud Bavarian baron."[574] The other nominees included Charles Bickford for the comedy *The Farmer's Daughter* (Loretta Young would walk away with the "Best Actress" award for her role in that film), and three very dramatic contenders: Robert Ryan in *Crossfire*; Richard Widmark in *Kiss of Death*; and Thomas Gomez in *Ride the Pink Horse*. During the announcement of the nominees during the ceremony, Gwenn got the biggest applause by far, an indication that he was surely going to win. The award was presented by Anne Baxter, who had won "Best Supporting Actress" for *The Razor's Edge* the year before. Gwenn gave a very endearing and heartfelt acceptance speech:

> *Thank you, Anne dear. Phew! Now I know there's a Santa Claus! You may laugh, ladies and gentlemen—it's not so easy to be certain, you know. He's a most elusive little fellow. He turns up in all sorts of places under all sorts of names and disguises. The first time I ever met him, he told me his name was George Seaton; and wonderful George Seaton had his revenge by bringing him to life. About a year and a half ago, he suddenly turned up at Culver City and told me his name was Metro-Goldwyn-Mayer. That was the day Metro agreed to loan me to TCF to make the picture. And now, I think it's time Santa Claus added a word to his name. I think he ought to call himself Santa Claus Incorporated. Santa Claus Inc. INC.! For then*

     PUBLICITY, PREMIERE, AND AWARDS

it would embrace all you wonderful, wonderful kind people who have done me the honor of making me stand here tonight. Thank you, all of you, for making the evening of my life such a happy one.

Lastly, *Miracle* was nominated for "Best Picture." It was up against another soon-to-be Christmas classic, *The Bishop's Wife*, and several weighty dramas: *Crossfire*, *Great Expectations*, and *Gentleman's Agreement*. Comedies have rarely been nominated in the Best Picture category, and, even when they are, they hardly ever win. The fact that it was considered for the award was high praise indeed from the Hollywood community. *Miracle* would lose out to *Gentleman's Agreement*, which won the top prize that year. But TCF would be the biggest winner of the evening, walking away with a total of seven awards: three for *Miracle*, three for *Gentleman's Agreement*, and one for *Mother Wore Tights*.

The big winners on Oscar night 1948: from left to right, Darryl F. Zanuck, Twentieth Century-Fox head of production who accepted for *Gentleman's Agreement*; Edmund Gwenn who won Best Supporting Actor for *Miracle on 34th Street*; Loretta Young who won Best Actress for *The Farmer's Daughter*; Ronald Colman who won Best Actor for *A Double Life*; and Celeste Holm who won Best Supporting Actress for *Gentleman's Agreement*. (Photofest)

Unbeknownst to Valentine Davies when he wrote *Miracle on 34th Street*, there had been actual judicial rulings on the existence of Santa Claus in 1927 and 1936. Had district attorney Thomas Mara and Judge Henry X. Harper known about these precedents, they could have saved themselves a lot of headaches. (Photofest)

Legally Speaking

In the early 1950s, Dr. James H. Barnett, then head of the sociology department at
the University of Connecticut, started an academic study of Christmas. His research
would eventually result in the publication of his book, *The American Christmas*, in 1954.
Miracle was of interest to him as a great example of a Christmas story in modern times, and so he
started a correspondence with Valentine Davies.

During Barnett's research, he had come across a ruling handed down in 1927 by Judge
John H. Hatcher of the West Virginia Supreme Court: "Ex Parte Santa Claus."[575] Details as to
why it was handed down or who requested it or if the court acted "ex officio" is unclear. Hatcher
begins with a brief history of Santa Claus and testifies of his goodness, concluding that "there
is no harm, and no guile [in him]—except perhaps in his manner of entering houses by way of
chimneys." He then discusses the then-current trend of people who want to modernize Santa
until he is just a "foxy grandpa out for a joy ride." Such people criticize him, saying his transportation is outmoded; instead of a sleigh, he should be using an airplane, or at least a car, to make
his deliveries. Hatcher comes to Santa's defense and points out that a sleigh and reindeer can go
anywhere, never run out of gas, never get a flat tire, or develop engine trouble. These people also
wonder why he can't enter through the front door like everyone else.

Far worse than the reformers, in Hatcher's opinion, are those who would abolish Santa
altogether. These people are "ruthless," like anyone who would steal from a blind beggar. He
questions why there are people who even want to do this. His conclusion: "Because they are liter-
al-minded. They will have none of make-believe. They demand proof of everything." He makes

it clear: "I warn them to keep out of our court." If it's proof they want, he declares, there is plenty. He says that there are millions of children who would be willing to testify that, on Christmas Eve, they have heard jingle bells, the crack of a whip, the "swish of the sleigh on the snow," or even Santa laughing. If you want further proof, what about the filled stockings on Christmas morning that were previously empty? That should be evidence enough to "satisfy any jury of our youthful peers on the issue of Santa Claus. *Res ipsa loquitur* [a Latin legal phrase that translates as "The thing speaks for itself]." He concludes by saying: "Let legislatures outlaw the law of evolution, if they must; let the Constitution be amended until it looks like a patchwork quilt; but rob not childhood of its most intriguing mystery—Santa Claus! Let him be to succeeding generations as he has been to us—a joyous faith of childhood, a pleasant indulgence of parenthood, and a happy memory of old age."

Hatcher's colleague, Judge Homer B. Woods, offered a concurring opinion. After quoting from the poem " 'Twas the Night Before Christmas," he declared that Santa Claus has a "vested right to be left undisturbed, at this season of the year, in his work of bringing joy and happiness to the world's children. The profane hand of the iconoclast who would interfere will be stayed by this court."

Barnett was intrigued by Hatcher's decision in light of its similarity to *Miracle*, especially given that it appeared twenty years before the motion picture was created. Obviously, both involve a decision by a judge on the validity of Santa Claus, but perhaps even more striking are the themes that Hatcher brings up, which are so effectively dramatized in *Miracle*. He was very curious if Davies had ever read or heard about this as an inspiration for *Miracle*. Davies had not, which is not surprising, since the decision did not get wide circulation, being printed only in the court syllabus and in the *Charleston Daily Mail*.[576]

A decade later, another ruling concerning Santa Claus was issued by Judge Michael. A. Musmanno, the presiding judge of the Allegheny County Court of Common Pleas in Pittsburgh: *In re Legality and Authenticity of Santa Claus* (Misc. No. 52 for 1936). In recent months, he had received several requests to make a ruling on the legal status of Santa Claus. At issue was whether men who worked as department store Santas should be arrested on the basis of false pretenses, for "deceiving the public, in that they purport to represent a personage that does not exist."

In his opinion, Judge Musmanno asked if anyone had ever seen Jack Frost, or Cupid, or Uncle Sam (and gave several examples of their deeds), and yet who could deny their existence? He further reasoned that if the courts can recognize John Doe, they can certainly recognize Santa Claus. The judge then said that he could personally attest to having seen Santa Claus, but could not say as much about John Doe. He declared that "Santa Claus is a reality recognizable by the law, and he will be protected in this court against all aspersions and insinuations to the contrary." He continued that "Santa Claus is not a figment of the imagination" but is the symbol of kindness, charity, and benevolence. He became a little philosophical in pointing out that "if there were no Santa Claus in the courts, there would be no justice, because Santa Claus represents the spirit of mercy, goodness and sympathy."

Judge Musmanno made it very clear that if anyone did file such a lawsuit on this issue, it would be dismissed, with the plaintiff paying all legal costs. He also warned that any doubter would be held in contempt of the court and would be sent to prison, "there to be kept in dungeon vile until his soul expands and the spirit of Christmas enters therein"—and would only be released on condition that he "shout with whole lungs and full heart 'Merry Christmas!' " Punishment indeed! Although the opinion was not published in the law reports, it was picked up by the Associated Press and published in several newspapers.[577] Despite its greater publicity, this case was also unknown to Davies.

In a somewhat ironic turn of events for a film that contains a court proceeding, TCF ended up having a couple of legal skirmishes in connection with *Miracle.* The first incident arose from the hearing scenes, filmed February 10 through 17. An actual court stenographer, Mr. Ettelson, had been hired through the A. A. Stenographic & Notary Company. He was hired as an actor, and since he was not a member of the Screen Actors Guild, a special waiver had to be obtained for him to appear in the film. He was paid $30 per day (the going rate for extras), but after his services were rendered, the company thought he should be compensated as a stenographer. The studio's legal department compromised by giving him $6.53 for some overtime.[578]

The second incident ended up being a much bigger headache, as it turned into a full-blown lawsuit involving claims of plagiarism. In October 1947, TCF was notified that Ralph J. Burns, author of a novel entitled *An Angel on Horseback*, was claiming that his work had been plagiarized and used in *Miracle.*[579] He subsequently filed *Burns v. Twentieth Century-Fox Film Corporation* in the US District Court for the District of Massachusetts in Boston.[580]

An Angel on Horseback was a modern romance novel that was published in November 1945 by Colonial Press, with Burns using the nom de plume "Ralph Byrne." The story centered around a young Swedish girl from Minnesota, Greta, who comes to Los Angeles to pursue an acting career. To support herself, she gets a job at Pollard's, one of the nicer department stores on Wilshire Boulevard. One day, lovely Greta goes horseback riding (hence, the title of the book) and is hit by an errant golf ball. This triggers an encounter with one of the golfers, a young doctor named Jimmy O'Farrell. Romance blossoms as they traipse and cavort around the playgrounds of Southern California. Of course, there are some challenges along the pathway to love. One of the most glaring is that Jimmy is Catholic while Greta is Protestant, and reconciling their religious differences seems almost unsurmountable. Additionally, a love triangle emerges when Lieutenant Anderson enters the picture, seeking Greta's affection. In the end, however, Greta converts to Catholicism after Jimmy joins the navy, and marriage is imminent.

The subject of the lawsuit concerned only six pages (pages 68–74) of the 234-page novel, which detail an episode at the store where Greta works. In the weeks before Christmas, Pollard's sets up a temporary toy department and hires a man to play Santa Claus. One day, the man playing Santa and Bill Henry, one of the store employees, bring some liquor to work, and the two

The author of the novel *An Angel on Horseback* sued Twentieth Century-Fox, claiming that Valentine Davies had plagiarized his scene of a drunk department store Santa Claus. He lost the lawsuit. (Author's collection)

take turns sneaking off to a dressing room to "brush their teeth." The man playing Santa, who is now clearly drunk, gets fresh with Greta, asking her to sit on his knee and tell him what she wants for Christmas. Then Bill starts giving toys away for free to kids in the store. Management finally gets wind of what is going on, and Greta, who is Bill's friend, helps him get out of the store in a Santa suit before he is caught. The drunk Santa ends up getting fired. There were a few more scenes in the department store, but Burns wasn't claiming any infringement on those. The majority of his novel (160 pages) focuses on the romantic activities of Greta and Jimmy.

Valentine Davies had to do a deposition on the TCF lot in mid-February 1948, and the court ruled two weeks later.[581] Judge Wyzanski, who wrote the opinion, didn't find any "credible evidence" that Davies or the studio had had any access to Burns's story, especially since Davies's

In its defense, Twentieth Century-Fox brought up the fact that a drunk Santa Claus is nothing new, and used its own film *Life Begins at Eight-Thirty* (1942) as an example. In the opening scene, actors Monty Woolley and Alec Craig are in front of the Marcy Herald Square department store. (Photofest)

first story outline was written months before Burns published his book (good thing he filed it with the Writers Guild!). The judge failed to see one "scintilla of the type of resemblance that gives rise to liability" between the two stories. He conceded that both take place in a retail setting at Christmas and feature a Santa Claus, but that's where the similarity ends.

To point out that this is a trope, he cites TCF's own 1942 film, *Life Begins at Eight-Thirty*, which features Monty Woolley as a drunk Santa in a department store (the studio's lawyers had identified this example as part of the defense). In a rare move, Judge Wyzanski took a cue from Judge Harper, noting that he "learned nearly to his cost that fantasy must be sharply distinguished from other types of thought." He goes on to point out that Burns's book is a romance, "entirely without whimsy," and *Miracle*'s "excursion into the never never world of Peter Pan [never] invaded one inch of the real world portrayed in [Burns's] book." The judge ruled in favor of TCF and ordered Burns to pay defendant's costs, plus attorneys' fees of $250.

The third (potential) legal issue involved the scene where Kris teaches Susan to act like a monkey, a scene that Natalie later said was one of her most vivid memories from the making of the film.[582] In the summer of 1948, Madaline Saenger, a resident of Burbank, wrote to TCF and claimed to be the originator of the monkey gestures that Kris teaches to Susan in the movie.[583] Saenger claimed that she taught these gestures to a three-year-old boy, who, in turn, taught them to Natalie Wood, who used them in *Miracle*, which Saenger claimed she had no right to do. According to Saenger, she owned the "rights" to these gestures that had been transferred to the boy, in the hopes that he would make it into a movie. She now wanted the studio to give this boy a part in a movie in exchange for using her monkey gestures. If not, she threatened to file suit. The handwritten letter and the absurdity of Ms. Saenger's claims were probably enough for the studio not to take this too seriously, but after the *Angel* case, it may have caused some jitters. There is no indication that any further action was taken by either side.

Luckily for TCF, the real-life legal problems were minimal and the studio prevailed in all of the legal skirmishes. TCF would also be grateful that there was limited publicity and that it didn't interfere with the movie's success. In any event, it is gratifying to know that the legal establishment—be it Judge Hatcher, Judge Musmanno, or Judge Harper—agreed and was willing to go on record and rule that Santa Claus does really exist!

This amusing scene of Kris teaching Susan how to be a monkey almost became the subject of a lawsuit. Natalie Wood later said that this was one of her most vivid memories about making the film. (Photofest)

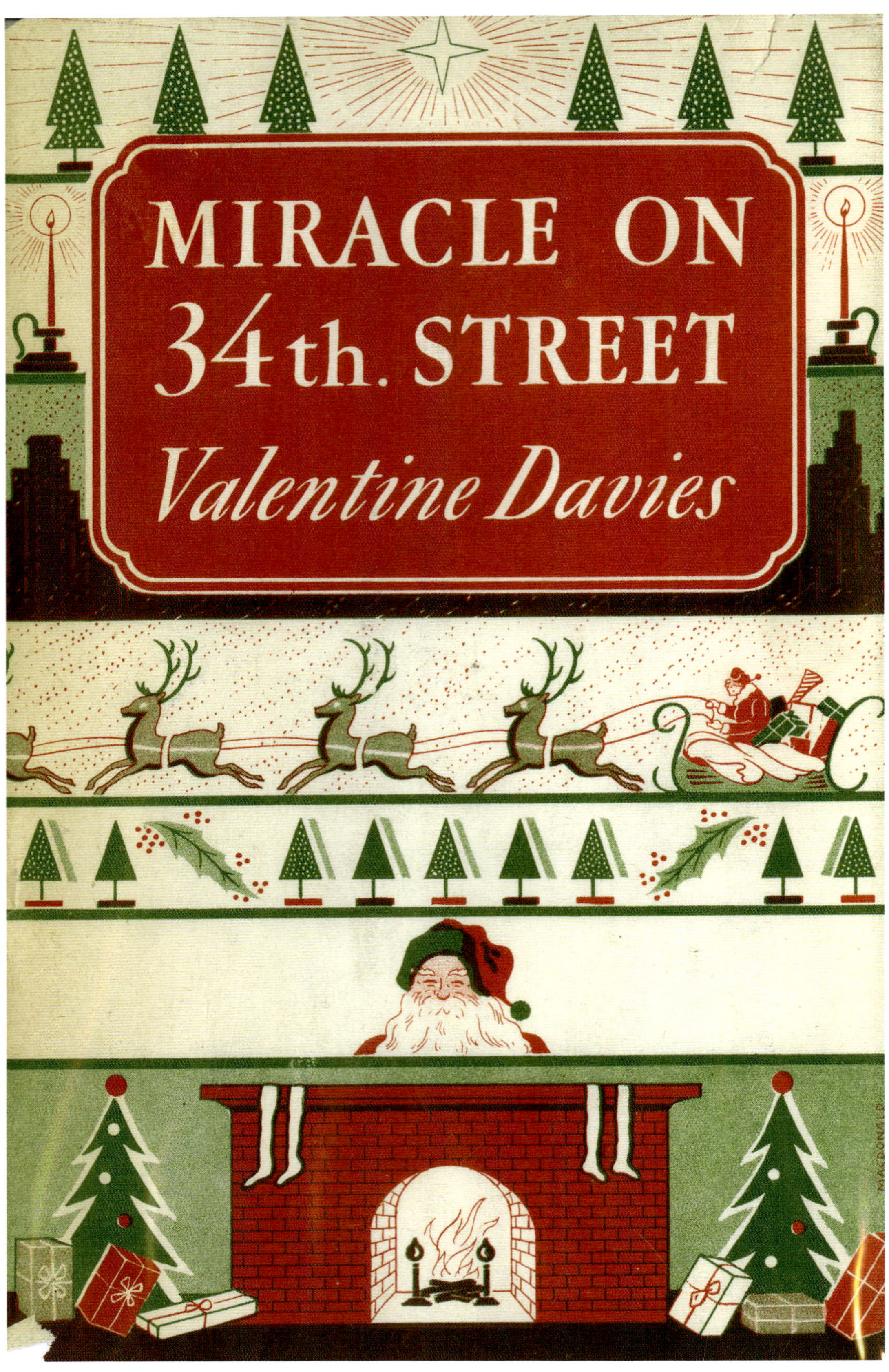

Even though the story was completely owned by Twentieth Century-Fox and the book was out in time to be promoted with the film, the original 1947 dust jacket did not feature any "tie-in" images from the film. This would remain the case for most of its publishing history. (Author's collection)

The Adaptations

The sheer number and variations of the adaptations based on the original *Miracle on 34th Street* film make it worthy of being called a franchise, though it has probably never been thought of as such. Through print, radio, television, theater, and film, the story has been retold, re-fashioned, extended, contracted, and modified in numerous ways for the various media interpretations. Some adaptations have incorporated elements from Valentine Davies's original story, reintroduced some of George Seaton's discarded scenes, or completely made up new plotlines. The adapters have always tried to do something different to make the story their own. But none of the adaptations has succeeded in eclipsing the first; in the case of *Miracle on 34th Street*, as Maureen O'Hara was proud to say, "The first one was the best one," and "is still the favorite. It hasn't been replaced by all the remakes. You can't recapture magic." [584]

THE BOOK

Since the dawn of cinema, literature has always provided a steady stream of source material for movies. Only occasionally does the flow go the other way, and when it does, it tends to be a simplified rehashing of the film. Valentine Davies's book of *Miracle on 34th Street* may be unique in the world of film–book adaptations simply because the book is not based on the movie, and the movie is not based on the book. As Davies indicates in his preface: "It was only after he [Kris Kringle] had come to life upon the screen that he was invited to appear within the covers of a book." [585] The movie and the book exist as separate, distinct iterations of the same story.

At some point in late 1946 or early 1947, while the movie was already in production, Davies shared his story with Walter M. Simpson, an old college friend, who, in turn, shared it with his friend, S. Spencer Scott, vice president and general manager at publisher Harcourt, Brace & Company.[586] By late January, Scott had read it and thought it was "a grand story," but that "it could be better written."[587] Nonetheless, he was "exceedingly anxious" to publish the story, and was bolstered by the fact that the book buyer at Macy's liked it.[588] However, since Davies had sold all of his interest in his story, TCF would need to grant permission. Davies approached producer William Perlberg about the possibility of doing a novel, and then Perlberg took it to Lew Schreiber, who, after consulting with the legal department, gave his approval in early February 1947.[589]

A couple of weeks later, Davies signed a book deal with Harcourt, Brace & Company, which provided a $1,500 advance and 10 percent royalty on book sales. The contract required a 45,000-word manuscript to be delivered within thirty days.[590] Harcourt agreed to title the book the same as the movie. Even though it appears that the studio had decided upon *Miracle on 34th Street* as the definitive title in January, in mid-February there was still some discussion, or at least "wishful thinking," on the part of the publisher, that it would be something else.[591] Scott had a particular aversion to "Miracle on 34th Street" as the title, saying that it "isn't good at all," because "in many cities, 34th Street has a far out in the country sound."[592] Apparently there had been some discussion of going back to "Mr. Kringle," or some variation thereof, but the studio vetoed that. Scott was really pushing for "Miracle on Herald Square" because "Herald Square means only one place."[593] Optimistically, he even typed that title on the contract with Davies, but had to cross it out.

There were a couple of hitches in the negotiations between Harcourt and TCF. Initially, the studio only wanted to give Harcourt publishing rights for five years. Scott found this too restrictive, and felt that Harcourt needed to take the long view, since Davies's story "might well become a classic and go on for years," which ended up being a very prescient statement.[594] The other hitch was that TCF instructed Harcourt to take out the copyright for the world market, and then later rescinded. One interesting stipulation of the contract was that if the sales of the book ever fell below four hundred copies per year, Davies would lose all legal interest and royalties in the book, and they would be transferred to TCF.[595]

Davies submitted his first draft of the manuscript in February. He then worked on a second draft. However, after reading the second draft, Scott preferred the first. Editor in chief Robert Giroux then edited the two drafts together and submitted the new version to Davies and TCF. Even though Scott liked Davies's first draft, he preferred Giroux's edited version even more.[596]

Davies's original story did not end up on the screen, and George Seaton's screenplay did not end up in the pages of the book. Davies made it very clear in his introduction that the development of the story was a collaborative effort between the two, and then, subsequently, each writer selected his favorite elements and created the narrative he liked best. One of the most interesting aspects of Davies's book is that he retained several of the scenes that were cut from the film. It opens with Kris in his room at the old folks' home, with Dr. Pierce; it has the Central Park scene with the reindeer; it has Kris's scheme to get Doris and Fred to spend the evening together; and it includes the Santa Claus lecture scene, where Kris embarrasses Mr. Sawyer. The story that made it on the screen is almost all there, with some additions and subtractions. It is an interesting look at how the film could have turned out.

The plan was to release the book at the same time as the film, in September 1947.[597] When TCF unexpectedly moved the film release date up to June, Harcourt was frustrated, because the book was still in production, and they would lose a crucial marketing opportunity if its release did not coincide with the premiere of the film. The publisher scrambled to get some copies printed in time for the New York premiere in June, and then gave it a national release on July 17, in time for the film's general release across the country.[598] Apparently, enough copies of the book were printed to hold an autograph party on June 9 at the May Company department store in downtown Los Angeles, to coincide with the opening of the film there. Even though it was a successful publicity event, it must have irked Valentine Davies just a bit; instead of him signing his own books, it was actor John Payne who was invited to do so![599]

The book, although technically a "tie-in" (published in conjunction with the movie), didn't utilize most of the normal cross-promotion conventions. It was featured in the pressbook, and theater owners were encouraged to coordinate "see the picture, read the book" promotions with booksellers, but the book cover showed no visual connection to the film.[600] The illustrated dust jacket featured a cozy fireplace, Santa Claus in his sleigh with reindeer, Christmas trees, and holly, but did not show any of the actors or images from the film. There was some attempt by Harcourt to use a picture of Edmund Gwenn as a frontispiece in the book, but that didn't materialize (his picture, however, was used in at least one advertisement for the book).[601] The only indication that there was a connection with the film was on the back cover, which said "Double Your Enjoyment: After You Read the Book—See the Picture," followed by cast credits. What is even more odd is that, throughout the book's long life, the cover never featured any images from the film, until the 1991 edition. That edition used the same cover photo of Natalie Wood hugging Edmund Gwenn that had appeared on the 1985 VHS tape release, and included a smattering of stills throughout, but these inclusions ended up being a one-off occurrence; later editions went back to using non-film-related artwork.

As for critical reviews of the book, Nona Balakian of the *New York Times* was not that impressed with it. She felt that it was a "harmless little extravaganza" that has some fun deriding the worlds of advertising, psychology, and politics, but that it "would hardly create competition for Charles Dickens come next yuletide."[602] Fanny Butcher of the *Chicago Tribune* liked it much better, finding it to be "a "whimsy without any whamsy," coupled with a nice dose of "happy satire." She found the writing "undistinguished," but felt that, if it had been more florid, the wonderful story might have gotten lost in the words.[603] The *Boston Globe* declared that "a trifle, it is, to be sure, but many will find it a delightful trifle," even though "in some ways the movie is better than the book."[604] *Newsweek* stated plainly, "It makes a lot more sense than most of us would like to admit."[605]

Bolstered by the popularity of the movie, the hardcover book sold well, at $1.75.[606] The printing for the original 1947 hardcover retail edition was 20,000 copies, and Macy's ordered 12,000 copies for its employees at cost, plus one cent.[607] One interesting detail about the first printing of the first edition is that Davies was not satisfied with the font used for Susan's letter to Kris, on page 104. A font had been selected to make it appear to be handwritten, but Davies thought that the selection looked too mature for Susan's handwriting, and so had the publisher replace it with a font that was more childlike for the second printing.[608]

The book was given a huge distribution boost when the Book-of-the-Month Club chose *Miracle* to be a selection for November, as well as a Christmas dividend book. The judges, obviously, really liked the story, with one (who was clearly not Balakian) declaring that he "personally liked it better than the Dickens classic," and another predicting that it would become standard fare in Christmas anthologies.[609] The Club ordered 440,000 copies for distribution to its members.[610] By December, there was a total of 477,000 copies of the book in print.[611]

In 1952, a paperback edition by Pocket Books, priced at just 25 cents, was issued in November, just in time for Christmas.[612] Davies was very "pleased" with how it turned out, and especially liked the drawings that embellished the beginning of each chapter.[613] In 1953 an Australian edition was issued that was Davies's favorite binding. He found the cover and interior illustrations "all delightful," and thought it to be "the most attractive" of any of the editions.[614] The only foreign-language edition made at the time was a French translation, *Le Miracle de la 34e Rue*, published in 1950 by Hachette, probably because the film, according to Davies, was "enormously popular and successful in France."[615] (It would eventually be translated into several foreign languages, including Por-

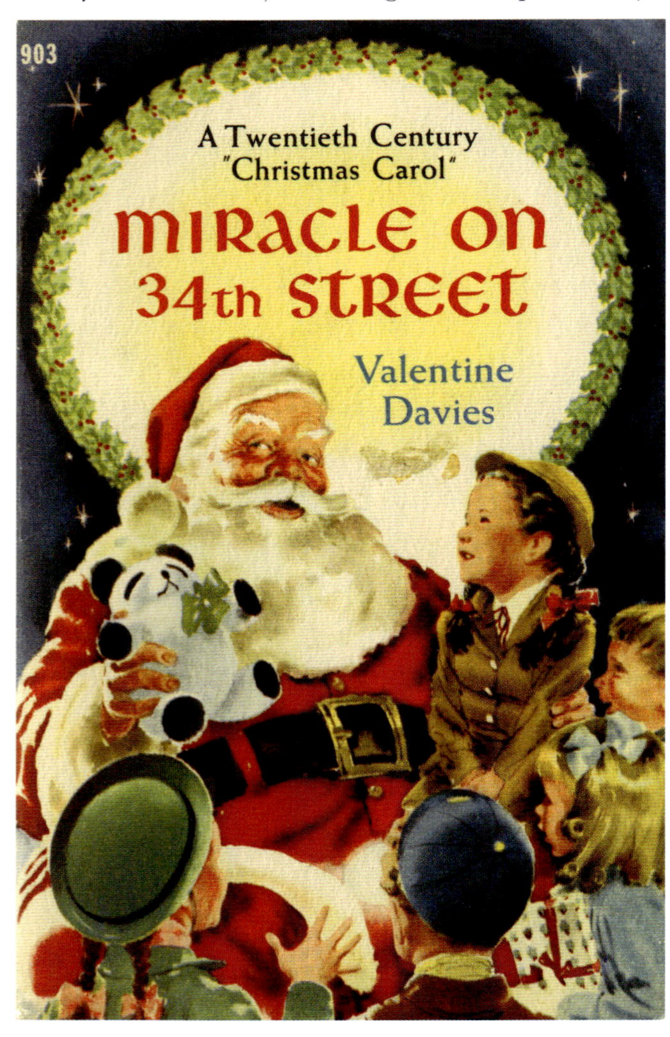

The popularity of *Miracle* as a novel led to a paperback edition by Pocket Books in 1952, which sold for 25 cents. (Author's collection)

This 1991 edition is the only one in *Miracle on 34th Street*'s long publishing history to carry a picture from the film on the cover. (Author's collection)

The endpapers of the 1959 special edition book of *Miracle on 34th Street* published by the Franklin Printing Company. (Author's collection)

tuguese (1990), German (1994), Japanese (2002), and Korean (2003).[616]) By 1951, sales had reached over half a million copies, and by 1954, a total of 750,000 copies had been sold.[617] A condensed version of the book appeared in the December 1956 issue of the British magazine *Home*, under the title "The Big Miracle," and a special illustrated edition by the Franklin Printing Company was issued in 1959, probably to coincide with the TV movie version that came out that year. The book was available in paperback throughout the 1960s and 1970s.

An impressive history by any standard, Davies's book has basically been in print ever since it was first published in 1947. Beginning in the 1980s, perhaps resulting from the popularity of the film's home video release, it has been republished at an almost dizzying rate. Davies had always wanted to do a nicely illustrated version of his book, but that never happened during his lifetime. In 1984, Davies's widow Elizabeth helped to make that "unfulfilled dream" come true, and with the help of artist Tomie dePaola, published a new illustrated edition.[618] Every few years, a new edition has surfaced, including children's books, novelizations of the 1994 John Hughes movie, and, in 2001, even a facsimile edition of the original 1947 book, which has been reissued several times since.

Since it was first published in 1947, *Miracle on 34th Street* has had an astounding publishing history, with upwards of fifty different editions and adaptations. The following list constitutes the most significant among them.

1947 First edition. Hardcover. Dust jacket features an illustration of a fireplace and other Christmas motifs on the front, with illustrations of Gimbels and Macy's and an ad for the film on the back. New York: Harcourt, Brace & Company. 120 pages.

1947 First edition, second printing. Hardcover. Under Davies's direction, the font for the letter written by Susan on page 104 is different from the one used for the first printing.

1947 Book-of-the-Month Club edition. Hardcover. Dust jacket features an illustration of a fireplace and other Christmas motifs on the front, with "So You Don't Believe in Santa Claus? The Critics Do!" and book reviews on the back. There were 440,000 copies of this edition printed, making it the most common of the early editions. New York: Harcourt, Brace & Company. 120 pages.

1950 French edition. Paperback. *Le Miracle de la 34e Rue* [Miracle on 34th Street]. "Les Meilleurs Romans Étrangers" [The best foreign novels] is printed across the top of the front cover, and "Traduit par Suzanne Pairault" [translated by Suzanne Pairault] is printed at the bottom. This was the first foreign-language edition. Paris: Hachette. 184 pages.

1952 Pocket Books edition, first printing. Paperback. Front cover features an illustration of Santa Claus surrounded by children, with number "903" in the upper left corner and the parade and balloons on the back. Illustrations by Frederick E. Banbery. This was the first paperback edition in English. New York: Pocket Books. 117 pages.

1953 Australian edition. Hardcover. Title changed to *There Is a Santa Claus*, with *Miracle on 34th Street* used as a subtitle. Front cover features an illustration of Santa Claus and a reindeer. Illustrations by Frank Hodgkinson. Issued with special mailing wrapper. This was Davies's favorite edition of his book. Sydney: Dymock's Book Arcade. 120 pages.

1959 Franklin Printing limited edition. Hardcover. Cover features an illustration of Santa Claus and snowflakes. Illustrations by James Reid. Limited numbered edition privately printed "outside of commerce" for select distribution. Primos, Pennsylvania: Franklin Printing Company. 85 pages.

1984 Illustrated edition. Hardcover. Dust jacket has illustration of Santa Claus with MACY'S written behind him on the front and a quote from Elizabeth Davies on the back. Introduction by Elizabeth S. Davies. Illustrations by Tomie dePaola. San Diego: Harcourt Brace Jovanovich. 118 pages.

1991 Harvest/HBJ illustrated gift edition. Paperback. Cover features an image of Natalie Wood and Edmund Gwenn from the 1947 film. Contains several stills from the film. This was the first edition to use images from the 1947 film. San Diego: Harcourt Brace Jovanovich. 144 pages.

2001 Facsimile of first edition. Hardcover. Includes a "Historical Note" by Anna Marlis Burgard and "A Note about Re-creating the Original Edition." The back inner flap contains a picture and biography of Valentine Davies. The font used for the second printing of the first edition was retained for the letter written by Susan on page 104. San Diego: Harcourt. 125 pages.

Before television provided the means to see reruns of movies on a regular basis, the most common way for people to experience a movie again was through dramatizations on the radio. During the 1940s, the "biggest, most important, most expensive drama anthology program on radio" at the time was the *Lux Radio Theatre* ("Lux" was a brand of soap made by Lever Brothers), hosted by William Keighley.[619] The show, which had been on the air for well over a decade, offered one-hour adaptations of popular Hollywood movies, and the producers were often able to get the original stars to appear. The shows were recorded live with an orchestra, and before a real audience. Although first approached by the *Ford Theater* to do an adaptation, the studio ended up going with *Lux*.[620] All four of the principal stars were available to appear, but, surprisingly, none of the supporting cast. The licensing agreement required a fee of $1,000 and a stipulation for an on-air announcement for the studio's new Tyrone Power picture, *Captain from Castile* (1947).[621] *Miracle* aired for the first time as a radio drama on Monday, December 22, 1947, on CBS.

The broadcast (episode #595) was scheduled for an hour, but the actual story only lasted for about forty-five minutes, with the ancillary content taking up the remaining fifteen minutes. Despite the run time being less than half of the original movie, writer Lance Arthur Smith was able to keep the story very much intact. The changes made were fairly insignificant; for example, instead of Fred inviting Kris to stay with him, it is Doris who arranges it; Doris is not at the court hearing, and so Kris goes back to Macy's to tell her about the outcome; and Susan's dream house is brand-new, with no previous occupants. Smith did throw in one fun detail about Kris's cane: During the competency test with

---

CAST OF THE 1947 *LUX RADIO THEATRE*[713]

Maureen O'Hara (Doris Walker)
John Payne (Fred Gailey)
Edmund Gwenn (Kris Kringle)
Natalie Wood (Susan Walker)
Joseph Kearns (Dr. Sawyer)
Alan Reed (Mr. Macy)
William Johnstone (Mr. Mara)
Herbert Butterfield (Judge Harper)
Herbert Rawlinson
Gil Stratton Jr.
Jack Carrington
Robert Griffin
Louise Fitch
Johnny McGovern
Sarah Berner
Stanley Farrar
Eddie Marr
Herbert Vigran
June Whitley
Phillip Bernard
Norma Jean Nilsson
John Milton Kennedy (announcer)
Barbara Lyon (intermission guest)
Louis Silvers (music)

Mr. Sawyer, Kris tells him, "I carved this cane out of a runner from one of my old sleighs."

The show was divided into three fifteen-minute acts, with commercials in between, and a "curtain call" with the stars. The commercial breaks artfully use Hollywood gossip to sell soap. The announcers begin with some banter about being at a cast party and running into Laraine Day, who talked about her new film, RKO's *Tycoon* (1947), with John Wayne, and also chatting with Rosalind Russell about her new period film, *Mourning Becomes Electra*. The announcers then discuss how soiled Rosalind's socks became during the filming, but luckily, they came clean with the use of Lux soap flakes! The second commercial break featured aspiring actress Barbara Bebe Lyon as the intermission guest, who had been visiting Celeste Holm on the set of *Gentleman's Agreement* at TCF. The two were having tea when Gregory Peck's dog came into the dressing room, bumping Celeste's elbow and causing some cream to spill on her outfit. But luckily, the studio wardrobe department uses Lux, and so stains like this are of no concern! During the "curtain call," the

Miracle on 34th Street would be adapted three times for *The Lux Radio Theatre*. This ad, featuring Twentieth Century-Fox star June Haver, is promoting the film *Summer Lightning* (aka *Scudda Hoo! Scudda Hay!*) which Natalie Wood filmed right after *Miracle*. (Author's collection)

cast chats briefly. John Payne lets everyone know that Edmund Gwenn was actually Macy's Santa Claus in the parade, to which Gwenn replies, "I've been Santa Claus so much, I'm beginning to really believe in myself!" Natalie Wood comes across as particularly cute. As contractually agreed, there was a plug for the film *Captain from Castile*.

The success of the 1947 broadcast brought another invitation to appear on the *Lux Radio Theatre* the following year, on December 20, 1948 (episode #637). All of the principals came back, with the exception of Natalie Wood, who was replaced by Marlene Aames. [622] The same script used in the 1947 show was used again. The commercials followed the same format, promoting Lux as the laundry soap of choice for the beautiful pajamas worn by Marta Toren in the new Universal film, *Rogues' Regiment* (1948). The intermission guest was Helena Sorrell, head dramatic coach at TCF, who marvels at how many things the wardrobe department washes with Lux, while plugging the new Betty Grable/Dan Dailey musical, *When My Baby Smiles at Me* (1948). There is also instruction on how to use Lux flakes to flock your Christmas tree.

One notable change to the 1948 Lux script is the line about Daniel D. Tompkins. In the film and in the 1947 broadcast, Kris incorrectly states that Tompkins was the vice president under John Quincy Adams, which he was not; he was the vice president under James Monroe. It was John C. Calhoun who was the vice president under John Quincy Adams. Apparently, someone finally pointed out this error and it was corrected.

The "curtain call" contains some fun banter between the cast. Gwenn declares: "If everyone believed in Santa Claus, peace would break out all over the world in thirty seconds," a nice thought for a world still recovering from the war. Maureen O'Hara chimes in with "I hope you won't be too busy to stop at my house. I'll have my stockings hung up," to which Gwenn gives a somewhat saucy reply: "I'll stop in, Maureen, but it seems rather futile: I couldn't possibly fill her stockings as well as she does." The program closed with plugs for the following week's show, an adaptation of TCF's *The Luck of the Irish* (1948), with Edmund Gwenn's cousin, Cecil Kellaway, as a leprechaun. There were also plugs for the studio's psychiatric hospital drama, *The Snake Pit* (1949), MGM's Lorenz and Hart biopic, *Words and Music* (1949), and John Payne's new Western at Paramount, *El Paso* (1949).

On December 23, 1949, *Miracle* again appeared as a radio drama but on the *Screen Directors' Playhouse* on NBC, which (much like the *Lux* show) featured adaptations of popular films, with closing remarks by the film's director and stars. It was sponsored by Macy's and publisher Simon & Schuster, who provided, respectively, Christmas stockings and children's books to the five hundred children in the studio audience. This adaptation differed substantially from the 1947 and 1948 *Lux Radio Theatre* plays, in that Edmund Gwenn was the only actor from the movie to appear in the cast, courtesy of MGM (where he was under contract). In addition, the story was trimmed considerably to fit a thirty-minute airtime. Surprisingly, the entire Thanksgiving Day parade scene was cut (Kris just walks into Macy's and asks for a job), and other scenes were reduced to the bare minimum of dialogue, to keep the story moving. During the courtroom scene, Fred allows Kris to give his own defense, and he delivers this poignant soliloquy:

> *Christmas [is] timeless and unchanging with the same deeper meaning it always has. Same summons to all men to have faith, not in any one faith, but to have faith in themselves, in mankind, in each other. Because if all the earth be laid in ruins, and all our yesterdays and all man's wonders become smoke and ashes, and man remains, well, then everything remains. For all we have on earth that matters is each other. And that's what Christmas is: a time for unselfishness, a time for each other, for goodwill and understanding, and deep respect for all our fellow men. Christmas isn't just once a year, Christmas is always; flowering, let's say, in late December. To the purest minds and the most immaculate souls among us, I mean the little children, he is Santa Claus because they believe he is, and that's good enough for me, Mr. Macy. That's good enough for me.*

In 1950, *Miracle* was brought back to the *Screen Directors' Playhouse* for a one-hour adaptation airing on December 21. Again, Edmund Gwenn was the only original cast member to return. The show was sponsored by RCA Victor (promoting their new television sets), Anacin pain reliever, and Bing Crosby and Bob Hope, promoting Chesterfield cigarettes (which must have bothered some parents, since the show was aimed at children!). The longer format provided enough time to tell the entire story in three acts, but there are some interesting variations to the storyline. In the courtroom scene, Kris conducts the examination of Thomas Mara Jr., and speaks most of the lines that belonged to Fred in the movie; but his eloquent speech on the meaning of Christmas was not repeated for this performance. The romance is a little more central, with a scene (taken from the book version) of Fred giving Doris an engagement ring. At the end, it is Fred who shows Susan a picture of her dream house and announces that he has an option to buy it if she and her mother want to move in. The music soundtrack was updated, with Leroy Anderson's then-new song "Sleigh Ride" heard during the parade scenes. One perplexing musical decision was the choice of "The Boar's Head Carol," which dates from the English Renaissance, for the opening sequence.

The 1950 radio broadcast on the *Screen Directors' Playhouse* featured commercials with Bing Crosby and Bob Hope advertising Chesterfield cigarettes. (Author's collection)

In private correspondence in 1951, Valentine Davies expressed his surprise at the popularity of his story: "I daresay you realize how rare it is for a motion picture to be revived at all, and I am sure that very few, if any, other film stories have been the bases of as many repeated radio broadcasts."[623] He probably was equally surprised when the State Department's radio program *Voice of America* requested permission to do a radio broadcast in Hebrew to air in Israel during the holiday season that year.[624]

There would be a three-year hiatus before *Miracle* was revived on American radio, this time brought back to the *Lux Radio Theatre* airing on NBC on December 21, 1954, as episode #902. For the third time, Edmund Gwenn would be the only original cast member to be featured. The show used the same script as the 1947 and 1948 broadcasts and, other than being hosted by Irving Cummings, was pretty much the same. This broadcast would mark the waning influence of radio as the nation literally turned its eyes to television. *Lux Radio Theatre*, after a twenty-year run, would end—but did continue on TV as the *Lux Video Theatre*.

On the other side of the world, there was another one-off radio show broadcast that year in Australia. It starred actor Tom Farley, who would go on to have a long career in Australian television, as Kris Kringle. Produced by E. Mason Wood, it aired the day after Christmas on the AW network as part of *The Caltex Theatre*.[625] The show was so popular that the station requested permission to do it again in 1955. The request, however, was denied, because of the TV movie that was going to be made for *The Twentieth Century-Fox Hour* later that year. TCF felt that any other adaptation might interfere with the promotion of the TV movie if the studio decided to broadcast it in Australia.[626]

In 2016, the San Diego Musical Theatre commissioned and staged *Miracle on 34th Street: A Live Musical Radio Play* with original music and lyrics by Jon Lorenz. The script was based on the 1947 *Lux Radio Theatre* show by Lance Arthur Smith.[627]

1955 TV Movie

The successful radio adaptations of *Miracle* paved the way for a television adaptation. Although the movie studios had initially feared the competition from television, by the mid-1950s, they had decided that if they couldn't beat 'em, they would join 'em, and so started providing content for broadcast. To make that foray into television, *The Twentieth Century-Fox Hour* was created. The series, hosted by Joseph Cotten and sponsored by General Electric, consisted mostly of one-hour adaptations of the studio's famous films. It alternated each week with another dramatic anthology series, *The U.S. Steel Hour*.[628]

The Miracle on 34th Street ("The" was added to the title for unknown reasons) was announced in late September of 1955, went into production in early October at the studio's Western Avenue lot, and aired as the sixth episode in the series on CBS on Wednesday, December 14, 1955, at 10:00 p.m. Eastern time (which probably kept a lot of children from seeing it, since it was on a school night!).[629]

Macy's and Gimbels enthusiastically participated and reprised their roles in the show. They also helped out with the advertising.. A week before the show aired, a sign went up on Macy's Herald Square store stating: "This Way to Gimbels" and "When Macy's Tells Gimbels, It's the Miracle on 34th Street." Gimbels, likewise, had a sign pointing the way to Macy's.[630] The two stores also placed a huge, two-page joint ad in the *New York Times* to promote the show and poke fun at their rivalry.[631] The other nod to reality was the inclusion of a real newspaper, for the first time in the franchise's history, the *Daily News*,—but they only got permission for that one paper, so the other featured newspaper, the *New York Chronicle*, was still fictitious.

The cast was solid, with the role of Kris Kringle going to Thomas Mitchell, who had become one of Hollywood's preeminent character actors with such roles as Scarlett O'Hara's father in *Gone with the Wind* (1939), Doc Boone in *Stagecoach* (1939), and Uncle Billy in *It's a Wonderful Life* (1946). He had recently become the second person to win the "Triple Crown of Acting," having received an Oscar, a Tony, and an Emmy (the first was Helen Hayes just a month before). In interpreting the role, Mitchell said he was trying "to play the Peter Pan of Santa Clauses," which explains his exuberance in the portrayal. [632]

The role of Doris went to perky Teresa Wright, who had found great success in Hollywood in the early 1940s (she had received Oscar nominations for each of her first three films), and had continued her success in the new medium of television on the various "playhouse" shows. She was reunited with Macdonald Carey, who played Fred, her co-star from *Shadow of a Doubt* (1943) a decade earlier. Carey would go on to become one of the mainstays of the long-running soap opera *Days of Our Lives*.

Susan was played by Sandy Descher, who, despite her young age, already had an impressive résumé, with roles in dramas such as *The Bad and the Beautiful* (1953) and *The Last Time I Saw Paris* (1954), and in the sci-fi classic *Them!* (1954). Ray Collins, who would soon be known to television audiences as Lieutenant Tragg on *Perry Mason*, played Judge Harper.

One other cast member of note is Herbert Heyes, who reprised his role as Mr. Gimbel, the only actor from the 1947 film to appear in this version. Since this was only eight years after the original film was made, several members of the production staff of the original film were still employees at the studio, and were also involved in this adaptation. These included cinematographer Lloyd Ahern, wardrobe director Charles LeMaire, and makeup man Ben Nye.

Veteran actor Thomas Mitchell was cast as Kris Kringle in *The Twentieth Century-Fox Hour* production of *Miracle*. Here he is with Earl Robie and Sandy Descher, who played Susan. (Photofes)t

John Monks Jr., who adapted the screenplay, had to cut the story in half to fit the allotted forty-five minute run time (there were six minutes of commercials, a six-minute behind-the-scenes tour of the TCF studio, and a three-minute spot on the studio's coming theatrical attractions), which is probably why the whole show feels rushed.[633] Overall, his screenplay includes all the major plot points, with one exception: He included the episode from Davies's original story, involving Dr. Sawyer giving a lecture on "Exploring the Myth of Santa Claus." Monks changes this scenario so that Sawyer is giving the lecture following Susan's school Christmas play, instead of at an employee lecture, and Doris and Susan are present in the audience. The battery occurs when Sawyer pronounces that "only stupid old men prancing around in white whiskers keep this ridiculous myth alive," and Kris comes out and hits him with his cane.

Monks made a few other minor changes. He included the venison story that had been deleted from the 1947 film. He also changed the post office's involvement. Instead of a postal employee coming up with the idea, Doris is the one who calls the postmaster and suggests that he deliver all the Santa letters in the dead-letter files to the courthouse. Another interesting small change (which is in the original story) is that Susan's dream house is discovered on the way to the Christmas Day party at the Brooks' Home, rather than on the way back. The screenplay adaptation was deemed successful enough to be nominated for the "Best Television Adaptation" Emmy that year.[634]

If nothing else, this version is an interesting look at how the movie studios were creating lower-cost productions for television. As TCF started going more and more on location for feature films like *Three Coins in the Fountain* (1954) (many scenes shot in Rome), the soundstages and backlot sets were getting used less and less—but they suddenly found new life as the backdrops for TV shows. Instead of going to New York, the 1955 *Miracle* uses the studio's "Old New York Street" for Kris to wander down in the opening scene; the TCF prop building served as the receiving area at Macy's; and "Suburban Street" on the backlot was the address of Susan's dream house. The production also economized by using some footage from the 1947 film, such as the shots of the parade, the panning shot of Gimbels and Macy's, some of the interior shots of Macy's, some of the insert shots of the newspapers, and the interior of the post office. All of these economies would become standard practice as TCF moved forward in television production.

The show was well received. *Variety* and the *Los Angeles Times* thought it was the best installment of *The Twentieth Century-Fox Hour* so far, because the story could be effectively trimmed down without losing too much of the plot, unlike some of the other adaptations of the studio's feature films. The *Variety* review stated that it was "slick without being brittle, warm without being slushy, and comic without being condescending," and gave much of this credit to director Robert Stevenson.[635] Incidentally, Stevenson, who had become one of television's top directors, would join forces with Walt Disney just a year later and become a star director there, beginning with his production of *Johnny Tremain* (1957).[636] He would go on to direct *Old Yeller* (1958), *The Absent-Minded Professor* (1961), *Mary Poppins* (1964), *That Darn Cat* (1965), and *The Love Bug* (1969), among others—almost every major live-action

Even though just forty-five minutes long, the 1955 TV movie was released theatrically outside the United States. Here is a poster from its release in Australia. (Author's collection)

hit the Disney studio made in the 1950s and 1960s.[637]

A few newspapers across the country printed a review which declared this version to be "an improvement over the original movie," because the condensed story "made it brighter and less saccharine."[638] The *Los Angeles Times*'s critic Walter Ames was also duly impressed. He hadn't seen the 1947 film, but declared, "If the movie version was any better than the TV version, it must have been a monumental work of drama."[639] Though few who have seen the original would agree with Ames, the Stevenson version does retain the flavor of the original and keeps much of the story intact. Future adaptations would not be so respectful.

Apparently it was one of the few times Thomas Mitchell actually watched his own films, something he normally did not do, feeling that "being disguised behind those whiskers, I might take a chance."[640] Somewhat surprisingly, this TV movie was released theatrically in Australia and in the UK as part of double feature bills.[641] Starting in 1958, it was retitled "Meet Mr. Kringle" when *The Twentieth Century-Fox Hour* went into syndication as *Hour of Stars*, probably to avoid confusion with the 1947 film that was also in syndication by then.[642]

CAST AND CREW OF THE 1955 TV MOVIE

CAST

Macdonald Carey (Fred Gaily [*sic*])
Teresa Wright (Doris Walker)
Thomas Mitchell (Kris Kringle)
Sandy Descher (Susan Walker)
Hans Conried (Mr. Shellhammer)
Ray Collins (Judge Harper)
Dick Foran (Thomas Mara)
John Abbott (Dr. Sawyer)
Don Beddoe (Mr. Macy)
Whit Bissell (Dr. Pierce)
Sara Berner (Woman Shopper)
Herbert Vigran (Postal Clerk)
Maudie Prickett (Miss Prossy)
Paul Smith (Store Clerk)
Herbert Hayes [his name is misspelled in the credits; it should have been "Heyes"] (Mr. Gimbel)
Louis Towers (Peter)
Earl Robie (Thomas Mara Jr.)

CREW

Director: Robert Stevenson
Producer: Jules Bricken
Writer: John Monks Jr., based on the screenplay by George Seaton, from a story by Valentine Davies
Director of photography: Lloyd Ahern
Art direction: Lyle Wheeler; Herman A. Blumenthal
Editorial supervision: Art Seid, ACE
Assistant director: Ed Bernoudy
Sound recording: E. C. Ward
Set decoration: Walter Scott, Ray Moyer
Wardrobe: Charles LeMaire
Women's wardrobe: Adele Balkan
Men's wardrobe: Richard James
Makeup: Ben Nye, Stanley Orr
Hair styling: Marsha Masa
Script supervisor: Pat Lamb

The second television movie was a live broadcast produced by Talent Associates and sponsored by Westclox that aired on Friday, November 27, 1959, the day after Thanksgiving, as part of NBC's *Special Tonight* series. It was in color, which was indicative of a prestige production, since color television was still in its infancy. The series, like *The Twentieth Century-Fox Hour*, was part of an anthology of one-hour adaptations of popular movies and other presentations.[643]

Macy's participated in the production and was prominently featured in the opening sequence, as the store where Kris tells the window dresser that the reindeer are in the wrong order. Macy's and Ideal provided the toys for the sets. The show was advertised during the Macy's Thanksgiving Day Parade, and even got a special plug from the star of the show, Ed Wynn, when he "stopped by" to chat with host Bill Wendell during the coverage. Susan Gordon (who played Susan) remembered the dress rehearsal taking place later that day in a studio located above a deli, with the smell of potato knishes wafting up through the floor. Apparently, food was on her mind, because she also remembered that the cast did not have a real Thanksgiving dinner, but instead (and somewhat appropriately) had TV dinners served to them in their dressing rooms.[644]

The show had a dependable cast. Ed Wynn, best known for playing Uncle Albert in *Mary Poppins* (1964) a few years later, got top billing as Kris Kringle. He played the role as a bumbling and goofy Santa, leaving little question of his doddering condition (he carries around a plastic candy cane). Television veterans Mary Healy

Miracle got its second TV movie adaptation in 1959, starring Ed Wynn as Kris Kringle. The show was performed live and broadcast in color. For decades, no recording was known to exist until a kinescope surfaced at the Library of Congress in 2005. (Author's collection)

A **TV GUIDE** CLOSE-UP 8:30 ② ③ ⑤ ⑥ ⑪ ⑫ ⑬ MIRACLE ON 34th STREET

SPECIAL **COLOR** Macy's is delighted with its new Santa, a jolly gent who claims to be old Kris Kringle himself. Then the store's executives learn a shocking fact—Kris has been recommending that customers buy their Christmas gifts at other New York City stores.

Harry Muheim wrote this one-hour adaptation of the 1947 movie, which starred Edmund Gwenn, Maureen O'Hara and John Payne. William Corrigan directs. (Live)

Cast

Kris Kringle	Ed Wynn
Fred Gailey	Peter Lind Hayes
Doris	Mary Healy
Susan	Susan Gordon
Sawyer	Orson Bean
Shellhammer	Loring Smith
Mr. Macy	Hiram Sherman
District Attorney	Larry Weber
Judge	John Gibson

The *Miracle on 34th Street* 1959 TV movie got a half-page in the November 21 issue of *TV Guide*. (Author's collection)

and real-life husband Peter Lind Hayes were cast as Doris and Fred. They come across as perhaps a bit bland, but don't detract; part of the problem could be that the condensed story doesn't allow much time to develop the romance between them. Relative newcomer Susan Gordon is more cute than skeptical as daughter Susan, but does fine in the role. Orson Bean as Dr. Sawyer gives a caricature performance which is a bit over-the-top.

Since the show was live, the action was confined to a television studio, with no exterior or on location shots; for example, the "parade scene" shows Fred and Susan at a window with sounds of the passing parade. Incidentally, the music heard during that scene—predictably, a big, brassy Sousa-esque march—was recorded and released on Columbia by Spencer Ross as "Thanksgiving Day Parade" and was the flipside to his hit instrumental song, "Tracy's Theme" (and the music heard over the opening and closing credits titled "Hop, Skip, Jump" also got released on his self-titled 1960 album as well).[645]

Once again, the story was abridged to fit the hour-long time slot, but this time, much was excised. Lots of the supporting characters, such as Alfred and Charlie Halloran, were not included. As with all of the adaptations, several things in the script were unnecessarily changed: instead of wishing for a house, Susan asks Kris for a large Christmas tree, and that her mother

Real-life husband and wife Peter Lind Hayes and Mary Healy played the roles of Fred and Doris. In line with the 1947 screenplay, Doris's apartment is given a modern decor. Susan Gordon played Susan. (Photofest)

In a rare move, the "Thanksgiving Day Parade" music from the 1959 *Miracle* TV movie was recorded and released by Spencer Ross as the flip side to "Tracy's Theme," which climbed the Billboard charts to #13 in early 1960. "Tracy's Theme" was from the soundtrack of a TV adaptation of *The Philadelphia Story*. (Author's collection)

In the 1959 TV movie, the Christmas Day scenes are replaced by Kris mysteriously appearing and disappearing from Susan's bedroom on Christmas Eve, complicating the question of "Is he or isn't he?" Ed Wynn played Kris and Susan Gordon played Susan. (Photofest)

and Fred will marry; Dr. Sawyer's son and wife are the ones that discover Kris is sending people to Gimbels instead of Mr. Shellhammer; Kris hits Dr. Sawyer with his cane because he won't let him out of his office, and so forth.

The show got good reviews. *Variety* compared it favorably to, and in the vein of, the 1897 editorial, "Yes, Virginia, there is a Santa Claus," and noted that Wynn gave a "believable" performance and kept the sentiment from getting "too mushy."[646] *The Hollywood Reporter* gushed quite a bit more, raving about Wynn's performance, the "brilliantly played smaller parts," the "excellent abridgement," and the "direction [that] avoided all temptations to go cutie-pie."[647] The latter review seems a bit excessive. Overall, the production is fine, but in no way eclipses the original.

One major drawback (which is not mentioned in the reviews) is that this version pushes the story into the realm of fantasy more than it should. For example, when Kris meets Fred for the first time, Kris already knows his name. Susan questions this, and he replies, "I just thought of it—imagination." How could he know this unless he really is Santa Claus? In the final scene, it's Christmas Eve, and Susan has just told Doris that she doesn't believe in Santa, and goes to bed upset. Kris then appears in her bedroom in his full regalia, with no explanation about how he got there. He tells Susan to peek out her bedroom door, where she sees Doris and Fred kissing, which revives her faith in him. He then mysteriously disappears. Again, how could he do this unless he really is Santa Claus? These questions are never answered, suggesting that he truly is a magical Santa.

One aspect that added to the show's attempt at realism was the inclusion of several real New York newspapers during the legal hearing scenes. Some of the newspapers that had declined to participate in the 1947 theatrical film had changed their minds and now allowed their mastheads to appear on the fictional news stories, including the *New York World-Telegram* and the New York *Daily News*. They didn't succeed in convincing the *New York Times* to have their paper featured, but they did get one additional paper, the *New York Herald-Tribune*, to agree to be featured.

The show was broadcast live, which was a bit of an anomaly by 1959—most producers had learned that filming productions paved the way for perpetual reruns—and in fact, this show featured one of the perils of doing a live show, when Ed Wynn stumbled over his lines as he starts talking to the little Dutch girl. For decades, no recording of the show was known to exist. Luckily, the TCF legal files explain the reason why. Talent Associates had paid a $55,000 licensing fee to do a one-time live broadcast of *Miracle*, and the contract allowed for it to be filmed for delayed and possible additional broadcasts within a thirty-day period.[648] After that period elapsed, TCF had the option to buy the program and assume all rights associated with it. If the option was not exercised, which apparently it was not, Talent Associates was supposed to destroy the recording.[649] This was understood to be the program's fate.

However, in 2005, Richard Finegan reported that he went searching through the inventory of a large collection that NBC had donated to the Library of Congress and found that a kinescope did exist.[650] This is probably not the official film made to potentially sell to TCF (it is in black-and-white), but it was probably recorded as part of a station's routine by someone who was not aware of the contract. After almost half a century, this version was made available, and Susan Gordon, who had never seen the show, finally got to see her performance for the first time.[651]

CAST AND CREW OF THE 1959 TV MOVIE

CAST	CREW
CAST	**CREW**
Ed Wynn (Kris Kringle)	Producer: David Susskind
Peter Lind Hayes (Fred Galey [*sic*])	Director: William Corrigan
Mary Healy (Doris Walker)	Adapted for television by Harry Muheim, based on a screenplay by George Seaton and a story by Valentine Davies
Orson Bean (William Sawyer)	Associate producer: Jacqueline Babbin
Loring Smith (Mr. Shellhammer)	Sets: Burr Smidt
Hiram Sherman (Mr. Macy)	Production supervisor: Renee Valente
Susan Gordon (Susan Walker)	Casting director: Liam Dunn
Lawrence Weber (Mr. Mara)	Unit manager: Richard K. Swicker
John Gibson (Judge Harper)	Technical director: O. Tamburri
Joey Walsh (Al)	Associate director: Marcia Kuyper
Arnie Freeman (Lou)	Lighting director: Leo Farrenkopf
William Post Jr. (Mr. Gimbel)	Music: Binny
Shirley Eggleston (Peter's mother)	Costumes: John Boxer
Frank Daly (The Bailiff)	Makeup: Dick Smith
William Griffis (First Santa Claus)	Hairstyles: Virginia Darcy
	Audio: Jim Blaney
	Video: Tony Nelle
	Toys courtesy of R. H. Macy Company and Ideal Toy Corporation

As early as 1954, TCF was investigating the possibility of turning *Miracle* into a musical.[652] TCF had long been the leader in Hollywood for musical productions, the studio of choice for such

Columbia released the *Here's Love* soundtrack as a deluxe album with a gatefold cover, copious liner notes, and a photo insert. It was supposed to be the big seller for the Christmas season of 1963, but it floundered. (Author's collection)

Broadway luminaries as Irving Berlin and Rodgers and Hammerstein, so it's not surprising that such discussions took place. Soon after the movie had been released, there had been inquiries about releasing an amateur theater script so that schools, churches, and community theaters could perform *Miracle* as a play. As the author of the book, Valentine Davies was constantly being asked about these theatrical rights, and was supportive of the venture, hoping that his son-in-law Richard Bracken would be allowed to do the play adaptation.[653] But since Davies had sold all of his interest in his story, he could only forward the requests to TCF. On at least one occasion, in the late 1940s, the studio did grant amateur performance rights to the Black Hawk Broadcasting Company (a school radio program) in Waterloo, Iowa. This entailed the rights to broadcast a one-off radio dramatization on KWWL.[654]

Year after year, the requests became so voluminous that Julian Johnson at TCF felt his file of accumulated letters and memos on the subject "would do credit to the negotiations for the purchase of the New York Central Railroad."[655] But the amateur version never came into being, for a couple of reasons. First, Davies and Seaton had approached publisher Samuel French, but were deterred by the demand for a 30 percent fee instead of the usual 20 percent.[656] More importantly, however, TCF was concerned that if an amateur version were released, it would undoubtedly be very popular, and would ultimately dilute the cachet of *Miracle* too much. Lew Schreiber stated unequivocally, "In the event that we ever wanted to develop the property into a musical, too wide and free use of the amateur dramatic rights would [make] further film development useless."[657]

It would be almost another decade before a musical version of *Miracle* emerged. The songwriting honors would ultimately go to the talented Meredith Willson, who had brought turn-of-the-century small-town Iowa to the stage in the form of *The Music Man*, and made it one of the biggest hits on Broadway in the 1950s.

Willson, born in 1902, was a gifted musician as a child and learned to play the piano, flute, and piccolo. After graduating from high school, he headed off to New York to attend the Institute of Musical Art (later renamed Juilliard), and by the early 1920s, he was touring the world with John Philip Sousa's band. He returned to New York and was first flutist in the New York Philharmonic under Arturo Toscanini for several years before heading to the West Coast in 1929, where he would be the conductor of the Seattle Symphony and work as a musical director for the American Broadcasting System for the Northwest. He then took a job as a music director for NBC in San Francisco, but continued to hop up and down the West Coast, conducting orchestras in Seattle, San Francisco, and Los Angeles.

NBC transferred Willson to Los Angeles, and he ended up being the musical director for the radio show *Maxwell House Coffee Time*. While there, he also scored films and received two Oscar nominations for his work on *The Great Dictator* (1941) and *The Little Foxes* (1941). During World War II, he joined the service and advanced to the rank of major, serving as head of the music division for the Armed Forces Radio Service.

Upon his return to civilian life, Willson continued working in radio and succeeded in getting his own radio shows, and even got his own television show in 1949. In addition to his film scores, Willson showed his amazing versatility by composing symphonies, commercial jingles for Jell-O and Canada Dry, and pop songs, including hits of the early 1940s, such as "You and I," made popular by Glenn Miller, and "Two in Love," a hit for Tommy Dorsey and young vocalist Frank Sinatra. His two most popular songs, which date from the early 1950s, are "May the Good Lord Bless You and Keep You" and "It's Beginning to Look Like Christmas" (the original title omitted the words "a Lot"). He is known to a couple generations of American schoolchildren for the song "Chicken Fat," which was the theme song for the youth fitness program initiated by President Kennedy in the early 1960s. Recorded by Robert Preston, it was a staple of physical education for decades in elementary schools. He was also an author of several books, as well, which included memoirs (*And There I Stood with My Piccolo; But He Doesn't Know the Territory*), a novel (*Who Did What to Fedalia?*), and advice for the musically inclined (*What Every Musician Should Know*). In short, Willson was an incredibly accomplished man, and as the author of one of the preeminent examples of pure Americana in the form of *The Music Man*, he seemed to be the perfect composer for adapting a classic film into a musical.

The Music Man was still playing on Broadway when Willson's follow-up hit, *The Unsinkable Molly Brown*, opened on Broadway in the fall of 1960. Both properties had attracted the attention of Hollywood; Warner Bros. had received the film rights for *The Music Man*, while several other studios were vying for *Molly*. With these two properties well on their way to the entertainment hall of fame, Willson started looking for a new project. He had been working on a backstage-themed musical called *The Understudy* in the spring of 1961, and even made a press announcement about it at the end of September. But shortly thereafter, the opportunity to adapt *Miracle* came up, and he apparently completely lost interest in *The Understudy*. Willson later said that he and producer Stuart Ostrow were looking for source material for a new musical and kept saying to each other, "If we could only find something a little off the ground—like *Miracle on 34th Street*," and kept looking around, until they decided to just do an adaptation of *Miracle* instead of trying to find something like it.[658]

Willson, however, had some doubts. Like Valentine Davies, he knew that the romantic relationship would be key to the success of the show, but wondered whether it would be robust enough to carry a musical. More importantly, he pondered, was the story already too dated; "would the space age—the age of disillusionment, of teenage gangsterism, of the assaulting of teachers and policemen, of jail sentences and pregnancies as Junior High status symbols—accept with any interest a story of a man who thinks he's Santa Claus?" The more he thought about it, the more he doubted he could make it work.

As he was getting ready to retire the idea, he was prompted to look up a quote from *Romeo and Juliet* that he had included in one of his outlines. He pulled out a book of Shakespeare that had belonged to his mother, and tucked inside was a newspaper clipping from long ago that read:

> *I hate these up-to-date, conscientious parents who insist on telling their children that Santa Claus is a myth. Of course, Santa Claus is a myth, but it is the most beautiful and sweetest myth that ever found place in rhyme and story. . . . [I]t has been revised and improved upon to suit steam-heated apartments, but it enchants just the same, and it always will.*

Apparently, this was the catalyst that prompted Willson to follow through with the project. He clearly thought that, by promoting the magic of Christmas, it might help, in some small way, a world beset with problems. This was probably the reason he updated the setting from the 1940s to the 1960s. By the end of November 1961, it was announced that Willson would be adapting *Miracle* into a musical and would write the book, music, and lyrics. TCF would help finance the stage production, share in the profits, and have an option for the film version.[659] As with the original film, they struggled to find an appropriate title, and considered *The Wonderful Plan*; *Wouldn't It Be Wonderful If*; and *Love, Love, Love*, before settling on *Here's Love*.[660]

Here's Love came out at a time when Broadway was starting to recycle Hollywood films as source material for musicals, many of which had begun as theatrical plays and were now coming full circle. Contemporaneous adaptations in the 1963–1964 season included *She Loves Me*, which was based on Frank Capra's 1940 Christmas-themed *The Shop Around the Corner*; *Tovarich*, based on the 1937 comedy of the same name, starring Charles Boyer and Claudette Colbert; *The Girl Who Came to Supper*, which had seen its most recent iteration as 1957's *The Prince and the Showgirl*, with Marilyn Monroe and Laurence Olivier; *110 in the Shade*, inspired by 1957's *The Rainmaker*, with Burt Lancaster and Katharine Hepburn; and *Hello, Dolly!*, based on the 1958 film *The Matchmaker*, with Shirley Booth as Dolly Levi.[661] So the concept of using a popular film like *Miracle* for source material wasn't without precedent.

In adapting *Miracle*, Willson, for the most part, kept the plot much the same as the movie, although he did make some odd changes. It starts with the parade and culminates with the legal hearing, but he altered the story in strange and unnecessary ways. For example, after Susan meets Kris for the first time and pulls his beard and starts to believe in him, Kris destroys it all by suggesting that she ask for one of the plastic alligators that Macy's over-bought for Christmas, which, in turn, crushes her belief. This goes against Kris's character in the movie; he explicitly states that this is something he would never do.

Following this episode, evidently drawing on George Seaton's discarded "anti-commercial" vignettes, Kris breaks into song, admonishing any entity with enmity toward another to stop it, with examples like CBS and NBC, cats and dogs, competing cigarette companies, and Mickey Mouse and Donald Duck—essentially, an effort to encourage love and goodwill rather than the opposite—and then leads everyone out of Macy's to go shopping at Gimbels. With his department store now empty, Mr. Macy is upset. Doris is trying to convince him that this "Here's Love" campaign is a good thing. Willson also changed it to be Mr. Shellhammer who fires Kris, not Doris. As one commentator has noted, in the movie, the goodwill Kris shows to customers by sending them to other stores inadvertently (and unintentionally) helps Macy's become more profitable. In the musical, Kris is encouraging people to shop at Gimbels just to show love. It just doesn't make much sense.[662]

The original Broadway cast of *Here's Love* included, from left to right; Craig Stevens, Janis Paige, and Laurence Naismith. Composer Meredith Willson is sitting in front. (Author's collection)

The other big change was the insertion of a dream sequence after Kris has told Susan about the "Imagine Nation." This takes place in Macy's toy department, when all of the toys come alive, similar to the dream in *The Nutcracker* ballet. We learn in this dream that Susan's birthday falls on Christmas, so she has never had a real birthday party. Several of the toys vie to be Susan's father, but they are all rejected by Doris. Fred then appears, and the dream ends.

Some other odd changes involve Susan's dream house. As Susan and Fred become close, she asks him to be her father, which he refuses, declaring that he will never marry. (Then why did he approach Susan in the first place if he didn't want to meet her mother?) He explains he certainly doesn't want a woman having access to his man-cave-retreat Connecticut farmhouse. He shows Susan a picture of his house, which she asks to keep, but he ultimately only lets her borrow it. At the end, Kris directs everyone to Macy's, where the "dream house" is a furniture display in the store where Doris and Fred kiss and fall in love.

Somewhat surprisingly, Willson also took what had been very sympathetic characters in the film and made them fairly unlikable. Instead of being a romantic, experienced lawyer looking to settle down to family life, Fred is a confirmed bachelor and an ex-marine who likes to gamble and who just got his law degree through a correspondence course. He is also a bit of a misogynist: He calls Doris a "witch" for not believing in Santa Claus, tells Susan in confidence that "Dames don't love anyone but themselves," and makes fun of women for always being late, in his song "She Hadda Go Back." He also comes across as a bit sketchy and creepy. Unlike in the movie, where he meets Susan with permission and under the supervision of Cleo, in *Here's Love*, he first approaches Susan on the street and is miffed when she doesn't respond to him; he then buys her a balloon and takes her to watch the parade. In another scene, he takes Susan to Central Park without telling Doris. Apparently, Willson was oblivious to the idea of "stranger danger," and, at the urging of producer Stuart Ostrow, changed his original idea of Fred taking Susan up on the roof to watch the parade.[663]

The character of Doris is also markedly different from the character in the film. Instead of being a disillusioned woman who is trying to protect her daughter from the unhappiness she has experienced, she comes across as quite unpleasant and controlling. In the bedtime lullaby "You Don't Know" that she sings to Susan, she describes herself as "locked in a nightmare" with a "heart full of hate." The song seems to be threatening Susan in an evil stepmotherly way when she coos, "You don't know what that is [i.e., to believe in a storybook world] and as long as I live / I promise you, you never will," all sung to a soft, lilting tune, making it all the more menacing. Willson also introduces indications of an unbalanced mother–daughter relationship, with Doris addressing Susan as "boss" and "captain" and Susan addressing Doris as "slave" and "crew." Doris also has a dislike of men to match Fred's dislike of women; as one critic observed, "She hates guys and he hates dames, but they get over it."[664] Perhaps Willson made the characters flawed so that he could effect a transformation by the end of the play, but they just come across as unlikable. All of these unnecessary changes ultimately affected the show's reception.

The cast was solid and deliberately chosen. Shirley Jones, who had just starred in the film adaptation of *The Music Man* (1962), was considered for the role of Doris, as was Michele Lee, but Janis Paige won out.[665] Paige, who had been in film and television throughout the 1940s and 1950s, had been the lead in the Broadway musical *The Pajama Game* a decade earlier, but had been out of the limelight long enough that this was considered a vehicle for her comeback. Jason Robards and Lloyd Bridges were both considered for Fred, but Craig Stevens, who had been a private eye on TV in the *Peter Gunn* series, was ultimately chosen, and would make his Broadway debut in the role. Fred Gwynne, who had starred as bumbling policeman Francis Muldoon in the hit TV show, *Car 54, Where Are You?* (which had just finished its run), returned to his theatrical roots in the role of Mr. Shellhammer, just a year before he became even more famous as Herman on *The Munsters*. Relative unknowns Laurence Naismith and Valerie Lee were cast as Kris Kringle and Susan, respectively. One supporting actor of note is David Doyle, who got the part of Mr. Sawyer. A decade later, he would be connected with *Miracle* again, appearing as Mr. Macy in the 1973 TV movie. One of the dancers was Michael Bennett, who would go on to create the huge Broadway hit, *A Chorus Line*.[666]

FASHIONS FEATURED IN *HERE'S LOVE*
AND AVAILABLE FOR PURCHASE AT MACY'S

Ladies' coats by Cuddlecoat
Chorus dresses and ensembles by Junior Sophisticates, Ted Brown, and Sportswhirl
Raincoats by March and Mendl
Millinery by Betmar
Scarves by Glentex
Handbags by Milch
Men's shirts by Eagle
Children's clothing by Joseph Love, O.K. Trouser Manufacturing Company, Northwood
Manufacturing Company, Peggy 'n' Sue Coats, Robert Bruce Sweaters, and Sandler Hats
Leather fashions by Bonnie Cashin of Philip Sills

Inspired by Kay Nelson's intention to use off-the-rack clothes in the original film, costume designer Alvin Colt worked with Macy's to provide many of the costumes. He developed the show's look and then collaborated with Macy's buyers to find clothing that would work, from regular ready-to-wear lines.[667] The result was that audiences not only got to see a Broadway musical, but they also got to see a fashion show, since the featured clothing was available for purchase at Macy's. Some of the brands represented included Cuddlecoat, Junior Sophisticates, Eagle, and Bonnie Cashin. One exception was for the elevator operators and salesclerks, who, in order to add some "pizazz" to the show, got special costumes unlike anything Macy's employees usually wore.

The production started with Norman Jewison as director, but Willson didn't like what he was doing and fired him; he then had producer Stuart Ostrow step in, and do double duty as producer and director.[668] Ironically, just a few years later, Jewison would be nominated for an Oscar for directing the film version of the musical *Fiddler on the Roof* (1971). *Here's Love* was first staged in Detroit at the Fisher Theatre, and opened (just like the movie) in the summer, on July 29, 1963, and did "unprecedented gross" receipts at the box office.[669]

Here's Love then went on to play the National Theatre in Washington, DC, where it was sold out for four weeks.[670] It opened on August 27, which happened to be the night before the big civil rights march in Washington. Opening night was such a "smash" hit that Ostrow let the cast and crew have the next day off so they could attend the rally on the Mall and hear Martin Luther King Jr.'s "I Have a Dream" speech in person.[671] Like the casting of Theresa Harris as Cleo in the film, the stage production took a low-key approach to fighting racism by casting Blacks in race-neutral roles. (The cast ended up being 10 percent Black, the idea being that, racially, it would represent New York City's actual demographics.[672]) It then went to the Shubert Theatre in

Fred (Craig Stevens), Susan and Kris toast Christmas: *Here's Love.*

Fred's hopes rise as he confides in Susan: *My Wish.*

To Kris and Macy it's beginning to look like: *Pine Cones and Holly Berries.*

Fred shows Doris: *Look, Little Girl.*

Some scenes from the Broadway production of *Here's Love* that appeared in the original cast album. Many of the costumes were provided by Macy's and were available for purchase at the store. (Author's collection)

Philadelphia for the last half of September, before opening on October 3, 1963, on Broadway at New York's Shubert Theatre, which was celebrating its fiftieth anniversary that year.[673]

Early reviews from the Detroit, Washington, and Philadelphia papers were ecstatic: Eight of the nine critics gave it rave reviews, and the ninth was still favorable—an impressive feat by any measure, but particularly so for a musical that was still in the works. The *Detroit Free Press* was incredibly laudatory, claiming "Meredith Willson has hit the peak of his career with the new musical . . . [and it] will always be remembered as one of the magnificent tender creativities of our time." Washington's *Daily News* named Willson "the great tour director of America's Sentimental Journey." The *Washington Post & Times-Herald* rallied with "down with Scrooge and up with Tiny Tim," and the *Philadelphia Enquirer* stated that "that 'Music Man' Meredith Willson has done it again."[674]

But the New York critics were not as exuberant. Howard Taubman of the *New York Times* thought it was too manufactured and just exploited an already-popular story, remarking, "The fantasy in the plot is not matched in the telling on the stage. 'Here's Love' does not soar and does not enchant."[675] *Variety* thought that Santa Claus was played with "expert simplicity" by Naismith, and that Paige was "excellent" in her role. Michael Kidd's choreography was considered a "lifesaver," often compensating for the more lackluster elements. And the costumes were deemed "a notable asset." Ultimately, the critic deemed it to be "a spotty show up to here in syrupy sentimentality," but predicted that it would have mass appeal and do well financially.[676]

Composer Meredith Willson incorporated his Christmas song "It's Beginning to Look Like Christmas" ("a Lot" was added to the title later) into the score of *Here's Love*. The song had been a big hit for Perry Como in the early 1950s and was already famous when the musical came out in 1963. (Author's collection)

So what went wrong? With a proven story and an accomplished composer, it seemed like all of the elements should have come together to make an amazing musical. First, this was Willson's first adaptation, and he clearly shouldn't have altered the story as he did; the changes were unnecessary, and ultimately affected the show's reception. Secondly, the music was not that good, which is a bad thing for a musical. *Here's Love* has a score that's a far cry from Willson's masterpiece, *The Music Man*, whose songs had already become ensconced in the American music lexicon by the early 1960s. The *New York Times* critic labeled the *Here's Love* score "pedestrian," and an overall "musically watery and emotionally sticky effort."[677] There are some brassy numbers reminiscent of "Seventy Six Trombones," but most of the music is fairly unremarkable; you certainly don't come away humming any of the tunes other than perhaps the "It's Beginning to Look a Lot Like Christmas" medley. *Variety* felt that the score was "disappointing," and that it was further hampered by the fact that, out of the four leads, only Paige was a singer. But the music wasn't really suited to her voice, and Stevens "simply cannot sing."[678]

The most enduring element of the show was the minor Christmas hit, "Pine Cones and Holly Berries." Willson wrote "Pine Cones" for the new score and incorporated it as the counterpoint in a medley with "It's Beginning to Look a Lot Like Christmas," a song he had written back in 1951, which became a big hit for Perry Como. The medley is sung in the play by Kris,

"Pine Cones and Holly Berries" has subsequently shown up on various Christmas albums, usually as a medley with "It's Beginning to Look a Lot Like Christmas," such as on the Living Voices 1965 album, *The Little Drummer Boy*. The most well-known version was recorded by The Osmonds for their 1976 Christmas album. (Author's collection)

"Pine Cones and Holly Berries" would be the only piece of original music from *Here's Love* that would have any traction. Mitch Miller recorded it as a single for the National Tuberculosis Association campaign in 1963. Even though there is no indication on the label, the recording was actually the medley with "It's Beginning to Look a Lot Like Christmas." (Author's collection)

Doris, and Mr. Shellhammer after Doris returns from Mr. Macy's office to rehire Kris; it's then reprised by Kris and Susan later on in the show. Although recycling popular songs in musicals is commonplace on Broadway today, it was very rare in the 1960s, and its inclusion was very much noticed. The *New York Times* critic quipped that "It's Beginning to Look a Lot Like Christmas" "glows like a true gem in these [musical] surroundings."[679]

The medley has turned out to be the most enduring piece of music from the play. It was selected as the 1963 Christmas Seal Appeal song by the National Tuberculosis Association, and released as a single by the ever popular Mitch Miller and his Sing-Along Gang, whose two previous Christmas albums had sold millions.[680] In the following years, it showed up on various Christmas albums, like the Living

Voices' *The Little Drummer Boy* in 1965, and, a decade later, on the *Osmond Christmas Album*, which is probably the best-known version. It likewise has become a popular choral piece for high school and university choirs.

Columbia Records had enough faith in the music to release a deluxe original cast album with a gatefold cover, color photo insert, and copious liner notes. It was one of only six Broadway musicals whose original cast album was released that season; eleven other shows didn't even make the cut.[681] Columbia positioned (and expected) it to be the key release for the Christmas season. Needless to say, it didn't sell well, especially in comparison to Columbia's other Christmas offerings that year, which included *The Andy Williams Christmas Album* (his first), Robert Goulet's *This Christmas I Spend with You*, The New Christy Minstrels's *Merry Christmas!*, and the Leonard Bernstein/Mormon Tabernacle Choir collaboration, *The Joy of Christmas*, all of which went on to become classics of the genre, leaving *Here's Love* mostly forgotten.[682] But the *Here's Love* album would eventually merit a reissue on compact disc in 1992, as it was, by that time, considered part of the classic Broadway catalog.

The cast was changed a few times. Janis Paige was replaced by Lisa Kirk, and Craig Stevens was initially replaced by Richard Kiley. And funny man Dom DeLuise replaced David Doyle as Mr. Sawyer.[683] But the most surprising replacement was John Payne. Though it is fairly common for an actor who played a part on Broadway to reprise a role in a film adaptation, it is perhaps singular for a Hollywood actor to reprise a character he originated on the screen in a musical stage adaptation of the movie. Payne, who had forsaken musical comedy for more dramatic roles after returning from his service in World War II, returned to the genre that had made him famous. He was the third replacement and appeared in the role just three weeks before *Here's Love* ended its run on Broadway, on July 25, 1964.[684] He would continue in the role on tour as part of the cast for the Los Angeles Civic Light Opera production later in 1964.

Three months into its run in December of 1963, in spite of its initial misgivings, the *New York Times* acknowledged that *Here's Love* was a "successful" show, and performances were selling out.[685] It ended up having a respectable run, and was on "The Big Ten" list of the best plays on Broadway from April to July.[686] It ran for nine

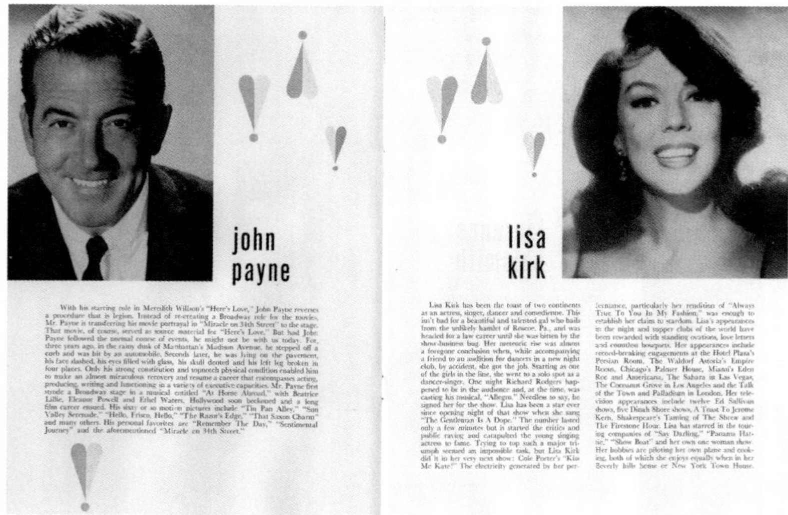

With his starring role in Meredith Willson's "Here's Love," John Payne reverses a procedure that is legion. Instead of re-creating a Broadway role for the movies, Mr. Payne is transferring his movie portrayal in "Miracle on 34th Street" to the stage. That movie, of course, served as source material for "Here's Love." But had John Payne followed the normal course of events, he might not be with us today. For, three years ago, in the rainy dusk of Manhattan's Madison Avenue, he stepped off a curb and was hit by an automobile. Seconds later, he was lying on the pavement, his face slashed, his eyes filled with glass, his skull dented and his left leg broken in four places. Only his strong constitution and topnotch physical condition enabled him to make an almost miraculous recovery and resume a career that encompasses acting, producing, writing and functioning in a variety of executive capacities. Mr. Payne first strode a Broadway stage in a musical entitled "At Home Abroad," with Beatrice Lillie, Eleanor Powell and Ethel Waters. Hollywood soon beckoned and a long film career ensued. His sixty or so motion pictures include "Tin Pan Alley," "Sun Valley Serenade," "Hello, Frisco, Hello," "The Razor's Edge," "That Saxon Charm" and many others. His personal favorites are "Remember The Day," "Sentimental Journey" and the aforementioned "Miracle on 34th Street."

Lisa Kirk has been the toast of two continents as an actress, singer, dancer and comedienne. This isn't bad for a beautiful and talented gal who hails from the unlikely hamlet of Roscoe, Pa., and was headed for a law career until she was bitten by the show-business bug. Her meteoric rise was almost a foregone conclusion when, while accompanying a friend to an audition for dancers in a new night club, by accident, she got the job. Starting as one of the girls in the line, she went to a solo spot as a dancer-singer. One night Richard Rodgers happened to be in the audience and, at the time, was casting his musical, "Allegro." Needless to say, he signed her for the show. Lisa has been a star ever since opening night of that show when she sang "The Gentleman Is A Dope." The number lasted only a few minutes but it started the critics and public raving and catapulted the young singing actress to fame. Trying to top such a major triumph seemed an impossible task, but Lisa Kirk did it in her very next show: Cole Porter's "Kiss Me Kate!" The electricity generated by her performance, particularly her rendition of "Always True To You In My Fashion," was enough to establish her claim to stardom. Lisa's appearances in the night and supper clubs of the world have been rewarded with standing ovations, love letters and countless bouquets. Her appearances include record-breaking engagements at the Hotel Plaza's Persian Room, The Waldorf Astoria's Empire Room, Chicago's Palmer House, Miami's Eden Roc and Americana, The Sahara in Las Vegas, The Cocoanut Grove in Los Angeles and the Talk of the Town and Palladium in London. Her television appearances include twelve Ed Sullivan shows, five Dinah Shore shows, A Toast To Jerome Kern, Shakespeare's Taming of The Shrew and The Firestone Hour. Lisa has starred in the touring companies of "Say Darling," "Panama Hattie," "Show Boat" and her own one woman show. Her hobbies are piloting her own plane and cooking, both of which she enjoys equally when in her Beverly hills home or New York Town House.

In a highly unusual move, John Payne reprised the role of Fred Gailey that he had made famous in the 1947 film in *Here's Love*. Lovely Lisa Kirk took over the role of Doris Walker from Janis Paige. (Author's collection)

months with 334 performances, more than any other musical on Broadway during the 1963–1964 season.[687]

The reception of *Here's Love* was tepid enough that TCF, whose option had expired six months after the show's opening, never moved forward with a film adaptation.[688] However, it did pave the way for an amateur play to finally be approved—twenty years later. The adaptation by Peter Troxell and Rita Faye Wadsworth was based on Davies's novel and published by the Dramatic Publishing Company as *Miracle on 34th Street, the Play*. It was first performed by the Mountain Community Theater in Ben Lomond, California, in 1982, and was received well enough that it has been consistently revived ever since by local and regional theaters.[689]

Here's Love has never been revived on Broadway or in the West End in London, but it has been performed regularly in regional theaters. It retained its original title until 2009, when the licensor, Music Theatre International (MTI), decided to rebrand it as *Meredith Willson's It's Beginning to Look a Lot Like Christmas*, capitalizing on the well-known song in the score. Just a couple of years later, in 2011, MTI changed the title again, going with the trend of adding "The Musical" to film properties that were previously not musically inclined; it has since been known as *Miracle on 34th Street: The Musical*, a clear marketing attempt to attract fans of the film.[690] Ironically, TCF has probably made more money from these amateur productions than it did on the Broadway production, which basically broke even.

1973 TV Movie

The third TV movie adaptation aired on CBS on Friday, December 14, 1973. Character actor Sebastian Cabot was selected to play Kris Kringle. Cabot was best known for his role as the butler Giles French in the sitcom *Family Affair*, which ran from 1966 to 1971. He had also worked for Disney as the narrator in the *Winnie the Pooh* animated short films, and had voiced parts in *The Sword and the Stone* (1963) and *The Jungle Book* (1967). Broadway's Tony Award–winning actress Jane Alexander, who was successfully transitioning to movies and television roles (she got an Oscar nomination for her first film role in *The Great White Hope* (1970)), was selected for the female lead. David Hartman, who had a leading role in the oddly titled medical drama, *The Bold Ones: The New Doctors*, was selected as the male lead just a few years before he became one of the original hosts of *Good Morning America*. Suzanne Davidson, who was just beginning her short show business career, was selected to play Susan. Her first role had been providing the voice of Karen in the Rankin/Bass animated special *Frosty the Snowman* in 1969.[691]

The supporting cast has lots of familiar faces from television, including Jim Backus (millionaire Thurston Howell III in *Gilligan's Island*), Tom Bosley (dad Howard Cunningham in *Happy Days*), James Gregory (Inspector Frank Luger in *Barney Miller*), David Doyle (manager Bosley in *Charlie's Angels*), and Roddy McDowall (who was in a little bit of everything). This would be Doyle's second association with the *Miracle* franchise; he had originated the role of Mr. Sawyer on Broadway in the musical version, *Here's Love*.

This version was turned into a two-hour special, which, without commercials, runs as long as the original feature film, yet it varies markedly from the original script. Apparently, "Doris" and "Fred" were considered outdated names by the 1970s (but Susan was not), and were changed to "Karen" and "Bill." Like all of the adaptations, writer Jeb Westbrook reworked the story. Most notably, he incorporated three of the unused/deleted scenes from the 1947 film script. The first is the scene at the Central Park Zoo. Instead of occurring before Kris heads over to the parade staging area, it is inserted after the parade is over. The scene doesn't include the boy being ignored by the reindeer, and so there is no contrast when they suddenly respond as Kris approaches, and hence, ends up having little impact.

The second scene included by Westbrook is of Kris and Bill going out to the Brooks' Home to pick up his things after Kris decides to move in with Bill. The scene involves Kris walking around the lounge, saying good-bye and asking residents what they want for Christmas. The scene does not show Kris's room (which was supposed to look like Santa's workshop), nor does it include the car ride home, where Bill explains what happened to Susan's father, and so, overall, really does not serve the plot and ends up being a bit extraneous.

A third scene that Westbrook included is one Seaton created for his first draft of the screenplay: the Kris/Sawyer battery, as part of the cafeteria scene. In this version, Mr. Sawyer sits down at the table with Kris and Alfred and starts giving his Santa-Claus-is-a-delusion speech. Kris becomes infuriated and throws a pie in Sawyer's face, which leads to his legal troubles. It's an interesting change, because the battery was debated by Davies and Seaton for the 1947 film. Davies had preferred a more comical incident to humiliate Sawyer, thinking that it was more in line with Kris's character, but Seaton changed it to a battery (albeit, a slight one), for the screenplay to illustrate that Kris could be considered to have "violent tendencies." Changing the battery to slapstick comedy undermines the accusation against Kris. Can we really believe that the State of New York is going to lock someone up because he threw a pie in someone's face?

Westbrook also made some significant changes to other scenes as well. One odd change is the fulfillment of Susan's dream house: Instead of Kris orchestrating the discovery of the house on Christmas Day, Bill is the one who does it. After revealing her wish to Kris, Kris tells Bill, who then finds such a house that his friend is selling. He meets Karen for dinner the night before the hearing and brings a real estate purchase contract for her to sign, along with a proposal of marriage. This undercuts the significance of Kris as the miracle worker; in fact, he doesn't end up doing anything for Susan.

A second significant change occurs when Susan writes the letter to Kris during the hearing. Instead of mailing it herself, she gives it to Bill to deliver to Kris. Bill then comes up with the idea to orchestrate the delivery of letters from the US Post Office (instead of a quick-witted postal employee) during the hearing. No coincidences are going to happen in this version of *Miracle*!

As with the other adaptations, several minor yet unnecessary changes were made. Bill has a girlfriend named Celeste who shows up when Karen and Susan first visit Bill in his apartment

Sebastian Cabot as Kris Kringle getting those reindeer in the right order in the 1973 TV movie. (Photofest)

during the parade, but then she completely disappears from the story; Dr. Pierce wants an emphysema machine instead of an X-ray machine for Christmas; the part of the Dutch girl is replaced by a Spanish-speaking girl; and Judge Harper declares that the hearing be closed to the public (was this done to avoid paying for extras to sit in the courtroom?).

Like the 1959 TV movie, the 1973 version crosses the line from reality to fantasy. After Mr. Macy's testimony, Kris and Bill are exiting the courthouse, and Kris tells him, "You gave me a couple of bad years back then," and talks about Bill wanting an erector set when he was six and not practicing the piano when he was eight. This exchange suddenly changes the story to complete fantasy; the audience is forced to believe that Kris is Santa Claus because there is no other explanation for his knowledge about Bill as a child. The production was also clearly set in movieland and avoided using any real names (other than Macy's and Gimbels). The Acme Toy Company is where you can get the best bike, and the featured newspapers are fictional: *New York Star-Standard*, *New York Dispatch*, and *New York Globe-Express*.

The soundtrack is more robust than any of the previous versions. The opening theme song is the somewhat catchy and exuberant "Miracles," the first theme song for a *Miracle* adaptation to include lyrics. Another original song, "Open Your Eyes and Dream," was written for Kris to sing to Susan. Lush instrumental versions of classic Christmas songs like "White Christmas," "The Christmas Song," and "Silver Bells" are heard throughout, and hearken back to the postwar origins of the story.

Variety seemed to sum up this version well when it declared that it "came a couple of reindeer lengths' short of the original [1947 film], scoring well enough in its intent and spirit but not quite up to snuff in its magic," adding that the "emotional wallop got lost among the tinsel."[692] After seeing this version, George Seaton thought it was, like the musical version, too cute and too sentimental.[693] Cabot is likable and believable as Kris Kringle, though his wig is a bit distracting at times. Alexander and Hartman are fine, but the romance comes across as a bit bland and matter-of-fact. Roddy McDowall as Mr. Sawyer, like Orson Bean in the 1959 version, is over-the-top. A maniacal temper tantrum during the consultation with Kris shows that the character has been changed from a professional who feels he is being ignored to a person with definite mental health issues. Another drawback is the Alfred character. Instead of the kind, pudgy Brooklynite in the original, this Alfred is awkward, kind of slimy and creepy, and has really bad hair (it's not clear whether they were trying to make him look unattractive or whether it was just 1970s hair).

Perhaps the standout feature of the 1973 version is the on location photography. Not only is there good footage of the parade, but there are also behind-the-scenes shots of the parade preparations and including the inflating of the big balloons. The film includes a nice tour of Macy's Herald Square store, and lots of terrific shots of Radio City Music Hall, the Rockefeller Center tree and ice-skating rink, and decorated department-store windows that really capture Christmas in New York City in the early 1970s.

1994 Feature Film

Almost fifty years after the original film was released, and over twenty years since any kind of adaptation had been made, TCF announced a feature film remake of *Miracle* in the fall of 1993, to be written and produced by John Hughes.[694] He had been approached about doing a remake a few years previously, but it had never materialized.[695]

A scene of Kris feeding reindeer in Central Park was included in Seaton's original script but eventually was cut out. The scene was partially revived for the 1973 TV movie with Sebastian Cabot. (Photofest)

Hughes had been an editor with *National Lampoon* magazine and became involved with the publication's movie projects, which helped him segue into the film industry.[696] After two of his scripts had been made into the box office hits *National Lampoon's Vacation* (1983) and *Mr. Mom* (1983) a decade earlier, Hughes had experienced a meteoric rise in Hollywood. In just a little over a decade, he had written, produced, or directed (in some cases all three) twenty-five films, including some of the most iconic movies of the 1980s: *Sixteen Candles* (1984), *Pretty in Pink* (1986), *The Breakfast Club* (1985), *Ferris Bueller's Day Off* (1986), and *Planes, Trains, and Automobiles* (1987). But Hughes was probably offered the chance to do a new version of *Miracle* based on the fact that he

CAST

Sebastian Cabot (Kris Kringle)

Jane Alexander (Karen Walker)

David Hartman (Bill Schaffer)

Suzanne Davidson (Susan Walker)

Jim Backus (Mr. Shellhammer)

Roddy McDowall (Dr. Sawyer)

Tom Bosley (Judge Harper)

David Doyle (Mr. Macy)

Ellen Weston (Celeste)

Roland Winters (Mr. Gimbel)

Barry Greenberg (Alfred)

James Gregory (district attorney)

Jason Wingreen (Halloran)

Conrad Janis (Dr. Pierce)

Pepe Serna (Y leader)

Janice Carroll (Mrs. Adams)

Gloria Leroy (mother #1)

Darryl Zwerling (floorwalker)

Jack Bernardi (shop owner)

Burt Mustin (Roy)

Liam Dunn (zookeeper)

CREW

Director: Fielder Cook

Producer: Norman Rosemont

Written by: Jeb Westbrook, based on the screenplay by George Seaton, from a story by Valentine Davies

Production designer: Jan Scott

Film editors: Gene Milford, Robert A. Daniels

Director of photography: Earl Rath

Director of photography (New York): Andrew Laszlo, ASC

Production managers: Paul Rapp, Roger Rothstein

Assistant director: Russell Vreeland

Script supervisor: Bonnie Prendergast

Set decorator: Robert Freer

Makeup: Mike Moschella

Hairstylist: Vivienne Walker

Costume supervisor: Mickey Sherrard

Prop master: Bill Bates

Sound mixer: George Maly

Gaffer: Larry Gilhooly

Key grip: Bill Martin

Music arranged and conducted by: Sid Ramin

Music editor: John Caper

Song: "Miracles" music by Sid Ramin and lyrics by Tony Velona

Song: "Open Your Eyes and Dream," music by Arthur Siegel and lyrics by June Carroll

Sound editing: Lee Osborne Film Services

Titles: Westholmer Company

Jane Alexander, Suzanne Davidson, and David Hartman starred in the 1973 TV movie.

had written and produced the Christmas movie, *Home Alone* (1990), which had become one of the highest-grossing films in history, and spawned a very successful sequel, *Home Alone 2: Lost in New York* (1992), just a couple of years later.

When *Miracle* was announced, the hope was to get director Chris Columbus on board to replicate the *Home Alone* success, but Columbus did not end up being part of the project. Instead, Les Mayfield, who had mostly worked on several "making-of" documentaries for popular films like *Back to the Future* (1985) and *Who Framed Roger Rabbit?* (1988), was chosen to direct. He had only directed one feature film, the Sean Astin/Brendan Fraser modern caveman comedy, *Encino Man* (1992).

Celebrated actor and director Richard Attenborough was cast as Kriss (a second "s" was inexplicably added to his name) Kringle and was given top billing. Attenborough had been acting in and directing films for over fifty years, and had just appeared in the first *Jurassic Park* (1993). The romantic leads were played by rising stars Elizabeth Perkins as Dorey (apparently a more hip name than Doris)

Despite a good cast with Richard Attenborough as Kriss and Mara Wilson as Susan, the 1994 updated remake of *Miracle on 34th Street* failed to capture the magic. (Photofest)

and Dylan McDermott as the Fred character, with the name changed (also inexplicably) to Bryan Bedford. Perkins was a trained stage actress and had appeared in a couple of films before getting her breakout role as Tom Hanks's girlfriend in *Big* (1988). McDermott had appeared in significant films such as *Steel Magnolias* (1989) and *In the Line of Fire* (1993) with Clint Eastwood. The role of Susan went to cute little Mara Wilson, who had been in several commercials, but had really gotten noticed after appearing as one of the children in *Mrs. Doubtfire* (1993) the previous year.

The supporting roles went to several accomplished character actors, such as William Windom as president of the department store, C. F. Cole; J. T. Walsh as district attorney Ed Collins; and Robert Prosky as Judge Harper, among others. Alvin Greenman, who played Alfred in the 1947 film, got a cameo as the doorman at Dorey and Bryan's apartment building. He is the

　　　　　　　　　　　　　　　　　　　　　　　　　　　　　　THE ADAPTATIONS

Following his huge success as the writer and producer of the first two *Home Alone* movies, John Hughes tried to update *Miracle on 34th Street*, but it didn't work. (Photofest)

only actor to appear in both the 1947 and 1994 feature films.

The choice to do a remake was an interesting one for Hughes, because he had mostly worked with his own original material. He was obviously fond of the original version; he included a clip of it in *Home Alone*, when Kevin wakes up to find his family gone. He publicly stated that he wanted to be "real careful" with *Miracle* because it was such a cherished film, and he hoped that his remake would be a "companion to the original," as if Kris Kringle had come back in modern times.[697] Like everyone else who has made an adaptation, Hughes took it upon himself to rework the screenplay. His version deviates more from the original than any of the others, and ended up being longer than any of the others, as well, with a running time of almost two hours.

From the beginning of the film, there is the uneven application of real and fictional elements. Noticeably absent from this production is Macy's as the department store. When the production was getting under way in the spring of 1994, Macy's announced that it would not be participating in the movie, stating, "We feel the original stands on its own, and there was nothing to be improved upon," which was a bit surprising, because this had not been their attitude toward the previous three television movies.[698] This posed a somewhat serious problem, because the title of the film indicates a physical location, and there is only one department store on 34th Street that hosts a Thanksgiving Day parade in New York City.

Instead of changing the title or switching the locale to another city, such as Chicago, where much of the action was filmed, Hughes opted to mask what was clearly supposed to be Macy's with the fictional Cole's (which was an awkward choice for a name, since there is an actual regional mid-range department store based in Wisconsin called Kohl's). This also posed a problem when it came to depicting the parade. Even though this is the Cole's parade, we all know that this is supposed to be the Macy's Thanksgiving Day Parade. Hughes even filmed it at 77th Street and Central Park West, where the Macy's parade always starts. (For the 1947 film, George Seaton had deliberately fought using a fictional store because it detracted from the realism that is necessary in order for the story to be believable.)

These fictional elements are compounded by the art direction. Unlike the 1947 film that went to New York to make the story more realistic, there was a concerted effort by Hughes and Mayfield for the movie to have somewhat of a classic look that was a bit nostalgic. The 1994 film does not capture life in New York in the early 1990s, but rather takes a cue from the grand tradition of Hollywood production design, where everyone and everything looks beautiful: the people, the department store, the apartments, the clothing, the courtroom, etc. Perkins noted, "What

Macy's declined to participate in the 1994 theatrical remake of *Miracle* and so the fictional Cole's department store was created. But it was clearly just a guise; they still had the parade start at Central Park West and 77th Street where the Macy's parade always starts, and Macy's is the only department store left on 34th Street! (Photofest)

we've tried to do is create a look and a feel and a style of language which is reminiscent of a time long past, and yet at the same time is very contemporary."[699] For example, the costume designer specifically did not allow contemporary ski parkas in the parade scenes, but dressed everyone in traditional wool coats, "to ensure that the film had a timeless feel." The date-night scene is right out of a 1940s romantic comedy, with Dorey and Bryan waltzing through the city to the tune of Kenny G's *Have Yourself a Merry Little Christmas*, in what could be a commercial for Christmas in New York. You see it all: bustling streets with holiday shoppers, a romantic dinner, the tree at Rockefeller Center, and ice-skating in Central Park. These decisions hamper the story by transforming the setting into a mythical New York instead of the real one, which makes it even more of a fantasy.

This is somewhat tempered by the use of real newspapers, including the *Houston Chronicle*, the *Rocky Mountain News*, the *Arizona Republic*, and the *New York Post* (the third time in the franchise's history that real newspapers were featured); by Kriss being featured on *Good Morning America*; and by some very obvious product placement for Sony, 7UP, and Cartier. But all in all, the mixture of the real and the unreal makes the audience unsure as to whether we are in a fictional world or not.

The principal cast of the 1994 remake of *Miracle*, from left to right: Richard Attenborough, Mara Wilson, Dylan McDermott, and Elizabeth Perkins. (Photofest)

The soundtrack was also done in a very traditional Hollywood way and very much conveys that "This is a Christmas movie," which detracts from any attempt at realism. The original score by Bruce Broughton is lush and romantic, and underscores most of the action in the film, very similar to how music was used in the 1973 TV movie. There is some musical homage to the 1947 film, with the use of "Santa Claus Is Comin' to Town" and "Jingle Bells," as well as a nod to composer Meredith Willson with the use of his song, "It's Beginning to Look a Lot Like Christmas." These songs are performed by the likes of Natalie Cole, Dionne Warwick, Ray Charles, Aretha Franklin, Elvis Presley, and Sarah McLachlan, whose "Song for a Winter's Night" reminds us that we are definitely watching a 1990s film. Incidentally, there was a new song that the Bee Gees were commissioned to write for the film, but it did not end up being used. It was titled "Miracles Happen," and ended up a few years later as a track on their 1997 album, *Still Waters*.[700]

Hughes made some changes that were unnecessary. He got rid of the opening scene of Kriss pointing out the reindeer in the wrong order, which had been preserved in every other adaptation. Hughes reduced or removed most of the supporting character roles. Mr. Shellhammer is reduced substantially, only appearing briefly at the beginning and at the end. Mr. Sawyer is completely gone, and has been replaced by a motley crew from Cole's competitor, Shopper's Express. Gone are sympathetic Alfred, politico Charlie Halloran, and even Thomas Mara Jr., who doesn't get to testify in court. One tender change was in substituting a deaf girl for the Dutch girl.

Like other adaptations, Hughes did incorporate ideas that had not made it into the 1947 film. The reindeer scene in Central Park is preserved, but, like the 1973 TV movie, no contrast is shown as to why this is remarkable. He also includes Bryan explaining to Kriss what happened to Susan's father. Hughes also made Susan substantially greedier than any previous Susan. She asks Kriss not only for a house (and a mighty large one at that!), but she also asks for a father *and* a brother.

Hughes dramatically expanded the romantic relationship between Dorey and Bryan, much like Davies and Seaton had orginally intended, but he doesn't let the romance blossom right before us. It's clear that there is already a relationship, and a bit of a rocky one at that. Susan doesn't get the chance to scheme to get Bryan invited to Thanksgiving dinner. Instead of their potential marriage being the culmination of all that Christmas magic, there is an awkward proposal and rejection that somehow results in a wedding a week or so later, after Dorey has made it very clear that she is not interested in Bryan. It all seems a bit of a stretch.

The biggest and most problematic change that Hughes made was the courtroom scene. Hughes sends Kriss to Bellevue on the same charge that Seaton does—namely, battery—but then Hughes goes off on quite a tangent. In the 1947 film, Kris fails the psychiatric evaluation because he believes the person he is trying to help (Doris) has turned on him. Hughes changes Kriss's motivation for failing the test to just the fact that he "disgraced" himself, which seems silly, since he was provoked and is the victim, and there is no reason that a good lawyer couldn't have gotten him off by arguing that he acted in self-defense. Instead of Bryan looking like a fool for defending Kriss, the district attorney looks ridiculous when he brings a live reindeer in the courtroom and asks Kriss to make him fly. Bryan's closing argument—that Judge Harper should rule to maintain "a lie that draws a smile or a truth that draws a tear"—is one bizarre argument indeed. Clearly, he doesn't have any faith in his client.

The 1947 film moves the hearing along with the need to, first, prove the existence of Santa Claus, and second, to prove that Kris Kringle is indeed the *only* Santa Claus. These aims seem to get lost in the 1994 film. Unlike the testimony of Thomas Mara Jr. in the 1947 film, which undermines the arguments of his district attorney father, the testimony of cute little Daniel does nothing of the sort. He's just one kid pointing out a man that looks like Santa. In the 1947 film, there is nothing to make us question Kris's sanity except for his claim of who he is. Seaton wanted to leave it up to the audience to decide if this is Santa Claus or not. But in Hughes's version, the decision is made for the viewers when Kriss declares that "my workshops . . . are invisible. . . . [T]hey are in the dream world." This happens again after the hearing ends, when Kriss tells the district attorney that he ripped his pants on the old television antenna on the attorney's roof. Like the 1959 and 1973 TV movies, these few lines force the audience to accept him as Santa Claus because there is no explanation given as to how or why Kriss would otherwise have that experience or knowledge. Hughes pushes us all the way into fantasy land.

Perhaps even more bizarre is Judge Harper's ruling. Hughes dispenses with the plot device of the US Postal Service intervening to prove the case, and instead invents something completely new and, frankly, strange. The idea that Bryan comes up with is odd enough, but the fact that he thinks the judge is going to come to the exact same conclusion when Susan gives him a dollar bill is far-fetched. In the original, Judge Harper needs to follow the law, but is able to justify his actions in light of the support from the USPS. Without the presence of the Charlie Halloran character, Judge Harper has no sounding board, and we are unaware of his motivations. But this Judge Harper declares that, if the United States government can issue currency that says "In God

Instead of the defense counsel looking ridiculous for defending Kriss, the prosecutor does when he brings in a reindeer and asks Kriss to make it fly. John Hughes rewrote the entire hearing scenes and the logic just doesn't work. (Photofest)

We Trust," without ever having proven the existence of God, "then the state of New York by a similar demonstration of the collective faith of its people can accept and acknowledge that Santa Claus does exist, and he exists in the person of Kriss Kringle." The district attorney has not proven anything, and Bryan has not proven anything. The reasoning just falls apart.

The preview audiences reacted favorably to the film, with TCF chairman Peter Chernin announcing that "It tested higher than any film in the studio's history," which now seems a bit hard to believe.[701] The film got a big splashy premiere at Radio City Music Hall in New York on November 15, 1994, which included a thirty-minute stage show by the Rockettes, reminiscent of the premiere of the 1947 film at the Roxy.[702] It was then released three days later with great expectations in 1,190 theaters, so it could play over the Thanksgiving holiday.[703] And then, it just bombed. Opening weekend, it only pulled in $2.7 million.

Panicked, TCF decided to offer an unprecedented money-back guarantee: If you didn't like it, you could send in your ticket stub for a refund.[704] Part of the lackluster reception was certainly due to the fact that Disney had released *The Santa Clause* (1994) with Tim Allen the week before, and that film was extremely well-received; if moviegoers were going to go see a Christmas movie, it would be that one. *The Santa Clause* had earned $27.5 million after just five days, while *Miracle* was only at $8.3 million after ten days.[705] By December 26, the disparity was quite stark: *Miracle* had brought in just over $16 million after six weeks in the theater, and *The Santa Clause* had brought in over $126 million after seven weeks.[706] It was pretty clear which Santa Americans preferred that year.*

Reviews were mixed. Siskel and Ebert, surprisingly, gave it "two thumbs up."[707] *Variety* liked Attenborough and Wilson, and predicted that it would do reasonably well and go on to "join the Christmas club of movies in perpetual year-end television rotation," which it did.[708] *Boxoffice* acknowledged it has "enchanting moments," but "remains too grounded in real-world concerns to work as the fantasy it intends to be."[709] *Screen International* found it to be "glaringly predictable," and that "its look and feel [are] too cloying."[710]

The most insightful review came from Kenneth Turan of the *Los Angeles Times*. He pointed out that Hughes did not just do a remake of *Miracle*, but rather an update, and in the process,

---

*In what appears to be an intentional gibe at the 1994 remake, *The Santa Clause* includes a reference to the original 1947 film. Right after the TV spot on how to make the perfect Christmas dinner, the announcer says "And now we return to the most cherished of Christmas movies: *Miracle on 34th Street* starring Natalie Wood." The dig was certainly heightened by the remake's poor ticket sales.

made "it cruder and more vulgar to match the tenor of modern times. . . . Although attracted to the original's innocence, they [Hughes and Mayfield] eventually lost faith and ended up tampering with its purity in small but ruinous ways."[711] The "ruinous ways" included Hughes's introduction of crass elements, like seeing the drunk Santa's rear end as he climbs into the sleigh; innuendo about Kriss and one of the female elves at the store; accusations that Kriss has inappropriate relationships with children; and a bunch of Santa Clauses getting drunk at a bar. At the outset of the production, Hughes had stated, "I feel if I can't take a Hollywood classic further, then I won't do it."[712] Obviously, he did do it, but didn't realize his limitations when working with *Miracle*. As with the other adaptations, he was unable to make the story better than it already was.

Many critics thought Richard Attenborough and Mara Wilson were the best things about the 1994 remake of *Miracle on 34th Street*. (Photofest)

CAST

Richard Attenborough (Kriss Kringle)

Elizabeth Perkins (Dorey Walker)

Dylan McDermott (Bryan Bedford)

Mara Wilson (Susan Walker)

J. T. Walsh (Ed Collins)

James Remar (Jack Duff)

Jana Leeves (Alberta Leonard)

Simon Jones (Mr. Shellhammer)

William Windom (C. F. Cole)

Robert Prosky (Judge Harper)

Kathrine Narducci (Mother)

Mary McCormack (Myrna Foy)

Alvin Greenman (The Doorman)

Allison Janney (The Woman)

Greg Noonan (Commander Coulson)

Byrne Piven (Dr. Hunter)

Peter Gerety (Cop)

Jack McGee (Tony Falacchi)

Joe Pentangelo (Bailiff)

Mark Damiano II (Daniel)

Casey Wurzbach (Grandson)

Jennifer Morrison (Denice)

Peter Siragusa (Cabbie)

Samantha Krieger (Sami)

Horatio Sanz (Orderly)

Lisa Sparrman (Mrs. Collins)

Kimberly Smith (Court Clerk)

Mike Bacarella (Santa)

CREW

Director: Les Mayfield

Producer: John Hughes

Executive producers: William S. Beasley and William Ryan

Written by: John Hughes, based on the screenplay by George Seaton, from a story by Valentine Davies

Production designer: Doug Kramer

Art director: Steve Arnold

Set decoration: Leslie E. Rollins

Film editors: Raja Gosnell

Director of photography: Julio Macat

Makeup: Ben Nye III

Hairstylist: Bunny Parker-Adamson

Costume Designer: Kathy O'Rear

Music: Bruce Broughton

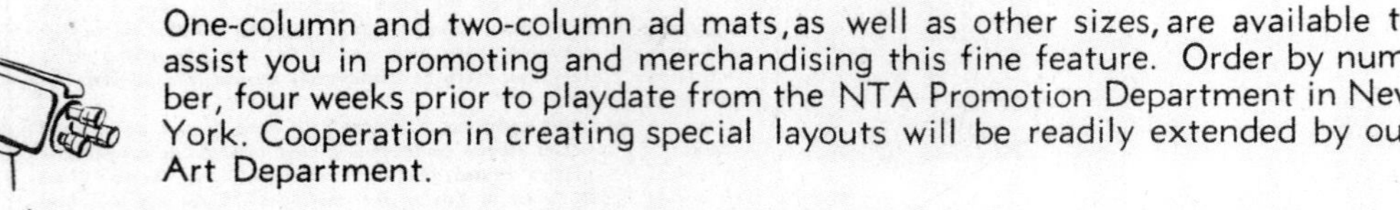

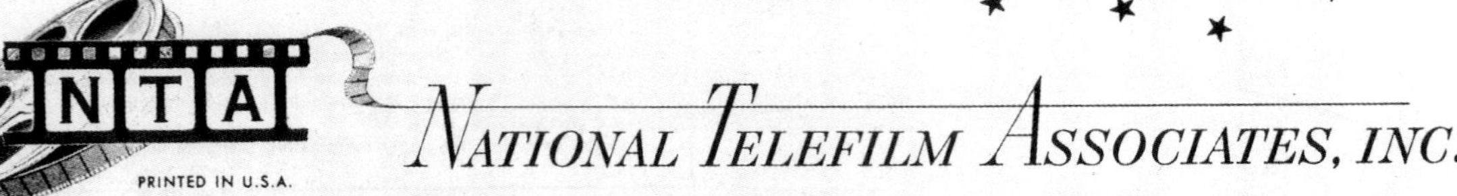

Miracle began its long history as a syndicated film on television in 1956 thanks to the National Telefilm Associates that licensed it from Twentieth Century-Fox. Here are some sample ads from the advertising brochure sent to local television stations. (Author's collection)

C H A P T E R   1 0

The Legacy

THE FILM: BECOMING A PERENNIAL FAVORITE

*M*iracle was a big hit when it was released in 1947, a commercial and a critical success, but perhaps more impressive is that it has endured over the years. Although the filmmakers wanted to make a good movie, *Miracle*'s continued popularity was a bit of surprise. In the early 1970s, when Seaton was looking back on his career, he recalled thinking that it wouldn't "do too much," and then "wham," it was huge.[714] Its staying power, with the theatrical rebookings, the radio shows, and the book sales, was already evident by the early 1950s, when Davies astutely pointed out that "on the basis of the past five years there is every indication that both the book and film version will develop into perennials.[715] In 1955, *Boxoffice* magazine, a trade publication for theater owners, looked back at the previous twenty-three years of awarding the "*Boxoffice* Blue Ribbon Award." Voters were asked to select the 23 best films from the 278 that had won the award since its inception in 1932. Not surprisingly, *Miracle* made the list, right along with *Snow White and the Seven Dwarfs* (1937) and *The Wizard of Oz* (1939).[716] It even got a presidential endorsement when Dwight D. Eisenhower indicated that it was his favorite movie.[717] With a big boost from television and home video releases, *Miracle* would continue to attract a wide audience, and go on to become as much a part of the holiday season as *A Christmas Carol* and Frosty the Snowman.

In the early days of television, the Hollywood movie studios considered their films to be in a separate class from the content being created for television, and were wary of allowing their film libraries to be broadcast on the airwaves. This attitude changed in the mid-1950s, when it became clear that television was here to stay. (In the spring of 1956, the US Department of Commerce concluded that 75 percent of US households owned a television.[718]) This led several of the major film studios to change their minds and allow their finest films to be broadcast.[719]

In May of 1956, TCF made the bold move of leasing fifty-two of their best features from the 1935–1947 period (out of 650 films made during that time frame) to National Telefilm Associates (NTA) for a ten-year period. NTA was part of National Affiliated Television Stations, Inc., a consortium of independent television stations with backing from General Electric. NTA was created to provide management, marketing, financial assistance, and access to a film library to local TV stations.[720] NTA would be responsible for the marketing and distribution of the TCF catalog titles to television stations in the United States, Canada, Cuba, and along the Mexican border. TCF would get a minimum of $45,000 per film title.[721] *Miracle* was one of the films in the package, and thus began its long life as a yuletide television favorite.[722] By the mid-1970s, it was the most requested title in NTA's library.[723]

TCF was the first major studio to enter the home entertainment market by licensing films from its catalog to Magnetic Video Corporation, in 1977. As one of TCF's most popular syndicated films, it is not surprising that *Miracle* was part of the early offerings, first released on video in 1980.[724] It would go on to become one of the studio's "evergreen" titles, an industry term for a film that consistently sells, year in and year out. It would be consistently repackaged and made available in every new home entertainment format, a privilege only acccorded to select films. TCF would acknowledge Miracle's status when it included it in the deluxe box set issued in 2010 consisting of the studio's best films to celebrate the seventy-fifth anniversary of the merger of Twentieth Century Pictures and Fox Film Corporation.

In the early 1980s, after almost thirty years on television, *Miracle*'s ratings were starting to drop. Since the mid-1960s, television shows had been shot almost exclusively in color. More and more, black-and-white content was being relegated to the late-late-show time slots, and attracting fewer and fewer advertising dollars, as prime-time viewers preferred color programming.[725] TCF decided to try and bring *Miracle* back as a star prime-time attraction by colorizing it, a process

Twentieth Century-Fox was the first major Hollywood studio to put films from its catalog on home video. *Miracle on 34th Street* was first released on VHS in 1980.

After airing for decades on TV as a black and white movie, Twentieth Century-Fox tried to attract a bigger audience by colorizing the film. The scheme worked and attracted three times the viewership than it previously had.

that was very much in its infancy. A Canadian company, Colorization Inc., had released the first such colorized movie in August 1985, the Cary Grant comedy *Topper* (1937), which ended up making a phenomenal $2 million in syndication and subsequent video sales.[726] TCF was hoping for similar success with *Miracle* and hired California-based Color Systems Technology, Inc., for the project. It was Color Systems' first foray into this new realm. Gene Allen, who had won the Academy Award for art direction for *My Fair Lady* (1964), oversaw the process. The company was able to use materials in Macy's corporate archive, such as color photographs of the parade and the store from the 1940s, to provide color samples. The president of the company was cognizant of the need to be attentive to detail: "There are some things that just have to be accurate—Maureen O'Hara's eyes, for example." The project took about forty-five days to complete, at a cost of $188,000.[727]

The gimmick worked. The colorized version of *Miracle* first aired during the holiday season of 1985, and viewership skyrocketed, attracting almost three times as many viewers as the black-and-white version had the previous year.[728] In fact, the colorized version of *Miracle* ended up being the highest-rated syndicated movie of 1985.[729] Since the response was so good (as well as the advertising revenue), TCF decided to reserve the colorized version exclusively for television syndication for almost a decade. When it was finally released on home video, it sold 2.4 million copies in just a couple of months, and was the eighth-highest-selling video of 1993.[730]

But colorization also brought a fury of criticism, the likes of which had never been seen. For decades, there hadn't been much complaint about films running on TV in altered form—with commercial breaks, or the "panning and scanning" of widescreen films, to fit the 4:3 television ratio. But colorization, which seriously changed the look, brought a swift and vitriolic response. Patently, it was an argument about the aesthetics of film as art. Many felt it was akin to "touching up the *Mona Lisa*," and that "technology and greed . . . emasculate films."[731] Prominent film personalities, such as Woody Allen and Sydney Pollack, decried the practice as a bastard-ization of film classics. Legendary director John Huston, who was completely outraged when his film *The Maltese Falcon* (1941) was colorized, compared it to selling his children into slavery. Frank Capra and James Stewart publicly denounced the colorization of *It's a Wonderful Life*, even though the new color version would sell eighty thousand VHS tapes.[732]

Soon, major industry groups, such as the Directors Guild of America, the Writers Guild of America, the American Society of Cinematographers, and the American Film Institute, were all vocal opponents of colorization, even though, by 1987, only twenty-five films had undergone the process.[733] The studios felt completely justified in trying to monetize movies that had not brought in any revenue for years. Furthermore, as Max Youngstein, former chairman at United Artists, glibly remarked, everyone knows that moviemaking is "90 percent making money and at best 10 percent an art form."[734] One film personality who was not opposed was Fran Lee, the ac-tress who played the woman who is sent to Gimbels in the 1947 *Miracle*. She wrote a letter to the editor of the *New York Times* and said that she had watched herself for thirty-five years in black-and-white; when she saw the colorized film, she thought it "brought a liveliness to the screen," and she was all for it.[735]

Only later did it come out that the guilds' campaign against colorization was an out-growth of an ongoing battle between them and the studios. The guilds were aware of all the new income the studios were generating from the sales of films on cable and home video, and they wanted to get higher royalty payments. Elliott Silverstein of the Directors Guild admitted, "There was a direct bridge between those negotiations and the campaign against colorization. We needed a platform."[736] The guilds felt that, by joining the fight over colorization, they would enlist public sympathy and hopefully sway the studios to give them what they wanted.

The debate raged on in the mid-1980s and got a lot of coverage, as politicians, celebrities, talk-show hosts, and journalists all joined in the conversation. The culminating event was Ted Turner's colorization of (gasp!) *Casablanca* (1942) in November of 1988, which he admitted he did just to stoke the controversy.[737] He aired it on his cable channel, SuperStation WTBS, but, unlike *Miracle*, with its huge ratings, *Casablanca* did not attract a high viewership. After that, the battle over colorization just seemed to fizzle. When Turner created the Turner Classic Movies station in 1994, he did an about-face and advertised to viewers that movies would be "uninterrupted, uncolorized, and commercial-free!"[738]

The controversy had led to Senate hearings, with testimonies from filmmakers and actors. There was hope that President Ronald Reagan, a former actor himself, would weigh in on be-half of the guilds, but he did not. As was expected, the guilds lost, and the studios won. The end result was that President Reagan signed into law the National Film Preservation Act in the fall of 1988, which, ultimately, did nothing more than establish the National Film Preservation Board and create the National Film Registry, "as an attempt to safeguard classic films and respond to the heated, two-year debate over" colorization, although some people didn't like the idea of the

1985 VHS

This tender image of Susan giving Kris a hug was included in some of the original poster art when the film was released in 1947. However, since Edmund Gwenn and Natalie Wood were considered supporting cast members, the image was a minor detail, with the faces of Maureen O'Hara and John Payne being much more prominent. But things changed: Ever since the 1985 video release,, this image has served as the basis for all advertising art. (Photofest)

1993 VHS

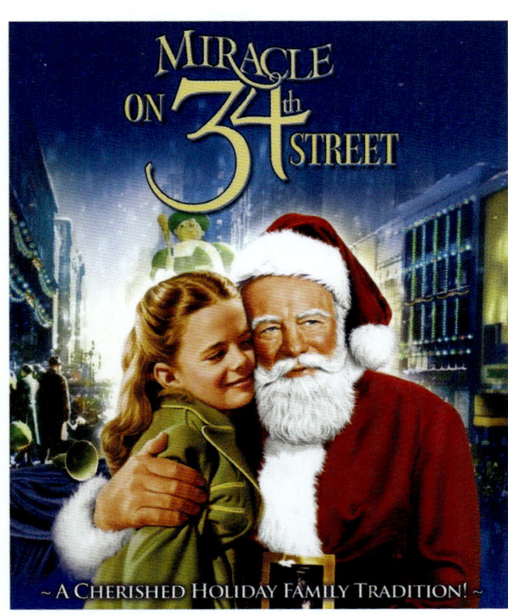
2009 Blu-Ray

NFPB deciding which films were worth preserving. [739]

Surprisingly, despite being one of the catalysts that brought colorization and film preservation into the forefront, the colorized version of *Miracle* did not provoke the hue and cry that *Casablanca* (1942) and *The Maltese Falcon* (1941) did. Even more interesting is the fact that it took another twenty years for *Miracle* to be added to the National Film Registry, which occurred in 2005, bringing the total up to 425 films at the time.[740]

MACY'S AND GIMBELS: KEEPING MIRACLE ALIVE

As *Miracle* has become an enduring property for TCF, its association with Macy's and Gimbels has provided ongoing marketing opportunities for those retailers. When Macy's did their big flower show in 1953—a stunning display by all accounts, with over 2.1 million flowers on the main floor—Gimbels was duly impressed, and, just like in the movie, encouraged everyone to go to Macy's. In an action that is probably unparalleled in retail history, Gimbels took out an ad in the *New York Times* stating that "Gimbels tells Macy's that Macy's flower show is the greatest miracle to hit 34th Street since 34th Street and miracles (and Gimbels and Macy's) were invented" and that "it's just plain silly" if New Yorkers don't go see it.[741] The ad caused quite a stir. Fictional movies are one thing, but no one could really believe that Gimbels actually *paid* for an advertise-

---

MIRACLE ON 34TH STREET HOME ENTERTAINMENT RELEASES

1980	VHS cassette edition of the original black-and-white version (Magnetic Video)
1985	VHS cassette edition of the original black-and-white version (CBS/Fox)
1987	LaserDisc edition of the original black-and-white version (CBS/Fox)
1993	VHS cassette edition of the "Exclusive Color Version" (TCF Fox Video)
1993	LaserDisc edition of the "Exclusive Color Version" (TCF Fox Video)
1997	VHS cassette of the fiftieth anniversary edition digitally mastered by THX (TCF Home Entertainment)
1997	LaserDisc fiftieth anniversary edition of the original black-and-white version (TCF Home Entertainment)
1999	DVD edition of the original black-and-white version (TCF Home Entertainment)
2006	DVD two-disc set edition of the original black-and-white and colorized versions (TCF Home Entertainment)
2009	Blu-ray edition of the original black-and-white version (TCF Home Entertainment)
2014	Blu-ray sixty-fifth anniversary edition of the original black-and-white version (TCF Home Entertainment)
2017	Blu-ray + Digital HD seventieth anniversary edition of the original black-and-white version (TCF Home Entertainment)
2020	Blu-ray + Digital HD edition of the original black-and-white version (Disney/Buena Vista)

---

ment to encourage people to go to Macy's. The *New York Times* even declared, "Gimbels Loses Its Head and Does Tell Macy's."[742] In response, Macy's took out a big ad confirming that the flower show "*is* the miracle on 34th Street, and 'Nobody but Nobody said it more prettily than Gimbels.' "[743]

The reciprocation brought cooperation when the first TV movie premiered on *The Twentieth Century-Fox Hour*. Macy's and Gimbels took out a double-page ad with cartoon drawings of the stores that featured arrow signs pointing "This Way to Gimbels" and "This Way to Macy's," with a plug for the show.[744]

Although the phrase had existed before, "Miracle on [fill in the blank] Street" certainly became more popular. Macy's would continue to use the film title in various advertisements, such as in a 1956 appliance ad: "Macy's . . . *The Miracle on 34th Street*. It's the miracle 1956 General Electric magnetic door refrigerator."[745] Other retailers on 34th Street felt completely fine poaching the phrase (certainly justified, because they too had helped promote the film), like Baker's, who ran an ad in 1958 for their patent-leather high-heeled shoes at $6.99 to $7.99: "No wonder smart New Yorkers have hailed the new Baker's as the modern miracle on 34th Street!"[746] Or Saks-34th, which was located right between Macy's and Gimbels, who advertised a "dazzling polished cotton" dress at $5.98 as "*our* miracle on 34th Street."[747] Bargain stores appropriated the phrase as well, like the Hearns store up in the Bronx, which advertised its super basement bargains as the "Miracle on 149th Street," and the Supermart Affiliate Surprise Store on Front Street in Keyport, New Jersey, which stated " 'Miracle on 34th Street'—That was nothing compared to the 'Miracle on Front Street,' where miracles and bargains go hand in hand!"[748]

In 1999, Macy's Herald Square store used *Miracle* as the basis for their Christmas windows, and invited Maureen O'Hara as the guest of honor to unveil them. Six windows were designed featuring scenes from the movie, at a cost of about $75,000 each. The windows were a bit of a throwback, not only because they featured a fifty-year-old movie, but also because it was the first time in many years that Macy's had used animated figures in their window displays. The window designer had learned that Macy's had introduced animated windows at their store in 1899, at the dawn of the twentieth century, and thought it would be a nice homage to usher in the twenty-first century.[749] The windows were unveiled on November 18, 1999, followed by O'Hara holding an autograph party in Santaland on the eighth floor, to sign copies of the VHS cassette.[750] The window displays were later permanently installed there. In 2004, O'Hara was invited back again to sign copies of her autobiography, and was given a star on Macy's Walk of Fame, also located on the eighth floor of the store.

A few years later, in honor of its 150th anniversary, Macy's highlighted *Miracle* by including the clip of Susan telling Kris that they buy all of their clothes there in a special retrospective commercial.[751] During the holiday season that year, the Herald Square store introduced a thirty-minute musical show in the puppet theater on the ninth floor, titled *Miracle on 34th Street . . . at Macy's*. The show featured seven new songs, with music by Wesley Whatley, and book and lyrics by William Schermerhorn.[752] The story is told in flashback, with Susan as an old lady reminiscing about the time Kris Kringle came into her life when she was a child. It was a professional show, with marionettes by The Puppetworks, Inc., and featured recorded vocals by Broadway stars Brian Stokes Mitchell and Victoria Clark.[753] The show was a cute, condensed adaptation with some decent songs, and at $5 per person, it was by far the cheapest ticket on Broadway (and provided a nice respite for harried shoppers). The song "I Believe," sung in the show by Doris, was the standout number, and ended up getting some traction after being recorded by Disney actress Tiffany Thornton, in a duet with Kermit the Frog.[754] The puppet show was revived as an attraction at Christmastime for a few years after.

In 2012, Macy's reinvigorated the connection between *Miracle* and their store with the release of a new special commercial, "Another Miracle on 34th Street," which had Kris returning to Macy's as an employee. It featured celebrities who were in then-current Macy's ads, including singers Justin Bieber and Taylor Swift, designer Tommy Hilfiger, lifestyle maven Martha Stewart, and real estate mogul and television personality Donald Trump, combined with footage of Edmund Gwenn from the movie. The commercial is cute, with Bieber asking to be taken off the naughty list, and

Macy's has enjoyed the affiliation with *Miracle on 34th Street* for decades. (Author's collection)

Macy's created this homage to *Miracle* as part of the "Believe" campaign, inviting customers to write a letter to Santa. (Author's collection)

When Macy's started the "Believe" campaign in 2008, it was based on "Yes, Virginia, There Is a Santa Claus," but four years later it was redefined to be based on *Miracle on 34th Street*. (Author's collection)

Trump questioning Kris as to whether he is the real Santa Claus. The commercial concludes with Kris declaring to Trump, "If I can win you over, there's still hope."

Macy's had been doing a "Believe" Christmas campaign since 2008, which had originally been based on the renowned 1897 editorial in the *New York Sun*, "Yes, Virginia, There Is a Santa Claus."[755] Beginning in 2012, "Believe" became a reference to Susan's repetition of the word in the film. Macy's has consistently used the "Believe" campaign during the Christmas season ever since.

Although Gimbels got second billing in *Miracle*, it did get featured in a couple of other films. The flagship Gimbels store in New York can be seen in all of its holiday glory in the 1967 comedy *Fitzwilly*, starring Dick Van Dyke and Barbara Feldon, in which the store becomes the object of a heist on Christmas Eve. A generation later, director Jon Favreau gave Gimbels a starring role in his 2003 Christmas film, *Elf*. Although he did not use the actual Gimbels exterior (he substituted the Textile Building on Fifth Avenue and 30th Street), through post-production CGI, the Gimbels name is prominently displayed on the marquee, providing a nice homage to *Miracle*, and to a legendary store in American retail history.[756]

In what seems to go against everything *Miracle* stands for, TCF decided to license the film to make branded merchandise in the 1990s and 2000s. In 1998, dolls of Kris and the little Dutch girl were issued by Exclusive Toy Products, but they did not have a very accurate likeness. Due to the popularity of Christmas villages, TCF partnered with Kmart and Enesco to create a *Miracle* village, with Santa's parade float, a department store that kind of looks like Macy's Herald Square, a post office, a courthouse, and Susan's dream house. Several ornaments have also been issued, and in 2008, TCF partnered with Hallmark to create a line of cards based on the film.[757] Notably absent from all of these products are Maureen

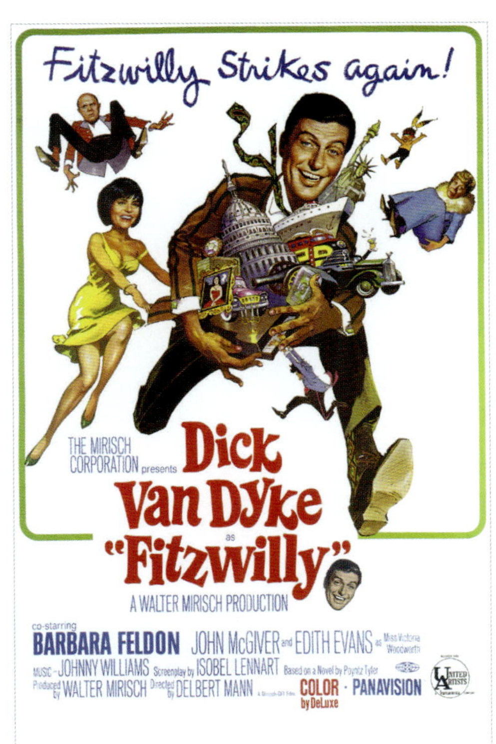

Gimbels can be seen in all of its 1960s Christmas splendor in the Dick Van Dyke/Barbara Feldon comedy *Fitzwilly* (1967), when it became the victim of a heist. (Photofest)

O'Hara, John Payne, and Natalie Wood, since TCF would have to get permission from those stars to include their likenesses; hence, the merchandise was usually just focused on Edmund Gwenn, who did not leave an estate.

THE CAST AND CREW: AN EPILOGUE

Miracle ended up being a highlight in the careers of many of the people involved in its creation. In the decade following *Miracle*, Valentine Davies would stick around TCF, finishing his seven-year contract as a screenwriter by working on some nice pieces of Americana, such as the screenplay of his own baseball comedy story, *It Happens Every*

In a nostalgic nod to *Miracle*, Gimbels finally got a starring role in a big Christmas movie when director Jon Favreau selected it as the name for the department store in his 2003 film *Elf,* starring Will Ferrell and James Caan. (Photofest)

Spring (1949), for which he would get another Oscar nomination, and the aforementioned *Chicken Every Sunday* (1949). He reworked the scripts for several film musicals, including *Three Little Girls in Blue* (1946; a remake of *Moon Over Miami*), *You Were Meant for Me* (1948; a remake of *Orchestra Wives*), and *On the Riviera* (1951; a remake of *Week-End in Havana*).

After TCF, Davies worked at Paramount, Universal, and MGM, writing screenplays for such films as the William Holden/Grace Kelly feature, *The Bridges of Toko-Ri* (1955), which was produced and directed by William Perlberg and George Seaton, and the Bob Hope/Lana Turner comedy, *Bachelor in Paradise* (1961). His most famous post-TCF effort was *The Glenn Miller Story* (1954), starring James Stewart and June Allyson. He wrote the story and the screenplay, and would again be nominated for an Academy Award. That filmed sparked a flurry of musical biopics throughout the rest of the 1950s, including his own *The Benny Goodman Story* (1956), which would be the only full-length film he directed during his career. He got one more Oscar nomination for his 1956 documentary, *The House Without a Name.* He was serving as the president of the Academy of Motion Picture Arts and Sciences at the time of his untimely death at age fifty-five, in 1961. After his passing, the Writers Guild of America established an award in his honor.

Valentine Davies would get another Oscar nomination for his story that was made into *It Happens Every Spring* (1949), starring Ray Milland. (Photofest)

Valentine Davies wrote the screenplay for the popular biopic *The Glenn Miller Story* (1954), starring James Stewart and June Allyson. As a follow-up he wrote and directed *The Benny Goodman Story* (1955) with Steve Allen as the famous bandleader. (Photofest)

Perlberg and Seaton would also stay at TCF for a few more years, sometimes paired together and sometimes working individually. When Seaton's contract came up for renewal during the filming of *Miracle*, he was compared to other first-rate directors like Otto Preminger, Lamar Trotti, and Henry King.[758] At the time, he was earning $3,000 per week.[759] Perlberg and Seaton wanted to work together exclusively as a production team. TCF did not want to allow this, so the two men approached Paramount, which was happy to accommodate their request.[760]

The move ended up being a good one. While there, the Perlberg-Seaton partnership would become one of the premier independent production teams in Hollywood, creating such films as *The Bridges of Toko-Ri* (1955), *Teacher's Pet* (1958), *The Counterfeit Traitor* (1962), and *36 Hours* (1965).[761]

Although Alfred Hitchcock is often credited with making Grace Kelly a star, it was actually Seaton who wrote the screenplay and directed her Oscar-winning performance in *The Country Girl* (1954), for which he also won the Oscar for Best Screenplay. He would serve as president of the Screen Writers Guild in 1947–1948; vice president of the Screen Directors Guild in 1950–1951; and as president of the Academy of Motion Picture Arts and Sciences for three consecutive terms, from 1955 through 1958. During his tenure in the latter, Seaton had the opportunity of directing a film for the Colonial Williamsburg organization as an orientation film for the historic site. Titled *Williamsburg: The Story of a Patriot* (1957), it starred a young Jack Lord, prior to his achieving TV fame in *Hawaii Five-O* a decade later. It is very possibly the longest continuously running film in history.

Late in his career, Seaton wrote and directed *Airport* (1970), which launched the disaster-movie phenomenon of the 1970s, and would remain Universal's biggest moneymaker until *Jaws* came out in 1976.[762] Seaton passed away in 1979.

Perlberg was committed to helping the next generation of filmmakers, and advocated to get full-credit film-production classes going at UCLA and USC, being a lecturer at both universities. He also served as the first president of the Screen Producers Guild.[763] He died in 1968.[764]

Miracle, in many ways, came at the apex of Maureen O'Hara's early career. She was one of Hollywood's top actresses, making several films a year, and constantly in the public's eye. As *Miracle* wrapped up, she was able to renegotiate her contract with TCF and doubled her salary—from $2,000 to $4,000 per week—resulting in one of the best contracts in the industry (the same compensation as TCF's biggest male star, Tyrone Power).[765]

Following *Miracle*, O'Hara filmed *The Foxes of Harrow* (1947) with Rex Harrison. She would continue to have

The Bridges at Toko-Ri (1955), starring William Holden and Grace Kelly was one of the early successes produced by William Perlberg and George Seaton after leaving Twentieth Century-Fox and moving to Paramount. (Photofest)

Although Grace Kelly is best remembered for her work with Alfred Hitchcock, it was George Seaton who directed her in *The Country Girl* (1954), which won her the Academy Award for Best Actress. Here she is on Oscar night with Marlon Brando who won for Best Actor. (Photofest)

William Perlberg produced and George Seaton directed Clark Gable and Doris Day in the journalism-based comedy *Teacher's Pet* (1958). (Photofest)

George Seaton directed *Airport* (1970), the first of the 1970s disaster films. (Photofest)

In the second of five films they made together, John Wayne and Maureen O'Hara were directed by John Ford in the Irish-themed *The Quiet Man* (1952). O'Hara would now have two holiday classics to her credit. She would later quip: "When I'm nailed into the box and long gone you'll still be seeing [*Miracle on 34th Street*] every Christmas and *The Quiet Man* every March." (Photofest)

hit movies, such as the comedy *Sitting Pretty* (1948) with Robert Young, and she would play Natalie Wood's mother again, in *Father was a Fullback* (1949), before leaving TCF and becoming a freelancer.

O'Hara co-starred with John Payne again for the fourth and final time in the period adventure *Tripoli* (1950), about the early days of the US Marine Corps. The film was directed by her husband, Will Price. The experience did not help their rocky marriage, and they divorced a couple of years later.[766] O'Hara would have another hit film when John Ford called on her again to appear in the Irish-themed *The Quiet Man* (1952). She was teamed with John Wayne, the second of their five films together, and the film would become a classic—almost required viewing on St. Patrick's Day. She now had two acknowledged holiday perennials to her credit, and would later say, "When I'm nailed into the box and long gone, you'll still be seeing [*Miracle on 34th Street*] every Christmas and *The Quiet Man* every March."[767]

A decade later, O'Hara would show off her comedic skills and give her career another huge boost when she appeared as Hayley Mills's hip mom in *The Parent Trap* (1961). She would continue to be a major star throughout the 1960s, until retiring from film in the early 1970s, when she got married for the third time to Charlie Blair, who became the love of her life. She briefly came out of retirement in the 1990s to star opposite John Candy in *Only the Lonely* (1991), and made some TV movies, including *The Christmas Box* (1995). As late as the 1990s, she was still very much identified with *Miracle.* She would often tell this story:

> *Just before Christmas, I was in New York, and I was coming home from Mass in the middle of the day and about five young kids came up behind me, and they pulled on my coat and they said, "You're the lady that knows Santa Claus,*

aren't you?" and I turned around and I said, "Yes, I know Santa Claus very, very well." [768]

Maureen O'Hara passed away in 2015 as one of Hollywood's legendary grandes dames.

Miracle would be John Payne's last film at TCF, marking the end of a chapter of his career. His contract with the studio ended in September of 1947, and he never made another movie there.

After leaving TCF, he delved into gritty crime dramas and Westerns, and in the late 1950s, he even produced and starred as Vint Bonner in his own Western TV show, *The Restless Gun*. Apparently, he liked co-starring with redheads, and appeared in several pictures with Rhonda Fleming. His marriage to Gloria DeHaven, after six years and two children, would end in divorce in 1950.[769] Payne's third marriage, to Alexandra Beryl Crowell, would be his longest, lasting the rest of his life.[770]

Tragedy literally hit Payne in the early 1960s when he was struck by a car while crossing Madison Avenue at 61st Street in New York City (in a bizarre coincidence, at the same intersection seen in the opening sequence of *Miracle*). He was hit with enough force to throw him into the air, causing him to land on the car and smash the windshield. He broke his leg, was badly bruised, cut his head and face, and got glass in his eyes. He would require plastic surgery, and live with scars for the rest of his life.[771] It took a long time to recover, and curtailed his professional activities for several years.

Nonetheless, in 1964, Payne would take over the role of Fred in the touring company of *Here's Love*, the Broadway musical based on *Miracle*. In the early 1970s, he reunited with his former TCF co-star, Alice Faye, in a touring theater revival production of the 1920s musical *Good News*.[772] He would appear periodically as a guest star on various television shows into the 1970s.

Payne was always fond of *Miracle* and wanted to do a sequel; he even told O'Hara that he had written a

In contrast to their first picture *To the Shores of Tripoli* (1942) about modern life in the US Marine Corps, Maureen O'Hara and John Payne's fourth and final picture together, *Tripoli* (1950), would focus on the early days of that branch of service. Payne would be the handsome lieutenant, O'Hara would be the beautiful gold digger, and pirates and mayhem along the Barbary Coast would keep the action moving forward. (Photofest)

Maureen O'Hara got a complete makeover as a hip mother to Hayley Mills (times two) in *The Parent Trap* (1961). The role reinvigorated her career for another decade. (Photofest)

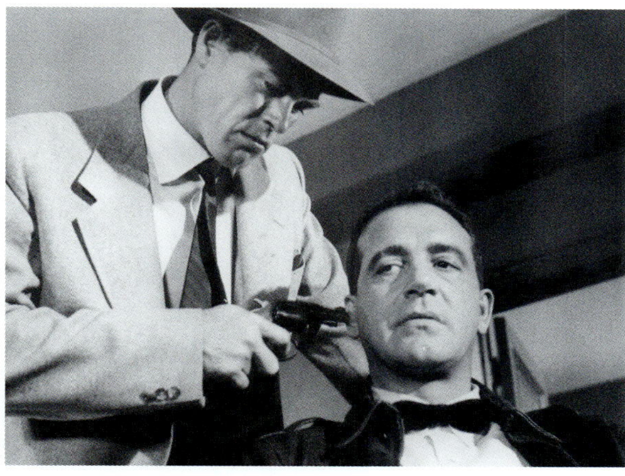

Following *Miracle*, in an attempt to get away from his image as a musical-comedy actor, John Payne did a series of gritty film noirs in the late 1940s and early 1950s. Here he is in *99 River Street* (1953) with Jack Lambert. (Photofest)

John Payne also starred in several Westerns, such as *Silver Lode* (1954,) and eventually got his own western TV show. (Photofest)

One of John Payne's best film noirs was actually shot in color with the beautiful Rhonda Fleming and Arlene Dahl. (Photofest)

script although, to date, it has never surfaced.[773] Despite the fact that he had almost sixty films to his credit when he passed, his obituary in the *New York Times* read: "John Payne, 77, Actor, Is Dead; Lawyer in 'Miracle on 34th Street.' "[774] In fact, *Miracle* would be listed as a major accomplishment in the obituaries of almost every person connected with the film, including George Seaton, Gene Lockhart, Jack Albertson, Harry Antrim, Jerome Cowan, James Seay, Arthur Jacobson, and Lloyd Ahern.[775]

Kris Kringle would become Edmund Gwenn's signature role for the rest of his life. "I've had many letters addressed to Santa Claus, care of MGM, sent to me. I'd no idea that my work in *Miracle on 34th Street* meant so much. Naturally, I'm pleased and a little awed."[776] After the movie, Gwenn received many requests from department stores to come and appear as Santa Claus, and he did accept on some occasions, such as at a Christmas pageant sponsored by Neiman Marcus in Dallas, in 1948.[777] He joked that he was now being typecast.[778]

He would stay active in film for another decade, appearing in another twenty films and receiving another Oscar nomination for the TCF film, *Mister 880* (1950), in which he played a counterfeiter who eludes capture by the FBI. His last film credit was in Hitchcock's *The Trouble with Harry* (1956). Right before Gwenn died, in 1959, George Seaton went to visit him in the hospital. He was hooked up to various medical devices, and looked very uncomfortable. Seaton offered a sympathetic line, saying "It must be hard" to be in this situation. Gwenn retorted, "But not as hard as playing comedy." He died a few seconds later.[779]

Natalie Wood would continue to be at TCF for several more months. She had been filming *The Ghost and Mrs. Muir* (1947) simultaneously during the filming of *Miracle*, and then, when both of those wrapped up (*Miracle* on February 22, and *Ghost* on March 13), she stayed on to play June Haver's little sister in *Scudda Hoo! Scudda Hay!* (1947).[780] She was able to take the transition from child star to young actress in stride. She ended up starring in revered classics during each stage of her career: as a little girl, she appeared in *Miracle*; as a teenager, she appeared opposite iconoclast James Dean in *Rebel Without a Cause* (1955), and picked up her first Oscar nomination; and then as an adult, she was in *West Side Story* and *Splendor in the Grass* (both 1961), garnering another Oscar nomination for the latter. For her third Oscar nomination, she would once again play a character associated with Macy's department store (this time as a salesclerk) in the romance *Love with the Proper Stranger* (1963), co-starring Steve McQueen. She continued to be one of Hollywood's top actresses through the 1960s.

She married three times—the first time to Robert Wagner, the second time to Richard Gregson, and the third time, to Robert Wagner again. She would have a daughter by each husband. Just as *Miracle* was starting its annual broadcasts on television in 1981, Wood tragically died under mysterious circumstances while yachting near Catalina Island on Thanksgiving weekend.

Edmund Gwenn would get a second Oscar nomination for his role as a counterfeiter in *Mister 880* (1950). (Photofest)

Edmund Gwenn would finish his illustrious film career appearing in Alfred Hitchcock's *The Trouble with Harry* (1956) with John Forsythe. (Photofest)

Maureen O'Hara and Natalie Wood got to play a mother and daughter again a few years after *Miracle* in the Twentieth Century-Fox film *Father Was a Fullback*, released in 1949. Fred MacMurray played the titular father. (Photofest)

Natalie Wood got the plum role of Maria in the classic musical *West Side Story* (1961). It was one of the biggest hits that year and walked away with the Oscar for Best Picture. (Photofest)

Natalie Wood's appearance in *Rebel Without a Cause* (1955) with James Dean provided the perfect transition to more adult roles. She ended up being nominated for an Oscar. (Photofest)

All grown up, Natalie Wood found herself back at Macy's in *Love with the Proper Stranger* (1963) but, instead of visiting Santa, she was a salesgirl in the pet shop on the fifth floor. Her she is discussing difficult decisions with Steve McQueen. The role got her another Oscar nomination. (Photofest)

Miracle on 34th Street succeeds on many levels, but ultimately its message that the "intangibles" like kindness, joy, and love are the only things that are worthwhile has resonated with audiences and kept it relevant through the years. (Photofest)

Conclusion

After more than seventy-five years, *Miracle on 34th Street* has become part of the fabric of Christmas in America. It is regularly featured on critics' "best of" lists in a number of genres, including Christmas, fantasy, family, and inspirational films. Despite all of the adaptations, it is the original black-and-white film that has prevailed as the preferred version of the story. This was confirmed when Twentieth Century-Fox released it on Blu-ray in 2009, and did not include the colorized version or the 1955 TV movie, as it had in the past—a somewhat daring move, since special features usually add value. But it didn't seem to matter; three subsequent Blu-ray editions have not included them either, and the film still sells. The message is clear: The devotees of *Miracle on 34th Street* want the original film as it was originally conceived, in all of its black-and-white glory.

So what makes *Miracle* so endearing and so enduring? There are a few obvious reasons. For one, it's an entertaining film that is perfectly crafted. No doubt this is due to director George Seaton's nurturing of the story, from a simple "what if" idea into a well-developed screenplay, which he then translated onto the screen just as he had envisioned it. He ingeniously fashioned the clever story to play at two levels, with an appealing Santa plotline for children, and sophisticated humor to be relished by adults. It has a wonderful cast of delightful characters, each of whom is worth the price of admission. Particularly noteworthy are the children, who all give adorable performances, which is quite a feat for a director, since one bad child actor can often ruin an entire film. The nice production values and on location photography of the Macy's Thanksgiving Day Parade provide a glimpse of vintage New York that is also a treat.

A second obvious reason is that it's a Christmas movie, and Americans love Christmas movies—especially good Christmas ones, plain and simple. But the fact that it is about Christmas contributes to another reason for its longevity, which was completely unintended by the director: It has become nostalgic. George Seaton had wanted to make, in essence, a docudrama that was grounded in the real world; everything was supposed to be as authentic as possible, without an ounce of nostalgia. But by complete happenstance, because it was a Christmas movie that was released in a postwar world, and subsequently seen on TV every yuletide, year after year by millions of baby boomers (and their children), it's now one of the most nostalgic films in existence, a reminder of the merry little Christmases that they used to know back in the 1940s. The nostalgia is compounded by the fact that Natalie Wood grew up with that generation, and they "knew" her as she blossomed into a beloved movie star. For many, the yearly ritual of watching her as a little girl is like reconnecting with a childhood friend; even though they are all grown up, it gives them the chance to reminisce about how life once was when they were all kids.

Aside from just being a great little Christmas movie, another major reason that the film has endured is that Seaton succeeded in creating a very relatable human drama. As one critic pointed out, "It's one of those somewhat rare films which strike such a responsive note because it's based on natural, everyday life," and full of characters that are "especially real."[781] Seaton captured so many little episodes of family life throughout the film that feel very authentic and very universal. He effectively portrays some of the frustrating moments of parenting, like Peter's mother traipsing around the city, trying to find a certain toy for her son; Mrs. Mara telling Tommy to go get some scissors so he doesn't hear what his parents are talking about; and Mr. Mara being stuck between a rock and a hard place when his own words come back to haunt him as his son testifies about Santa Claus. In Doris, he exemplifies the difficulties of a single mother who has the responsibility of raising a daughter by herself while juggling a career.

Seaton also created some wonderful vignettes depicting a variety of marriages. He shows Mr. Shellhammer as a husband who has to manipulate his wife so she will say yes to having Santa Claus stay with them; Mr. Sawyer telling everyone that he is in a happy marriage when he clearly is not; and Mrs. Harper being critical of her husband and siding with the grandchildren when her husband is just trying to do his job.

In addition, Seaton also accurately depicted some of the difficulties people face in their professional lives, like Doris making an executive decision to let Kris go, only to find out that that's exactly what her boss didn't want, and then having to try and rectify the situation. He shows Judge Harper's dilemma of carrying out the duties of his job while being faced with the unpleasant consequences of such a course of action. Fred faces the all-too-common internal debate so many people experience, as to whether they should stay in a steady job because it pays well, or whether they should pursue something they really want to do. Almost every human, at some point, will experience at least one of these episodes in his or her own life.

In addition to being a wonderful human drama, *Miracle* also resonates on a deeper level because it gets at the heart of what Christmas should be all about. Despite being set in a patently commercial setting, the movie's message is not about consumerism or corporate profits; in fact, it encourages just the opposite. Susan's wish is not for toys, but rather for a stable home environment; and Fred quits his lucrative legal job to help the helpless. Through the characters of Fred and Doris, the film communicates that logic, reason, and the cold, hard facts are not the things that should be ruling our lives. In one of the most famous lines from the movie, Fred tells Doris that "Faith is believing in things when common sense tells you not to," which stresses the importance of hope. But perhaps the more important message of the film is when he tells her that she needs to realize that the "lovely intangibles" like "kindness and joy and love . . . are the only things that are worthwhile"; everything else is of little value. It is Doris's wholehearted adoption of these "lovely intangibles" that effectuate the change in her.

The film also demonstrates how, by small and simple actions, one person (in this case, it just happens to be someone who thinks he's Santa Claus) can be an influence for good on other people. Like many of the great Christmas stories, from *A Christmas Carol* to *The Gift of the Magi* to *The Grinch Who Stole Christmas*, *Miracle* is ultimately a narrative about how the spirit of Christmas can transform a person for the better.[782] Perhaps that's why so many of the audiences who first saw the film clapped at the end. *Miracle* unabashedly proclaims that there is an antidote to the negativity and the purveyors of doom and gloom in the world.[783] Perhaps it is this message that has made *Miracle on 34th Street* a Christmas classic, and has kept us coming back year after year.

Appendix A

THE *MIRACLE ON 34TH STREET* SEVENTY-FIFTH ANNIVERSARY ON-LOCATION TOUR

Since much of *Miracle* was filmed on location, you can still go visit many of these places. Here's where you can go, seventy-five years on.

Begin your tour on the northeast corner of Madison Avenue and 62nd Street in Manhattan. This is where Kris begins his walk during the opening credits.

Cross the street to the west side and continue down Madison Avenue, until you reach 61st Street, where you can turn right and walk halfway down the block to 19 East. This is where the Lillian Schary Waldman Interior Decoration store was in the film. (The building is gone, and the site is now occupied by a Tom Ford clothing boutique.)

You can then experience a deleted scene. After correcting the order of the reindeer in the window display, Kris walked over to Central Park Zoo to feed the reindeer. Of course, there are no reindeer in the zoo, but you can visit some of the other animals as a substitute.

It was while he was at the zoo that Kris heard the strains of "Jingle Bells" and wandered through Central Park, over to the parade route. You can do that too (while streaming a symphonic version of "Jingle Bells" on your mobile device for the full effect), and find your way over to 77th Street and Central Park West. There, you can stand on 77th Street between the American Museum of Natural History and the New York Historical Society. This is where Doris and Kris first meet.

You can then walk the forty-three-block parade route down Central Park West, turning onto Broadway and continuing, until you reach 34th Street. As you pass

The intersection of Madison Avenue and 62nd Street is where *Miracle on 34th Street* begins. (Author's collection)

This artful lamppost (or perhaps its predecessor) can be seen during the opening credits as Kris walks down Madison Avenue. (Author's collection)

The 1946 parade route started here at Central Park West and 77th Street. The area still looks very much the same with the New York Historical Society on the left, the American Museum of Natural History in the middle, and the Beresford apartment building towering in the background. (Author's collection)

the stately apartment buildings, you can decide which one you think Doris and Fred lived in. If you want, you can stop at 253 West 58th Street, where an apartment on the third floor was used for filming. For full reenactment effect, stream "Sabres and Spurs," "National Emblem March," and a marching band version of "Santa Claus Is Comin' to Town" as you promenade.

Another stop you can make along the way is at the northeast corner of Seventh Avenue and 50th Street, where, in the 1940s, the Hotel Taft and Roxy Theatre complex was located. The building now hosts a hotel and condominiums. The lobby of the Roxy occupied the south end of the first floor of the Taft Hotel, and then the auditorium extended in the back, along 50th Street. This is where *Miracle* had its world premiere and played for a month in June 1947. You can stand here and pretend you are waiting four deep in line to be one of the 21,171 people who saw *Miracle* on its opening day. The Roxy was tragically torn down in 1960, and America lost one of its

The parade route continued down Central Park West. Which building do you think Fred and Doris lived in? (Author's collection)

greatest theaters. It was memorialized in the November 7, 1960 (page 46), issue of *Life* magazine, with actress Gloria Swanson (whose movie *The Love of Sunya* was the first movie to play here in 1927) in a dramatic pose amid the rubble. The theater was replaced by (what else?) a boring office building.

Once you arrive at Macy's on 34th Street, heading west, note the canopies that are still there. These can be seen when Kris arrives at Macy's at the end of the parade, and when Dr. Sawyer gets Kris into the limousine under false pretenses to go to Bellevue. Since this is a film-related tour, make sure to stop and read the plaque about halfway down the block, which states "Here the Motion Picture Began: On the night of April 23, 1896, on this site in Koster & Bial's Music Hall, Thomas A. Edison with the "Vitascope" first projected a moving picture."

After digesting this fascinating little fact, continue walking down and cross over to the southwest corner of

The canopies along 34th Street at Macy's are still recognizable from the film. (Author's collection)

34th Street and 7th Avenue. You can then look up (and take a picture if you want) of the street sign, with Macy's facade in the background, just as we see it in the movie (except, apparently, it's no longer smart to be thrifty—that's been removed from Macy's—and Seventh Avenue is now also known as Fashion Avenue).

With a few additions and subtractions, the corner of 34th Street and Seventh Avenue still looks much like it did in 1946. (Author's collection)

You can then enter Macy's. Understandably, most of the store has been renovated during the past seventy-five years, and does not appear as it does in the movie, but if you do go during December, you can still experience the crowds of holiday shoppers as depicted in the film.

There are still some traces of *Miracle* in the store. We know that the North Pole Annex in 1946 was on the seventh floor, just as you exited the bank of elevators on the west side of the store, and the facing on the walls appears to be the same as it was in 1946. The bank of escalators located behind the elevators has definitely not been updated. You can briefly see Mr. Sawyer and Mr. Shellhammer getting off the "up" escalators on the seventh floor before they escort Kris to Bellevue.

You can then go up to the eighth floor, where Santa now sits in residence during the Christmas season. There is now a display dedicated to *Miracle on 34th Street* here. Maureen O'Hara came and unveiled these animated displays when they were created for the street-level Christmas windows in 1999. They were subsequently moved up here to be a permanent fixture. The windows depict four scenes from the movie: Kris correcting the order of the reindeer; Fred and Susan watching the parade go by; Kris sitting on his throne; and the postal workers delivering the letters in the courtroom. There is a faux movie theater marquee and a *Miracle* movie

Make sure to stop and read about this interesting little piece of film history. (Author's collection)

In 1946, the North Pole Annex was located in the area in front of this bank of elevators on the west side of the 7th floor. (Author's collection)

poster, and the film is on a constant loop that you can stop and watch if you want.

After completing your tour of Macy's, you can exit through the doors on Broadway, turn right, and walk down to the old Gimbels store. It took up the frontage from 32nd Street to 33rd Street on the

Mr. Shellhammer and Dr. Sawyer can be seen getting off the 7th floor "up" escalators before escorting Kris to Bellevue. The escalators look very much like they did in 1946. (Author's collection)

On the 8th floor of Macy's, stop and see this permanent display of animated windows created as an homage to the film. (Author's collection)

The stately New York County Supreme Courthouse, located at 60 Centre Street in lower Manhattan, is where Kris's sanity hearing took place. (Author's collection)

The rotunda of the New York County Supreme Courthouse still looks much the same as it did when *Miracle* was filmed here in 1946. (Author's collection)

west side of Sixth Avenue. It is now unrecognizable from the way it appeared in the film, because it has been covered in glass paneling, but if you walk down 32nd or 33rd Street, you can see what the building looked like, since these facades have not been modernized.

You can then head over to First Avenue, where you will find the old Bellevue psychiatric hospital building to which Kris was taken. It is located on the northeast corner of the intersection with 29th Street. The exterior was filmed, but got cut from the final version.

You can then head down (on foot or by subway) to the New York County Supreme Courthouse at 60 Centre Street in Lower Manhattan. This is where Kris's sanity hearing took place. The exterior looks much the same as it did in the film. As it is a public building, you can go inside as long as you are willing to go through a security check. The courthouse was completed in 1927, and was a little less than twenty years old when *Miracle* was filmed

Although the courtroom scenes were not shot on location, the Twentieth Century-Fox art department did a pretty good job capturing the look and feel of the actual courtrooms in the New Your County Supreme Courthouse, of which this is one. (Author's collection)

Though the shot of Doris and Kris on the steps of the courthouse was a process shot created back at the studio, the footage was shot from this angle. (Author's collection)

here. You will instantly recognize the beautiful rotunda, where Dr. Sawyer tries to persuade Fred to avoid anything that will bring publicity. Take some time to view the murals, which were completed during the 1930s as part of the Works Progress Administration. You can then go peek into one of the courtrooms on the upper floors. You will be impressed at how similar they look to the courtroom that was re-created at the Twentieth Century-Fox lot in Los Angeles. (For more information on the building, check out their website: https://history.nycourts.gov.)

If you are really adventurous and want to explore the greater New York metropolitan area, you can go see Susan's dream house. It is located at 24 Derby Road in Port Washington (not in Manhasset, where Fred said he wanted to live, but still on Long Island).[784] It is adjacent to the Nassau Knolls Cemetery. The house is clearly recognizable; the only major change is a large dormer that was added to the roof on the second floor. The interior, of course, was a set back at the TCF lot, so there's no reason to try to go inside. If you do decide to visit the house, remember that this is a private residence, so please be respectful.

One place that you will never find, should you go looking for it, is the Brooks' Memorial Home for the Aged, purportedly located at 126 Maplewood Drive in Great Neck on Long Island (according to Kris's employment card). The facade, which we see Doris and Susan enter on Christmas Day, was not real, but the result of special effects done by TCF expert, Fred Sersen. Another example of movie magic.

It is always fun to see the locales where a film was made and we are lucky that so many are still extant. Hopefully this little romp around New York will let you experience some of the magic of *Miracle on 34th Street.*

<h1 align="center">Appendix B</h1>

<h2 align="center">FILMING LOCATIONS INFORMATION SHEET</h2>

```
A-512                        "MIRACLE ON 34TH STREET"  Art Dir.Irvine
PERLBERG-PRODUCER            GEORGE SEATON,DIRECTOR
Hall-Prod.Mgr.(Golden)      A.Jacobson-Asst.Dir.
Clarke-Cameraman             PICTURE STARTED 11/26/46  Key Grip-Faxon

    51201 INT.DORIS & FRED'S APT.,PROC. 1/6-7-8-9-___   FOLDED STG.14
                (10-11-13-15-16-20-21-22-24-25-27
  F 51202 INT.COURTROOM__2/10-11-12-13-14-15________   FOLDED    " 14
    51203 EXT.NEW YORK LOC.11/26-27-28-29-30-12/1-2-    SHOT  LOC.
                (3-4-5-6-7-8-9-10-11-12-13-14-15-17-18-
  F 51204 INT.JUDGE HARPER'S CHAMBERS______2/19        FOLDED STG. 3
  F 51205 INT.MACY'S 7TH FLOOR______1/18-23-28-29      FOLDED  "   B
  F 51206 INT.DORIS' OFFICE__________1/30-31-2/3-4      FOLDED  "   3
  F 51207 INT.SAWYER'S OFFICE _______1/31________       FOLDED  "  14
  F 51208 EXT.DORIS' APT., PROC. ____1/17________        SHOT   "  14
  F 51209 INT.MACY'S CAFETERIA ______2/1 ________        SHOT   "  14
  F 51210 INT.LIMOUSINE PROC.________1/17________       FOLDED  "  14
  F 51211 EXT.COURTHOUSE PROC._______1/17________       FOLDED  "  14
  F 51212 INT.TOY DEPT. ______________1/29________      FOLDED  "   B
    51213 INT.CHRIS' RM., MEMORIAL HOME_________          OUT   "   6
  F 51214 INT.MEMORIAL HOME,L.F.______2/5-6-7_____      FOLDED  "   6
  F 51215 INT.DOCTOR'S OFF.,BELLEVUE 2/8________        FOLDED  "  14
  F 51216 INT.CHRIS' RM., BELLEVUE__2/6-7________       FOLDED  "   6
                (Psychiatrist Sitting Rm)
  F 51217 INT.FRED'S CAR, PROC.________1/29-2/8________ FOLDED  "  14
  F 51218 INT.SHELLHAMMER'S APT.______2/1______________ FOLDED  "  14
    51219 EXT.REINDEER PEN______________________________   OUT   VENTURA
  F 51220 INT.CHRISTMAS HOUSE________2/21______________       STG.
                (Incl.Hall,Stairs,Liv.Rm.)
  F 51221 INT.EXAM RM.________________1/31_____________ FOLDED STG.
                (Macy's Hospital)
  F 51222 INT.JUDGE HARPER'S LIV.RM._2/20______________        "   6
  F 51223 EXT.MEMORIAL HOME-SIGN______2/22____________ BLACK FCXE
  F 51224 INT.DORIS' OFF. RETAKE______3/1_____________    SHOT  STG. 3
  F 51225 INT.MARA'S APT.______________2/28___________    SHOT   "   6
  F 51226 EXT.N.Y.ST.__________________3/1____________    SHOT  STG. 3
```

One of only a handful of original production documents to survive from Miracle on 34th Street (aside from the legal files), this art department set construction sheet lists the dates of filming and the locations (and, incidentally, spurred the writing of this book). Due to staining, the original is difficult to read and so the information has been retyped to recreate the original. "F" indicates that set construction was completed; "51201, 521202," etc. references the production number "512" and the set numbers "01, 02," etc.; "INT." and "EXT." indicate whether the shot was an interior or an exterior shot in the script; "PROC." refers to a special effects "process" shot with rear projection; "BLACK FCXE" refers to a special effects shot; "FOLDED" refers to the breaking down of a set; and "LOC" refers to shooting on location. The stage information for the "CHRISTMAS HOUSE" and "EXAM RM-(Macy's Hospital)" is missing due to a paper tear on the original.

Appendix C

WARDROBE DESCRIPTIONS

How accurate is the colorized version? Here are color descriptions of the costumes from the original wardrobe continuity books. Note that there was not complete or consistent information for all wardrobe changes, so there are some gaps. Descriptions of costumes from the deleted scenes are included.

MAUREEN O'HARA (DORIS)
Change #1
(parade, and Fred's apartment)

Suit: two-piece brown wool, white bead trim
Coat: camel hair
Hat: tan beaver cloth, brown satin sequin trim band
Shoes: brown kid leather, bow trim
Hose: dark nylons
Scarf: green and brown silk, large square
Gloves: tan fabric
Bag: tan kid leather, gold emblem
Ring: silver (to cover wedding ring)

Change #2
(on phone in Doris's apartment)

Robe: navy blue flannel
Slippers: medium blue

Change #3
(Susan meeting Kris at Macy's; in Mr. Macy's office)

Dress: two-piece gray with black trim, coat fastened in this scene
Sweater: black bouclé
Jewelry: silver ring and earrings
Hose: dark nylons
Shoes: black suede

Change #4
(meeting with Dr. Pierce)

Dress: two-piece suit, brown wool, white bead trim
Hose: dark nylons
Shoes: brown kid, bow trim
Ring: silver
Earrings: pearl

Change #5
(dinner at Doris's apartment)

Blouse: white crepe, gold lamé trim
Skirt: brown wool from Change #1
Apron: light green and black, cotton
Hose: dark nylons
Shoes: brown kid, bow trim
Ring: silver

Change #6
(deleted Sunday brunch scene)

Skirt: brown wool
Blouse: tan stripe
Apron: blue plaid
Hose: dark nylons
Shoes: brown kid leather, bow trim
Ring: silver

Change #7 / 7A
(deleted searching-for-Kris scenes)

Dress: three-piece gray and black suit
Sweater: black bouclé
Hat: black felt, black ribbon band
Gloves: black fabric
Bag: black kid, shoulder
Hose: dark nylons
Shoes: black suede

Ring: silver
Earrings: silver

Change #8
(deleted nightmare scene)

Dress: powder-blue flannel
Mules: light blue and silver
Handkerchief: white, lace trim
Ring: silver

Change #9
(Dr. Sawyer's office and in the infirmary)

Dress: two-piece gray with black trim; jacket open
in this scene
Sweater: black bouclé
Hose: dark nylons
Shoes: black suede
Ring: silver
Earrings: silver

Change #10
(argument in Doris's apartment)

Dress: black wool with lace collar
Shoes: black suede
Hose: dark nylons
Necklace: two-strand pearl
Ring: silver
Earrings: pearl button

Change #11
(writing the letter to Kris; courtroom)

Dress: two-tone blue wool, gray-blue and navy
Coat: camel hair
Beret: large navy felt
Gloves: black fabric
Bag: navy, shoulder
Hose: dark nylons
Ring: silver
Earrings: pearl

Change #12
(Christmas Eve, courtroom)

Dress: three-piece gray and black wool
Hat: small black felt
Gloves: black fabric
Sweater: black bouclé
Bag: shoulder, gold emblem
Hose: dark nylons
Shoes: black suede
Ring: silver
Earrings: silver

Change #14 and 14A
(Christmas Day)

Dress: aqua blue wool
Coat: nutria fur (Maureen O'Hara's own coat)
Hat: light beaver with nutria fur trim
Gloves: tan fabric
Bag: tan kid leather, short straps
Hose: dark nylons
Shoes: brown kid leather, bow trim
Scarf: print chiffon, sequin trim
Necklace: two-strand pearl
Ring: silver

John Payne (Fred)
Change #1
(Fred's apartment)

Suit: gray, single-breasted, with red-and-blue-
thread stripe
Shirt: gray
Tie: blue with red and light blue small figures
Shoes: brown
Handkerchief: white

Change #2
(Susan meeting Kris at Macy's)

Suit: brown, double-breasted
Shirt: tan
Tie: brown with red and yellow figures

Overcoat: gray herringbone
Shoes: light brown
Gloves: pigskin
Scarf: blue
Handkerchief: white

Change #3
(dinner at Doris's apartment)

Suit: brown, double-breasted
Shirt: tan
Tie: maroon with figures
Shoes: brown
The following articles of clothing were added for the deleted scenes of Fred taking Kris out to the Brooks' Home to collect his things:
Overcoat: navy
Hat: brown
Gloves: pigskin
Scarf: red, blue, yellow, and green plaid

Change #4
(Fred's bedroom)

Pajamas: light tan, rayon
Slippers: heel-less alligator

Change #5
(deleted Sunday-brunch scene)

Suit: brown, three-piece, single-breasted
Shirt: tan
Tie: maroon knit
Shoes: light tan oxford
Handkerchief: white

Change #7
(deleted searching-for-Kris and nightmare scenes)

Suit: dark green flannel, single-breasted, no vest
Shirt: blue
Tie: navy, white dot
Shoes: black
Overcoat: dark gray herringbone, three-button
Hat: brown

Change #8
(Fred's office)

Suit: brown, three-piece, single-breasted
Shirt: tan
Tie: red with tan and red teardrop figures
Shoes: brown oxfords

Change #9
(courtroom)

Suit: plain gray, two-piece
Shirt: white
Tie: maroon with design
Socks: black
Shoes: black
Handkerchief: white
The following articles of clothing were added for the argument in Doris's apartment:
Overcoat: gray herringbone
Hat: brown

Change #10
(second day of hearing)

Suit: gray with red-and-blue stripe, two-piece
Shirt: white
Tie: four-in-hand silk, dark blue, with small red and white figures
Shoes: black oxfords
Handkerchief: white

Change #11
(Christmas Eve, courtroom)

Suit: two-piece, single-breasted
Shirt: tan
Tie: four-in-hand silk, with red and tan hexagon figures
Shoes: light brown oxfords
Handkerchief: white

Change #12
(Christmas Day)

Suit: blue with chalk stripe, two-piece
Shirt: blue oxford

Tie: blue and white pattern
Shoes: dark brown
Overcoat: navy raglan
Scarf: blue wool, plain
Gloves: pigskin

Edmund Gwenn (Kris)
Change #1
(opening sequence)

Suit: brown tweed, orange stripe
Shirt: white
Tie: orange-and-tan wool check
Shoes: black
Coat: black, double-breasted
Hat: black homburg
Gloves: tan pigskin
Handkerchief: white
Cane

Change #4
(Sawyer's office; dinner at Doris's apartment)

Suit: brown tweed, three-piece, single-breasted
Shirt: white
Tie: orange-and-brown wool check
Shoes: black

Change #7 (Susan's bedroom)

Suit: gray flannel, three-piece
Shirt: white
Tie: maroon
Shoes: black
Handkerchief: white

Change #10
(courtroom)

Suit: dark blue, three-piece, single-breasted
Tie: four-in-hand, maroon wool

Natalie Wood (Susan)
Change #1
(Fred's apartment)

Dress: turquoise jersey
Sweater: pink (Natalie Wood's own)

Socks: brown, design top
Shoes: brown oxfords (Natalie Wood's own)

Change #2
(meeting Kris at Macy's)

Dress: turquoise jersey (same as Change #1)
Coat: red and green plaid wool
Socks: brown
Shoes: brown oxfords (Natalie Wood's own)
Hat: green felt
Gloves: red kid

Change #3
(dinner at Doris's apartment)

Pajamas: cotton print, two-piece
Robe: blue flannel, pink trim
Shoes: pink kid

Change #4
(deleted Sunday-brunch scene)

Dress: navy blue jersey
Ribbons: blue satin
Socks: brown, design top
Shoes: brown oxfords (Natalie Wood's own)

Change #5
(deleted nightmare scene)

Nightgown: light blue cotton, white eyelet trim
Robe: light blue flannel, pink trim
Shoes: pink kid

Change #6
(writing the letter to Kris)

Dress: turquoise jersey (same as Change #1)
Socks: brown, design top
Shoes: brown oxfords (Natalie Wood's own)

Change #7
(Christmas Day)

Dress: powder blue, lace trim
Socks: brown, design top
Shoes: black patent-leather Mary Janes
Coat: red wool, beaver trim
Gloves: beaver and kid mitts

Acknowledgments

Special thanks to (in alphabetical order):

Leighton Bowers, director of the Western Costume Research Library, for providing access to the wardrobe continuity books.

James D'Arc, for his help with images.

Stephanie Lundeen, for proofreading the manuscript.

David Miller, of the Twentieth Century Fox legal department, for providing access to the legal files.

Joel Parham, librarian at the Twentieth Century Fox Research Library, for his help with research.

Brian Passantino, for giving me a copy of the 1994 feature film version of *Miracle*.

Rick Rinehart, editor at Rowman & Littlefield, for approving the book.

David Wills, for his help with images.

A Note on the Sources

The original Twentieth Century-Fox production files are believed to have been discarded back in the early 1970s, around the same time that the publicity photographs were saved and put on deposit at UCLA. Since the production files are no longer extant, other sources were consulted. The Twentieth Century-Fox legal files (TCFLF) formed the basis for much of the information contained in the book. They were accessed in 2018, before the sale of TCF to Disney in 2019, and hence, their current location is unknown. The Valentine Davies papers at the Academy of Motion Picture Arts and Sciences (AMPAS) Margaret Herrick Library provided the other large corpus of archival material. The archive at Western Costume holds the original wardrobe continuity books. Most of the other information has been culled from published sources.

Endnotes

1   Jane Galbraith, "Now the Miracle is Off 34th Street, Macy's Says 'No Thanks' to a Remake of the Classic, So the Film Moves to Chicago," *Newsday,* (Combined Editions, Long Island, New York, April 18 1994. p.B13.

2   "Top Holiday Songs of 2022," www.ascap.com. ASCAP has published an annual list for several years. Accessed December 26, 2022.

3   "Skouras Outlines Plans for 20 of 25 on 20th-TCF Sked," *Hollywood Reporter,* February 20, 1947, p. 1.

4   [Davies, Valentine.] "Biographical sketch," V. D. papers, folder 72, AMPAS. This is a two-page sketch that appears to have been written by Davies himself.

5   [Davies, Valentine.] "Biographical sketch."

6   [Davies, Valentine.] "Biographical sketch."

7   Valentine Davies, "Why I Believe in Santa Claus, *Book News,* Christmas 1947, p. 5.

8   Davies, "Why I Believe in Santa Claus," p. 5.

9   Helen Colton, "George Seaton on Top," *New York Times*, November 14, 1948, p. X5; George Seaton, "Oral History with George Seaton, by David Chierichetti, January–June 1974," American Film Institute, 1974, p. 92.

10   Untitled "chronological statement" comparing the timeline of the creative process of *Miracle on 34th Street* to that of *An Angel on Horseback*, prepared for the litigation of *Burns v. Twentieth Century-Fox Film Corporation*. Accompanying cover letter from George Wasson to Harold Collins, February 5, 1948, TCFLF. The actual date that Davies shared his idea was January 24, 1945; "parties are certain of this date." *Twentieth Century-Fox Film Corporation Official Directory*, Los Angeles: Twentieth Century-Fox, 1946, p. 4, Twentieth Century-Fox Research Library.

11   Seaton, "Oral History with George Seaton by David Chierichetti," p. 92.

12   Davies, "Why I Believe in Santa Claus," p. 5.

13   Untitled "chronological statement" comparing the timeline of the creative process of *Miracle on 34th Street* to that of *An Angel on Horseback*.

14   Letter from Valentine Davies to James Barnett, July 9, 1951. V. D. papers, folder 72, AMPAS.

15   [Davies, Valentine.] "Mr. Kringle," [1945], TCFLF. This is the first written version of the story and is identified on the untitled chronological statement prepared for litigation as the "First Outline." It is twenty pages long and is a synopsis of fifty-two scenes.

16   Letter from Valentine Davies to Mr. Murrett, December 2, 1952, V. D. papers, folder 72, AMPAS.

17   Letter from Valentine Davies to James Barnett, July 9, 1951.

18   [Davies, Valentine.] "Mr. Kringle," [1945], TCFLF.

19   Letter from Valentine Davies to James Barnett, July 9, 1951.

20   Memo from Jason S. Joy to Lew Schreiber, April 22, 1947; Memo from Robert H. Patton to "Files," August 13, 1947; Memo from George Wasson to Mr. T. R. Frazer, August 15, 1947. TCFLF.

21   "Assignment" contract signed by John C. Eagan, MD, February 26, 1947, TCFLF.

22 Untitled "chronological statement" comparing the timeline of the creative process of *Miracle on 34th Street* to that of *An Angel on Horseback*.

23 Untitled "chronological statement" comparing the timeline of the creative process of *Miracle on 34th Street* to that of *An Angel on Horseback*; Letter from B. C. Roos of Beverly Management Corporation to Mr. Patton of TCF Legal Department, August 14, 1946, TCFLF.

24 Colton, "George Seaton on Top," p. X5.

25 "Lone Ranger Dead, Auto Hit Trailer," *New York Times*, April 9, 1941, p. 27.

26 "Perlberg-Seaton," *The Independent Film Journal*, June 30, 1956, p. 58.

27 "Writer-Director Seaton Double-Checks Himself!" *Miracle on 34th Street* [pressbook], Los Angeles: Twentieth Century-Fox, [1947], p. 25.

28 Untitled "chronological statement" comparing the timeline of the creative process of *Miracle on 34th Street* to that of *An Angel on Horseback*.

29 Untitled "chronological statement" comparing the timeline of the creative process of *Miracle on 34th Street* to that of *An Angel on Horseback*; "Notes . . . 'Kris Kringle,' " [undated], V. D. papers, folder 73, AMPAS. This is the second story outline, and is referred to in the legal records as a "step-sheet."

30 Untitled "chronological statement" comparing the timeline of the creative process of *Miracle on 34th Street* to that of *An Angel on Horseback*. The seventy-eight-page full-length version is referred to as the "First Full Handwritten Version."

31 Valentine Davies, "Author's Note," *Miracle on 34th Street* (New York: Harcourt, Brace & Company, 1947).

32 Untitled "chronological statement" comparing the timeline of the creative process of *Miracle on 34th Street* to that of *An Angel on Horseback*; Perlberg received a copy of the story on July 18, 1946.

33 *Twentieth Century-Fox Film Corporation Official Directory* (Los Angeles: Twentieth Century-Fox, 1946), p. 2, Twentieth Century-Fox Research Library.

34 "United States Census, 1910," William Perlberg in house of Israel Perlberg, Bronx Assembly District 34, New York, New York, United States; citing enumeration district (ED) 1561, sheet 3B, family 51. Available at www.familysearch.org. Accessed January 18, 2023.

35 "Perlberg-Seaton," *The Independent Film Journal*, June 30, 1956, p. 58.

36 Letter from Valentine Davies to Mr. and Mrs. Frank Bevan, July 26, 1946, V. D. papers, folder 73, AMPAS; Untitled "chronological statement" comparing the timeline of the creative process of *Miracle on 34th Street* to that of *An Angel on Horseback*.

37 Memo from Darryl Zanuck to Valentine Davies, June 5, 1947, V. D. papers, scrapbook #3, AMPAS.

38 Seaton, "Oral History with George Seaton by David Chierichetti," p. 91.

39 Sylvia Shorris and Marion Abbott Bundy (quoting Arthur Jacobson), *Talking Pictures with the People Who Made Them* (New York: The New Press, 1994), p. 20.

40 Seaton, "Oral History with George Seaton by David Chierichetti," p. 91.

41 *Chicken Every Sunday* would not go into production until 1948, even though it was listed as an upcoming production on 1946 and 1947 press releases. John Payne, Maureen O'Hara, Jeanne Crain, and Henry Fonda were all considered for the roles (*Variety*, October 23, 1946, p. 17; October 30, 1946, pp. 6, 25). According to cinema-

tographer Charles Clarke, Zanuck felt that it would be a more successful picture if filmed in color, but, due to the limited availability of Technicolor cameras, they couldn't. It was eventually filmed in black-and-white. See Charles G. Clarke, *Highlights and Shadows: The Memoirs of a Hollywood Cameraman* (Metuchen, NJ, and London: Scarecrow Press, 1989), p. 161.

42   Letter from Valentine Davies to Mr. and Mrs. Frank Bevan, July 26, 1946, V. D. papers, folder 73, AMPAS.

43   Rudy Behlmer, ed., *Memo from Darryl F. Zanuck: The Golden Years at Twentieth Century-Fox* (New York: Grove Press, 1993), p. 119.

44   Memo from Darryl Zanuck to Valentine Davies, June 5, 1947, V. D. papers, scrapbook #3, AMPAS.

45   Davies, "Why I Believe in Santa Claus," p. 5.

46   Memo from Lew Schreiber to George Wasson, August 7, 1946, TCFLF.

47   Telegram from E[dwin] P. Kilroe to George Wasson, August 26, 1946; Telegram from Donald A. Henderson to F. L. Metzler, September 3, 1946, TCFLF.

48   Memo from George Wasson to F. L. Metzler, et al., October 1, 1946, TCFLF.

49   Memo from George Wasson to Mr. [Lew] Schreiber, September 17, 1946, TCFLF.

50   "Flashes . . . Keeping Up with the Studios," *Box Office Digest*, November 9, 1946, p. 4.

51   "Writer-Director Seaton Double-Checks Himself!" *Miracle on 34th Street* [pressbook], p. 25.

52   Letter from Valentine Davies to James Barnett, July 9, 1951, V. D. papers, folder 72, AMPAS.

53   William R. Weaver, "Miracle on 34th Street," *Motion Picture Herald*, May 10, 1947, p. 3621.

54   Telegram from Edwin P. Kilroe to George Wasson, January 8, 1947; Letter from V. F. Sullivan of the *Daily News* to Mr. Henry Klinger, January 14, 1947, TCFLF.

55   Letter from V. F. Sullivan of the *Daily News* to Mr. Henry Klinger, January 14, 1947, TCFLF.

56   Telegram from George Wasson to E[dwin]. P. Kilroe, January 2, 1947, TCFLF.

57   Memo from William Perlberg to George Wasson, January 6, 1947, TCFLF.

58   Letter from Earl Wilson to Twentieth Century-Fox, January 16, 1947, TCFLF.

59   Letter from Marvin Berger of the *New York Post* to Jules Field, January 28, 1947, TCFLF.

60   Final script dated January 2, 1947, p. 108.

61   Letter from Paul J. G. Kidd of Hiram Walker & Sons, Inc., to William F. Sittel, December 27, 1946.

62   Untitled "chronological statement" comparing the timeline of the creative process of *Miracle on 34th Street* to that of *An Angel on Horseback*; Davies worked on the *Miracle* screenplay as a studio employee from October 28 to November 11, 1946.

63   Behlmer, ed., *Memo from Darryl F. Zanuck*, p. 120.

64   Letter from [Valentine Davies] to George [Seaton], December 2, 1946, V. D. papers, folder 73, AMPAS.

65   Behlmer, ed., *Memo from Darryl F. Zanuck*, p. 120.

66   Valentine Davies, "This is the Time," Valentine Davies Papers, Yale University Library, GEN MSS 1150, Box 1, p. 24.

67   Letter from [Valentine Davies] to George [Seaton], November 19, 1946, V. D. papers, folder 73, AMPAS.

68   Letter from Joseph T. Breen to Jason Joy, November 7, 1946, Production Code files for *Miracle on 34th Street*, AMPAS.

69   Letter from Joseph T. Breen to Jason Joy, dated November 21, 1946.

70   Memo from T. R. Frazer to All Departments, November 8, 1946, TCFLF.

71   "L.A. to N.Y.," *Variety*, November 27, 1946, p. 4.

72   Seaton, "Oral History with George Seaton by David Chierichetti," p. 103.

73   Untitled "chronological statement" comparing the timeline of the creative process of *Miracle on 34th Street* to that of *An Angel on Horseback*; Memo from Lew Schreiber to George Wasson, August 21, 1946, TCFLF.

74   Maureen O'Hara, with John Nicoletti, *'Tis Herself: A Memoir* (New York: Simon & Schuster, 2004), pp. 7–10.

75   O'Hara, *'Tis Herself: A Memoir*, p. 12.

76   *This is Your Life* [TV show] featuring Maureen O'Hara and her family. Episode originally aired March 27, 1957. Available on www.youtube.com. Accessed December 26, 2022.

77   O'Hara, *'Tis Herself: A Memoir*, pp. 15–17.

78   Lupton A. Wilkinson, "Hollywood Careers Hold Sober Lessons for Hopeful Job Hunters Everywhere," *Christian Science Monitor*, April 10, 1940, p. 7; "Redhead On Her Own," *Silver Screen*, November 1941, p. 26.

79   O'Hara, *'Tis Herself: A Memoir*, pp. 18–19.

80   Louis Berg, "Frozen Champagne," *Los Angeles Times*, March 30, 1947, p. 11. This statement explains why details differ in the various accounts of this encounter.

81   Aubrey Malone, *Maureen O'Hara: The Biography* (Lexington: University Press of Kentucky, 2013), p. 11.

82   O'Hara, *'Tis Herself: A Memoir*, p. 19.

83   O'Hara, *'Tis Herself: A Memoir*, p. 20.

84   *This is Your Life* [TV show] featuring Maureen O'Hara and her family, March 27, 1957.

85   Gladys Hall, "All the World Will Be Talking About Her!" *Silver Screen*, March 1940, p. 40.

86   Hall, "All the World Will Be Talking About Her!," p. 40; *This is Your Life* [TV show] featuring Maureen O'Hara and her family, March 27, 1957.

87   O'Hara, *'Tis Herself: A Memoir*, p. 23.

88   Malone, *Maureen O'Hara: The Biography*, p. 15.

89   O'Hara, *'Tis Herself: A Memoir*, p. 31.

90   O'Hara, *'Tis Herself: A Memoir*, pp. 46–47.

91   "Redhead On Her Own," p. 26.

92   Hall, "All the World Will Be Talking About Her!," p. 40.

93   O'Hara, *'Tis Herself: A Memoir*, pp. 33–34, 75.

94   Ben Maddox, " 'I Want to be Loved,' Says Maureen O'Hara," *Photoplay*, April 1942, p. 41; O'Hara, *'Tis Herself:*

A Memoir, p. 77.

95 O'Hara, *'Tis Herself: A Memoir*, pp. 59–62.

96 O'Hara, *'Tis Herself: A Memoir*, p. 67.

97 Marjorie Kent Candee, ed., *Current Biography* (New York: H. W. Wilson, 1953), p. 462.

98 Maureen O'Hara, "Feature Audio Commentary by Maureen O'Hara" (August 24, 2006). *Miracle on 34th Street*, Los Angeles: Twentieth Century Fox Home Entertainment, two-disc DVD set, 2006.

99 Candee, ed., *Current Biography*, p. 462.

100 Berg, "Frozen Champagne," p. 11; O'Hara, *'Tis Herself: A Memoir*, p. 15.

101 O'Hara, "Feature Audio Commentary by Maureen O'Hara" (August 24, 2006).

102 "Chatter," *Daily Variety*, August 21, 1946, p. 2; Maureen O'Hara, *AMC Backstory: Miracle on 34th Street*, Los Angeles: Twentieth Century Fox Home Entertainment, two-disc DVD, 2006.

103 O'Hara, *'Tis Herself: A Memoir*, p. 98.

104 "Ill in Pix," *Daily Variety*, September 12, 1946, p. 11.

105 "Old Race Story," *Daily Variety*, September 19, 1946, p. 1.

106 Memo from Lew Schreiber to George Wasson, August 20, 1946. There is additional correspondence between TCF and RKO, August–September, 1946, TCFLF.

107 "Maureen O'Hara and Daughter Leave for Ireland October 23," *Variety*, October 9, 1946, p. 79.

108 "TCF to Star O'Hara in Story by Davies," *New York Times*, October 9, 1946, p. 34.

109 Harry Brand, "Vital Statistics on 'Miracle on 34th Street' " [press release], Los Angeles: Twentieth Century-Fox, February 21, 1947.

110 "Europe to N.Y. Maureen O'Hara," *Variety*, November 20, 1946, p. 4; O'Hara, *'Tis Herself: A Memoir*, pp. 112–13. Doris Walker's job title is never identified in the film itself, but the pressbook identifies her as a "personnel manager." *Miracle on 34th Street* [pressbook], Los Angeles: Twentieth Century-Fox, [1947], p. 25.

111 O'Hara, *'Tis Herself: A Memoir*, p. 115.

112 Untitled "chronological statement" comparing the timeline of the creative process of *Miracle on 34th Street* to that of *An Angel on Horseback*.

113 "TCF to Star O'Hara in Story by Davies," p. 34.

114 "Paramount Plans 'Catalina' Musical," *New York Times*, November 15, 1946, p. 27.

115 Behlmer, ed., *Memo from Darryl F. Zanuck*, p. 119.

116 Helen Weller, "Let's Pretend You're Mrs. John Payne," *Motion Picture*, September 1945, p. 31.

117 Howard Sharpe, "Bewildered Knight," *Photoplay combined with Movie Mirror*, October 1942, p. 28.

118 Ida Zeitlin, "The Best Son a Mother Ever Had," *Modern Screen*, December 1942, p. 27.

119 Sharpe, "Bewildered Knight," p. 28.

120 Sharpe, "Bewildered Knight," p. 28.

121 Sharpe, "Bewildered Knight," p. 28; Weller, "Let's Pretend You're Mrs. John Payne," p. 31.

122 Weller, "Let's Pretend You're Mrs. John Payne," p. 31.

123 Sharpe, "Bewildered Knight," p. 28.

124 Sharpe, "Bewildered Knight," p. 28.

125 Zeitlin, "The Best Son a Mother Ever Had," p. 27.

126 John Fuller, "Make Way for John Payne," *Hollywood*, November 1942, p. 22.

127 Sharpe, "Bewildered Knight," p. 28.

128 Sharpe, "Bewildered Knight," p. 56.

129 Zeitlin, "The Best Son a Mother Ever Had," p. 27.

130 Sharpe, "Bewildered Knight," p. 56.

131 Sharpe, "Bewildered Knight," p. 56.

132 Sharpe, "Bewildered Knight," p. 56.

133 Sharpe, "Bewildered Knight," p. 56.

134 "Payne Won Battle of Man Over Voice," *Miracle on 34th Street* [pressbook], Los Angeles: Twentieth Century-Fox, [1947], p. 26.

135 Fuller, "Make Way for John Payne," p. 22.

136 Fuller, "Make Way for John Payne," p. 22.

137 Fuller, "Make Way for John Payne," p. 22.

138 Liza, "The Girls He Leaves Behind Him!," *Screenland*, February 1943, p. 33.

139 Liza, "The Girls He Leaves Behind Him!," p. 33.

140 Fearless, "The Truth About Stars' Pasts," *Photoplay combined with Movie Mirror*, August 1942, p. 65.

141 Sara Hamilton, "Love, Honor and Good-by [*sic*]," *Photoplay combined with Movie Mirror*, April 1942, p. 31.

142 Sharpe, "Bewildered Knight," p. 56; Hamilton, "Love, Honor and Good-by," p. 31.

143 O'Hara, *'Tis Herself: A Memoir*, p. 80.

144 Fuller, "Make Way for John Payne," p. 22.

145 Ruth Waterbury, "The Difference Is You," *Photoplay combined with Movie Mirror*, March 1945, p. 32.

146 Liza, "The Girls He Leaves Behind Him!," p. 33.

147 Waterbury, "The Difference Is You," p. 32.

148 "Just for Variety," *Daily Variety*, December 7, 1946, p. 7.

149 Memo from George Wasson to Lew Schreiber, et al., August 12, 1947, TCFLF.

150 Behlmer, ed., *Memo from Darryl F. Zanuck*, p. 119.

151 George Benjamin, "Sentimental Journey," *Modern Screen*, September 1947, p. 50.

152 Seaton, "Oral History with George Seaton by David Chierichetti," p. 115.

153 Untitled "chronological statement" comparing the timeline of the creative process of *Miracle on 34th Street* to that of *An Angel on Horseback*.

154 "Births 1877 July–December A–Z," *Index to the Civil Registration of Births, Marriages, and Deaths for England and Wales, 1837–1980.* Great Britain, Registrar General. Filmed by the Genealogical Society of Utah, Salt Lake City, Utah. Accessed on www.familysearch.org October 4, 2022; *Who's Who in the Theatre* incorrectly states that Gwenn was born in 1875, and, in some editions, that he was born in Glamorgan, Wales. The British civil registration conclusively shows him born in London in 1877. John Parker, ed., *Who's Who in the Theatre: A Biographical Record of the Contemporary Stage*, 9th ed., rev. (New York: Pitman Publishing Corporation, 1939).

155 Parker, ed., *Who's Who in the Theatre*, p. 728.

156 Parker, ed., *Who's Who in the Theatre*, p. 728.

157 Theodore Strauss, "The Wookey at Home," *New York Times*, October 12, 1941, p. X1.

158 Strauss, "The Wookey at Home," p. X1.

159 Strauss, "The Wookey at Home," p. X1.

160 "Rogue and Vagabond," London: *The Era*, April 20, 1895, p. 10.

161 Parker, ed., *Who's Who in the Theatre*, p. 728.

162 Candee, ed., *Current Biography*, p. 263.

163 Strauss, "The Wookey at Home," p. X1.

164 "Edmund Gwenn Is Dead at 84; Famed For His Character Roles," *New York Times*, September 7, 1959, p. 15; Strauss, "The Wookey at Home," p. X1.

165 Strauss, "The Wookey at Home," p. X1.

166 Parker, ed., *Who's Who in the Theatre*, p. 728.

167 "Three Star Classic," *Time*, December 21, 1942, p. 45.

168 Gladwin Hill, "Edmund Gwenn Goes Californian," *New York Times*, September 17, 1950, p. 113.

169 Hill, "Edmund Gwenn Goes Californian," p. 113.

170 "Understudy for Santa," *Photoplay*, December 1947, p. 10.

171 "TCF to Star O'Hara in Story by Davies," p. 34.

172 Shorris and Bundy, *Talking Pictures with the People Who Made Them*, p. 20.

173 Edmund Gwenn wardrobe test shot, October 1, 1946, *Miracle on 34th Street* Wardrobe Continuity Books, Western Costume Research Library.

174 Seaton, "Oral History with George Seaton by David Chierichetti," p. 103.

175 "California Birth Index, 1905–1995," Department of Health Services, Vital Statistics Department, Sacramento, California. Natalie Zacharenko (with no middle name) is listed as born on July 20, 1938, in San Francisco. Available at www.familysearch.org. Accessed January 23, 2023; "Birth + Marriages + Deaths," *San Francisco Examiner*, July 27, 1938, p. 13; Natalie's mother apparently used various Russian and English versions of the name "Marie" throughout her life, including Maria, Musia, Marusia, and Mary. Suzanne Finstad, *Natasha: The*

Biography of Natalie Wood (New York: Harmony Books, 2001), p. 33. On the US Census and her petition for naturalization, both from 1940, she reported her name as "Marie," and so that is what is used in this book.

176 "United States Census, 1940," San Francisco City Assembly District 25, San Francisco, California, United States; citing enumeration district (ED) 38-352 sheet 3B, family 66. Available at www.familysearch.org. Accessed January 23, 2023. Marie S. Zacharenko (wife), Olga A. Tatuloff (stepdaughter), and Natalie N. Zacharenko (daughter) listed in household of Nicholas S. Zacharenko;

177 Finstad, *Natasha: The Biography of Natalie Wood*, p. 14.

178 "United States of America Petition for Naturalization, no. 651571" for Nicholas Stephen Zacharenko, Marie Stephen Zacharenko, and Natalie Nicholas Zacharenko, March 26, 1940. Western District, Naturalization Records, 1853–1957. Available at www.familysearch.org. Accessed January 23, 2023.

179 Finstad, *Natasha: The Biography of Natalie Wood*, p. 15.

180 Finstad, *Natasha: The Biography of Natalie Wood*, p. 33.

181 Bob Lardine (quoting Natalie Wood), "A Star Is Born Again," *Daily News* (New York), *Sunday News Magazine*, February 11, 1979, p. 12.

182 Agreement for loan of Natalie Wood from Universal to TCF, signed by H. Brewster and Lew Schreiber. A handwritten date of "January 7" followed by a typed "1947" appears at the top, but the dates of "11/19/46" and "11/29/46" and "12/2/46" are found at the bottom. This appears to be a duplicate copy of the original sent to TCF, TCFLF.

183 Finstad, *Natasha: The Biography of Natalie Wood*, p. 18.

184 There is the possibility, supported by some startling evidence (namely the film itself), that Natalie Wood's film debut actually occurred six months earlier in another film directed by Irving Pichel called *The Moon is Down*. About forty-five minutes into the film, a young girl named Kari is questioned by a Nazi. The girl, who speaks no lines, gets a couple of minutes of screen time along with an adorable close-up shot—and she looks very much like Natalie Wood. That said, there are some issues that make this a problematic claim. According to the art department set construction sheet in the studio archives, *The Moon is Down* was in production from November 16, 1942 through January 4, 1943 with retakes continuing until the end of January. The village set that had been constructed for *How Green Was My Valley* (1941) at TCF's Century Ranch (now Malibu Creek State Park) was used for the exteriors of the Norwegian village in *Moon* and filming on that set was done just before Thanksgiving on November 17, 20, 21, 23, 24, and 25, in 1942. Natalie would have been about four and a half years old and her family would have just moved from San Francisco to Santa Rosa. For her to appear in *Moon*, her mother would have had to make the trek from northern California to Los Angeles just after getting settled in their new home, finagle an audition for her, complete the paperwork for her to appear in the film, and then make arrangements for her to be at the Century Ranch during the week of filming there. This is all very plausible since Marie Gurdin was very much a stage mother, but was it possible? Could she have actually managed to pull that off in her circumstances? The answer is maybe. But what is even more perplexing about this possibility is that no person who was contemporary with the events has ever made any mention of Wood's participation in the movie. If Natalie's mother had pulled that off, why didn't she ever publicize it and make it known? Director Pichel, as the story goes, "discovered" her for *Happy Land* and then subsequently used her in *Tomorrow is Forever* and *The Bride Wore Boots*. If the Kari character was indeed Natalie Wood, it would be reasonable to assume that Pichel would remember using her in *Moon* when he met her on the set of *Happy Land* just six months later – she couldn't have looked that much different. However, in an article in *Silver Screen* magazine in 1947 in which he discusses Natalie's discovery, he does not mention *Moon* at all. And it isn't mentioned in any other contemporary articles about her either. Furthermore, Natalie never mentioned it and neither did any of her biographers, including

her sister and daughter. How could such a significant film debut be completely forgotten by everyone? It only makes sense if it isn't Natalie in the film. The claim of Wood's participation in *Moon* appears to have originated with Michael Barson in his article on Irving Pichel for *Encyclopedia Britannica* (see www.Britannica.com). Without further evidence to provide confirmation, it will be left up to the viewer to decide."

185 "10-Year-Old S. R. Girl Gets Chance at Role in Movies!," *Press Democrat* (Santa Rosa, California), July 28, 1942, p. 1.

186 " 'Cinderella Girl' to Arrive Tomorrow," *Press Democrat* (Santa Rosa, California), October 23, 1942, p. 1; "City Welcomes Child Actress with Rally," *Press Democrat* (Santa Rosa, California), October 25, 1942, p. 1.

187 Dick Moore (quoting Ann Rutherford), *Twinkle, Twinkle, Little Star* (New York: Harper & Row, 1984), p. 21.

188 Moore, *Twinkle, Twinkle, Little Star*, p. 21.

189 Faith Service (quoting Irving Pichel), "Modern Pied Piper," *Silver Screen*, February, 1947, p. 53.

190 Moore, *Twinkle, Twinkle, Little Star*, pp. 19–21.

191 Service, "Modern Pied Piper," p. 53.

192 Finstad, *Natasha: The Biography of Natalie Wood*, pp. 27–28.

193 Service, "Modern Pied Piper," p. 53.

194 Service, "Modern Pied Piper," p. 53.

195 Finstad, *Natasha: The Biography of Natalie Wood*, p. 32. This story comes from Robert Redford.

196 Service, "Modern Pied Piper," p. 53.

197 Lardine, "A Star Is Born Again," p. 14.

198 "Academy Nominations Outlook," *Newsweek*, February 26, 1962, p. 54.

199 Moore, *Twinkle, Twinkle, Little Star*, p. 59.

200 Shorris and Bundy (quoting Arthur Jacobson), *Talking Pictures with the People Who Made Them*, p. 20. Jacobson's account is muddled; he seems to be conflating Irving Pichel's story with Seaton's and his own, making his story a bit suspect.

201 Untitled "chronological statement" comparing the timeline of the creative process of *Miracle on 34th Street* to that of *An Angel on Horseback*.

202 Letter from George Wasson and Frank Ferguson to Donald Henderson, March 12, 1947, TCFLF.

203 Letter from [Valentine Davies] to George [Seaton], November 1, 1946. V. D. papers, folder 73, AMPAS.

204 Hedda Hopper, "Looking at Hollywood," *Los Angeles Times*, November 9, 1946, p. A5.

205 Agreement for loan of Natalie Wood from Universal to TCF, signed by H. Brewster and Lew Schreiber.

206 Harry Brand, "Press Releases: Natalie Wood, the sensational eight year old . . . ," Los Angeles: Twentieth Century-Fox, [November 1946], p. 1, AMPAS; Hedda Hopper, "Looking at Hollywood," *Los Angeles Times*, November 23, 1946, p. A5.

207 "Reviews," *Variety*, May 7, 1947, p. 18.

208 Doug McClelland (quoting Maureen O'Hara), *Forties Film Talk: Oral Histories of Hollywood, with 120 Lobby Posters* (Jefferson, NC: McFarland & Company, 1992), p. 312.

209 Ronald L. Smith, *Who's Who in Comedy: Comedians, Comics and Clowns From Vaudeville to Today's Stand-Ups* (New York: Facts on File, Inc., 1992), p. 6. *Who's Who in Comedy* incorrectly lists his birth year as 1910. See the "Massachusetts State Vital Records 1841–1920" database available at www.familysearch.org, which lists his birthdate as June 16, 1907. (Accessed November 22, 2022).

210 John W. Straus, *Macy's Thanksgiving Day Parade: Floating in History* [documentary], *Miracle on 34th Street*, two-disc DVD, Los Angeles: Twentieth Century Fox Home Entertainment, 2006.

211 Contract between Twentieth Century-Fox and Fred Irving Lewis to play Mr. Macy, December 6, 1946 (later canceled), TCFLF.

212 "Ann Sothern to Co-Star in 'Indian Summer' for RKO," *Motion Picture Herald*, January 4, 1947, p. 25; "Briefs from the Lots," *Variety*, January 1, 1947, p. 7.

213 "Crystal Gardens to Open with Two Musical Comedies," *New York Times*, June 21, 1903, p. 25; "Frolicsome Lambs" *Variety*, September 26, 1908, p. 16; "United States World War II Draft Registration Cards, 1942," available on www.familysearch.org, Harry T Antrim, 1942; citing NARA microfilm publication M1936, M1937, M1939, M1951, M1962, M1964, M1986, M2090, and M2097 (Washington, DC: National Archives and Records Administration, n.d.).

214 "New Shows Next Week: Harry Antrim," *Variety*, March 21, 1913, p. 19.

215 "Correspondence: Chicago," *Variety*, December 19, 1908, p. 25; "Unique Painter at Empress," *Los Angeles Times*, August 27, 1913, p. 119.

216 "Resuming as Act," *Variety*, February 11, 1925, p. 4; "Stage," *Los Angeles Times*, July 22, 1917, part III, p. 3.

217 "Obituary: Harry Antrim," *Variety*, January 25, 1967, p. 71.

218 "Burlesque Reviews," *Variety*, August 23, 1923, p. 42.

219 Marriage record report no. 96558 for Ernest W. Hayden and Lela May Bliss, dated September 29, 1923, "Colorado Statewide Marriage Index, 1853–2006," State of Colorado, Division of Vital Statistics. Available on www.familysearch.org. Accessed January 24, 2023.

220 "Obituaries: Harry Hayden," *Variety*, July 27, 1955, p. 127.

221 "Rose-Marie," *Variety*, September 10, 1924, p. 60.

222 "Dance and Drama School Notes," *Los Angeles Times*, July 1, 1934, p. A7.

223 "Harry Hayden and Co.," *Variety*, December 18, 1929, p. 43.

224 "Dance and Drama School Notes," *Los Angeles Times*, July 1, 1934, p. A7.

225 "Little Theatres," *Hollywood Reporter*, September 9, 1938, p. 9.

226 "Lela Bliss's Pic Debut," *Hollywood Reporter*, October 11, 1935, p. 7.

227 "Bliss for 'Story,' " *Hollywood Reporter*, November 14, 1946, p. 6.

228 Betty White, *Here We Go Again: My Life in Television* (New York: Simon & Schuster, 1995), p. 18; Donald Spoto, *Marilyn Monroe: The Biography* (New York: HarperCollins, 1993), p. 129.

229 "Obituaries: Harry Hayden," *Variety*, July 27, 1955, p. 127.

230 "Births in the Town of Norwich, Connecticut," p. 178 in "Connecticut [Births and] Deaths, 1640–1955" database; Jerome Cowan, questionnaire, February 15, 1917, "Connecticut, Military Census Questionnaire, 1917,"

database. Available at www.familysearch.org. Accessed January 25, 2023.

231 Jerome Palmer Cowan, in "New York City Marriage Records, 1829–1938," database. Available on www.family-search.org. Accessed January 25, 2023; "Jerome Cowan, Character Actor Who Played in 100 Films, Dead," *New York Times*, January 26, 1972, p. 40.

232 Cowan, questionnaire, February 15, 1917, "Connecticut, Military Census Questionnaire, 1917"; "Obituaries: Jerome Cowan," *Variety*, February 2, 1972, p. 71.

233 "Legitimate Out of Town Reviews: 'The Blimp,' " *Variety*, February 8, 1923, p. 18; "New Acts This Week: Dorothy Russell and Co. 'My Evening Star,'," *Variety*, June 28, 1923, p. 24; "Cast for 'Money,'," *Variety*, August 2, 1923, p. 16.

234 "Obituaries: Jerome Cowan," *Variety*, February 2, 1972, p. 71.

235 "Engagements" and "Rialto, Hoboken, Reopens," *Variety*, September 8, 1926, pp. 30, 42; "Birmingham Stock," *Variety*, October 30, 1929, p. 73.

236 "Frankie and Johnnie," *Variety*, October 1, 1930, p. 71.

237 "Plays on Broadway: Just to Remind You," *Variety*, September 15, 1931, p. 54; "Plays on Broadway: Marathon," *Variety*, January 31, 1933, p. 52.

238 "Warners Have Smash Legit in 'Boy Meets Girl,' " *Hollywood Reporter*, November 29, 1935, p. 1.

239 "Jerome Cowan Here," *Hollywood Reporter*, July 11, 1936, p. 3.

240 "Goldwyn Tests Jerome Cowan for 'Dead End,' " *Hollywood Reporter*, December 2, 1936, p. 15; "Goldwyn Keeps Cowan," *Hollywood Reporter*, November 27, 1936, p. 6.

241 Thomas F. Brady, "RKO to Make Film of Hodgins Novel," *New York Times*, February 11, 1947, p. 36.

242 Britannica, T. Editors of Encyclopedia. "Thomas E. Dewey," *Encyclopedia Britannica*, March 20, 2022. https://www.britannica.com/biography/Thomas-E-Dewey. Accessed October 13, 2022.

243 "Obituaries: Jerome Cowan," *Variety*, February 2, 1972, p. 71.

244 Rob Edelman and Audrey Kupferberg, *Meet the Mertzes* (Los Angeles: Renaissance Books, 1999), pp. 22–27.

245 Edelman and Kupferberg, *Meet the Mertzes*, p. 31.

246 Edelman and Kupferberg, *Meet the Mertzes*, p. 33.

247 Thomas F. Brady, "News of the Screen: Other Castings Today—Frawley and Lockhart," *New York Times*, January 10, 1947, p. 16.

248 "Gist Quitting Academia to Return to Pix, TV Biz," *Variety*, January 3, 1973, p. 128.

249 "Columbia Doing It Again for Minority Journalists," *Broadcasting*, June 18, 1973, p. 74.

250 "Film School: Skill Allied to Teamwork," *Screen International*, May 7, 1977, p. 30.

251 "Obituaries: Agnes Moorehead," *Variety*, May 8, 1974, p. 286.

252 Telegram from George Wasson to Edwin Kilroe, TCFLF.

253 "20th Signs Greenman," *Hollywood Reporter*, February 6, 1951, p. 6.

254 "20th Signs Greenman," p. 6; "Down among the Sheltering Palms," *Variety*, April 1, 1953, p. 6.

255 "Miracle on 34th Street" story on *Entertainment Tonight*. Aired December 1994. Available on www.youtube.com, titled "December 1994 Entertainment Tonight Clip (Alvin Greenman)." Accessed November 10, 2022.

256 Barry Monush, *Screen World Presents the Encyclopedia of Hollywood Film Actors from the Silent Era to 1965* (New York: Applause, 2003), p. 305.

257 Edwin Schallert, "Cathy Carter Groomed as Light Comedy Star," *Los Angeles Times*, November 20, 1946, p. A5; Porter Hall out of the hospital and into "The Big Heart" for 20th-TCF, "Chatter–Hollywood," *Variety*, December 4, 1946, p. 55.

258 "Up-to-the-Minute Casting News," *Hollywood Reporter*, January 8, 1947, p. 13.

259 Sam Thomas, ed., *Best American Screen-Plays. First Series. Complete Screenplays* (New York: Crown, Inc., 1986), p. 174.

260 "Obituaries," *Variety*, New York, September 15, 1971, p. 79.

261 Hedda Hopper, "Looking at Hollywood," *Los Angeles Times*, April 27, 1948, p. 22.

262 "Up-to-the-Minute Casting News," *Hollywood Reporter*, February 17, 1947, p. 16.

263 Anna Rothe, ed., "Lockhart, Gene," *Current Biography* (New York: H. W. Wilson, 1950), p. 346.

264 Rothe, ed., "Lockhart, Gene," *Current Biography*, p. 347.

265 Rothe, ed., "Lockhart, Gene," *Current Biography*, p. 346.

266 Brady, "News of the Screen: Other Castings Today—Frawley and Lockhart," p. 16.

267 Rothe, ed., "Lockhart, Gene," *Current Biography*, p. 347.

268 Carol Hughes, "Thelma Ritter's Road to Stardom," *Coronet*, September 1951, p. 85.

269 Hughes, "Thelma Ritter's Road to Stardom," p. 87.

270 Hughes, "Thelma Ritter's Road to Stardom," p. 88.

271 "From the Production Centres," *Variety*, December 11, 1946, p. 34.

272 Hughes, "Thelma Ritter's Road to Stardom," p. 89.

273 Seaton, "Oral History with George Seaton by David Chierichetti," p. 99.

274 Hughes, "Thelma Ritter's Road to Stardom," p. 85.

275 Milton Z. Esterow, "Thelma Ritter, Back Home, Gives Her Views on Some New Theatre Trends," *New York Times*, September 1, 1957, p. 63.

276 "Jas. Seay, DeMille Find, Signed to Para Contract," *Hollywood Reporter*, October 23, 1939, p. 4.

277 "Up-to-the-Minute Casting News," *Hollywood Reporter*, November 18, 1946, p. 13.

278 "United States Census, 1920," New York, Westchester County, Yonkers, 9 Ward, Enumeration District 261, sheet 1A, line 38, under William Koerlin household. Available on www.familysearch.org. Accessed February 8, 2023.

279 "Low-Budgeted Features Scores," *Los Angeles Times*, July 11, 1942, p. 7.

280 Ed Sullivan, "Little Old New York," *Daily News* (New York), December 27, 1943, p. 24; Hugh Dixon, "Hollywood," *Pittsburgh-Post Gazette*, July 24, 1945, p. 20.

281 Cheryl Cheng, "Child Actor Anthony Sydes Dies at 74," *Hollywood Reporter*, June 24, 2015. www.hollywoodre-

porter.com. Accessed January 28, 2023.

282 *Who Was Who in the Theatre, 1912–1976*, vol. 4 (Detroit: Gale Research Company, 1978), p. 2378; Philip Tonge, "Actor Reviews His 50 Years of Stage, Movies, Television," [Columbus, Georgia] *Ledger-Enquirer*, December 5, 1955, p. 12; "Obituaries," *Variety*, February 4, 1959, p. 79; "New York, County Naturalization Records, 1791–1980," certificate number 158893. Available on www.familysearch.org; "New York, New York City Marriage Records, 1829–1938," Philip Tonge and Anna Hahn, 1923. Available on www.familysearch.org. Accessed January 12, 2023.

283 "Call Bureau Cast Service 'Miracle on 34th Street,' " [cast and crew list], April 4, 1947. TCF Research Library.

284 Ralph M. Hower, *History of Macy's of New York, 1858–1919* (Cambridge, MA: Harvard University Press, 1943), summarized from pp. 3–31.

285 Robert M. Grippo, *Macy's: The Store. The Star. The Story* (New York: Square One Publishers, 2009), p. 26.

286 Hower, *History of Macy's of New York, 1858–1919*, p. 113.

287 Hower, *History of Macy's of New York, 1858–1919*, p. 65; Grippo, *Macy's: The Store. The Star. The Story*, p. 32.

288 Grippo, *Macy's: The Store. The Star. The Story*, p. 44.

289 Grippo, *Macy's: The Store. The Star. The Story*, p. 60.

290 Hower, *History of Macy's of New York, 1858–1919*, p. 220; Grippo, *Macy's: The Store. The Star. The Story*, p. 55.

291 Hower, *History of Macy's of New York, 1858–1919*, summarized from pp. 123–24, 211–13, 226–27.

292 There is a plaque on the 34th Street facade of Macy's that declares "Here the Motion Picture Began: On the night of April 23, 1896, on this site in Koster & Bial's Music Hall, Thomas A. Edison with the 'Vitascope' first projected a moving picture."

293 Hower, *History of Macy's of New York, 1858–1919*, pp. 318–19.

294 "Macy's A World Giant," *Kansas City Star*, March 30, 1947, p. 1.

295 Michael J. Lisicky, *Gimbels Has It!* (Charleston, SC: The History Press, 2011), pp. 41–42.

296 Robert Hendrickson, *The Grand Emporiums: The Illustrated History of America's Great Department Stores* (New York: Stein and Day, 1979), pp. 156, 161; *The WPA Guide to New York City* (New York: Random House, 1982 reprint [1939]), p. 217.

297 *The WPA Guide to New York City*, p. 217.

298 Hower, *History of Macy's of New York, 1858–1919*, pp. 345–348.

299 Grippo, *Macy's: The Store. The Star. The Story*, p. 97.

300 "J. I. Straus Made Head of R. H. Macy," *New York Times*, May 1, 1940, p. 44.

301 Grippo, *Macy's: The Store. The Star. The Story*, p. 105.

302 "Macy's A World Giant," *Kansas City Star*, March 30, 1947, p. 1.

303 Hendrickson, *The Grand Emporiums*, p. 69; "Macy's Purchase in Toledo," *New York Times*, January 4, 1924, p. 27.

304 "Macy's A World Giant," *Kansas City Star*, March 30, 1947, p. 1.

305 Louis Sobol, "34th Street," reprint of King Features Syndicate "New York Cavalcade" column in *New Dynamo*, Los Angeles: Twentieth Century-Fox, May 17, 1947, p. 6.

306 "Macy's A World Giant," *Kansas City Star*, March 30, 1947, p. 1.

307 "Macy's A World Giant," *Kansas City Star*, March 30, 1947, p. 1.

308 "Sales Record at Macy's," *Kansas City Times*, November 15, 1946, p. 11; "Macy's A World Giant," *Kansas City Star*, March 30, 1947, p. 1.

309 "Macy's A World Giant," *Kansas City Star*, March 30, 1947, p. 1.

310 Colton, "George Seaton on Top," p. X5.

311 Lisicky, *Gimbels Has It!*, p. 132.

312 Lisicky, *Gimbels Has It!*, p. 47.

313 Sobol, "34th Street," p. 6.

314 Hendrickson, *The Grand Emporiums*, p. 72.

315 Lisicky, *Gimbels Has It!*, p. 42.

316 Margaret Case Harriman, *And the Price is Right* (Cleveland and New York: The World Publishing Company, 1958), p. 137.

317 Harriman, *And the Price is Right*, p. 139.

318 Telegram from George Wasson to E[dwin]. P. Kilroe, January 7, 1947, TCFLF.

319 Memo from George Wasson to Files, January 27, 1947, TCFLF.

320 *Manhattan New York City Telephone Directory Fall–Winter 1946*, New York Telephone Company, 1946, p. 1092.

321 Hendrickson, *The Grand Emporiums*, p. 352. The Bronx store was on Third Avenue at 150th Street and the store in Newark was at Broad and Cedar Streets.

322 Hendrickson, *The Grand Emporiums*, p. 390.

323 Memo stamped December 3, 1946, TCFLF.

324 Associated Press. "No More Miracles on 34th Street: Gimbels Gone," Deseret News, September 28, 1986, p. A5.

325 "Costs Up 63% Over '46," *Variety*, June 11, 1947, p. 3.

326 "Hollywood Takes It on the Lam," *Variety*, June 11, 1947, p. 3.

327 Colton, "George Seaton on Top," p. X5; Seaton, "Oral History with George Seaton by David Chierichetti," p. 95.

328 Letter from William Howard (vice president of Macy's) to TCF, August 30, 1946, TCFLF.

329 "Industrial Movies Come of Age," *Business Week*, October 9, 1937, p. 35.

330 Hopper, Hedda. "Looking at Hollywood," *Los Angeles Times*, April 27, 1948, p. 22.

331 Letters from Bernard Gimbel to TCF, November 16, 1946, and November 27, 1946, TCFLF; Colton, "George Seaton on Top," p. X5; Seaton, "Oral History with George Seaton by David Chierichetti," p. 95; Clarke, *Highlights and Shadows*, p. 164.

332 Telegram from George Wasson to E[dwin] P. Kilroe, January 7, 1947; Letter from George Wasson to Harry J. McIntyre, January 2, 1947; Letter from Harry J. McIntyre to George Wasson, January 30, 1947; Telegram from George Wasson to E[dwin] P. Kilroe, January 7, 1947, TCFLF.

333 Brand, "Vital Statistics on 'Miracle on 34th Street' " [press release], p. 3.

334 O'Hara, *'Tis Herself: A Memoir*, p. 116.

335 Brand, "Vital Statistics on 'Miracle on 34th Street' " [press release], p. 3; "20th Century-Fox News," [undated press release] circa December 1946; "New Yorkers Unobservant—Star Grateful!" *Miracle on 34th Street* [pressbook], Los Angeles: Twentieth Century-Fox, [1947], p. 29.

336 William L. Bird Jr., *Holidays on Display* (New York: Princeton Architectural Press, 2007), p. 8.

337 Lisicky, *Gimbels Has It!*, p. 34.

338 Robert M. Grippo and Christopher Hoskins, *Macy's Thanksgiving Day Parade* (Charlotte, NC: Arcadia Publishing, 2004), p. 11.

339 Grippo and Hoskins, *Macy's Thanksgiving Day Parade*, p. 11.

340 Grippo and Hoskins, *Macy's Thanksgiving Day Parade*, p. 24.

341 Grippo and Hoskins, *Macy's Thanksgiving Day Parade*, p. 53.

342 A. H. Weiler, "Random Notes About People and Pictures," *New York Times*, December 8, 1946, p. 89.

343 O'Hara, "Feature Audio Commentary by Maureen O'Hara" (August 24, 2006).

344 O'Hara, "Feature Audio Commentary by Maureen O'Hara" (August 24, 2006); "Temperatures Yesterday," *New York Times*, November 29, 1946, p. 1.

345 Grippo and Hoskins, *Macy's Thanksgiving Day Parade*, p. 54.

346 Brand, "Vital Statistics on 'Miracle on 34th Street' " [press release], p. 1.

347 "Bargain Hunters Elbow Stars as Film is Shot in New York's Macy's," *Miracle on 34th Street* [pressbook], Los Angeles: Twentieth Century-Fox, [1947], pp. 26–27; Straus, *Macy's Thanksgiving Day Parade: Floating in History* [documentary].

348 Shorris and Bundy, *Talking Pictures with the People Who Made Them*, p. 21.

349 Seaton, "Oral History with George Seaton by David Chierichetti," p. 99.

350 "Quiet!," *Miracle on 34th Street* [pressbook], Los Angeles: Twentieth Century-Fox, [1947], p. 26.

351 Shorris and Bundy, *Talking Pictures with the People Who Made Them*, p. 21.

352 Straus, *Macy's Thanksgiving Day Parade: Floating in History* [documentary].

353 [Macy's Parade advertisement], *New York Times*, November 27, 1946, p. 7.

354 Phil M. Daly, "Along the Rialto," *Film Daily*, November 27, 1946, p. 3; "Seaton Unit in N.Y. Monday for 'My Heart,' " *Hollywood Reporter*, November 14, 1946, p. 11; Hedda Hopper, "Hollywood," [New York] *Daily News*, November 15, 1946, p. 36; Weiler, "Random Notes About People and Pictures," p. 89.

355 Weiler, "Random Notes About People and Pictures," p. 89.

356 Released in 1945, with lyrics by Foster Carling; Jones did include "with apologies to Tchaikovsky" on the cover of the album.

357 Shorris and Bundy, *Talking Pictures with the People Who Made Them*, p. 21.

358 Clarke, *Highlights and Shadows*, p. 162.

359 Seaton, "Oral History with George Seaton by David Chierichetti," p. 100.

360 Brand, "Vital Statistics on 'Miracle on 34th Street' " [press release], p. 1.

361 Grippo and Hoskins, *Macy's Thanksgiving Day Parade*, p. 24.

362 Robert Sullivan, ed., *America's Parade: A Celebration of Macy's Thanksgiving Day Parade* (New York: Time, Inc., 2001), p. 86.

363 Day player agreement for Ritter, signed November 29, 1946, for part of "4th Woman," Thelma Ritter and Joseph Aloysius Moran Papers, folder 44, AMPAS.

364 Brand, "Vital Statistics on 'Miracle on 34th Street' " [press release], p. 2; Clarke, *Highlights and Shadows*, p. 163.

365 "Hollywood Heaven!," *Miracle on 34th Street* [pressbook], Los Angeles: Twentieth Century-Fox, [1947], p. 28; "Macy's Goes Hollywood as 20th Century-Fox Shoots Scenes for 'The Big Heart'!" *The Macy Star: A Supplement to Sparks the Macy Magazine*, vol. 1, no. 27, December 11, 1946, [page 1]. Other Macy's employees that assisted included Lee Wallace from Public Relations; Leigh Allen, John Snedaker, and Judson Cox from Display; Vincent Keane of Maintenance; Carl Plehaty and Tom Quinn from the Chief Engineer's Office. Porters, protection representatives, and receiving men also helped out.

366 Fred Freed, "Macy's Santa Claus," *Esquire*, December 1946, p. 133. According to the American Film Institute Catalog, in 1964, Charles W. Howard, who had worked as a Santa Claus at Macy's for many years, claimed to be a consultant on *Miracle*, but no contemporary source can confirm this.

367 Seaton, "Oral History with George Seaton by David Chierichetti," p. 101.

368 Irving Hoffman, "Tales of Hoffman," *Hollywood Reporter*, March 31, 1947, p. 31.

369 Clarke, *Highlights and Shadows*, p. 163.

370 "Seventh Floor—Magic Carpets!," and "Bargain Hunters Elbow Stars as Film is Shot in New York's Macy's," *Miracle on 34th Street* [pressbook], Los Angeles: Twentieth Century-Fox, [1947], pp. 26–27

371 Brand, "Vital Statistics on 'Miracle on 34th Street' " [press release], p. 2.

372 "New Yorkers Unobservant—Star Grateful," *Miracle on 34th Street* [pressbook], Los Angeles: Twentieth Century-Fox, [1947], p. 29.

373 "Macy's A World Giant," *Kansas City Star*, March 30, 1947, p. 1.

374 Straus, *Macy's Thanksgiving Day Parade: Floating in History* [documentary].

375 Shorris and Bundy, *Talking Pictures with the People Who Made Them*, p. 22.

376 "Bargain Hunters Elbow Stars as Film is Shot in New York's Macy's," p. 27.

377 Clarke, *Highlights and Shadows*, p. 163.

378 "Macy's A World Giant," *Kansas City Star*, March 30, 1947, p. 1.

379 Straus, *Macy's Thanksgiving Day Parade: Floating in History* [documentary]; "Seventh Floor—Magic Carpets!," *Miracle on 34th Street* [pressbook], Los Angeles: Twentieth Century-Fox, [1947], Pressbook, p. 26.

380 "Macy's Goes Hollywood as 20th Century-Fox Shoots Scenes for 'The Big Heart'!," p. 1.

381 Seaton, "Oral History with George Seaton by David Chierichetti," p. 101.

382 O'Hara, *'Tis Herself: A Memoir*, p. 117.

383 O'Hara, *'Tis Herself: A Memoir*, p. 117.

384 "Oriental Splendor" [Macy's ad], *New York Times*, November 29, 1946, p. 49.

385 [Macy's advertisement], *New York Journal-American*, December 20, 1946.

386 O'Hara, *'Tis Herself: A Memoir*, p. 117.

387 Clarke, *Highlights and Shadows*, p. 164.

388 Seaton, "Oral History with George Seaton by David Chierichetti," p. 97.

389 "Executive Tweet!," *Miracle on 34th Street* [pressbook], Los Angeles: Twentieth Century-Fox, [1947], p. 25. The exact dates of filming at Macy's are not known. The article in Macy's internal newsletter is dated December 11, 1946, and so filming was completed by then. "Macy's Goes Hollywood as 20th Century-Fox Shoots Scenes for 'The Big Heart'!," p. 1.

390 "WPA Rents Space in Long Island City," *New York Times*, September 10, 1941, p. 39; *Manhattan New York City Telephone Directory, Fall–Winter 1946*, New York Telephone Company, 1946, p. 1277.

391 Shorris and Bundy, *Talking Pictures with the People Who Made Them*, p. 23.

392 Memo from R. A. Klune to William Perlberg, December 30, 1946, TCFLF.

393 O'Hara, *'Tis Herself: A Memoir*, p. 116.

394 On the filming location sheet it is listed as "BLACK FCXE [effects]."

395 Radie Harris, "Broadway Runaround: Add Arrivals," *Daily Variety*, November 22, 1946, p. 14.

396 "Notables, Society Out for Preem of 'Razor's Edge,' " *Daily Variety*, November 20, 1946, p. 6.

397 Harris, "Broadway Runaround: Add Arrivals," p. 6.

398 "Maureen O'Hara Reception," *Film Daily*, December 10, 1946, p.7.

399 "Names at AMPA Lunch," *Variety*, December 11, 1946, p. 27; "Coming and Going," *Film Daily*, December 10, 1946, p. 2; Report of in *Film Daily*, December 16, 1946, p. 8.

400 "O'Hara Extends N.Y. Stay," *Hollywood Reporter*, December 13, 1946, p. 8; "Maureen O'Hara Home," *Hollywood Reporter*, December 20, 1946, p. 4.

401 Brand, "Vital Statistics on 'Miracle on 34th Street' " [press release], p. 3; Ed Sullivan, "Little Old New York," *Daily News* (New York), December 11, 1946.

402 "Engine Fails; 54 on Airliner Safe," *Daily News* [New York], December 17, 1946, p. 59.

403 Untitled "chronological statement" comparing the timeline of the creative process of *Miracle on 34th Street* to that of *An Angel on Horseback*.

404 Memo, dated October 1, 1946, TCFLF.

405 "TCF to Star O'Hara in Story by Davies," p. 34; John Gray Peatman, "Radio and Motion Picture Songs," *Hollywood Reporter Anniversary Issue*, September 23, 1946, p. 298. Confusingly, this also happened to be the working title of another film TCF had in development, to be produced by Gene Markey, based on his story "No Wedding Ring," and to star Victor Mature and newcomer Nancy Guild. That project ended up being canceled. "My Heart Tells Me," *The Daily Film Renter*, October 31, 1946, p. 46. "Markey Shelves 'Heart,' " *Hollywood Reporter*, October 9, 1946, p. 9.

406 Affidavit by George Seaton, March 19, 1947, TCFLF.

407 Affidavit by George Seaton, March 19, 1947, TCFLF; " 'Big' Race is On," *Hollywood Reporter*, November 15, 1946, p. 9; The second draft of the script, dated November 16, 1946, reflects the title change as well. Jock MacGregor, "London Observations," *Showmen's Trade Review*, June 28, 1947, p. 24.

408 "Minutes of meeting with all departments, December 3, 1946," p. 12, TCF Advertising Department. Charles Schlaifer papers, Skouras correspondence, folder 1, AMPAS.

409 Telegram from Walt[er Simpson(?)] to George Seaton, December 3, 1946, V. D. papers, folder 73, AMPAS. The sender is presumably Walter Simpson, who connected Davies with Harcourt, Brace & Company, which resulted in the book version being printed.

410 "Briefs From the Lots," *Variety*, December 18, 1946, p. 15.

411 " '34th Street' Latest in 20th-TCF Titles," *Hollywood Reporter*, January 24, 1947, p. 6; Memo from George Wasson to Files, January 27, 1947, TCFLF.

412 "Studio Size-Ups," *Film Bulletin*, February 3, 1947, p. 17.

413 Final script, January 2, 1947, p. 61, V. D. papers, folder 68, AMPAS.

414 "Acting Angered Dad; Gwenn Makes It Pay," *Miracle on 34th Street* [pressbook], Los Angeles: Twentieth Century-Fox, [1947], p. 29.

415 "Lights! Camera! . . . Bubble!" *Miracle on 34th Street* [pressbook], Los Angeles: Twentieth Century-Fox, [1947], p. 28.

416 Brand, "Vital Statistics on 'Miracle on 34th Street' " [press release], p. 2.

417 Straus, *Macy's Thanksgiving Day Parade: Floating in History* [documentary].

418 Brand, "Vital Statistics on 'Miracle on 34th Street' " [press release], p. 2.

419 "Added Space for Duel," *Showmen's Trade Review*, February 1, 1947, p. 44; "Chatter," *Variety*, January 22, 1947, p. 63; "From the Production Centres," *Variety*, January 29, 1947, p. 26.

420 O'Hara, "Feature Audio Commentary by Maureen O'Hara" (August 24, 2006).

421 Donfeld, "Recalling the Happy Times with Natalie Wood," *Los Angeles Times*, September 30, 1983, p. F8.

422 Finstad, *Natasha: The Biography of Natalie Wood*, p. 51.

423 Robert Hyatt, *AMC Backstory: Miracle on 34th Street*, Los Angeles: Twentieth Century Fox Home Entertainment, two-disc DVD, 2006.

424 "John Payne laid up with flu while 'It's Only Human' shot around him," "Chatter," *Variety*, January 22, 1947, p. 63; "Payne Ill; Switch Sked," *Daily Variety*, January 17, 1947, p. 9; "Natalie out of *Miracle* for at least a week because of a bad cold," "Cold Stops Moppet," *Hollywood Reporter*, February 3, 1947, p. 14.

425 "Grounded!," *Miracle on 34th Street* [pressbook], Los Angeles: Twentieth Century-Fox, [1947], p. 28.

426 Letter from [Valentine Davies] to George [Seaton], November 19, 1946, V. D. papers, folder 73, AMPAS.

427 Letter from [Valentine Davies] to George [Seaton], December 2, 1946, V. D. papers, folder 73, AMPAS.

428 Thomas, ed., *Best American Screen-Plays. First Series. Complete Screenplays*, p. 186.

429 Thomas, ed., *Best American Screen-Plays. First Series. Complete Screenplays*, p. 199.

430 "Stars Look In," *Daily News* (New York), December 19, 1946.

431 See appendix B.

432 Clarke, *Highlights and Shadows*, p. 165.

433 "Up-to-the-Minute Casting News," *Hollywood Reporter*, February 11, 1947, p. 11; "Up-to-the-Minute Casting News," *Hollywood Reporter*, February 13, 1947, p. 12.

434 Letter from [Valentine Davies] to George [Seaton], November 1, 1946, V. D. papers, folder 73, AMPAS.

435 Seaton, "Oral History with George Seaton by David Chierichetti," p. 93.

436 Brand, "Vital Statistics on 'Miracle on 34th Street' " [press release], p. 3.

437 O'Hara, "Feature Audio Commentary by Maureen O'Hara" (August 24, 2006).

438 O'Hara, "Feature Audio Commentary by Maureen O'Hara" (August 24, 2006).

439 George Seaton, *The Big Heart* temporary script, November 16, 1946, V. D. papers, folder 68, AMPAS.

440 Thomas, ed., *Best American Screen-Plays. First Series. Complete Screenplays*, p. 202.

441 Memos, December 23, 1946, and December 27, 1946, TCFLF.

442 "Rambling Reporter," *Hollywood Reporter,* February 24, 1947, p. 2.

443 McClelland (quoting Natalie Wood), *Forties Film Talk*, p. 314.

444 "O'Hara Off to Ohio," *Hollywood Reporter*, February 15, 1947, p. 15; "Chatter" *Daily Variety*, February 22, 1947, p. 2.

445 "Ill in Pix," *Daily Variety,* February 28, 1947, p. 14; "Understudy for Santa," *Photoplay*, December 1947, p. 10.

446 "*Life* Goes to Mike Romanoff's Restaurant," *Life*, October 29, 1945, p. 141.

447 "Mike's Place," *Time*, November 6, 1950.

448 Memo from George Wasson to Files, January 27, 1947; Letter from Michael Romanoff to TCF, January 27, 1947, TCFLF.

449 Memo from Lyonel Kahne to George Wasson, December 30, 1946, TCFLF.

450 "New French Cabinet Upheld by Deputies," *New York Times,* December 23, 1932, p.1; "Our Speed Praised in Child Labor Ban," *New York Times,* July 20, 1933, p. 21; "Roosevelt Orders War on Kidnapping by Federal Forces," "Captive of Thug Leaps from Moving Car; Robber is Killed in Duel with Policeman," *New York Times,* July 27, 1933, p. 1; "Earth Forces Laid to Cosmic Impulse," *New York Times,* July 27, 1933, p. 19.

451 Hopper, "Looking at Hollywood," *Los Angeles Times*, March 21, 1947, p. A3; Shorris and Bundy, *Talking Pictures with the People Who Made Them*, p. 23; Seaton, "Oral History with George Seaton by David Chierichetti," p. 102.

452 Letter from George Seaton to Walter [Simpson?] dated April 22, 1947, V. D. papers, folder 72, AMPAS.

453 Seaton, "Oral History with George Seaton by David Chierichetti," p. 102.

454 Clarke, *Highlights and Shadows*, p. 164.

455 "Music Cue Sheet and Continuity Report with Copyright Status [for] Miracle on 34th Street–English Dialog Version," May 1, 1947, TCFLF.

456 Jack D. Grant, " 'Miracle on 34th Street' Delightful Surprise Hit," *Hollywood Reporter*, May 2, 1947, p. 3.

457 Music cue sheet, May 1, 1947, TCFLF.

458 Memo to E[dwin] P. Kilroe, May 10, 1947, TCFLF.

459 Memo from Frank Tresselt to George Wasson, March 11, 1947; Memo from Frank Tresselt to George Wasson, May 1, 1947.

460 Memos from Frank Tresselt to George Wasson, March 25, 1947, TCFLF.

461 Memo, November 26, 1946, TCFLF.

462 Music Cue Sheet and Continuity Report with Copyright Status, May 1, 1947; Memo from Frank Tresselt to George Wasson, January 17, 1947, TCFLF.

463 Thomas, ed., *Best American Screen-Plays. First Series. Complete Screenplays*, p. 195.

464 Memo from Frank Tresselt to George Wasson, January 7, 1947, TCFLF.

465 Memo from Frank Tresselt to George Wasson, March 25, 1947, TCFLF.

466 Letter from Joseph Breen to Jason Joy, April 29, 1947, Production Code files for *Miracle on 34th Street*, AMPAS.

467 National Legion of Decency, *Motion Pictures Classified by National Legion of Decency: February 1936–October 1959* (New York: National Legion of Decency, 1959), p. 152.

468 Letter from Joseph Breen to TCF, June 10, 1947, Production Code files for *Miracle on 34th Street*, AMPAS.

469 The local censor board in Ohio objected on May 24, 1947, to the scene with the drunken Santa Claus. Letter from Joseph Breen at MPAA, June 10, 1947.

470 Screen Credits, undated; Memo from Hector Dods to George Wasson, April 19, 1947; Letter to TCF from Johnson and Tannenbaum, attorneys, September 4, 1947, TCFLF.

471 Seaton, "Oral History with George Seaton by David Chierichetti," p. 102; O'Hara, *'Tis Herself: A Memoir*, p. 118; McClelland (quoting Natalie Wood), *Forties Film Talk*, p. 314; Fanny Butcher, "Jingle Bells! Santa Makes a Jolly July," *Chicago Sunday Tribune* (Chicago Sunday Tribune Magazine of Books), July 20, 1947, part 4, p. 3.

472 See articles in *Variety*, such as "National Boxoffice Survey," July 16, 1947, p. 3.

473 "Macy's Goes Hollywood as 20th Century-Fox Shoots Scenes for 'The Big Heart'!," p. 1. "Since it is most appropriate for Thanksgiving and Christmas time, the film will be held for release until next fall."

474 The following paragraph summarized from: Gerald Horne, *Class Struggle in Hollywood 1930–1950* (Austin: University of Texas Press, 2001).

475 "Black and White Christmas Seen for Nation's Screens," *Hollywood Reporter*, December 18, 1946, p. 1.

476 [Macy's advertisement], *New York Journal-American*, December 20, 1946.

477 "20th Has 21 of 24 Pictures on '47 Sked Ready," *Hollywood Reporter*, January 22, 1947, p. 4; "Product Status," *New Dynamo*, Los Angeles: Twentieth Century-Fox, February 8, 1947, p. 18; "Product Status," *New Dynamo*, Los Angeles: Twentieth Century-Fox, February 15, 1947, p. 18; "Product Status," *New Dynamo*, Los Angeles: Twentieth Century-Fox, March 1, 1947, p. 34.

478 See schedules in *Motion Picture Daily* from February 6, 1947, p. [8] to March 28, 1947, p. [8].

479 Letter from S. Spencer Scott to Walter M. Simpson, May 3, 1947, V. D. papers, folder 72, AMPAS; "Easing of Color Print Shortage," *Film Daily*, February 10, 1947, p. 1.

480 " '34th Street' Is in the Bag," *New Dynamo*, Los Angeles: Twentieth Century-Fox, April 26, 1947, p. 3; *Miracle* first appears on schedule in *Motion Picture Daily*, April 30, 1947, p. 10; Telegram from E[dwin]. P. Kilroe to George Wasson, May 7, 1947; Telegram from George Wasson to Edwin P. Kilroe, May 6, 1947, TCFLF; Harry Hansen, "Book with a Movie Genesis Brings Santa Out in July," *Chicago Sunday Tribune*, June 15, 1947, "Magazine of Books" section, part 4, p. 8.

481 " '34th Street' Is in the Bag," p. 3; "Skouras Sees Higher '47 Foreign Income," *Film Daily*, May 21, 1947, p. 1; Memo from George D. Stephenson to "Files" dated April 28, 1947, TCFLF.

482 William R. Weaver, "Miracle on 34th Street," *Motion Picture Herald*, May 10, 1947, p. 3621; Jack D. Grant, " 'Miracle on 34th Street' Delightful Surprise Hit," *Hollywood Reporter*, May 2, 1947, p. 3.

483 "Miracle on 34th Street," *Variety*, May 7, 1947, p. 18.

484 Grant, " 'Miracle on 34th Street' Delightful Surprise Hit," p. 3.

485 "Reviews: Miracle on 34th Street," *Film Daily*, May 2, 1947, p. 10.

486 "Publicity" section, "Miracle on 34th Street" [advertising approach memo] p. [7], TCF Advertising Department, Charles Schlaifer papers, Skouras correspondence, folder 1, AMPAS. The memo indicates that the article appeared in the March 30, 1947, edition of *This Week*, but that has not been verified.

487 "Macy Tie-up" section, "Miracle on 34th Street" [advertising approach memo] p. [1], TCF Advertising Department, Charles Schlaifer papers, Skouras correspondence, folder 1, AMPAS.

488 Advertising Billing, Miracle on 34th Street, March 7, 1947, TCFLF.

489 "RKO Starts Newspaper Ads on 'Miracle' Trailer," *Boxoffice*, June 21, 1947, p. 42.

490 The studio head is played by Charles Tannen, and three of the four other actors have been identified as Harry Seymour, George E. Stone, and Gene Nelson.

491 "New Kind of Kidding Trailer," *Variety*, May 14, 1947, p. 18.

492 "No Matter How Palatable, Exhibs Balk at Lengthy Trailers; 20th's Longie," *Variety*, July 9, 1947, p. 24.

493 "Macy Tie-up" section, "Miracle on 34th Street," p. [5].

494 *Film Daily*, May 16, 1947, p. 11; *Film Daily*, May 12, 1947, p. 6; *Boxoffice*, May 31, 1947, p. 76; *Film Daily*, May 13, 1947, p. 2.

495 "Sluggish Pace in N.Y. Puts Cramp in New Pix," *Variety*, May 21, 1947, p. 11; "Report on Preview at New York Roxy," *New Dynamo*, Los Angeles: Twentieth Century-Fox, May 24, 1947, p. 2.

496 "Preview Audiences Are Echoing Trade's Enthusiastic Reaction to '34th Street,' " *New Dynamo*, Los Angeles: Twentieth Century-Fox, May 24, 1947, p. 2. Previews were held at the Delaware theater in Albany; the Fenway theater in Boston; the United Artists theater in Chicago; the RKO-Palace theater in Cleveland; the Wisconsin theater in Milwaukee; the TCF theater in Detroit; the TCF theater in St. Louis; the Joy theater in New Orleans; the Albee theater in Cincinnati, and three Kansas City theaters.

497 Sobol, "34th Street," p. 6.

498 " '34th Street' Is in the Bag," p. 3.

499 *Miracle on 34th Street* [pressbook], Los Angeles: Twentieth Century-Fox, [1947], p. 21.

500 Phil M. Daly, "Along the Rialto," *Film Daily*, June 5, 1947, p. 6.

501 "New York's Millions Flooded with Millions of Messages in Ace Campaign on 'Miracle,' " *Showmen's Trade Review*, June 21, 1947, p. 12.

502 *Miracle on 34th Street* [pressbook], Los Angeles: Twentieth Century-Fox, [1947], p. 20.

503 Daly, "Along the Rialto," June 5, 1947, p. 6; *Miracle on 34th Street* [pressbook], Los Angeles: Twentieth Century-Fox, [1947], p. 20.

504 [Gimbels ad], *New York Times*, June 4, 1947, p. 14.

505 Daly, "Along the Rialto," June 5, 1947, p. 6.

506 "Inside Stuff—Pictures," *Variety*, July 2, 1947, p. 20.

507 Daly, "Along the Rialto," June 5, 1947, p. 6.

508 "Radio-TV Merger Approved by F.C.C.," *New York Times*, January 18, 1952, p. 33; Grippo, *Macy's: The Store. The Star. The Story*, p. 106.

509 Daly, "Along the Rialto," June 5, 1947, p. 6.

510 "Around Clock Air Plays for '34th St.,' "*Film Daily*, May 26, 1947, p. 1.

511 Daly, "Along the Rialto," June 5, 1947, p. 6.

512 *Miracle on 34th Street* [pressbook], Los Angeles: Twentieth Century-Fox, [1947], p. 21.

513 Daly, "Along the Rialto," June 5, 1947, p. 6.

514 "Inside Stuff—Pictures," *Variety*, May 21, 1947, p. 24; "New York's Millions Flooded with Millions of Messages in Ace Campaign on 'Miracle,' " p. 12; Daly, "Along the Rialto," June 5, 1947, p. 6.

515 "Miracle on 34th Street" [ad], *New York Times*, June 4, 1947, p. 35.

516 "Memorial Day Ups N.Y.," *Variety*, June 4, 1947, p. 13.

517 "Memorial Day Ups N.Y.," p. 13; Average ticket price in America in 1947 was $ .34 ("20th-TCF Sliding Scale Plan Gets a Trial in 25 Theatres," *Box Office*, July 19, 1947, p. 10).

518 "Miracle on 34th Street" [ad]. *New York Times*, June 4, 1947, p. 35; Joel Whitburn, *Pop Memories: 1890–1954* (Menomonee Falls, WI: Record Research Inc., 1986), pp. 38, 285.

519 "20th-TCF's Roxy Nixes Lund's Mention of M-G In 'Mam'selle' Tie-up," *Variety*, June 18, 1947, p. 1.

520 Bosley Crowther, "The Screen," *New York Times*, June 5, 1947, p. 32.

521 Daly, "Along the Rialto," June 5, 1947, p. 6.

522 "Chatter–Hollywood," *Variety*, May 21, 1947, p. 63.

523 " 'Miracle' is Rave of New York!" *New Dynamo*, New York: Twentieth Century-Fox, June 7, 1947, p. A.

524 "New York's Millions Flooded with Millions of Messages in Ace Campaign on 'Miracle,' " p. 12; "Miracle on 34th Street" [advertising campaign plan], undated, Charles Schlaifer papers, folder 1, AMPAS; Daly, "Along the Rialto," June 5, 1947, p. 6.

525 Letter from J. Clarence Davies to Valentine Davies, June 6, 1947, V. D. papers, folder 73, AMPAS.

526 "New Pix Help B'way," *Variety*, June 11, 1947, p. 13.

527 "Heat Dulls N.Y. But 'Ruth'-Como Sock 102G," *Variety*, June 18, 1947, p. 18.

528 "Heat Melts B'way H.O.s But Can't Scare 'Ghost,' 144G," *Variety*, July 2, 1947, p. 9.

529 "Memorial Day Ups N.Y.," *Variety*, June 4, 1947, p. 13; "Heat Melts B'way H.O.s But Can't Scare 'Ghost,' 144G," p. 9.

530 Memo from Charles Schlaifer to Spyros Skouras, July 30, 1947, Charles Schlaifer papers, folder 1, AMPAS.

531 "National Boxoffice Survey," *Variety*, June 18, 1947, p. 3

532 "A Box Office Miracle Everywhere!" [ad] *Variety*, June 18, 1947, p. 14.

533 "National Boxoffice Survey," *Variety*, July 16, 1947, p. 3.

534 *Miracle on 34th Street* [pressbook], Los Angeles: Twentieth Century-Fox, [1947], p. 21; "NRDGA Tie-in of 7,500 Stores Highlight of 20th-TCF Ad-Pub. Campaign for '34th St.' " (*Film Daily*, May 14, 1947, p. 8).

535 "K. C. Perking; 'Hucksters' $30,000, Near New High; "Miracle' 19G, 'Beach' 13G," *Variety*, July 23, 1947, p. 16.

536 "Open Forum," *Hollywood Reporter*, September 23, 1947, p. 9.

537 "Inside Stuff—Pictures," *Variety*, October 22, 1947, p. 22; " 'Miracle' Flops, 'Crossfire' Tops In Detroit Week," *Hollywood Reporter*, September 3, 1947, p. 14; "Transit Strike's End No Aid to Frisco," *Variety*, July 2, 1947, p. 8.

538 "Inside Stuff—Pictures," *Variety*, October 22, 1947, p. 22.

539 "Top Grossers of 1947," *Variety*, January 7, 1948, p. 63.

540 " 'Amber' Draws 8,715,610 Fans, Sets 372 Records in 3 Weeks," *Hollywood Reporter*, November 11, 1947, p. 4.

541 Letter from Valentine Davies to James Barnett, October 23, 1951, V. D. papers, folder 72, AMPAS.

542 Rose Felswick, "Comedy at the Roxy a Delightful Picture," *New York Journal-American*, June 5, 1947.

543 "The Stage & Screen," *The Commonweal*, June 6, 1947, p. 189.

544 James Mason Brown, "Seeing Things," *The Saturday Review*, July 12, 1947, p. 22.

545 "There is a Santa Claus," *Newsweek*, June 2, 1947, p. 85.

546 "Reviews," *Variety*, May 7, 1947, p. 18; "There is a Santa Claus," *Newsweek*, June 2, 1947, p. 85.

547 Bosley Crowther, "The Screen," *New York Times*, June 5, 1947, p. 32.

548 Hedda Hopper, "Looking at Hollywood," *Los Angeles Times*, August 4, 1947, p. 10.

549 Cecelia Ager, "A Miracle that Makes Neighbors of Us All," *New York Post PM Magazine*, June 5, 1947; "Miracle on 34th Street," *New Republic*, June 2, 1947, p. 36.

550 Lee Mortimer, " 'Miracle on 34th St.,' Is Really That," *Daily Mirror* (New York), June 5, 1947.

551 Louella Parsons, " 'Miracle' Film Renews Faith," *Los Angeles Examiner*, June 14, 1947.

552 Bosley Crowther, "The Screen," *New York Times*, June 5, 1947, p. 32.

553 Ager, "A Miracle that Makes Neighbors of Us All."

554 Kate Cameron, " 'Miracle on 34th St.,' A Love of a Picture," *Daily News* (New York), June 5, 1947, p. 52.

555 Brown, "Seeing Things," p. 22.

556 Chuck Gray, "John Mason Brown Reviews New Plays," *Dayton Daily News*, October 22, 1947, p. 17.

557 Archer Winsten, " 'Miracle on 34th Street' A Commercial Fairy Tale," *New York Post*, June 5, 1947, p. 28.

558 "Movie of the Week: *Miracle on 34th Street*, Or, Yes, There Is a Santa Claus," *Life*, June 16, 1947, p. 65; Brown, "Seeing Things," p. 22.

559 "Review Digest," *Boxoffice*, "BookinGuide," July 5, 1947, p. [11].

560 Eileen Creelman, "The New Movies," *New York Sun*, June 5, 1947.

561 Velma West Sykes, "20ᵗʰ-TCF 'Miracle on 34ᵗʰ Street' Awarded Blue Ribbon for July," *Boxoffice*, August 9, 1947.

562 Jack Alicoate, ed. *The 1948 Film Daily Yearbook of Motion Pictures*, 1948, p. 157; Bosley Crowther, " 'Ten Best' Films," *New York Times*, December 28, 1947, p. X1; Philip K. Scheuer, "Picture Parade Put on Review," *Los Angeles Times*, December 28, 1947, p. C1; Kate Cameron, "Ten Best Pictures of 1947," *Daily News* (New York), December 28, 1947, section 2, p. 114; Leo Mishkin of the *Morning Telegraph* (New York) selected *Miracle* as one of the ten best reported in " 'Gentleman's Agreement' Tops Mishkin's '10 Best,' " *Hollywood Reporter*, December 23, 1947, p. 2.

563 " 'Best Years' Wins Film Daily's Poll," *New York Times*, January 12, 1948, p. 15. The poll covered films released between November 1946 and November 1947, which explains why *The Best Years of Our Lives* is on the list.

564 "Film Critics Hold 'Agreement' Best," *New York Times*, December 30, 1947, p. 17; "Rubin Accepts Award for 'The Yearling,' " *Boxoffice*, January 31, 1948, p. 14.

565 "National Board Picks 'Verdoux' Year's Best," *Boxoffice*, December 20, 1947, p. 10.

566 "Film Critics, Big Grossers Concur on '47 'Best' Lists," *Variety*, January 14, 1948, p. 7.

567 "Annual Award Winner" [ad]," *Boxoffice*, January 10, 1948, p. A18.

568 *Look* magazine awards footage, Straus, *Macy's Thanksgiving Day Parade: Floating in History* [documentary].

569 "Rosalind Russell and Peck Get Top Honors in Look Awards," *Hollywood Reporter*, February 4, 1948, p. 1; "*Look* Awards Plaques on Bob Hope Show," *Boxoffice*, February 7, 1948, p. 41.

570 "H'd [Hollywood] Foreign Press Hands Out Awards," *Hollywood Reporter*, March 11, 1948, p. 3.

571 "Correspondents Pick Hollywood's 'Bests,' " *Boxoffice*, March 13, 1948, p. 59; "Golden Globe Awards Increased from 8 to 12," *Hollywood Reporter*, February 27, 1948, p. 4; "H'd [Hollywood] Foreign Press Hands Out Awards," p. 3.

572 Behlmer, ed., *Memo from Darryl F. Zanuck*, p. 121.

573 O'Hara, "Feature Audio Commentary by Maureen O'Hara" (August 24, 2006).

574 Seaton, "Oral History with George Seaton by David Chierichetti," p. 103.

575 J. H. Hatcher and Homer B. Woods, "Ex Parte Santa Claus," *Charleston Daily Mail*, December 18, 1927, p. 1. The decision was printed in the newspaper, but apparently was also printed in G. C. Guff, *The Syllabus Service of the Supreme Court of Appeals of West Virginia*, vol. 6, December 23, 1927. The author has not been able to confirm this second source.

576 Letter from Valentine Davies to James Barnett, July 9, 1951, V. D. papers, folder 72, AMPAS.

577 Mark W. Podvia, "Yes, Pittsburgh, There is a Santa Claus" [paper], 2003, https://papers.ssrn.com. Accessed January 10, 2023. Podvia's paper reprints the entire decision. The original opinion is held in Judge Musmanno papers at the Duquesne University Gumberg Library. Musmanno went on to serve on the Supreme Court of Pennsylvania; "Decrees Santa Claus a Living Reality," *New York Times*, December 23, 1936, p. 19.

578 Letter from Frost E. Stockslager to TCF, February 20, 1947; Letter from George Wasson to David Ettleson, March 19, 1947, TCFLF.

579 Telegram from Harry J. McIntyre to George F. Wasson, October 7, 1947, TCFLF.

580 *Burns v. Twentieth Century-Fox Film Corporation*, 75 F. Supp. 986 (D. Mass. 1948).

581 Letter from Robert Patton to Valentine Davies, February 6, 1948, V. D. papers, folder 73, AMPAS.

582 Erskine Johnson, "Early American Fort Puzzles British Lad," *Mirror-News* (Los Angeles), July 7, 1956, p. 6.

583 Letter from Madaline Saenger to Sirs [TCF] dated July 7, 1948, TCFLF.

584 O'Hara, *AMC Backstory: Miracle on 34th Street*; *News Times*, Television News, December 12, 1995, quoted in Malone, *Maureen O'Hara: The Biography*, p. 193.

585 Davies, "Author's Note," *Miracle on 34th Street* (1947).

586 Valentine Davies, "Historical Note," *Miracle on 34th Street* [facsimile edition] (San Diego: Harcourt, Inc., 2001), p. 122; Letter from S. Spencer Scott to Walter Simpson [1947]. V. D. papers, folder 72, AMPAS.

587 Letter from S. Spencer Scott to Walter Simpson [1947], V. D. papers, folder 72, AMPAS; Letter from S. Spencer Scott to Walter Simpson, dated January 28, 1947, V. D. papers, folder 72, AMPAS.

588 Letter from S. Spencer Scott to Walter Simpson, dated January 28, 1947, V. D. papers, folder 72, AMPAS.

589 Memo from Lew Schreiber to George Wasson, February 5, 1947, TCFLF.

590 Agreement between Valentine Davies and Harcourt, Brace & Company relative to *Miracle on 34th Street* ("Herald Square" crossed out), February 18, 1947, TCFLF.

591 Letter from S. Spencer Scott to Valentine Davies, February 18, 1947, V. D. papers, folder 72, AMPAS.

592 Letter from S. Spencer Scott to Walter Simpson, February 11, 1947, V. D. papers, folder 72, AMPAS; Letter from S. Spencer Scott to Valentine Davies, February 18, 1947, V. D. papers, folder 72, AMPAS.

593 Letter from S. Spencer Scott to Valentine Davies, February 18, 1947, V. D. papers, folder 72, AMPAS.

594 Letter from S. Spencer Scott to Walter Simpson, March 5, 1947, V. D. papers, folder 72, AMPAS.

595 Memo from Lew Schreiber to George Wasson, March 21, 1947, TCFLF.

596 Davies, "Historical Note," *Miracle on 34th Street* [facsimile edition, 2001], p. 123. Letters from/to S. Spencer Scott, March/April 1947, V. D. papers, folder 72, AMPAS.

597 Letter from S. Spencer Scott to Valentine Davies, March 25, 1947, V. D. papers, folder 72, AMPAS.

598 Letter from S. Spencer Scott to Walter Simpson, June 3, 1947, V. D. papers, folder 72, AMPAS; Hansen, "Book with a Movie Genesis Brings Santa Out in July," part 4, p. 8.

599 "Autograph Party. John Payne in Person. May Company Downtown. Book Department Street Floor," [ad from unidentified newspaper]; Photographs of event, V. D. papers, scrapbook # 4, AMPAS.

600 *Miracle on 34th Street* [pressbook], Los Angeles: Twentieth Century-Fox, [1947], p. 23.

601 Harcourt, Brace & Company, "Miracle on 34th Street" [book ad], *New York Times*, December 14, 1947, p. BR24.

602 Nona Balakian, "Two Tales: One Miracle, One Cynical," *New York Times*, August 3, 1947, p. BR23.

603 Butcher, Fanny, "Jingle Bells! Santa Makes a Jolly July," *Chicago Sunday Tribune Magazine Review of Books*, July 20, 1947, part 4, p. 3.

604 "Off the Beaten Path," *Boston Daily Globe*, July 24, 1947, p. 15.

605 "Other Books," *Newsweek*, July 28, 1947, p. 87.

606 Harcourt, Brace & Company, "Miracle on 34th Street" [book ad], p. BR24.

607 Letter from Valentine Davies to James Barnett, October 23, 1951; Letter from S. Spencer Scott to Walter Simpson [1947], V. D. papers, folder 72, AMPAS.

608 Valentine Davies, "A Note about Re-creating the Original Edition," *Miracle on 34th Street* [facsimile of first edition] (San Diego: Harcourt, 2001), ISBN: 0-15-216377-8.

609 Harry Scherman, ed., "Miracle on 34th Street," *Book-of-the-Month Club News*, October 1947, p. [1].

610 "Literati," *Variety*, December 10, 1947, p. 69; Letter from Valentine Davies to James Barnett, October 23, 1951, V. D. papers, folder 72, AMPAS. *Variety* lists the print run at 400,000, but Davies tells Barnett it was 440,000.

611 Harcourt, Brace & Company, "Miracle on 34th Street" [book ad], p. BR24.

612 Letter from Valentine Davies to Eugene McCarty, February 27, 1952, V. D. papers, folder 72, AMPAS.

613 Letter from Valentine Davies to Mr. Freeman Lewis, January 30, 1953, V. D. papers, folder 72, AMPAS.

614 Letter from Valentine Davies to Mr. M. H. Forsyth of Dymock's Book Arcade LTD, publisher of the Australian edition, 1953, V. D. papers, folder 72, AMPAS.

615 Letter from Valentine Davies to James Barnett, October 23, 1951, V. D. papers, folder 72, AMPAS.

616 *Milagre na Rua 34* (Acigi); *Das Wunder von Manhattan* (Fischer-Taschenbuch-Verl); 34 choome no kiseki [English transliteration of Japanese] (Asunaro shobo).

617 Letter from Valentine Davies to James Barnett, October 23, 1951, V. D. papers, folder 72, AMPAS; Letter from Valentine Davies to Frank McCarthy [of TCF], June 6, 1954, V. D. papers, folder 72, AMPAS.

618 Valentine Davies, *Miracle on 34th Street*. Introduction by Elizabeth Davies, Illustrations by Tomie dePaola (San Diego: Harcourt Brace Jovanovich, 1984).

619 Lux Radio Theatre page by Old Time Radio Researchers Group on the Internet Archive. https://archive.org/details/OTRR_Certified_Lux_Radio_Theatre. Accessed December 15, 2022.

620 Letter from Donald Severn to Irving Kahn, December 21, 1947, TCFLF.

621 Memo from Lew Schreiber to George Wasson, November 28, 1947; Letter from TCF to Kenyon and Eckhardt, Inc., September 19, 1947, TCFLF.

622 *Miracle on 34th Street* [script for radio play that aired on December 20, 1948]. Lux Radio Theatre Collection, AMPAS.

Cast list:

Maureen O'Hara (Doris Walker)

John Payne (Fred Gailey)

Edmund Gwenn (Kris Kringle)

Joseph Kearns (Dr. Sawyer)

Willard Waterman (Mr. Macy)

Marlene Aames (Susan Walker)

William Johnstone

Herbert Butterfield

Howard McNear

Norman Field

Gil Stratton Jr.

Cliff Clark

Larry Dobkin

Louise Fitch

Johnny McGovern

Sarah Berner

Eddie Marr

Herbert Vigran

June Whitley

Jeanine Anne Roose

Helena Sorrell (TCF dramatic coach—intermission guest)

623 Letter from Valentine Davies to James Barnett, October 23, 1951, V. D. papers, folder 72, AMPAS.

624 Memo from George Wasson to Lew Schreiber, November 28, 1951, TCFLF. From the correspondence it appears that this broadcast was made and aired, but it has not been confirmed.

625 "Actor Tom Farley" [photo caption], *The Age* (Melbourne), December 23, 1954, p. 18; "Father Christmas Story in AW Hour," *The Age* (Melbourne), December 23, 1954, p. 15.

626 Letter from Valentine Davies to J. Ridley, June 20, 1955, V. D. papers, folder 72, AMPAS.

627 "Miracle on 34th Street: A Live Musical Radio Play Based on the 1947 Lux Radio Hour Broadcast," Show Perusal, September 2, 2022, p. [5]. broadwaylicensing.com/shows/holiday/miracle-on-34th-street/. Accessed November 7, 2022.

628 Tim and Earle Marsh, *The Complete Directory to Prime Time Network TV Shows 1946–Present* (5th ed.) (New York: Ballantine, 1992), p. 924; "TCF Television Productions, Inc." [ad], *Hollywood Reporter*, March 1, 1956, p. 9.

629 "Remake of 'Miracle' Set for Television," *Los Angeles Times*, September 26, 1955, p. 30.

630 Murray Illson, "Macy's Tells Gimbels, and Truce Rules 34th Street Until Thursday," *New York Times*, December 9, 1955, p. 29; "This Way to Gimbels. Watch 'The Miracle' Tonight at 10," [ad], *New York Times*, December 14, 1955, p. C21.

631 "This Way to Gimbels. Watch 'The Miracle' Tonight at 10," pp. C20–21.

632 Hedda Hopper, "Drama. Jim Piersall Story Stars Tony Perkins," *Los Angeles Times*, January 7, 1956, p. A6.

633 Philip K. Scheuer, "TV's Flicka Gallops in Studio Where Tom Mix Rode Tony," *Los Angeles Times*, August 21, 1955, p. D2; "20th Century-Fox Hour to Debut Oct. 5," Opelousas, Louisiana: *Daily World*, September 11, 1955, p. 23.

634 "Emmy Award Nominations Announced," *Broadcasting, Telecasting*, February 27, 1956, p. 93.

635 "20th Century-Fox Hour," *Variety*, December 21, 1955, p. 25.

636 "Congratulations Robert Stevenson," [ad] *Hollywood Reporter*, July 18, 1956, p. 5.

637 "20th Century-Fox Hour," *Variety*, December 21, 1955, p. 25.

638 "TV Program Notes," Baltimore: *Evening Sun*, December 14, 1955, p. 48; "Gold Mine and Little Girl," Munster, Indiana: *The Times*, December 14, 1955, p. C4.

639 Walter Ames, " 'Miracle on 34th Street' First Christmas Fare; Perry Gets Top Singer," *Los Angeles Times*, December 14, 1955, p. 34.

640 Hedda Hopper, "Drama: Jim Piersall Story Stars Tony Perkins," *Los Angeles Times*, January 7, 1956, p. A6.

641 "Hoyts Mayfair—'Smiley,' " *Sydney Morning Herald*, December 8, 1956, p. 19; "Amusements," *Sydney Morning Herald*, December 18, 1956, p. 12; "Granada, Willesden," *Marylebone and Paddington Mercury*, December 7, 1956, p. 2.

642 "Tuesday, November 4, 1958—Afternoon," *Los Angeles Times*, November 2, 1958, p. 158; Marsh and Marsh, *The Complete Directory to Prime Time Network TV Shows 1946–Present* (5th ed.), p. 414.

643 Minus the commercials from sponsor Westclox, it runs about fifty-two minutes.

644 Susan Gordon, *Susan Gordon Q&A* [video], Super Mega Show, Fairfield, New Jersey: July 10, 2010. https://susangordon.info under "Calendar Year 2010" and on www.youtube.com Accessed on December 13, 2022.

645 Spencer Ross, *Spencer Ross and His Orchestra; Saxophone Solos by Jimmy Abato*. Columbia CS 8325, 1960.

646 "Miracle on 34th Street," *Variety*, December 2, 1959, p. 35.

647 "TV Review: Special Tonight ('Miracle on 34th Street')," *Hollywood Reporter*, November 30, 1959, p. 11.

648 Letter from Harry J. McIntyre to Frank Ferguson, July 31, 1959, TCFLF.

649 Memo from Frank Ferguson to Lew Schreiber, August 7, 1959, TCFLF.

650 Richard Finegan, " 'Miracle on 34th Street' Rare Live TV Version Found," *Classic Images*, Muscatine, Iowa: *Muscatine Journal*, December 2005, p. 22. A kinescope is "a film of a TV screen showing a live broadcast" (www.merriam-webster.com).

651 Gordon, *Susan Gordon Q&A* [video].

652 Letter from Julian Johnson to Valentine Davies, August 19, 1954, V. D. papers, folder 72, AMPAS.

653 Letter from Valentine Davies to Miriam Howell, December 3, 1954, V. D. papers, folder 72, AMPAS.

654 Letter from Lew Schreiber to Black Hawk Broadcasting Company, December 20, 1948; Letter from George Wasson to T. Frazer, January 1, 1949, TCFLF.

655 Letter from Julian Johnson to Valentine Davies, June 24, 1954, V. D. papers, folder 72, AMPAS.

656 Correspondence attached to letter from Valentine Davies to Miriam Howell, December 20, 1954, V. D. papers, folder 72, AMPAS.

657 Letter from Julian Johnson to Valentine Davies, August 19, 1954, V. D. papers, folder 72, AMPAS.

658 Meredith Willson, "How come 'Here's Love?' " [liner notes], *Meredith Willson's Here's Love: The New Musical* KOS-2400 [original cast recording], New York: Columbia Masterworks, 1963.

659 "Film to Become Musical," *New York Times*, November 2, 1961.

660 " 'Miracle on 34th Street' Legit Next for Willson," *Hollywood Reporter*, November 29, 1961; Milton Esterow, "Wilson to Adapt Movie for Stage," *New York Times*, November 30, 1961; "Masquers Extol 'The Music Man,' " *Hollywood Reporter*, June 4, 1962, p. 3; "Wouldn't It Be Wonderful If"; Dominic McHugh cites a February 27, 1962, letter from Rosemary to Meredith Willson in his book, *The Big Parade*. Dominic McHugh, *The Big Parade: Meredith Willson's Musicals from The Music Man to 1491* (Oxford, UK: Oxford University Press, 2021, p. 168.

661 "Broadway Musicals that Were Once Movies," *New York Times*, August 11, 1963, p. 89.

662 McHugh, *The Big Parade*, p. 183.

663 Letter from Stuart Ostrow to Meredith Willson, November 7, 1962, quoted in McHugh, *The Big Parade*, p. 177.

664 Louis Cook, " 'Here's Love' a Happy Package," *Detroit Free Press*, July 31, 1963, p. 4B.

665 McHugh, *The Big Parade*, p. 177.

666 Stuart Ostrow, *Present at the Creation, Leaping in the Dark, and Going Against the Grain* (New York: Applause Books, 2006), p. 28.

667 Marilyn Bender, "Fashions for a Musical Will Be Sold at Macy's," *New York Times*, August 6, 1963, p. 24.

668 Ostrow, *Present at the Creation*, p. 27.

669 "Papers Love Willson's 'Here's Love,' " Mason City, Iowa: *Mason City Globe-Gazette*, August 29, 1963, p. 3.

670 Ostrow, *Present at the Creation*, p. 52.

671 Ostrow, *Present at the Creation*, p. 28.

672 Richard Spong, "Sure-fire Success 'Here's Love' Has a Special Integrated Cast," Mason City, Iowa: *Mason City Globe-Gazette*, September 18, 1963, p. 23.

673 "Papers Love Willson's 'Here's Love,' " Mason City, Iowa: *Mason City Globe-Gazette*, August 29, 1963, p. 3.

674 Louis Cook, " 'Here's Love' a Happy Package," *Detroit Free Press*, July 31, 1963, p. 4B; "Papers Love Willson's 'Here's Love,' " p. 3; " 'Here's Love' Breaks All Records for Musicals," Mason City, Iowa: *Mason City Globe-Gazette*, September 18, 1963, p. 32.

675 Howard Taubman, "Theater: Musical by Meredith Willson," *New York Times*, October 4, 1963, p. 28.

676 "Shows on Broadway: 'Here's Love,' " *Variety*, October 9, 1963, p. 54.

677 John S. Wilson, "Shows on Disks," *New York Times*, February 16, 1964, p. X16; John S. Wilson, "The Old Outshines the New in Disked Shows," *New York Times*, November 24, 1963, p. 42.

678 "Shows Out of Town—'Here's Love,' " *Variety*, July 31, 1963, p. 104.

679 Wilson, "The Old Outshines the New in Disked Shows," p. 42.

680 " 'Here's Love,' Keys Col's Xmas Drive," *Variety*, October 2, 1963, p. 57.

681 Wilson, "The Old Outshines the New in Disked Shows," p. 42; "ASCAP, With 17 Upcoming Musicals Hitting Biggest B'Way Tally Since '30s," *Variety*, September 18, 1963, p. 55.

682 " 'Here's Love,' Keys Col's Xmas Drive," p. 57.

683 "Legit Signings," *Variety*, February 26, 1964, p. 79.

684 " 'Here's Love' to Close July 25," *New York Times*, July 2, 1964, p. 28.

685 Louis Calta, "Broadway Issues a Plea to Santa," *New York Times*, December 21, 1963, p. 16.

686 "The Big 10," *New York Times*, March 1, 1964, p. X3; June 7, 1964, X1; July 19, 1964, p. X1.

687 "Closing the Record Book on 1963–64," *New York Times*, June 28, 1964, p. X3.

688 Memo from Frank Ferguson to Frances Richardson and Richard Huckans, June 19, 1962, TCFLF.

689 Peter Troxell and Rita Faye Wadsworth, et al., *Miracle on 34th Street, the Play* (Woodstock, IL: Dramatic Publishing, 2010, p. 6.

690 mtishows.com/show_detail.asp?showid=000042 in the Wayback Machine on web.archive.org. See show index on archived webpages for December 16, 2008, for *Here's Love* on December 16, 2008; January 29, 2009, for "Meredith Willson's It's Beginning to Look a Lot Like Christmas"; and April 9, 2011, for "Miracle on 34th Street: The Musical." Accessed November 7, 2022.

691 Davidson had never been credited with the role, and her participation was only revealed in the Mark Evanier commentary on the *Frosty the Snowman Deluxe Edition* DVD/Blu-ray released in 2018.

692 "Miracle on 34th Street," *Variety*, December 19, 1973, p. 28.

693 Seaton, "Oral History with George Seaton by David Chierichetti," p. 103.

694 "Hughes Works New 'Miracle,' " *Hollywood Reporter*, October 22, 1993, p. 1.

695 "Hughes Recruits 'Damn Yankees' for Retro Slate," *Hollywood Reporter*, November 24, 1993, p. 1.

696 Hughes Gets ShowEast DeMille Award," *Hollywood Reporter*, October 19, 1994, p. 7.

697 "Hughes Recruits 'Damn Yankees' for Retro Slate," p. 1.

698 Galbraith, "Now the Miracle is Off 34th Street, p. B13.

699 "Miracle on 34th Street" [press release], Twentieth Century Fox, 1994, p. 7.

700 Melinda Bilyeu, et al., *The Bee Gees: Tales of the Brothers Gibb* (London: Omnibus Press, 2001), p. 623.

701 " 'Miracle' Screening Makes Believers of Fox," *Hollywood Reporter*, October 14, 1993, p. 7; Stephen Galloway, "Fox Says Enjoy 'Miracle' or Get Your Money Back," *Hollywood Reporter*, November 23, 1994, p. 3.

702 " 'Street' Sales," *Hollywood Reporter*, October 18, 1994, p. 3.

703 Galloway, "Fox Says Enjoy 'Miracle' or Get Your Money Back," p. 3.

704 Galloway, "Fox Says Enjoy 'Miracle' or Get Your Money Back," p. 3.

705 Duane Byrge, " 'Santa' Puts Ho-Ho in B.O.," *Hollywood Reporter*, November 28, 1994, p. 1.

706 "Domestic Box Office," *Variety*, January 2, 1995, p. 18.

707 "Miracle on 34th Street" [ad] *New York Times*, December 4, 1994, p. H30.

708 Leonard Klady, "Miracle on 34th Street," *Variety*, November 14, 1994, p. 48.

709 "Miracle on 34th Street," *Boxoffice*, January 1, 1995, p. 72.

710 Patricia Dobson, *Screen International*, December 2, 1994, p. 16.

711 Kenneth Turan, "The 'Miracle' of 1947, 47 Years Later," *Los Angeles Times*, November 18, 1994, p. OCF1.

712 "Hughes Recruits 'Damn Yankees' for Retro Slate," p. 1.

713 *Miracle on 34th Street* [script for radio play that aired on December 22, 1947]. Lux Radio Theatre Collection, AMPAS.

714 Seaton, "Oral History with George Seaton by David Chierichetti," p. 140."

715 Letter from Valentine Davies to James Barnett, October 23, 1951, V. D. papers, folder 72, AMPAS.

716 Velma West Sykes, "23 Years of Industry Service by the Blue Ribbon Award," *Boxoffice*, July 2, 1955, pp. 88–89.

717 "Around the Clock with Eisenhower," *Collier's*, March 5, 1954, p. 30.

718 "Three Out of Four Homes Equipped with TV Sets," *Hollywood Reporter*, May 16, 1956, p. 1.

719 Ely Landau, "Don't Look Now, Boys, But There's a Celluloid Revolution Going On," *Variety*, July 27, 1955, p. 30.

720 "TV Stations to Get Aid from New Group," *New York Times*, March 19, 1955, p. 21.

721 "20th-TCF Dips into Its Backlog," *Hollywood Reporter*, May 16, 1959, p. 1.

722 "CKLW Slates New Series of Films," *Detroit Free Press*, December 2, 1956, p. 86.

723 Harry Haun, "What's Right with the Movies," New York: *Sunday News*, December 21, 1975.

724 "20th-Fox First Major Studio to Enter Home Vidtape Market with Pix," *Variety*, August 10, 1977, p. 3.

725 Vernon Scott, "Color Comes to 'Casablanca,' " UPI Archives: Entertainment, November 19, 1985, Gale General OneFile.

726 Gary R. Edgerton, "The Germans Wore Gray, You Wore Blue," *Journal of Popular Film and Television*, 27:4, 2000, p. 26.

727 "A 'Miracle' of Technology," *New York Times*, November 27, 1985, p. C22.

728 Eugene Secunda, "Is Movie Colorization a Moral Issue for Broadcasters?" *Broadcasting*, May 25, 1987; Bill Desowitz, "Colorized '34th'a Ratings Hit," *Hollywood Reporter*, December 5, 1985, p. 1.

729 " 'Public Reaction Has Been Excellent,' said Young," UPI Archives: Entertainment, October 18, 1986, Gale General OneFile.

730 "Top-Selling Videos of 1993," *Hollywood Reporter*, December 27, 1993, p. 1.

731 Andrew L. Yarrow, "Action But No Consensus on Film Coloring," *New York Times*, July 11, 1988, p. C13.

732 Vernon Scott, "Director John Huston, Crusty in Defense of Black-and-White Movie Classics," UPI Archives: Entertainment, November 13, 1986, Gale General OneFile; Vernon Scott, "Colorization Debate Rages On," UPI Archives: Entertainment, June 16, 1987, Gale General OneFile.

733 Scott, "Colorization Debate Rages On."

734 Secunda, "Is Movie Colorization a Moral Issue for Broadcasters?"

735 Fran Lee, "Color Her Pleased," *New York Times*, December 3, 1986, p. A30.

736 Edgerton, "The Germans Wore Gray, You Wore Blue," p. 27.

737 Edgerton, "The Germans Wore Gray, You Wore Blue," p. 29.

738 Edgerton, "The Germans Wore Gray, You Wore Blue," p. 31.

739 Yarrow, "Action But No Consensus on Film Coloring," p. C13.

740 "Librarian of Congress Adds 25 Films to National Film Registry," December 20, 2005, www.loc.gov. Accessed December 20, 2022.

741 "Does Gimbels Tell Macy's? No, Gimbels Tells the World" [ad], *New York Times*, May 6, 1953, p. 8.

742 Meyer Berger, "About New York: Gimbels Loses Its Head and Does Tell Macy's," *New York Times*, May 6, 1953, p. 33.

743 "This is the Miracle on 34th Street," [ad], *New York Times* May 7, 1953, p. 7.

744 "This Way to Gimbels. Watch 'The Miracle' tonight at 10," [ad], *New York Times*, December 14, 1955, p. C21.

745 "Macy's . . . The Miracle on 34th Street. It's the miracle 1956 General Electric magnetic door refrigerator," *New York Times*, December 14, 1955, p. 18.

746 "Pointed Patents" [ad], *Daily News* (New York), March 20, 1958, p. 531.

747 "Saks-34th" [ad], *Daily News* (New York), June 1, 1958, p. 158.

748 "Hearns Basement Super Bargains 'Miracle on 149th Street,' " *Daily News*, September 21, 1949; "Supermart" [ad], *Asbury Park Press* (New Jersey), March 25, 1955, p. 28.

749 Kathryn Shattuck, "Windows, Do They Do Windows!," *New York Times*, November 14, 1999, p. CY4.

750 "Relive the Magic of 'Miracle on 34th Street' in Macy's Herald Square Broadway Windows!" [ad], *New York Times*, November 14, 1999, p. 5.

751 [Celebrating 150 Years] Macy's commercial, 2008. Available on www.youtube.com. Accessed January 26, 2023.

752 "The Magic of Macy's: Macy's Celebrates the Holidays with Communities Across the Country" [press release], New York: Macy's Inc., November 21, 2008. Available at www.macysinc.com via the Wayback Machine at www.internetarchive.org. Accessed January 26, 2023.

753 A live recording of the show, titled "Macy's 'Miracle on 34th Street' Puppet Show," which appears to have been made in 2011, is available on www.youtube.com. Accessed January 26, 2023.

754 " 'I Believe,' Muppet Music Video, The Muppets," available on www.youtube.com. Accessed January 26, 2023.

755 Stuart Elliott, "Macy's Melds Past and Present in a Marketing Paean to a Christmas Movie Classic," *New York Times*, November 6, 2012, p. B4.

756 Joey Hadden, "Photos Show What the Iconic Locations In 'Elf' Look Life [*sic*] in Real Life," www.insider.com/elf-real-life-movie-locations-new-york-city-2020-11. Accessed December 5, 2022.

757 Sam Thielman, "TCF Properties Are in the Cards at Hallmark," *Variety*, July, 28, 2008, p. 4.

758 Memo from Lew Schreiber, August 20, 1946, TCFLF.

759 Memo on George Seaton contract, January 2, 1947, TCFLF.

760 Seaton, "Oral History with George Seaton by David Chierichetti," p. 134.

761 "Death of a Showman," *Variety*, November 6, 1968, p. 4.

762 Alfred E. Clark, "George Seaton, Director, Dead," *New York Times*, July 29, 1979, p. 36.

763 "Perlberg-Seaton," *The Independent Film Journal*, June 30, 1956, p. 58.

764 "William Perlberg," *Variety*, November 6, 1968, p. 71.

765 O'Hara, *'Tis Herself: A Memoir*, p. 119.

766 Candee, ed., *Current Biography* (New York: H. W. Wilson, 1953), p. 462.

767 Maureen O'Hara, appearing on *The Tonight Show with Johnny Carson*, May 17, 1991. Available on www.youtube. com. Accessed January 21, 2023.

768 O'Hara, *The Tonight Show with Johnny Carson*, May 17, 1991.

769 Cal York, "Inside Stuff," *Photoplay*, April 1950, p. 8; "Gloria De Haven Wins Divorce," *New York Times*, February 10, 1950, p. 32.

770 Peter B. Flint, "John Payne, 77, Actor, Is Dead; Lawyer in 'Miracle on 34th Street,' " *New York Times*, December 8, 1989, p. D17; "Obituaries," *Hollywood Reporter*, December 8, 1989, p. 57. In the *Hollywood Reporter* obituary it states that Payne claimed credit for discovering the story of *Miracle* in a magazine and insisting that TCF make it. *Miracle* never appeared in a magazine prior to filming; Payne's memory was clearly muddled.

771 "John Payne Hit by Car," *New York Times*, March 2, 1961, p. 18; "John Payne's Condition Reported Still Serious," *Hollywood Reporter*, March 7, 1961, p. 2.

772 Louis Calta, "News of the Stage," *New York Times*, October 14, 1973, p. 67.

773 O'Hara, *'Tis Herself: A Memoir*, p. 117.

774 Flint, "John Payne, 77, Actor, Is Dead," p. D17.

775 Clark, "George Seaton, Director, Dead," p. 36; "Obituaries: Harry Antrim," *Variety*, January 25, 1967, p. 71; "Jerome Cowan, Character Actor Who Played in 100 Films, Dead," *New York Times*, January 26, 1972, p. 40; "Obituaries: James Seay," *Variety*, April 12, 1993, p. 11; "Obituary: Edmund Gwenn," *The Times* (London), September 8, 1959; "Obituaries: Arthur Jacobson," *Variety*, October 25, 1993, p. 68; "Obituaries: Lloyd Ahern," *Hollywood Reporter*, January 16, 1984, p. 45.

776 McClelland (quoting Edmund Gwenn), *Forties Film Talk*, p. 309.

777 Memo from George Seaton to George F. Wasson, December 11, 1948, TCFLF.

778 McClelland (quoting Edmund Gwenn), *Forties Film Talk*, p. 309.

779 Thomas, ed., *Best American Screen-Plays. First Series. Complete Screenplays*, p. 170.

780 Letter from George Wasson and Frank Ferguson to Donald Henderson, March 12, 1947, TCFLF.

781 "Christmas Film Clicks in July," *Spokane Chronicle*, July 26, 1947, p. 14; "Ticket Buyers Acclaim '34th Street,' " *New Dynamo*, New York: Twentieth Century-Fox, May 24, 1947, p. 1.

782 Ted Byfield, "If You Think Christmas Is about Giving, Then Take a Closer Look," *Alberta Report*, December 23, 1996.

783 Butcher, "Jingle Bells! Santa Makes a Jolly July," part 4, p. 3.

784 Annie Wilkinson, "The House that Santa Found: 'Miracle on 34th Street' Partly Shot on Long Island," *Long Island Press*, December 23, 2019. The House That Santa Found: Miracle on 34th Street Partly Shot on Long Island (longislandpress.com). Accessed January 5, 2023.

About the Author

Jeffrey Paul Thompson is a graduate of Brigham Young University where he received degrees in the humanities and in law. He also has a master's degree in library and information science from the University of California, Los Angeles. He worked as an archivist at Twentieth Century Fox from 2005 to 2016 and is a co-author of the official corporate history *Twentieth Century Fox: A Century of Entertainment* published by Rowman & Littlefield in 2017. During his time in Los Angeles, he has served on the board of Hollywood Heritage, interned with the Academy of Motion Picture Arts & Sciences, and volunteered for the Los Angeles Historic Theatre Foundation and the American Cinematheque. He currently works as an archivist for Fox Corporation, the successor entity of Twentieth Century Fox.